1695

Ethnic America

ETHNIC AMERICA

A HISTORY

THOMAS SOWELL

Basic Books, Inc., Publishers   New York

Library of Congress Cataloging in Publication Data

Sowell, Thomas, 1930–
   Ethnic America.

   Includes bibliographical references and index.
   1.   Minorities—United States—History.
2. United States—Ethnic relations.   I.   Title.
E184.A1S688   973'.04   80–68957
ISBN 0-465-02074-7   AACR2

To Birdie and Lacy, and the memory of Ruth

Contents

I

Introduction

Chapter 1

THE AMERICAN MOSAIC

THE PEOPLING of America is one of the great dramas in all of human history. Over the years, a massive stream of humanity—45 million people—crossed every ocean and continent to reach the United States. They came speaking every language and representing every nationality, race, and religion. Today, there are more people of Irish ancestry in the United States than in Ireland, more Jews than in Israel, more blacks than in most African countries. There are more people of Polish ancestry in Detroit than in most of the leading cities in Poland, and more than twice as many people of Italian ancestry in New York as in Venice.

The sheer magnitude of American ethnic communities makes them autonomous cultures with lives of their own—neither copies of some "mainstream" model nor mere overseas branches of some other country's culture. Chow mein, the St. Patrick's Day parade, and the Afro hairdo all originated on *American* soil. Far from taking direction from overseas, American ethnic communities have supplied leadership to their countries of origin. The first president of Ireland, Eamon de Valera, was born in Brooklyn. Israeli Prime Minister Golda Meir was

3

born in Milwaukee. Liberia was for more than a century ruled by the descendants of freed American Negro slaves.

The massive ethnic communities that make up the mosaic of American society cannot be adequately described as "minorities." There is no "majority." The largest single identifiable ethnic strain are people of British ancestry—who make up just 15 percent of the American population. They barely outnumber German Americans (13 percent) or blacks (11 percent). Millions of Americans cannot identify themselves at all ethnically, due to intermixtures over the generations.[1]

The setting in which the history of all these peoples unfolded is no less impressive than the numbers and varieties of the peoples themselves. The United States is one of the largest cultural-linguistic units in the history of the world. From San Francisco to Boston is the same distance as from Madrid to Moscow. Yet here there is one language, one set of laws, and one economy in an area that, in Europe, is fragmented into a multitude of nations, languages, and competing military and political blocs. The size and cohesion of the American society are all the more remarkable because of the diverse origins of the people who make it up. As a unified nation, the United States is older than Germany or Italy. As for size, Texas is larger than France, Colorado is larger than Great Britain, and Italy is only two-thirds the size of California. The United States as a whole is larger than the Roman Empire at its greatest expansion.

The mixture of unity and diversity runs through American history as through American society today. No ethnic group has been wholly unique, and yet no two are completely alike. Each group has its own geographic distribution pattern, reflecting conditions when they arrived on American soil and the evolution of the industries and regions to which they became attached. Even the ages of American ethnic groups vary widely. Mexican Americans and Puerto Ricans have median ages of less than twenty years, while the average Irish American or Italian American is more than thirty years old, and Jewish Americans are over forty. These age differences reflect not only current fertility patterns—some groups are composed disproportionately of children—but also historic *changes* in fertility patterns that have caused the successive generations to be of drastically altered size in some groups.

Incomes, occupations, and unemployment rates differ substantially among American ethnic groups, as do rates of crime, fertility, and business ownership. The *explanation* of those differences is complex and in many ways surprising. None of the easy explanations fits all the facts. Color has obviously played a major role in determining the

4

fate of many Americans, and yet a black ethnic group like the West Indians earns more than a predominantly white ethnic group like the Puerto Ricans, and the Japanese earn more than whites in general. The initial wealth of a group and its time of arrival are obviously important, as many wealthy "old families" show, but the Jews arrived late and penniless in the nineteenth century and are now more affluent than any other ethnic group.

THE ECONOMIC PICTURE

The incomes, occupations, and unemployment rates of American ethnic groups are too different from one another to be described by any generalization. Moreover, it is as misleading in the economic area as in other areas to think of them as "minorities" who fall below some "majority," or national average, in socioeconomic terms. A number of ethnic groups exceed the national average in socioeconomic status.

Family Income Index
(U.S. Average = 100)

Jewish	172
Japanese	132
Polish	115
Chinese	112
Italian	112
German	107
Anglo-Saxon	107
Irish	103
TOTAL U.S.	100
Filipino	99
West Indian	94
Mexican	76
Puerto Rican	63
Black	62
Indian	60

SOURCE: U.S. Bureau of the Census and National Jewish Population Survey.[2]

Many factors are responsible for these economic differences among the various groups. Age is a major factor that is often overlooked. Ethnic groups that differ in average age—by ten or twenty years in some cases—have vastly different percentages of their population in the older age brackets, where people in professional and other high-income occupations are concentrated. For example, about 20 percent of American Indians are age forty-five or older, while *twice* that percentage of Polish Americans are that old.[3] Higher income occupations typically require either long periods of education or long years of experience, or both, so it is not surprising that older ethnic groups earn more than younger ethnic groups. What is misleading is when these gross differences are regarded as showing either the extent of employer discrimination or of ethnic "ability." Comparisons of the earnings of thirty-year-old males show a narrower spread among ethnic groups, and when the comparison is between thirty-year-old males with the same education, the differences become even smaller.

In a country as vast as the United States, with very different economic conditions in different regions, the average income of an ethnic group depends to some extent on how the group is distributed among the regions. Differences between members of the same ethnic group located in different places are often greater than the difference between the national average income and the average income of the group as a whole. There are regional differences, not only in income, but also in such things as fertility, IQ, and the rate of return on educational investment.[4]

Discrimination has obviously influenced the incomes of American ethnic groups. All have been discriminated against to one degree or another. Yet some of the most successful—such as the Orientals—have experienced worse discrimination than most, and the extraordinary success of the Jews has been achieved in the face of centuries of anti-Semitism. The *moral* offensiveness of discrimination has attracted much attention, but whether its *cause-and-effect* role is equally important is another question. There are also difficulties in distinguishing current employer discrimination from past discrimination in schooling, whose effects may still be present years later. These complex questions will be considered in the chapters that follow.

Education is also an obvious influence on income. For every ethnic group, finishing college means an income above the national average. In recent years, even long-standing black-white income differences have been eliminated among college-educated young people with similar family characteristics.[5] The amount of education varies greatly from one ethnic group to another, and variations in educational quality add to these differences. Those groups with the largest quantity of education—Jews and Orientals—also tend to be educated in higher quality institutions and in the more demanding and higher paid fields, such as the natural sciences, medicine, and law.[6]

The diversity of American ethnic groups in economic terms is equally apparent in such social characteristics as fertility, longevity, crime, IQs, and alcoholism.

As in the general society, fertility tends to be greatest where people are poorest: "The rich get richer, and the poor have children." In general, those ethnic groups with the lowest incomes—blacks, Puerto Ricans, American Indians, and Mexican Americans—have the highest fertility rates, while Jews and Orientals have too few children to reproduce themselves. Another striking pattern is that the more successful members of low-income groups have even *fewer* children than equally successful members of the general population. That is, high-income blacks, Indians, and Hispanics have unusually low fertility rates. For example, Mexican American women who have completed high school have *fewer* children than any other women with the same education, even though Mexican Americans as a group have the highest fertility rate of any American ethnic group.[7] The causes of this phenomenon are not nearly so clear as the effects of it.

When those individuals who have struggled upward from poverty to affluence die off without fully reproducing themselves, it means that much of their struggle has to be repeated from scratch in the next generation because they leave few descendants to start off with the advantages made possible by their success. In other words, a part of the "human capital" accumulated by low-income ethnic groups perishes with each generation, making the group's upward mobility more difficult for lack of the money, experience, personal contacts, and other advantages that their more successful members could pass on to their offspring.

High fertility directly lowers the standard of living of a group by spreading a given income more thinly among family members. Mexican Americans average lower incomes per capita than blacks, even though blacks earn less, because Mexican-American families are larger.[8] This contributes to the Mexican Americans' poorer housing and lesser education than blacks—and, of course, much less than the general U.S. population. High fertility is also correlated with lower scores on mental tests by the children, who must receive smaller shares of parental time. Half of all black males who failed the army mental tests came from families of six or more children.[9] Whatever the cultural bias of the mental test, such bias would apply equally to blacks from small families, so the *difference* in failure rates is significant.

Fertility rates in general have changed drastically over the years, and the relative positions of various ethnic groups have been reshuffled as well. As of 1910, Jewish women in the thirty-five- to forty-four-year age bracket had the same number of children (5.3) as Mexican Americans, and more than blacks (4.2), the Irish (3.3), or the national average (3.4). By 1969, however, Jewish fertility in the same age bracket had been more than cut in half (2.4), while Mexican-American fertility had been reduced only moderately (4.4), as had that of blacks (3.6) and the Irish (3.1).[10] This means a V-shaped distribution of ages among the Jews, with the older generations spread out at the top, followed by progressively fewer younger age individuals, leading to a high average age for the group as a whole.

Rates of unemployment, crime, and fertility are all strongly influenced by age. Unemployment varies so much by age that, despite a generally higher unemployment rate among blacks than among whites, whites *under twenty* have consistently had higher unemployment rates than blacks in the prime twenty-five- to forty-four-year-old bracket. Similarly, most violent crime is committed by males under twenty-five, so that groups with a high proportion of their members in the crime-prone age brackets tend to have high crime rates for this reason, even aside from other factors that may be at work. The magnitude of this effect may be suggested by the fact that, although black crime rates are several times those of whites, the black and white crime rates become very similar when people of the same age and socioeconomic condition are compared.[11]

Like fertility rates, IQ scores differ substantially among ethnic groups at a given time, and have changed substantially over time—reshuffling the relative standings of the groups. As of about World War I, Jews scored sufficiently low on mental tests to cause a leading "expert" of that era to claim that the test score results "disprove the popular belief that the Jew is highly intelligent."[12] At that time, IQ scores for many of the other more recently arrived groups—Italians, Greeks, Poles, Portuguese, and Slovaks—were virtually identical to those found today among blacks, Hispanics, and other disadvantaged groups.[13] However, over the succeeding decades, as most of these immigrant groups became more acculturated and advanced socioeconomically, their IQ scores have risen by substantial amounts. Jewish IQs were already above the national average by the 1920s, and recent studies of Italian and Polish IQs show them to have reached or passed the national average in the post-World War II era. Polish IQs, which averaged eighty-five in the earlier studies—the same as that of blacks today—had risen to 109 by the 1970s.[14] This twenty-four-point increase in two generations is greater than the current black-white difference (fifteen points).

Social attitudes about race and ethnicity have changed considerably over time, especially in the post–World War II era. Jews, who had been excluded from many top university faculties, came ultimately to be overrepresented on such faculties. Professional sports that had once excluded blacks came to be dominated by black athletes. Anti-Oriental laws, which had flourished for decades in California, were repealed in popular referendums. Intermarriage rates among people of Irish, German, and Polish ancestry exceeded 50 percent of all their marriages, with Italian intermarriage rates falling just below 50 percent and Japanese Americans not far behind. Attitude surveys and election results show similar patterns of growing mutual acceptance.[15]

The road toward pluralism and cosmopolitanism has been long and rocky. The intergroup animosities of the nineteenth century—among European ethnic groups or between nativists and immigrants of European or Oriental ancestry—frequently erupted in violent confrontations in which the loss of life exceeded anything seen in mid-twentieth-century versions of "race riots."[16] An anti-immigrant political party called the Know-Nothings achieved a brief but spectacular success in the 1850s, electing six governors and dominating several state legislatures.[17] Later revivals of the same intolerant spirit culminated in national legislation all but cutting off immigration in the 1920s. The tragic history of slavery, Jim Crow laws, and lynchings against blacks is all too familiar. Yet what is peculiar about the United States is not that these intergroup animosities have existed here—as they have existed for thousands of years elsewhere—but that their intensity has lessened and in some respects disappeared.

Ethnic groups themselves have changed in ways that made their acceptance easier. The high rates of crime, disease, dependence on charity, and lack of personal hygiene that characterized many nineteenth-century immigrant groups passed with their acculturation to American norms and with the improvement of cities themselves, as sewer systems replaced backyard outhouses and eventually indoor plumbing brought running water into the tenements by the end of the nineteenth century (although bathtubs remained a rare luxury even then). Before that, the smells and diseases of the slums were overpowering realities. Moderate heat waves were literally fatal in tenements that were far more overcrowded and unventilated than the slums of today. People who could not speak English, or who could not read or write in any language, were far more common then. Religious animosities were so fierce as to retard the development of public education,[18] as well as to provide the spark for riots and the fuel for long-smoldering political rivalries. Protestant-Catholic clashes led to fifty deaths in one day in 1871.[19] In earlier times, there were similar antagonisms and violence against Mormons, Quakers, and others.[20]

American pluralism was not an ideal with which people started but an accommodation to which they were eventually driven by the destructive toll of mutual intolerance in a country too large and diverse for effective dominance by any one segment of the population. The rich economic opportunities of the country also provided alternative outlets for energies, made fighting over the division of existing material things less important than the expansion of output for all, and rewarded cooperative efforts so well as to make it profitable to overlook many differences.

TIME AND PLACE

The many ethnic groups that make up the American people did not arrive at the same time or locate in the same places. Each group typically had its own era during which its immigration to America was concentrated. Irish immigration to the United States peaked about 1850, while Jewish immigration peaked half a century later, and Mexican-American immigration peaked half a century after that. Geographic distribution has been equally diverse. Scandinavians settled in the upper Midwest, Orientals along the West Coast, Cuban refugees in Florida, Mexican Americans in the Southwest, and the Scotch-Irish along the Appalachian region from western Pennsylvania down through the Carolinas. Those groups that arrived virtually penniless from Europe—the Irish, the Italians, and the Jews—settled right in the northeast ports where they arrived. Blacks were concentrated in the South.

Since each of these regions has its own characteristic economic activities, the fate of each of these groups became intertwined with the fate of wheat farming or steel production, railroading, cotton manufacturing, etc. Because economic conditions in the country as a whole were different in different eras, each group faced a different set of opportunities and constraints upon arrival. The subsequent economic history of each group reflected the influence of time and place, as well as the cultural heritage that it brought to America.

Present-day differences are still heavily influenced by location. The average family income of blacks in New York State is more than double that of blacks in Mississippi. Mexican Americans in the Detroit metropolitan area earn more than twice as much as Mexican Americans in the metropolitan areas of Laredo or Brownsville in Texas. American Indians in Chicago, Detroit, or New York City make more than double the income of Indians on reservations. These differences within the same ethnic group are greater than the differences between any ethnic group and the larger society.[21] Location matters.

The geographic distribution of ethnic groups affects not only their incomes but also their life-styles in general. American Indians in the rural Midwest average about two children more per family than American Indians in the urban Northeast. Blacks outside the South have consistently had smaller families and higher IQs than blacks living in the South. Even within a given city, a given ethnic group has widely varying patterns of income, crime, broken homes, etc., by neighborhood—whether the ethnic group is Jewish, Italian, Mexican, etc., in origin.

There are many historic reasons for differences in the geographic distribution patterns of American ethnic groups, and for their arrival at one period of history rather than another.

The change from wind-driven ships to steam-powered ships caused a drastic change in the origins of immigrants to America. In the era of wind-driven ships, European immigrants came almost exclusively from northern and western Europe. With the advent of steam-powered ships, suddenly immigration was overwhelmingly from southern and eastern Europe—people with greater cultural and religious differences from the U.S. population, at a time when religious differences were of major social and political importance.

In the era of wind-driven ships, an ocean voyage on a passenger vessel was beyond the financial means of most immigrants. They could reach America only in the hold of a cargo vessel returning from its deliveries in Europe. This meant that mass immigration was possible only from areas with large-scale trade with the United States— northern and western Europe, but not eastern or southern Europe.

American shipments to Europe were usually bulky agricultural cargoes and their imports were much smaller sized European manufactured goods, so that there was excess space on the return voyage. This space was where the immigrants were packed in, in makeshift quarters without adequate ventilation, toilet facilities, or enough food or water, in either quantity or quality. The voyage was long—and unpredictable. Depending upon the winds, it might take from one to three months. The longer the voyage took, the weaker the people became from inadequate food and water and the more susceptible they became to diseases that could spread quickly in the crowded hold of a cargo ship.

The routes traveled by cargo ships depended upon the pattern of trade. This meant that the immigrants did not select their destinations but landed wherever the ship was going. For example, the Irish came to America in vessels that carried lumber from the northeastern United States, so that is where they landed when the ships returned. Many Germans took cargo vessels that carried cotton to Le Havre and returned to New Orleans—where empty space on Mississippi riverboats returning to northern cargo shipping points carried the Germans through the upper Mississippi Valley to settle in such places as Cincinnati, St. Louis, and Milwaukee. The American beer industry was created by the Germans in the latter two cities, with Budweiser originating in St. Louis and numerous other brands in Milwaukee.

The economic conditions that happened to exist in the region of settlement were particularly important for those groups too poor to relocate. For example, the Irish who landed in Boston found a city with very little industry or other opportunities for working-class people. Most American working-class groups avoided Boston for that reason, but this was where many of the Irish found themselves in the middle of the nineteenth century, and they suffered the economic consequences for years to come. The very large numbers of the Irish who arrived in a few northeastern cities (notably New York and Boston) within a very few years (the 1840s and 1850s), and most of them crowded into a single occupation (unskilled labor), created special problems of absorption into the economy and society. As canal and railroad building proceeded in the Northeast, poverty-stricken Irishmen took on the hard and dangerous jobs involved. Many settled in the cities and towns along the routes of the canals and railroads. Their present-day geographic distribution continues to reflect these early settlement patterns.

The change from wind-driven ships to steam ships drastically altered the pattern of American immigration. The time of the voyage shrank from a variable thirty to ninety days to a dependable ten days, and it now became economically feasible for working-class people to travel on ships specializing in passengers rather than cargo. No longer were immigration patterns tied to trade patterns. These developments changed both the size of the immigration and its origins. The number of immigrants rose from 5 million in the pre-Civil War era to 10 million in the next thirty years, and to 15 million in the next fifteen years. The change in countries of origin was equally dramatic: 87 percent of the immigrants were from northern and western Europe in 1882, but twenty-five years later, 81 percent were from southern and eastern Europe.[22] Slavic, Jewish, and Mediterranean peoples became important elements of the American population for the first time.

Blacks were of course brought to the United States involuntarily, and their destinations were chosen by others, but it was not a random choice. Blacks were concentrated in the South, whose climate and soil were suited to the kinds of crops that could be produced under the restrictive conditions of slavery. After the invention of the cotton gin in 1793, slavery in the United States became overwhelmingly cotton-producing slavery, and the geographic distribution of the black population shifted even more so toward the South, concentrating in the cotton-growing lands of Mississippi, Alabama, Georgia, and northern Louisiana. Even after the end of slavery, the concentration of blacks in a region that was to remain poorer than the rest of the country was an enduring economic handicap. Today, that half of the black population which lives outside the South earns about 50 percent higher income than the half still located in the South. Obviously, the income of the black population as a whole is lower because of its geographic distribution, aside from all other considerations.

Some immigrants to the United States simply settled in those parts of the country closest to their places of origin—the Orientals in Hawaii and on the West Coast, Mexican Americans in the Southwest, and Cubans in Florida. The concentrations of Puerto Ricans and West Indians in and around New York City reflect the accessibility of air and shipping routes in the twentieth century.

AN OVERVIEW

Each ethnic history is distinctive, and yet all were influenced by similar factors of age, location, time of arrival, and the skills and cultures they brought with them to American shores. The current economic position of American ethnic groups covers a wide range, and yet no group is unique, nor as unusual as comparison with a statistical "national average" might suggest. For each group, there are others in similar circumstances, whether the comparison is by income, IQ, or fertility.[23] The national average itself is nothing more than a lumping together of large differences.

Each group has changed in America, and American society has changed in many ways. The most dramatic example is that today there are people sitting in Congress and on the Supreme Court whose ancestors were brought here as slaves. Among the world's leading scientific, political, and economic figures today are Americans whose immigrant ancestors were once dismissed as "the beaten men of beaten races." Nothing has so vindicated the untapped potential of ordinary people as the American experience.

The assimilation of American ethnic groups has not been a one-way process. Much of the vernacular, food, music, and other cultural characteristics of the American society today were once ethnic peculiarities but are now part of the common heritage. Gershwin, the Kennedys, Andrew Carnegie, Joe DiMaggio, and O. J. Simpson are American phenomena rather than ethnic figures. Groups have not vanished in a melting pot, but neither they nor the country are the same as they were.

How and why American ethnic groups have developed as they have is the story of the chapters that follow.

II

Americans from Europe

Chapter 2

THE IRISH

THE IRISH were the first great ethnic "minority" in American cities. Much of their early history set the classic pattern of the newcomer to the urban economy and society. When the Irish began arriving in the 1820s, and especially after their massive immigration in the 1840s and 1850s, they began at the bottom of the urban occupational ladder—the men as manual laborers, the women as maids. They crowded into the poorest quality housing—far worse than slum housing today—and lived under conditions that readily communicated disease, fire, and such social problems as violence, alcoholism, and crime. The native public's reaction to the Irish included moving out of neighborhoods *en masse* as the immigrants moved in; stereotyping them all as drunkards, brawlers, and incompetents; and raising employment barriers exemplified in the stock phrase, "No Irish need apply." The jobs the Irish did find were those considered too hard, too menial, too dirty, or too dangerous by others. The hardships of their lives may be summed up in a nineteenth-century observation that "You seldom see a gray-haired Irishman." Their average life expectancy was forty years.

With painful slowness, the Irish rose over the generations. Their

17

first successes were in politics, where some achieved influential positions by the middle of the nineteenth century and within a few decades became dominant in big city political "machines" in Boston, New York, and other metropolitan areas. These successes brought prosperity and prominence to a few, but had little immediate impact on the economic conditions of most Irish Americans. As late as the 1890s, most of the men were still laborers and most of the women domestic servants.

Even the most famous Irish American family, the Kennedys, rose slowly at first. The first Kennedy arrived from Ireland in 1848 a laborer, and lived and died a laborer.[1] His son achieved enough modest success to send the grandson to college, and that grandson—Joseph P. Kennedy—made the fortune that enabled the great-grandsons to achieve fame and to become a tragic legend in American politics.

For most Irish Americans, what has been achieved, after more than a century, has been a rise to the level of other Americans in income, occupations, IQ, and other indicators of socioeconomic position.[2] Social acceptance came slowly and generally followed their achievements rather than being a precondition. A more genial public image of the Irishman replaced the harsh earlier stereotypes. How it all happened is a long and complex story that began, for most, in peasant cottages in Ireland.

IRELAND

A French traveler in the early nineteenth century returned from a trip that included America and Ireland and wrote:

I have seen the Indian in his forests and the Negro in his chains, and thought, as I contemplated their pitiable condition, that I saw the very extreme of human wretchedness; but I did not then know the condition of unfortunate Ireland.[3]

This was not mere rhetoric. Slaves in the United States had a longer life expectancy than peasants in Ireland, ate better, and lived in cabins built of sturdier materials, with more space, ventilation, and privacy, than the huts of contemporary Irish peasants.[4] It is unnecessary to attempt to say who was worse off on net balance. The mere fact that

The Irish

such a comparison could be made indicates something of the desperate poverty of Irish peasants in the 1830s.

While the Irish were legally free, they lived as a conquered people in their own land. British rulers controlled their political life, and British settlers dominated the agrarian economy, having confiscated most of the land and rented some of it back to Irish tenant farmers. The British landlords were more than economic interests. They were a social and political power. In the eighteenth century, their power had been so great that they could physically punish Irish peasants, who dared not raise a hand in self-defense. They could even send for a peasant's wife or daughter to spend the night with them.[5] Some students of this earlier era have questioned whether there was more than a technical difference between slavery and the subjugation of the Irish peasant.[6] Again, it is unnecessary to decide. The severity of the oppression is indicated by the mere fact that such a question could be debated.

In earlier centuries, Ireland had been a nation of some accomplishment in crafts and even learning. In pre-Christian times, the Celtic culture was "hostile to literacy,"[7] although it did use its own version of the Latin alphabet. Ireland was just outside the area of the Roman Empire, and for many centuries it remained on the periphery of Europe and hence culturally insular as well as politically isolated. Internal dynastic struggles and external invasions repeatedly disrupted Irish life and prevented the emergence of a strong, unified nation. In the early fifteenth century, the British king's effective control of Ireland extended only along a narrow strip of land about thirty miles long and twenty miles wide on the east coast around Dublin.[8] For centuries, the history of Ireland was a history of sporadic bloody uprisings and bloody repressions. Six hundred prisoners were slaughtered by the British on one occasion.[9] Contempt was mixed with antipathy. The Irish were referred to as "mere Irish" or "wild Irish." Even the rare compliment to an Irish leader was in such terms as "a great man, as savages go."[10]

One of the climactic events in Irish history was the rebellion of 1641, in which thousands of Protestants were massacred, followed by Cromwell's massacres of thousands of Irish Catholics. In the fighting, which lasted for more than a decade, more than half a million people—about 40 percent of the total population of Ireland—died from war, famine, or disease.[11] The British victory in Ireland was followed by so-called penal laws, depriving the Irish of many basic rights. Irish Catholics could neither vote nor be elected to public office, nor practice law, nor be a student or faculty member at a university. Irish Catholic children could not be educated legally, nor could Catholic churches function freely and openly, nor could Catholics own any significant property or exercise basic legal or political rights. The openly avowed purpose of these laws was to keep the Irish subjugated and impoverished. In the words of the great statesman Edmund Burke, the penal laws in Ireland constituted "a machine of as wise and elaborate contrivance for the impoverishment and degradation of the people, and the debasement in them of human nature itself, as ever proceeded from the perverted ingenuity of man."[12] The British conquerers were much more successful in keeping the Irish poor than in destroying their resistance.

Clandestine, grass-roots organizations of all sorts developed among the Irish to serve their religious, educational, and political needs. Catholic priests often went "underground" to serve their parishioners; schools were secretly conducted, and vigilantes struck against those forcibly collecting tithes among Catholics to support Protestant churches, against landlords evicting tenants—or against indigenous Irishmen collaborating with the enemy. Not only did the Irish develop considerable *organizing* skills from having to provide themselves with a range of institutions normally provided by the government; they developed skills in circumventing governmental institutions that they regarded as illegitimate oppressions. Both kinds of skills were later to prove useful in the development of Irish political power in America.

The oppressive penal laws were relaxed in the later eighteenth century and finally repealed in 1829, largely due to the political genius of Daniel O'Connell, who organized the Catholics and eventually left the British little choice other than repeal or civil war.[13] The term "Catholic Emancipation" has been applied to the repeal of these laws, and its historic significance may be suggested by the fact that the event was celebrated even in the United States, where the Liberty Bell was cracked by its ringing on that occasion.

The Irish were not simply a "lower class" in the sense of being people with less wealth or education. Their position was more castelike, in the sense that no efforts—or even achievements—would lift them to a plane of equality with others in the society as it was structured. Indeed, so inappropriate were higher level positions considered for them that law and custom combined to impede any such rise. Moreover, the property rights system in Ireland, whether by intention or design, undermined the initiative of Irish tenant farmers by making

20

any improvements they made on the land the property of the land-owner. The moral and economic impact of all this reached well beyond the time and place of these laws. Like other groups who went through generations under conditions in which they had little to gain or lose from their own actions, the Irish suffered not only the immediate losses from these laws but also longer run losses from a social pattern of reduced initiative. The "laziness" or "improvidence" of the Irish became a familiar refrain among contemporaries in Ireland—and later in America—and among sympathizers as well as critics, both scholarly and popular. The point here is not to assign blame but to recognize a factor that was to have a continuing influence on the history of the Irish immigrants in America.

Another feature of life in Ireland was to have a continuing influence after immigration to America. Ireland produced some of the finest whiskey in the world, and the economic and social climate produced ample reasons for drinking it. In the eighteenth century, "when whiskey was cheaper than bread,"[14] drunkenness was common among both the rural and the urban Irish population. Similar alcohol consumption patterns were observed even earlier, however, in Ireland[15]—and would be again among Irish American immigrants and their descendants.[16]

The general poverty of the Irish was sporadically accentuated by crop failures and famines, beginning in the 1830s. At the same time, there began a general increase in emigration, which would eventually cause Ireland to lose a higher proportion of its population this way than any other nation.[17] The climax of these crises was the Great Famine of the 1840s. An international potato blight reached Ireland in 1845, destroying much of the crop that year and in the next few succeeding years.[18] Since one-fourth of the total arable land in Ireland was used for growing potatoes,[19] the effect on the Irish—especially the Irish poor—was devastating. A million people died of starvation or starvation-related diseases and epidemics. Even more emigrated.[20] Altogether, about a third of the total population of Ireland disappeared in a few years in the mid-1840s. By 1914, the population of Ireland was one-half what it had been in the 1840s.[21]

The magnitude of the population loss was matched by the magnitude of the misery of the immigration process. The bulk of the immigrants to the United States came in the hold of cargo ships—ships built with little or no regard for the needs of passengers. There were no toilet facilities, for example, so that filth, odor, and disease were common.[22] Each emigrant was given a shelf to sleep on, three feet wide and six feet long—"still reeking from the ineradicable stench left by the emigrants of the last voyage"[23]—and these shelves were stacked up with just over two feet of space between them. About half the ships took on ordinary river water for drinking, and it was often brackish or muddy. Less than 2 percent of the ships had a medical officer on board. Most ships made no effort to segregate the sexes, and women were so vulnerable to molestation at night that many slept sitting up on their bundles of belongings rather than lie down on the shelves.

Inadequate food, water, and sanitation made ocean crossings dangerous to health and life. In the most disastrous year of all, 1847, about 20 percent of the huge famine immigration died en route to America or upon landing.[24] This was about 40,000 dead—mostly young people in the prime of life. By comparison, the loss of life among slaves transported from Africa in British vessels in the nineteenth century was about 9 percent.[25] While no other year was nearly so bad as 1847, epidemics of typhus, cholera, and other fatal diseases broke out repeatedly and unpredictably, and shipwrecks were sufficiently common that more than forty emigrant ships went down in the Atlantic in the 1850s.[26]

IRISH IMMIGRANTS IN AMERICA

The Irish who came to America came from a country where more than four-fifths of the population were rural,[27] where even the "urban" areas were mostly tiny villages,[28] and where most communities were simply "clusters and scatters of mud cabins on every plain and hillside."[29] The country lacked coal and iron, essential to modern industry, and the economic policies of the British government had the effect of inhibiting or destroying whatever other industries Ireland could develop.[30] Some idea of the general British attitude toward the Irish may be shown by the fact that food continued to be shipped from Ireland to England during the great Irish Famine of the 1840s.

Although the cost of a trip to the United States in the hold of a cargo vessel was less than ten pounds sterling[31] (less than fifty dollars at contemporary exchange rates), the poorest of the Irish could not afford even that, so that immigration was very low from the poorest fourth of the Irish population. Those a notch above them on the economic scale emigrated in large numbers,[32] often by selling their belongings, using up savings, and spending money sent by relatives already in America. From one-third to three-quarters of the Irish immigration to America in the 1830s and 1840s was financed by money sent from North America.[33]

Although the immigrants from Ireland were not the very poorest by Irish standards, they were destitute by American standards. They generally had virtually no money beyond their passage fare and so settled in the American ports of debarkation—notably Boston and New York—and usually not far from where the ships docked. The Irish immigrants typically lacked any skill of use in an urban economy, and were wholly unacquainted with the essentials of urban living. Still they had some advantages: most of them spoke English[34] (the native Irish language, Gaelic, having died out under British rule), probably more than half were literate,[35] and they were familiar with Anglo-Saxon institutions, which had been imposed on them. They had also developed their own ability to organize politically and had a cadre of trusted social and political leaders in their priests, who had been forced to acquire experience with secular organization as a result of the persecution that the Catholic church had suffered along with the Irish people. Moreover, the Irish had a sense of identity and cohesion as a people oppressed by foreigners in their native land.

Unlike more tentative immigration patterns, in which the men go first and later send for their wives and children, the nineteenth-century Irish immigration was of whole families—generally a sign of permanent commitment from the outset. They had already made the decision to become Americans when they got on the boat.

The Scotch-Irish

The first emigrants from Ireland, before the famines of the 1830s and the 1840s, were predominantly the Protestant settlers of Scottish ancestry in Ulster County—the "Scotch-Irish," as they called themselves in America, to distinguish themselves from the later Celtic immigrants. The Scotch-Irish immigration began in colonial America; was much smaller than the later immigration of the indigenous Irish; and included many more skilled workers, small businessmen, and educated people. Still it was basically an immigration of people of modest means, and many financed their voyage by agreeing to work as indentured servants for a number of years after arrival, to repay fares advanced by prospective employers or shipping companies.

The Scotch-Irish settled in a long band running roughly south from central Pennsylvania through the Shenandoah Valley of Virginia and into the Piedmont region of the Carolinas.[36] Much of this was frontier territory when the Scotch-Irish settled it, and they became famous as frontiersmen and Indian fighters. The historic concentration of the Scotch-Irish in these areas is still apparent even in the twentieth century: two of the counties in the Shenandoah Valley claim to have more Presbyterians than all other denominations put together, and their telephone books have so many names beginning with "Mac" that they are listed in a separate category instead of under "M."[37]

The Scotch-Irish tended to be independent farmers but not plantation owners or slaveholders. Indeed, the few areas of antislavery thought in the antebellum South included those where the Scotch-Irish were concentrated. Abraham Lincoln's family came from such an area.

For all their fame as fighters and drinkers, the Scotch-Irish were also builders of churches and schools wherever they went. Both traditions went back to Scotland, which had one of the most widely educated populations of any country in Europe.

As time passed, the Scotch-Irish were absorbed into the general American population, except in isolated settlements where they formed a large majority. But there was no self-conscious movement to maintain their ethnic identity, as among the later Celtic Irish immigrants. Still, enough ethnic identity remained among enough of the Scotch-Irish to bring them into repeated conflict with the Irish Catholics in the nineteenth century, recreating in the United States their bitter historic conflict in Ireland. Orange Day—the celebration of the victory of William of Orange over the Catholics in Ireland—was a source of annual conflict in the United States, as the Scotch-Irish tried to hold public celebrations and the Celtic Irish tried to stop them. Nearly fifty people lost their lives in one Orange Day clash in 1871.[38] At various times and places, the state militia or the federal troops had to be called out to stop battles between these two groups.[39]

Sometimes in American history, the earlier immigrants from a given country have helped ease the adjustment of their later-arriving fellow countrymen. Nothing of this sort was possible between the Scotch-Irish and their Celtic fellow Irishmen, partly because of their different geographic distribution, but more fundamentally because of the bitter hostility between them, brought over from the Old World. The Irish immigrants had to make it entirely on their own.

24

The Irish

Eventually, the very term "Irish" or Irish American" came to mean only those people of indigenous or Celtic Irish ancestry, not the Scotch-Irish. More than half of the Irish were concentrated in four states: Massachusetts, New York, Pennsylvania, and Illinois. The sum total of the Irish Americans exceeded the total population of Ireland. There were more Irishmen in New York than in Dublin.[40] Altogether, more than 4 million people emigrated from Ireland to the United States in the nineteenth century.[41] But there were only about 85,000 Irishmen in the whole South.[42] The Irish were not only concentrated geographically in the Northeast; they were overwhelmingly urban in America, as they had been overwhelmingly rural in Ireland. More than four-fifths lived in urban communities.[43]

The building of roads, canals, and railroads eventually took large numbers of the Irish out of the few big cities in which they were concentrated and spread them out in smaller communities along the routes of these arteries.[44] Some of these communities, in fact, originated as shantytowns occupied by the Irish workmen.[45] Irishmen who joined the army sometimes settled near the military posts from which they were discharged.[46] But organized attempts to spread the Irish out into the agricultural countryside were generally unsuccessful. American agriculture on large isolated farms—especially on the frontier—was radically different from growing potatoes on small plots in close-knit little communities in Ireland. Aside from great differences in the skills needed and in the harsher American climate, the isolation implied by most American farming was foreign to the gregarious Irish, and a separation from other Irishmen would have meant for many a loss of the opportunity to attend a Catholic church. Despite numerous appeals and campaigns—extending into the twentieth century—the American Irish remained a largely urban people.[47]

As the Irish crowded into the northeastern urban centers, a pattern unfolded that was to be seen again and again with many later groups. Homes originally intended for single families were subdivided into tiny apartments into which many large families were crowded. Cellars and attics were also turned into dwellings. Makeshift housing was constructed in alleys. Such living patterns reflected not only the poverty of the Irish but also their being used to squalid living conditions in mud huts in Ireland.

Cleanliness was neither a cultural value nor a reasonable possibility for people forced to work at dirty jobs and lacking access to indoor running water. Sewage piled up in backyard privies until the municipal authorities chose to collect it, or else it ran off in open trenches, fouling the air and providing breeding grounds for dangerous diseases. The importance of proper garbage disposal, to keep the neighborhood from being overrun with rats, was one of many similar facts of urban life that every rural group new to the city would have to learn over the years, beginning with the Irish and continuing through many others until the present day. None paid a higher price than the Irish during their period of adjustment. Cholera, which had been unknown before, swept through Boston in 1849, concentrated almost exclusively in Irish neighborhoods.[48] In New York, cholera was also disproportionately observed in Irish wards.[49] In various cities, both tuberculosis and fire swept regularly through the overcrowded tenements where the Irish lived, and there was also a high rate of insanity among the Irish immigrants during the difficult early years of adjustment.[50] The incidence of tuberculosis in Boston varied closely with the proportion of the Irish living in a neighborhood.[51]

Patterns of alcoholism and fighting brought over from Ireland persisted in the United States. Over half the people arrested in New York in the 1850s were Irish[52]—usually for drunken or disorderly behavior, rather than for serious crimes. Police vans became known as "Paddy wagons" because the prisoners in them were so often Irish. "The fighting Irish" was a phrase that covered everything from individual brawls to mass melees (known as "Donnybrooks," for a town in Ireland) to criminal gangs and terrorist organizations like the "Molly Maguires," who murdered and dynamited on a mass scale in Pennsylvania until twenty of their leaders were hanged in 1876.

Irish neighborhoods were tough neighborhoods, in cities around the country. The Irish Sixth Ward in New York was known as "the bloody ould Sixth."[53] Another Irish Neighborhood in New York was known as "Hell's Kitchen," and another as "San Juan Hill" because of the battles fought there. In Milwaukee, the Irish section was called the "Bloody Third."[54] In New Orleans, the area called "Irish Channel" was "long notorious as one of the tougher parts of the city."[55] Where the Irish workers built the Illinois Central Railroad, people spoke of "a murder a mile"[56] as they laid the track.

The largest riot in American history was by predominantly Irish rioters in New York in 1863. Angry at the Civil War military draft, which bore more heavily on working-class people like themselves, the Irish rioted for several days, killing a thousand people in the process. But although the Irish were prominent—and perhaps paramount—in

The Irish

violence, they were by no means unique. Mass violence was common in nineteenth-century America,[57] and the Irish were among its victims, as anti-Catholic rioters invaded their neighborhoods to burn churches and homes and to attack people.[58]

The Irish put many efforts into self-improvement. Temperance societies struggled with the age-old problem of drink. Emigrant aid societies provided services designed to shield new arrivals from schemers trying to defraud them of their small sums of money. The Catholic church was active on many fronts, from education to charity to opposing terrorist organizations that others were afraid to oppose.[59] With all these efforts, the economic rise and social acceptance of the Irish were still slow. A state census in 1855 showed that one-fourth of the Irish working in New York City were domestic servants and another fourth laborers and other unskilled workers.[60] In Boston, almost two-thirds of the Irish were either unskilled workers or domestic servants.[61] Similar occupational patterns were found in Milwaukee, St. Louis, Detroit, New Orleans, and other cities.[62] No other contemporary immigrant group was so concentrated at the bottom of the economic ladder.[63] Even the proportion of the black population who were laborers and house servants in Boston in 1850 was much lower than among the Irish,[64] and the free blacks in mid-century Boston were in general economically better off than the Irish.[65]

The Irish were prominent not only in unskilled work but also in hard, dirty, and dangerous work, such as coal mining and the building of railroads and canals. Malaria was so common among canal diggers that it became known as "canal fever." Cholera and dysentery were also common—and deadly. Railroad building had so many fatalities that it was said that there was "an Irishman buried under every tie."[66] In the pre-Civil War South, Irish laborers were often used in work considered too dangerous for slaves, who represented a sizable capital investment.[67]

The jobs that the Irish immigrants held were not simply hard, dirty, and dangerous. They were also unsteady, as unskilled work often was and is. Once a canal or railroad had been built, the workers were out of a job. The same was true of many other construction jobs, seasonal work, and casual occupations. The Irishwomen's work as domestic servants and washerwomen was usually more steadily available than that of Irishmen—a situation later to be repeated among blacks.

As in Ireland itself, the poverty and improvidence of the Irish immigrants in America often reduced them to living on charity when hard times came. In early nineteenth-century Ireland, even before the famine, it was common for whole families of the poor to go "tramping about for months, begging from parish to parish."[68] Recourse to public charity was a well-established habit carried over to America. Expenditures for relief to the poor in Boston more than doubled from 1845 to 1855, during the heavy influx of the Irish,[69] after such expenditures had been relatively stable for years. In New York City in the same era, about 60 percent of the people in almshouses had been born in Ireland.[70] As late as 1906, there were more Irish than Italian paupers, beggars, and inmates of almshouses,[71] even though the Italians arrived a generation later and were generally poorer at the turn of the century. Radically different attitudes toward accepting charity existed in Ireland and Italy, and these attitudes apparently had more effect than their respective objective economic conditions in America. There were similar cultural differences in attitudes toward the abandonment of wives and children. In the 1840s, "it was almost automatically assumed that an orphan was Irish,"[72] and as late as 1914, about half the Irish families on Manhattan's west side were fatherless.[73] No such pattern appeared among the Italians.

But although both contemporary observers and later scholars frequently described the Irish immigrants as thriftless, the Irish also left a remarkable record of donations to the Catholic church and remittances to family members back in Ireland—all out of very low incomes. Money from America paid the fares of most of those who immigrated during the famine of the 1840s, and from 1848 to 1864, Irish Americans sent $65,000,000 to Ireland.[74] The Irish could and did save from their earnings, and were generous in donating these savings to their church and their families. Nevertheless, they were not good financial managers over time. Nor were they inhibited about resorting to public charity when in distress.

The low and precarious economic conditions of the nineteenth-century Irish were reflected in their living conditions—perhaps the worst of any racial or ethnic group in American history. As one account noted: "Though Jews and Italians lived five and ten to a room in roach-infested, dilapidated, and dark buildings, their conditions do not seem to have been as horrendous as those of the Irish."[75] By the time these later immigrants—and then blacks—reached the big cities, indoor running water was common, even if cold and in a spigot or toilet shared by many families. In the housing available to the early Irish immigrants, there was a "complete neglect of sewage and sanitation of any kind." The only water came from hydrants in the backyards, where crude outhouses were also located, "perpetually gushing over into the surrounding yards" and acting as "mighty carriers of disease." Garbage also collected in these yards, "which converted the few feet between adjoining buildings into storehouses of accumulated filfth."[76] Inside, rooms were small, unpainted, and typically had damp walls and leaky roofs. Repairs went undone for years. Closets were rare; belongings were either hung on pegs or simply scattered around. Washtubs provided whatever cleaning was received by clothes or people, for bathtubs "were unheard of."[77] Even attics only three feet high were rented out.[78] It was common in Irish slums for whole families to live "in a single room without sunlight or ventilation."[79] The crowding was so great that beds were shared by numerous adults, "sometimes wife and husband, brothers and sisters, in the same bed."[80] Slum streets were "ankle-deep in garbage," and sewage flowed in open trenches.[81]

Although the Irish immigrants (like other immigrants) had a disproportionate representation of young people in the prime of life, the mortality rate shot up after their arrival. Boston's mortality rate in 1850 was double that of the rest of Massachusetts, even though there were relatively fewer aged people in Boston. The difference was due to the extremely high mortality rate in the Irish neighborhoods.[82] Diseases that had become rare in America now flourished again. In 1849, cholera spread through Philadelphia to New York and to Boston—primarily in Irish neighborhoods.[83] There had not been a smallpox epidemic in Boston since 1792, but after 1845, it became a recurring plague, again primarily among the Irish.[84] The spread of the Irish into other neighborhoods meant, among other things, the spread of these and other diseases. The residential flight of middle-class Americans from the Irish immigrants[85] was by no means all irrationality.

LATER GENERATIONS

The Irish continued to immigrate to the United States in large numbers, even after the catastrophic famines of the 1840s had ended. So there were—and are—first-generation Irish Americans throughout American history. Yet the peak of Irish immigration to the United

States was reached in the mid-nineteenth century, and thereafter, second- and third-generation Irish Americans became an ever larger portion of the total picture.

How did these later generations fare? Given the desperate poverty of their immigrant forebearers, it may seem inevitable that they rose. And yet progress is by no means automatic or costless, and many parts of the world remain mired in the same poverty as their ancestors in centuries past.

Politics

One of the earliest and most spectacular rises of the Irish in America was in politics. Block voting of the Irish in the big cities, where they were often the largest single group, assured them political influence, evident as early as the 1830s.[86] But the political success of the Irish went far beyond this, including outright control of municipal political machines in many cities for many decades, long after other ethnic groups arrived and formed a numerical majority of the electorate. In Boston, Irish mayors began being elected in the 1880s.[87] In New York at the same time, the Irish were in control of the Tammany political machine[88]—an organization from which they had once been excluded, in the early nineteenth century.[89] Similar Irish political domination occurred in contemporary Chicago, Buffalo, Milwaukee, San Francisco, and other cities.[90] This Irish domination of American big city politics continued on into the twentieth century, including to the present day in some cities.

Irish political bosses included many picturesque, legendary figures, from John F. Fitzgerald ("Honey Fitz"), singing mayor of nineteenth-century Boston (and grandfather of President John F. Kennedy) to Richard J. Daley, mayor of twentieth-century Chicago for more than twenty years. Many were charming, beloved rogues, such as New York's mayor "Big Tim" Sullivan, "a warmhearted giant" who "collected graft from many sources and distributed food and clothes to the poor"—and whose funeral, in 1913, was attended by 25,000 people.[91] In a similar mold was James Michael Curley, who was mayor of Boston four times, a congressman for two terms, and governor of Massachusetts—as well as serving two terms in prison.[92]

The Irish did not simply take over the conventional apparatus of politics. They transformed American municipal politics. They changed the class composition of municipal government, putting the reins of power in the hands of men who had risen from the working class, and

The Irish

often from the slums. Moreover, the Irish political machines were accessible to people still in the working class and the slums—accessible not only to those seeking political careers, but accessible more broadly to members of the great urban masses who needed help in getting a job, or naturalization papers, or food or fuel to last through an emergency. The bewildering bureaucracies, regulations, and red tape confronting the poor and undereducated could be made responsive, or could be circumvented through the episodic interventions of political bosses. The earlier history of the Irish in Ireland provided them with both the skills and the attitudes required to operate outside the official rules while adhering to a separate, informal code of conduct. The Irish "brought to America a settled tradition of regarding the formal government as illegitimate, and the informal one as bearing the true impress of popular sovereignty."[93] Bribery, violence, and vote fraud were prominent features of the Irish political machines. However, they were not chaotic but highly organized and controlled. Irish political machines were built on loyalty to individuals and to the organization. Their guiding principle was the pragmatic desire to be elected, not any ideological program.

The goals of political machines have been the perquisites of power—salary, graft, and the ability to appoint followers and favorites to sought-after jobs. These jobs included not only the exalted positions but also many less spectacular posts still considered highly desirable by low-income people: policemen, firemen, clerks, schoolteachers, and other municipal jobs that were largely appointive in nineteenth-century municipalities. For example, in 1855 nearly 40 percent of New York City's policemen were immigrants, and about three-fourths of these immigrants were Irish.[94] By the late nineteenth century, the police forces and fire departments of all major American cities were controlled by Irish Americans.[95]

What tied these municipal political organizations together was neither philosophy nor a social vision, but the *quid pro quo*. Voters who loyally supported the machines could turn to it for help in time of trouble—which might cover anything from a threatened eviction to petty criminal charges to a need to avenge some insult. The businessmen who made contributions to the party or paid graft to the political boss could expect municipal regulations to be relaxed or his violations to be overlooked, and city contracts were more likely to come his way. The rank-and-file followers of the political boss could expect their years of getting out the vote, looking out for local constituents, and otherwise doing the bidding of the leader to be duly rewarded with slow but steady promotions up the hierarchy. Reciprocal loyalty was the key.

The highly controlled hierarchy of machine politics meant that each individual had to wait his turn for advancement—a pattern common in Ireland, where waiting patiently (and unmarried) to inherit the family farm was the custom. This also meant that whoever was at the top could stay at the top for many years, often for life. In its heyday, the Tammany machine in New York had just three leaders in half a century—all Irish. In Brooklyn, one man (also Irish) headed the machine for more than forty years—followed by another (Irish) man who ruled for a quarter of a century, until his death. In the Bronx, another Irish machine leader was in control for more than thirty years, until his death.[96] Similar longevity was common in Irish political machines in Chicago.[97]

Even more remarkable than such individual longevity was the even greater longevity of Irish political machines, long after the Irish were outnumbered by the other immigrant groups that came to America by the millions in the late nineteenth and early twentieth centuries. It was common for the Irish machines to continue in power, not only in the city as a whole, but even for Irish politicians to represent neighborhoods that were predominantly Italian[98] or Jewish,[99] or other ethnic groups. For example, the Nineteenth Ward in turn-of-the-century Chicago was about four-fifths Italian but was represented for years by an Irish politician named Johnny Powers.[100] Only after many years did the Irish politicians find it necessary to admit Jews and Italians to even low-ranking jobs in their political organizations. It was the 1890s before "ambitious young Jews were beginning to be accepted as Tammany hangers-on, messengers, and flunkies."[101] As late as 1907, Tammany had only one Jewish district leader.[102] Similarly, in Chicago and Boston, Italians were belatedly and grudgingly given low-level jobs, becoming "small cogs in the ward machine"[103] and being placed in ambiguous and compromising positions as go-betweens between their own people and the Irish political bosses.[104] Attempts of Italian and Jewish Americans to gain political control of their own communities were repeatedly beaten back by the more politically experienced Irish, on into the early twentieth century.[105]

The Irish had a number of advantages in political competition. First, they had a strong sense of group solidarity, going back for centuries in Ireland, where they had been a persecuted people in their own land. Jews and Italians had many more internal divisions, also pointing to their experience in Europe in centuries past. The Irish also had the advantage of arriving in America decades earlier, speaking English, and having a history of political awareness and organizational experience, even if clandestine. Finally, the culture of the Irish was one in which personal charm and fluency with words were highly valued[106]—obviously great assets in politics and in other areas where personality and articulation are important, such as law, show business, the labor movement, journalism, and the priesthood—all areas where the Irish also became very successful.[107]

The Irish were by no means the originators of corrupt politics. They were simply more successful at it, and performed with a warmer human touch. No small part of their success was due to the insensitivity of their political opponents to the desires and fears of the immigrant masses in the cities. Political "reform" movements were typically in the hands of upper-income, more educated people with values, goals, and styles very different from those of the working-class voters. Reform politicians typically had neither personal nor organizational roots in the low-income communities, so that even when they acted on behalf of the poor, it was with little mutual understanding and much unintended harm. The poor usually ended up preferring corrupt politicians, who understood them, to distant theorists, who did not.

The advantages of indigenous political leaders from within the immigrant communities still do not explain why they should be specifically Irish, long after great numbers of Jewish, Italian, Polish, etc. people constituted the bulk of the urban masses. The Irish advantages included speaking English—and often speaking it eloquently even when ungrammatically. The Irish were also unique among peoples from a peasant background in having had a history of political and organizational experience in Europe—in maintaining underground religious organizations and terrorist organizations. Other peasant masses, in Italy or Poland, for example, also suffered oppression, but not in the particular form that would make the Irish kind of underground activity an effective response. For example, the oppressors of Italian peasants were other Italians, not a different race with a different religion. The issue of race, religion, or country did not exist as an emotional nucleus for group solidarity. Among the Jews scattered through Europe, religion, culture, and race were factors promoting solidarity. But the Jews were so hopelessly outnumbered and isolated in each country that it would have been suicidal for them to engage in the kind of resistance and terrorism applied by the Irish, who were a large majority in their own country. In short, no other immigrant group had either the historical or organizational experience of the Irish or their gift for words and human relations, as demonstrated in many other fields besides politics.

In an era when religious differences were fiercely divisive, the Irish had the political advantage over other Catholic immigrants of being committed to the American principle of separation of church and state. They had lived under a state-established church—the Anglican church—in Ireland and had found it repellent. Other Catholics from countries with state-established churches had a very different experience and tradition, for there it was their own church that was established. While it was no political advantage to the Irish to be Catholic in Protestant America, their particular political view of church-state relations made them less politically vulnerable than other Catholics. While there were nativists who raised alarms about the dangers of the pope taking over the United States politically, such alarms had little to feed on in Irish-American theory or practice and lost credibility over time. Such accusations were resurrected against Al Smith in his 1928 bid for the presidency, but the great number of successful Irish Catholic candidates for other offices makes this less than a decisive example. Smith himself had of course been elected to other offices, including governor of New York, by a largely Protestant electorate. John F. Kennedy's election as president in 1960 marked the death knell of a political tactic that was already moribund.

Irish political machines have almost invariably been of the Democratic party, going far back into the nineteenth century. The Irish districts voted overwhelmingly Democratic—more so than any other ethnic group.[108] Other groups split their votes among the Whigs or the emerging Republican party. In the 1850s, there arose yet another political party, the American party—better known as "Know-Nothings"—based on opposition to immigrants in general and the Irish in particular.

The Know-Nothings were initially a secret order, from which the American party developed as a political arm. Nativist hostility to foreigners went back before this particular movement, but by the 1830s, such hostility appeared to be dying out. However, a great and sustained increase in immigration rekindled nativist feeling. Immigration to the United States had been well below 10,000 persons per year prior to the 1840s but soared over 100,000 in 1842, over 200,000 in 1847, and over 400,000 in 1854. The Irish were the largest single group of immigrants, and in many of the years of the 1840s and the 1850s, over half the immigrants to the United States came from Ireland.[109] The Irish

The Irish

were considered not merely to be foreigners, but an *unassimilable* group.[110] In an argument destined to be repeated many times about many groups, it was claimed that, although earlier immigrants could be absorbed into the mainstream of American life, the peculiar characteristics of this group made that impossible.

The nativist attack on foreigners—centering on the Irish[111]—cited their political corruption; their low standard of living, which was seen as a threat to the living standards of native American workers; and their overrepresentation among people in jail and receiving public charity. That the Irish were overwhelmingly Catholic was to become and remain a central source of discord—especially in the nineteenth century, when religious differences were very serious matters, politically and socially. One small but significant indication of the social importance of religious differences was that the intermarriage rate of the Irish in Boston in the 1860s was the lowest of all the immigrant groups—and even lower than black/white intermarriage rates at the same period.[112]

The Know-Nothings rode a rising tide of nativist feeling to spectacular political successes. Advocating tighter controls on immigration and naturalization, the Know-Nothings in 1855 elected six governors and controlled several state legislatures, as well as electing numerous congressmen.[113] Their decline was, however, almost as swift as their rise. One of their problems was that northern and southern branches of the party could not agree on the issue of slavery.

The Know-Nothings were, on most issues, a reform party, and the Irish were opposed to most reforms. The Irish sought to rise in the existing system, not to change it fundamentally. Democrats in general were, in this era, defenders of the status quo, while Whigs, Republicans, and the short-lived Know-Nothings were in favor of a variety of reforms, ranging from limitations on alcohol consumption to women's suffrage to the containment or abolition of slavery. Part of their hostility to the Irish was due to the fact that the Irish were seen as obstacles to the achievement of many reforms and social experiments.[114]

Economic Advancement

The spectacular success of Irish politicians in nineteenth-century American cities was by no means reflected in the economic conditions of contemporary Irish Americans as a whole. As late as 1890, 42 percent of the Irish were servants, and many of the others remained in unskilled labor.[115] In Boston in 1890, while 4 percent of native Americans and 5 percent of Germans worked in the professions, less than one-tenth of 1 percent of the Irish had such occupations.[116] While 31 percent of the native Americans did high-level white-collar work, only 6 percent of the Irish had advanced that far.[117] But although the economic conditions of the Irish compared unfavorably with some other groups, they were rising. Despite "pronounced similarities between the Irish and the Negroes"[118] in mid-century Boston, later generations of the Irish pulled ahead of blacks in skilled and white-collar occupations.[119] Still, the Irish were the slowest rising of the European ethnic groups.

With socioeconomic rise came internal differentiation. Some remained "shanty Irish," mired in poverty and squalor, while others became "lace curtain Irish," seeking amenities and respectability. The influx of new Irish immigrants continued to begin at the bottom of the economic ladder, but many of the second-generation Irish moved up from the positions held by their fathers. For example, while only 10 percent of first-generation Irishmen in Boston held white-collar jobs in 1890, nearly 40 percent of the second-generation Irish had achieved that at the same time. Conversely, while two-thirds of the older generation ended their careers as unskilled and semiskilled workers, at the same time only about one-third of their second-generation contemporaries ended their careers in such positions.[120]

As the Irish rose slowly through manual and white-collar occupations, many of their places at the bottom of the economic ladder were taken by members of other groups that now constituted the bulk of the massive new immigration to the United States from southern and eastern Europe after the Civil War. A whole pattern of ecological succession was set in motion, with later arriving groups (notably the Italians) slowly replacing the Irish in hard, dirty, and dangerous occupations and moving into the slums as the Irish began moving out. By 1910, the proportion of the Italians who were unskilled and semiskilled laborers in Boston was precisely the same as that of the Irish twenty years earlier.[121] Where the Irish had been slum tenants with Anglo-Saxon landlords, now there were increasingly Italian tenants with Irish slum landlords.[122] Where the older Americans had once fled as the Irish moved into their neighborhoods, now the Irish fled as blacks, Jews, and Italians moved in.[123] Where the Irish children had once been taught by Anglo-Saxon teachers, now increasingly Irish schoolteachers taught children who were Jewish or Italian.[124] Where the Irish immigrants had once been used as strikebreakers against unionized native workers, now Italian or black workers were used as strikebreakers against unionized Irish workers.[125]

The Irish

The pattern of ethnic ecological succession did not mean a complete repetition of one group's history in another group. Some groups moved upward at a faster pace than others. The Jews, for example, arrived in the United States with even less money than the Irish;[126] initially earned less than their Irish contemporaries; but then overtook and outdistanced the Irish in income, occupation, and education.[127] Moreover, there were numerous group differences, not only in the pace of economic advancement, but also in the channels through which advancement took place. The Irish advanced in politics, banking, union leadership, sports, and journalism; the Jews in business ownership, skilled trades, scholarship, and science.

The Irish seldom advanced through business entrepreneurship. Even though the Boston Irish had higher incomes than the Jews in that city in 1909, the Jews were nine times more heavily represented among businessmen[128]—even if, at that time, many of these businesses were petty peddling from pushcarts and the like. Where the first-generation Irish in their poverty became domestic servants and heavy, unskilled laborers, Jews sought other kinds of low-level jobs—jobs that permitted them to acquire a skill or learn to operate their own businesses later on. Italians also went into business more often than the Irish. Even in Irish-dominated Boston, not a single important office of the Chamber of Commerce was held by an Irishman, as late as 1929.[129]

There have been some highly successful businesses founded by Irish Americans, such as the Grace Steamship Lines, and Irish Americans invented the O'Sullivan rubber heel and the "hurricane lamp" for use on railroads.[130] However, the kinds of businesses in which the Irish have done well have typically been "businesses such as banking, where there is stress on personal qualities and the accommodation of conflicting interests, and not a little involvement in politics."[131] Bars and saloons are also businesses requiring a human touch, and the Irish have thrived in such businesses. But by and large, "the Irish have not been especially outstanding in the field of science and invention."[132]

The areas in which the Irish met their greatest success, and the channels through which the mass of the Irish advanced, were typically areas not requiring either business entrepreneurship or scholarly education. Neither of these were part of their history in Ireland, nor did they become prominent in the Irish-American pattern. The ancient Celtic culture was "hostile to literacy,"[133] and Ireland was the only major Western nation that did not build a single university during the Middle Ages.[134] Even a sympathetic historian of the Irish acknowledged that there has been "almost no intellectual tradition" among them.[135]

Against this background, it is perhaps not surprising that early twentieth-century Irish youngsters in New York finished high school at a rate less than one-hundredth of that of youngsters from a German or Jewish background.[136] At this point in history, the Irish were by no means underprivileged vis-à-vis the Jews, either economically or in terms of political power. Nor was the difference one of "ability," for as late as World War I Irish soldiers scored substantially higher on mental tests than did Jewish soldiers.[137] The importance of education was simply seen very differently by the two cultures, and had been for centuries. This apparently had more weight than the immediate objective circumstances, which at this point were all in favor of the Irish, compared to the Jews. In the late nineteenth and early twentieth centuries, the Irish in Boston had higher incomes than the Jews,[138] smaller families to support,[139] and a higher rate of literacy,[140] in addition to being dominant in politics. As late as 1950, Irish immigrants had the edge in education over Jewish immigrants, but the *children* of the Jewish immigrants went on to college more than twice as often as the children of Irish immigrants.[141]

Many Irish Americans rose to prominence in sports and entertainment—a pattern to be repeated by later ethnic groups living in poverty and without an intellectual or entrepreneurial tradition. There were idolized actors named Tyrone Power in both the nineteenth and twentieth centuries (father and son), famous singers from John McCormack to Bing Crosby, and sports heroes from John L. Sullivan to John J. McGraw to Knute Rockne and his "Gipper." The Irish dominated some sports—such as boxing, baseball, and track—but were not nearly as prominent in swimming or wrestling. The Irish distribution among sports was also a pattern later to be repeated by blacks. In the nineteenth century, it was usually a foregone conclusion that the heavyweight champion of the world would be Irish—Jack Kilrain, John L. Sullivan, and "Gentleman Jim" Corbett being the best known. In the twentieth century, Irish-American heavyweight champions included Jack Dempsey and Gene Tunney, and ended with James J. Braddock—whose loss of the title to Joe Louis marked the beginning of ethnic succession in boxing. The early Irish Americans were so successful in boxing and baseball that non-Irish boxers and ball players often took Irish names to help their careers.

Although scholarship was not a feature of Irish traditions, the use of words has been. Even among the mass of poor and uneducated Irish—

in both Ireland and America—pride in the expressive use of words has been common, whether called "a gift of gab," a talent for aphorism, or plain "blarney." Many famous writers come from this background, from journalists like Peter Finley Dunne (creator of Mister Dooley), David G. Croly (editor of the famous *New York World*), and sportswriter John Kiernan to novelists and playwrights from John O'Hara to Eugene O'Neill.

The point here is not to praise or blame whole peoples, nor even to rank or grade their performances. The point is much more general—to assess the role of enduring cultural values compared to more immediate "objective" conditions.

Intergroup Relations

Despite the ability of Irish politicians to win the votes of other ethnic groups in the nineteenth century, the general relations between the Irish populace and other groups were typically far from harmonious.

Perhaps the worst relations between any two groups in American history have been between the Irish and the Negroes. Chronic animosity between them erupted into numerous fights and riots for more than a century, in cities across the country, both at work and in the slums they often shared.[142] The famous draft riots of New York in 1863 saw rampaging Irishmen lynching Negroes on sight, often mutilating them, and even burning down an orphanage for black children.[143] The first blacks to move into Harlem were middle-class Negroes who left the black enclave in mid-Manhattan around the turn of the century to get away from the Irish living nearby.

The Irish had similar relations with other groups whose skins were white. In addition to their many bloody clashes with the Scotch-Irish, they were also involved in numerous riots and street battles against the Germans;[144] violence against the Italians in various cities;[145] and attacks on Jewish property, persons, and burial grounds in Boston and New York.[146] On the West Coast, the Irish led both physical assaults and political attacks on the nineteenth-century Chinese immigrants.[147]

The usual difficulties of determining the initiator of hostilities are not so great in some of these instances. Some of the groups with whom the Irish had numerous clashes were groups that lived relatively harmoniously with other groups. For example, the Jews and the Italians generally lived peaceably with each other,[148] although neither could get along with the Irish. The Chinese Americans seldom—if ever—attacked any other ethnic group. The historic hostility between blacks and the Irish goes back well before the Civil War, at a time when there was only a relative handful of free blacks, and it would have been suicidal for them to have launched unprovoked attacks on the numerous Irish. Germans sometimes initiated conflicts with the Irish, but on other occasions, "Irish rowdies interfered with German picnics, frequently for no apparent reason except to add excitement to an otherwise dull Sunday."[149]

The era when Irish immigration peaked, in the 1840s and 1850s, was an era when violence peaked in American cities—and not merely because of the Irish. Often mobs of nativists rampaged into Irish neighborhoods, attacking individuals and burning down homes and churches.[150] The general level of violence in the country was high.

Violence was not the only form of intergroup hostility involving the Irish. Institutions controlled by the Irish—notably municipal politics and the Catholic church—were institutions in which it was very difficult for the non-Irish to advance. Not only was it difficult for Jews or Italians to advance in the Irish political machines themselves, it was even difficult for them to get city jobs under the patronage system.[151] Only with the rise of civil service tests did Jews begin replacing the Irish in municipal jobs in New York City. A similar pattern of ethnic preserves was apparent in the Catholic church, where "a priest born in Baltimore of Italian parents, speaking English and Italian equally naturally, will see priests new from Ireland, promoted over him because he is a 'foreigner.'"[152] Although the Irish were only 17 percent of the Catholic population, they were 35 percent of the clergy and 50 percent of the hierarchy.[153] Over half of all Catholic bishops in the United States from 1789 to 1935 were Irish.[154] Protests by non-Irish Catholics over Irish control of the church caused the sending of a papal emissary to the United States and the establishment of churches and parochial schools for various ethnic groups, preferably staffed by members of those respective groups.

In addition to hostility between the Irish and specific ethnic groups, there developed in later generations a generalized hostility of Irish Americans toward "foreigners" in general.[155] With the Irish now having acquired a higher standard of living and a degree of respectability, the new immigrants were seen as being as much of a threat to them as they themselves had once been seen by an earlier generation of Americans.

Like other patterns found among the Irish in America, pervasive intergroup conflict seems less traceable to circumstances in the United States than to attitudes or traditions going back to their history in Ireland. The circumstances of the Irish immigrants in the United States were not very different from those of such later arriving groups as the Italians, who have peacefully coexisted with many very different kinds of other people. In Ireland, however, those whom an Irishman encountered in centuries past could be readily categorized as either (1) another Irishman or (2) a bitter enemy—disdainful, persecuting, and often violent. The group identity of the Irish was pronounced, before they set foot on American soil.

Against this background, it is all the more remarkable that the American Catholic church, although Irish dominated, has played an important conciliatory role among the various Catholic ethnic groups and even an important role in philanthropic activities among Negroes, reaching far back in history[156] and continuing on to the present.[157] While the south Boston Irish were rioting over the busing of black schoolchildren into their communities, Catholic parochial schools in cities across the country were operating in black neighborhoods with white—often Irish—priests and nuns, who were achieving remarkable educational results, far outstripping those in public schools in the same neighborhoods.

THE IRISH TODAY

With the rise of the Irish, and their growing social acceptance, has come both cultural and biological assimilation, making it difficult to determine precisely who is Irish today. While only about one-tenth of the Irish married outside of their own ethnic group in the 1860s, in the 1960s just over half of all Irish-American men married women from different ethnic backgrounds.[158] The descendants of the original immigrants from Ireland include many who may be classified under other ethnic groups today, or may be part of that half of the American population that cannot identify its ethnicity at all to the census surveyors.

Much of the data available on the Irish today are based on individuals who choose to identify themselves to the Census Bureau as Irish, and these may or may not be typical of the descendants of the original immigrants from Ireland. If it is the more upwardly mobile who assimilate more readily, those still readily identifiable as Irish (or Italian,

German, etc.) may be a residual population, less successful than the larger group from which they came.

Even with such reservations, however, it is clear that the Irish have risen from their initial poverty to reach (or surpass) American standards of income or education. Irish-American incomes have been about 5 percent above the national average in the 1970s.[159] Their years of schooling and their proportions in college are about the same as the U.S. population as a whole. The IQ scores of Irish Americans have been consistently just above the national norm of 100 for the past half century.[160] Alcoholism remains a striking characteristic among the Irish in America, as in Ireland. Various studies show them with rates of alcohol consumption and alcoholic diseases higher than among Negroes, Germans, Italians, Jews, or many other groups.[161] Family size among the Irish is the same as among other Americans,[162] despite popular stereotypes about large Catholic families. Irish Americans number about 16 million people, or about 8 percent of the total U.S. population.[163] Their voting patterns are now about the same as those of other Americans.[164] With the election of John F. Kennedy to the presidency in 1960, the "issue" of a Catholic president is dead.

The Irish have in fact become so Americanized that some lament that they have lost their distinctive qualities.[165] But becoming American can hardly be regarded as failure. It remains the dream of many around the world,[166] and was the dream of millions who first embarked on the perilous journey from Ireland.

Chapter 3

THE GERMANS

MORE THAN 25 million Americans are of German ancestry. This is more than for any other ethnic group except descendants of people from the British Isles, who originally colonized the country and who now number 29 million. Germans are the largest group to immigrate to America. They have played important roles in American history, and not merely because of their numbers. American industry, education, military defense, eating and recreational patterns all reflect the contributions and influence of German Americans. The very language of the country reflects that influence, in such words as kindergarten, delicatessen, frankfurters, and hamburgers. The Conestoga wagons in which American pioneers first crossed the great prairie were created by Germans. So was the Kentucky rifle of the frontiersman. The Christmas tree was a German tradition that became an American tradition. The leading American optical firm—Bausch and Lomb—was created by Germans, as were all of the leading brands of American beer. Suspension bridges and the cables that hold them were both created by a German-American engineer. Iron, steel, automobiles, pianos, lumber, chocolate bars, and petroleum are among the many products in which Americans of German ancestry were pioneers and dominant figures.[1]

The German military tradition gave the United States some of its leading generals down through history—including those generals who led American armies to victory against Germany in World War 1 and World War II—Pershing and Eisenhower.[2]

Large-scale immigration from Germany to the United States has not been concentrated in a few decades, like immigration from other countries, but has occurred in many different eras of American and German history. There were German communities in colonial America, and Germans were a significant proportion of all immigrants to the United States throughout the nineteenth century. More than 100,000 people emigrated from Germany to the United States in 1852 and in 1952, and in many other years in between.[3] There were fluctuations in the size of the immigration—varying with conditions in the United States and in Germany—but the flow has remained substantial for nearly two centuries. At various periods of history, the flow has been predominantly immigrants, at other times refugees. Sometimes the immigrants have been predominantly Catholic, sometimes predominantly Protestant, and sometimes predominantly Jewish. The regional origins of this emigration in Germany have also differed. The net result is that German Americans have been a highly diverse group—not only by such usual indications as class, religion, or region, but also differing greatly by how many generations they have been American.

GERMANY

A very substantial portion of the German immigration to America occurred when there was no Germany. It was not until 1871 that Prussia, Bavaria, Baden, Mecklenburg, Hesse, and other Germanic states were united by Bismarck to form the nation of Germany. However, the German language is recorded as far back as 750 AD[4] and Germanic peoples—who do *not* include the Huns[5]—as far back as the first century BC.

In the early days of the Roman Empire, the Germans were among the barbarian warriors on the northern frontier described by Julius Caesar. Over the centuries, through the shifting fortunes of war and politics, as well as migrations, some Germanic people acquired the civilization of the Romans, and ultimately influence in the Roman Empire.[6] In the later empire, German soldiers replaced Romans in the Roman legions, which were now often commanded by German generals,[7] who were sometimes de facto rulers behind figurehead Roman emperors.[8] At the same time, other German peoples on the northern frontiers of the empire continued to be a major menace to its existence. Many of the great battles in the declining phase of the Roman Empire were battles of Germans against other Germans. Within the empire, Germans were never fully accepted or fully assimilated. Intermarriage between Romans and Germans was forbidden.[9] The Roman aristocracy referred to Germans as "blond barbarians"[10] and denounced them for "the nauseating stink of their bodies and their clothing."[11] To some extent, Germans themselves were apologetic about their racial origins. For example, a tombstone among the Germans buried in Gaul referred to their ancestry as "part of the stain that baptism has washed away."[12] Other Germans simply returned the resentment and hatred that Romans felt toward them.

More than a thousand years of history—and the evolution of language, culture, and peoples—elapsed between these early Germans and the people who began immigrating to colonial America. Modern Germany—even before it became a nation—was in the forefront of Western civilization in science, the arts, music, literature, and philosophy. It was the home of Goethe, Beethoven, Kant, and Leibniz. Technology and craftsmanship were German hallmarks. Zeiss and Voigtlander were renowned names in optics long before they (and other German names) became famous in the later era of photography.

Germans, once disdained as inferior barbarians by the Romans, now easily surpassed the achievements of Italy, where "the glory that was Rome" had become only a memory and a bitter mockery of Italian weakness, disunity, and lagging technology and economy. In a still later era, the German ancestry that some had felt ashamed of in Roman times was to become an object of fanatical worship under Hitler and the Nazis.

Emigration from the German states (and later the German nation) ebbed and flowed with historic events.

The German states of the seventeenth and eighteenth centuries were separately ruled by petty princes and were in a state of turmoil. The Reformation and the Counter-Reformation had created religious refugees in both Catholic and Protestant German states, and the Thirty Years' War disrupted their economies, as well as reduced the total German population by about one-third.[13] A severe winter in 1708–09 destroyed the German wine industry for years to come.[14] In short, the domestic problems that often stimulate emigration were present in the German state. However, there were also restrictions and prohibitions on emigration, which led to much internal migration instead.[15]

Later, in the eighteenth and early nineteeth centuries, the currents of the French Revolution, the conquests of Napoleon, and the Restoration of autocratic rule by the Congress of Vienna after Waterloo all profoundly affected German emigration. About half the overseas German emigrants of the post-Waterloo era went to South America,[16] but from 1830 until World War I, most German overseas emigration was to the United States—as high as 90 percent or more in some years.[17]

The rise of liberal and radical opposition to German autocracy led to the abortive Revolution of 1848, after which many fled to escape persecution, or in despair of achieving greater freedom, or simply to find greater social and economic opportunity elsewhere. Nearly a million Germans moved to the United States during the decade of the 1850s.[18]

The presence of German settlements facilitated the movement of more Germans to the same country, and indeed often to the same region or city. But this depended on the good or bad experiences of earlier emigrants. The South American experiences of early German emigrants provided warnings to others in Germany to change their destinations.[19]

There were reductions of immigration to the United States associated with the American Civil War, the Franco-Prussian War in Europe, and especially World War I. But in between, German immigration to America was massive. During the decade of the 1880s, about a million and a half Germans moved to the United States.[20]

In the twentieth century, there were usually more immigrants to Germany than emigrants from Germany.[21] Even after the Nazi regime came to power in 1933, repatriated Germans exceeded those leaving. Those leaving, however, included some of the leading German intellectuals and scientists[22]—including a German Jew who would later give the United States the decisive military weapon of World War II, Albert Einstein, a pacifist who ushered in the nuclear age.

The Germans

GERMANS IN AMERICA

The Colonial Era

The earliest German immigration to America came in the form of individual Germans among the Dutch who, in 1620, settled New Amsterdam—which later became New York.[23] They were predominantly from peasant or artisan backgrounds or were people who had worked in cottage industries.[24] Some were also soldiers of the Dutch West Indies Company, carrying on an already long tradition of German mercenary soldiers. Later, in the seventeenth century, William Penn made a tour of Germany in 1677 to recruit immigrants for his colony of Pennsylvania. Religious toleration in Pennsylvania was a special attraction to those Germans whose religion differed from that of their respective established churches in their regions of Germany.[25] Pennsylvania thus attracted the first sizable German communities in America, largely from the Rhineland region.[26]

In 1683, thirteen Mennonite families established Germantown in Pennsylvania, now part of Philadelphia.[27] Many other German religious denominations and sects followed, including Calvinists, the Amish, and others virtually unknown to the larger society.[28] In 1742, Heinrich Muhlenberg arrived, and became the organizer of the Lutheran church in America and also founder of a prominent family[29] whose achievements included creation of Muhlenberg College, an outstanding institution in Pennsylvania.

Thus began the "Pennsylvania Dutch"—Dutch being in this case an American mispronunciation of the word *Deutsch* for German. By 1745, there were an estimated 45,000 Germans in Pennsylvania.[30] Most settled out on the frontier as it existed at that time, in order to acquire cheap land within their meager means. This made them vulnerable to Indian attacks, especially because of the reluctance of the colonial government to provide defense. Control of the government was largely in the hands of pacifist Quakers living safely in Philadelphia.[31]

In 1709, Germans established Neuberg—now called Newburgh—on the Hudson River, and then spread north into the Mohawk Valley. As in Pennsylvania, this was frontier territory, subject to Indian raids.[32] The Germans of the Mohawk Valley region came as indentured servants—people bound by contract to work for a certain number of years (usually three to seven) to pay off the cost of their transportation to America. At least half of the white population of colonial America came this way.[33] It was a scheme first tried with German and Swiss immigrants and later spread to the Scotch, the Irish, and others. The Germans who settled in the Mohawk Valley came as indentured servants of the British government, which paid half their transportation and settlement costs. More so than other groups, Germans left their home in groups, ranging from whole families to whole communities.[34]

The early German immigrants—both in New York and in Pennsylvania—came from the Palatinate,[35] a small region in the southwestern part of Germany, along the Rhine. Sixteen families of Palatines also settled in New Bern, North Carolina, in 1710.[36] Eighteenth-century South Carolina also carried on a brisk trade in German indentured servants from the Palatinate.[37]

Usually, a boat trip of several weeks on the Rhine to Holland preceded their transatlantic voyage. Then began their ocean travel, on wind-driven ships, averaging between eight and ten weeks on the water. Indentured servants were packed into small, ill-ventilated quarters on small ships perpetually pitching on the Atlantic waves—producing widespread seasickness among the passengers. The weakness and dehydration produced by seasickness made the ill-fed passengers particularly vulnerable to disease. Contemporary observers described the scenes below decks, "some sleeping, some spewing," some "devoured with lice," some "beset with boils, scurvy, dysentery, many cursing themselves and others." At night, there were "fearful crys" and the groaning of "sick and distracted persons," some of whom were "tumbling over the rest, and distracting the whole company...."[38] These were the more or less normal conditions. In extreme cases of ships delayed at sea by weather, the suffering and the casualties could be worse.[39] In 1749, two thousand Germans died at sea on voyages to Philadelphia alone.[40]

After a vessel docked in an American port, potential buyers of the passengers' indenture contracts came aboard. The indentured servants were brought out of their quarters, walked up and down to let the buyers see them, and sometimes feel their muscles and talk to them to form some opinion of their intelligence and submissiveness. Sometimes a middleman called a "soul driver" would buy a group of servants and then walk them through the countryside, selling their contracts here and there as opportunity allowed.[41] The society of the time attached no moral stigma to this trade in human beings, and it was openly engaged in by individuals of the highest rank and renown. George Washington purchased the contracts of indentured servants to work at Mt. Vernon, just as he owned slaves. As late as 1792, the new American government devised a plan to import indentured German labor to help construct the city of Washington.[42]

Deaths on the ocean voyage were so widespread among the Germans that many children were orphaned by the time the ships finally reached America. These orphans were either adopted by relatives in America or apprenticed out to someone to learn a trade. One of these German orphans, John Peter Zenger, was apprenticed to a printer and in later years went on to establish his own newspaper. In 1734, his editorial criticisms of the governor of New York led to his being arrested and tried for libel. His acquittal was one of the landmarks in the development of the doctrine of freedom of the press.[43]

Like helpless people everywhere, the indentured servants were preyed upon by the dishonest. Some ship captains provided inadequate food or sold them into longer periods of bondage than actually required to work off the cost of their transportation. Germans who could not understand English were especially vulnerable.[44]

Many Germans left their homes with no plans to become indentured servants, but found that the mounting costs of travel to Holland and then across the Atlantic were more than they had bargained for.[45] Others had family or friends in America whom they expected (or hoped) would pay their fare, and when this failed to happen, they were sold into indentureship.[46] The term "redemptioner" was used to describe the kind of person who came looking to have his fare redeemed in one way or another,[47] although there was no distinction made between such people and other indentured servants after both found themselves in that status.

And yet, they kept coming—and generally in ever larger numbers. The Germans arriving in the port of Philadelphia alone in the 1740s and 1750s added up to more than 60,000 people, conservatively estimated. An estimated one-half to two-thirds of these were indentured servants. Although indentured servants were subject to many of the restrictions and punishments that applied to slaves—including corporal punishment—they did have a few legal rights during their years of indentureship, and those years did come to a conclusion. Often indentured servants received a modest payment in cash or in kind upon reaching the time for freedom, and many were given land. This was not always the best or the safest land. In the Mohawk Valley or in western Pennsylvania, for example, it was land in frontier areas, near Indians unhappy at seeing their ancestral lands invaded. Many whites who settled in such areas were killed or carried off into bondage by the Indians.

However they came to America, and whatever their vicissitudes en route or after arriving, the early German settlers quickly established a reputation for hard work, thoroughness, and thriftiness. German farmers cleared frontier land more thoroughly than others and made it more productive.[48] They often began by living in sod houses, then log cabins, then finally stone farmhouses.[49] Their farm animals were not allowed to roam free but were also housed, in huge barns like those of their homeland. In the late eighteenth century, a contemporary observed:

A German farm may be distinguished from the farm of the other citizens of the state, by the superior size of their barns; the plain, but compact form of their houses; the height of their inclosures; the extent of their orchards; the fertility of their fields; the luxuriance of their meadows, and a general appearance of plenty and neatness in everything that belongs to them.[50]

Most of the early German immigrants had none of the highly developed scientific, technical, or intellectual skills associated with German achievements in the vanguard of Western civilization. What they did have were the discipline, thoroughness, and perseverance that made such achievements possible. They were renowned as "the nation's best dirt farmers."[51] The highly successful German farmers were paralleled by the achievements by German skilled craftsmen in colonial America. Glassmaking was—and is—a skill associated with German Americans. The first papermill was also set up by a German. The first Bible published in America was printed by a German, in the German language.[52]

The Pennsylvania Dutch were very un-German in two important respects: they were pacifists and distrusters of government. As Palatines, they were descendants of people from a province that had suffered especially severe and repeated devastations by contending armies during the Thirty Years' War.[53] They were also refugees from autocratic tyranny and religious persecutions. Moreover, the religious freedom of Pennsylvania—rare even in America at that time—had disproportionate attraction to pious and pacific religious sects. Germans of that era took little or no interest in government or politics.[54]

The early German settlers lived in self-isolation in farming communities made up of people of a particular religious denomination. They were socially separate from the larger society and internally separated by numerous religious divisions. The English language and the culture of the British settlers had little influence within the areas settled by Germans. They imported books from Germany and published newspapers and preached sermons in German.[55] With the passage of time, English slowly began to creep in, often with German sentence structure, to produce a peculiar local dialect known as Pennsylvania Dutch.[56] The most isolated of these German settlers were—and are— the Amish, who today still live in farm communities very much like those of the early settlers. Pious religious people who dress in old-fashioned black clothes, the Amish avoid modern ways, drive horse-drawn black carriages, and keep their children out of public schools as a means of preserving their way of life.

With the passage of time, most German settlers spread out geographically, learned to speak English, and both absorbed and contributed to American culture. Philadelphia scrapple, German chocolate cake, cole slaw, and sauerkraut were among their many contributions to American cooking. German farming settlements spread north and south through the great fertile valleys of the Appalachian mountain range. By the late eighteenth century, there was an almost unbroken chain of German frontier settlements stretching from the Mohawk Valley in upstate New York down through western New Jersey, central Pennsylvania, western Maryland, on down through the Shenandoah Valley in Virginia, through the Piedmont region of the Carolinas, and into Savannah, Georgia.[57] Names scattered through this region still reflect those early German settlements. Upstate New York has communities with such names as Palatine Bridge, Germantown, New Hamburg, and Rhinebeck, as well as a region of the Mohawk Valley known as German Flats.[58] New Jersey has its German Valley area[59] and Pennsylvania its Heidelberg, Germantown, Muhlenberg Park, and King of Prussia. Maryland has its Frederick and cities named for early German settlers, Hagerstown and Creagerstown. The name of the German province of Mecklenburg was repeated in Mecklenburg County, North Carolina, and the village of New Mecklenburg in Virginia. Not all the communities established by Germans had German names. Harper's Ferry in Virginia, Bethlehem in Pennsylvania, and Hope Settlement and Ebenezer in Georgia were among many German communities with non-German names.

As the German farming communities spread down through the Appalachian valley near the frontier, they found themselves often near the Scotch-Irish, who were frontiersmen par excellence. The Scotch-Irish often led the way into the untamed wilderness, hunting, fishing, clearing land, and fighting Indians,[60] with the Germans and others following after the area became more settled.[61] The Germans and the

Scotch-Irish were very different in temperament and behavior and generally kept quite separate from each other, even in adjacent settlements.[62] The Germans were noted for their order, quietness, friendliness, steady work, frugality, and their ability to get along with the Indians. The Scotch-Irish were just the opposite—quick-tempered, hard drinking, working intermittently, saving little, washing little, and constantly involved in feuds among themselves or with the Indians.[63] Religious differences also divided them. The early German settlers were usually pious Lutherans, Calvinists, and other strict Protestant sects that avoided strong language or strong drink, while the Scotch-Irish were Presbyterians and were given to hard liquor and language that pious people considered blasphemous. After a century of sharing hundreds of miles of the great valleys of the Appalachian range, there was still little racial intermixture between the Germans and the Scotch-Irish.[64]

About half of all the Germans in colonial America lived in Pennsylvania. Not all of these were farmers. Skilled workers were almost as numerous as farmers.[65] They not only performed a variety of tasks; they developed new products as well. Germans in the Pennsylvania Dutch country near Conestoga Creek produced a wagon for hauling farm produce, a wagon that was destined to play a major role in the later settlement of the western United States. The Conestoga wagon was a large and rugged vehicle, covered by canvas draped over high, arching hoops. It was eleven feet high, twenty-six feet long (counting the wagon tongue), weighed about 3,000 pounds, and required six strong horses to pull it.[66] In the eighteenth century, there were "great files of these enormous wagons lumbering into Philadelphia along the Lancaster Road, sometimes a hundred or more a day."[67] Although originally designed by German farmers to carry their produce to market, the covered wagons proved useful for many other purposes. In 1755, they were used by the British to carry military supplies during the French and Indian War. Later, the American army used the covered wagons during the Revolutionary War. The most famous role of the covered wagons came still later—transporting American pioneers across the great plains of the West toward the Pacific Ocean.[68] These were the wagon trains that braved the elements, forded the rivers, and pulled into circles to fight off Indians.

The Pennsylvania Dutch also developed a hunting rifle that was to play a very different role from that intended by these German pacifists. Unlike most European muskets of the time, German weapons had spiral grooves (called rifling) inside the barrel to produce greater accuracy. Some of these rifled muskets were brought to Pennsylvania by German immigrants. Here they developed a new rifle, with a very elongated barrel for even greater accuracy. This product of German craftsmen in Lancaster, Pennsylvania, was originally known as the Pennsylvania rifle. But it acquired fame in the hands of frontier sharpshooters like Daniel Boone and then became known as the "Kentucky Rifle." It later proved very effective in the guerrilla warfare used by Americans against the British during the Revolutionary War.[69]

The Revolutionary War and Independence

While other Americans split into Tory supporters of England and revolutionaries for independence in 1776, German Americans split into pacifists and revolutionaries. Mennonites and other German religious sects would not fight, but some paid extra taxes instead or engaged in medical or other duties consistent with their status as conscientious objectors.[70] However, the largest denominations among Germans, the Lutherans and the Reformed, had no prohibitions against the military, and many Germans from these groups fought in the revolution.[71]

There were about 300,000 Germans in the American colonies—about 10 percent of the total population.[72] Shortly after the war began, a volunteer company of Germans formed in Charleston, South Carolina, and four companies of infantry formed from the Germans around Reading, Pennsylvania. A German regiment was raised in Pennsylvania and Maryland. Four battalions of Germans were recruited in the Mohawk Valley. Germans served not only in the ranks but also in the highest levels of the American army. Peter Muhlenberg, son of the founder of the American Lutheran church, rose to become a general in the American army.[73] General von Steuben came from his native land for the express purpose of fighting in the Revolutionary War. He served with Washington at Valley Forge, and has been credited with introducing military discipline into the new American army. Turning undisciplined civilians into professional soldiers was a formidable task, and von Steuben was known to curse in both German and French—and to ask his aide to curse for him in English![74] Yet as drillmaster of the American army, he succeeded in creating an army capable of defeating professional British troops. General von Steuben also helped plan the successful siege of Yorktown.[75]

A number of other military officers came from the German states to America to fight in the Revolutionary War. One of these was Baron de Kalb, who died fighting while others fled at the Battle of Camden in

South Carolina.[76] One of the most dramatic fighters was a German-American woman named Maria Ludwig, who traveled with her husband, a gunner in the American army, and carried pitchers of water to soldiers in battle. She was nicknamed Molly Pitcher, and won fame by taking her husband's place at a cannon after he had been wounded. The inspiring example of her bravery was recognized by George Washington after the battle.[77]

The British brought nearly 30,000 German mercenary soldiers to the colonies to try to put down the American rebellion. These were not individual volunteers but soldiers sold or rented to the British by the rulers of various German principalities.[78] More than half came from the little state of Hesse-Cassell, so all German mercenaries in the Revolutionary War were lumped together by Americans as "Hessians." Some of these soldiers deserted to the American side during the war, and some remained in the United States after the war, settling in existing German communities. Just over half of the "Hessians" returned home.[79] Somewhere between 5,000 and 12,000 eventually became American citizens.[80] One of these soldiers, named Kuester, was an ancestor of General George Custer, the Indian fighter.[81]

Although the Germans were not numerically prominent in politics, there were some prominent German political figures. The first governor of Georgia was a German, Johann Adam Treutlen. So was the first treasurer of the United States, Michael Hillegas. The most prominent of these early German statesmen was from the Muhlenberg dynasty in Pennsylvania—Frederick Augustus Conrad Muhlenberg, first Speaker of the House of Representatives and as such one of the two men to sign the Bill of Rights.[82] Another member of the family, William Augustus Muhlenberg, later served in Congress for nine years.[83]

Another German American of the colonial period who achieved renown was John Jacob Astor, who came to the United States in 1783, at the age of twenty. He was the son of a butcher, had little education, and arrived with only twenty-five dollars and a few flutes. He became a fur trader and, a quarter of a century after his arrival, organized the American Fur Company, as well as speculating in New York real estate. Both activities proved highly profitable, and his fur company became the leading such enterprise in the Great Lakes, the Rocky Mountain region, and ultimately the Pacific Northwest.[84] His trading post in Oregon was the first American settlement on the Pacific Coast.[85] He became the richest man in America, leaving an estate estimated at about 20 million dollars.[86]

The Germans

Nineteenth-Century Immigrants

There was little emigration from Germany in the early years of the new American nation.[87] It was 1828 before there were as many as a thousand German immigrants arriving in America in one year. But by 1832, there were more than 10,000, and by 1836, there were more than 20,000. This was still only a foretaste of the massive emigration from Germany that was to surpass 50,000 in 1846 and surpass 200,000 in 1854.[88]

Initially, this emigration was from the same region of Germany as the earlier emigration of the colonial era. But with the passing decades, a more regionally, socially, and intellectually diversified German population arrived in the United States. They also became more regionally dispersed in a growing America. In the years 1830 through 1834, virtually all overseas German emigrants were from southwest Germany, but a decade later, only about one-third were from that region, and in the 1860s, less than one-sixth of the German emigrants were from that region.[89] Since the overwhelming bulk of all Germans who emigrated overseas during this era went to the United States,[90] similar proportions would apply to German immigrants to America.

Many factors lay behind the rising emigration from Germany—the easing of emigration restrictions in the German states,[91] dwindling farm size in those regions (such as the Palatinate) where land was subdivided among heirs rather than being entailed whole to a single heir,[92] the elimination of common village land to the detriment of peasants,[93] and unemployment among artisans caused by the rise of the factory system and by the competition of British goods after trade was resumed following the end of the Napoleonic Wars.[94] Despotism in the German states after the nobility was restored by the Congress of Vienna also provoked both uprisings and emigration.[95] There were also many enthusiastic accounts of life in America written in German and circulated in Germany by literally dozens of German authors.[96] Letters from relatives in the prosperous German-American farming communities likewise spread information and enthusiasm about the United States in Germany. The replacement of sailing ships by steamships in the middle of the nineteenth century also made America more accessible. More than 5 million Germans immigrated to the United States in the nineteenth century—more than from any other country.[97]

About three-quarters of all the German immigrants in the early 1820s were men,[98] suggesting initially a tentative or exploratory kind of immigration. Later, the emigrants from Germany included large

55

proportions of children,[99] indicating that whole families were now coming to America with the intention of making this their home.

The occupations of the immigrants varied somewhat from province to province and from decade to decade. The earlier immigration continued to be heavily peasant farmers from southwest Germany. As of the 1840s, about half of the immigrants were peasants and day laborers. In the middle and later nineteenth century, there were rising numbers of industrial workers and artisans,[100] reflecting both the regional changes in the immigration sources and the rising importance of industry in Germany as a whole. In the last quarter of the nineteenth century, the proportion of German immigrants from an agricultural background declined from about one-third in the early 1870s to little more than one-fourth in the mid 1890s. There was a corresponding rise in the proportions that had worked in industry, commerce, and trade.[101] Still, as late as 1900, most of the farmers in America were of German ancestry.

Many of the German immigrants of the nineteenth century sought the frontier, for its cheap land, as their predecessors had done in the eighteenth century. However, the frontier itself had moved farther west by now. Those who came in the nineteenth century tended to settle in the upper Mississippi and Ohio valleys, as those of a century earlier had settled in the Appalachian valleys. German farmers tended to settle along the rivers and lakes of the region and to seek wooded areas, which provided them with building materials and fuel.[102] They were disproportionately concentrated along the rivers—the Mississippi, the Missouri, the Ohio, the Miami, and the Kentucky—and along the south shores of the Great Lakes.

The increasingly urban portion of the new wave of immigration created large concentrations of Germans in Cincinnati, St. Louis, Milwaukee, and other cities of the region. There were also smaller communities founded by and composed largely of Germans, and carrying such names as Frankfort (Kentucky), Berlin (Wisconsin), and Westphalia (Michigan). Ohio had its Frankfort and Berlin also, as well as Dresden, Potsdam, Strasburg, and other communities with German names—including the inevitable Germantown, which also appeared in Illinois, Wisconsin, Kentucky, and Tennessee, as it had a century earlier in Pennsylvania. As in the East, the more pious religious sects gave their communities biblical names—Bethlehem, Nazareth, and Canaan, for example, in Ohio.[103] Sometimes the first settlers of a particular community were from a specific region of Germany. Frankfort, Kentucky, was founded by people from Frankfurt in Germany,[104] and Grand Island, Michigan, was first settled by Schleswig-Holsteiners.[105]

Access to the upper Midwest was provided by the Mississippi and its connecting waterways. Many Germans sailed from the French port of Le Havre, which imported cotton from New Orleans. Shipping that existed primarily to carry cotton in one direction was utilized by the Germans to travel in the opposite direction. This was true not only for crossing the Atlantic but also for travel within the United States. Following in reverse the route of cotton shipments, the German immigrants landed at New Orleans and then sailed up the Mississippi on boats that had brought cotton to New Orleans from the Mississippi Valley region.[106] Others reached the same region across northern routes from the eastern port cities to the Great Lakes, and some came by train.[107]

Whereas the German immigration of the eighteenth century had been concentrated in Pennsylvania, and then in a band stretching north and south along the Appalachians, by the middle of the nineteenth century, more than half of all German-born persons in America lived in the upper Mississippi and Ohio valleys, concentrating in the states of Ohio, Illinois, Wisconsin, and Missouri.[108] This was still true as late as 1900, when about a million and a half German-born people lived in that region, out of a total German-born population of about two and a half million in the country as a whole at that time.[109] The total German origin population—German-born plus native Americans of German ancestry—was about 8 million in 1900.[110]

Germans were also a part of the pioneering settlers into the Pacific Northwest. An estimated one-fourth of the people in Oregon today are of German ancestry. In 1857, Germans founded Anaheim in southern California, near Los Angeles. There, they established the cultivation of oranges, long a dominant crop in that region.[111]

Whether in a rural or an urban setting, concentrations of Germans perpetuated the German language and German culture for generations. Often this reflected residential as well as cultural isolation. In nineteenth-century Milwaukee, German residential patterns "involved minimal neighborhood contact with either natives or Irish."[112] Buffalo, New York, had an even higher degree of residential separation of Germans.[113] Germans in Baltimore likewise "lived in their own world, cut off from their American surroundings."[114] In Cincinnati, Germans were concentrated in an area known as "Over the Rhine."[115] Hermann, Missouri (near St. Louis), was known as "Little Germany," and its street names were written in German.[116] In Texas as well, "Germans did not mingle much with the American population," and the two groups observed each other from a distance, "with unfeigned curiosity, often tempered with mutual contempt."[117]

In mid-nineteenth-century America in general, according to a contemporary, a German settlement typically "becomes a nucleus of a pure German circle, which is born, marries, and dies within itself, and with the least possible mixture of Anglo-Americans."[118] Mid-century America had 27 *daily* German-language newspapers in 15 cities, and well over two hundred other publications in German.[119] Cincinnati alone had four German newspapers.[120]

German-language publications continued to flourish on into the early twentieth century, when there were nearly 3.5 million readers for 49 monthly publications, 433 weekly publications, and 70 daily publications.[121]

Many features of the German culture besides language were brought to America. With the passing generations, as the German language slowly faded away, many of the cultural features of German-American life became features of American life in general. Along with the Christmas tree, the frankfurter, the hamburger, and beer became fixtures of the American way of life. Like many ethnic foods, the hot dog was an improvisation in America (like chop suey and chow mein among the Chinese), rather than a direct import from the homeland. German street vendors selling cooked wieners in nineteenth-century Cincinnati produced the combination roll and frankfurter that became famous as the all-American hotdog.[122] Oatmeal was also created by a nineteenth-century German American[123] and was perhaps as widely used although not nearly so popular as the hotdog.

German urban workers in the nineteenth century brought many skills with them. They were carpenters, bakers, blacksmiths, butchers, shoemakers, printers, and tailors, among their many skilled occupations. Half or more of all employed Germans were skilled manual workers in mid-century Milwaukee, St. Louis, Detroit, New York, Jersey City, and Boston. A substantial additional number were in nonmanual occupations. Very few were unskilled laborers—less than half the proportion found among the Irish in the same cities.[124] In mid-nineteenth-century Philadelphia, only 14 percent of the German workers were day laborers, the occupations of from one-half to two-thirds of the Irish in the same city.[125]

Many German immigrants brought with them skills required for brewing beer—and the concentrated German population provided a large market for it. American brews did not satisfy them. In Milwaukee, where more than one-third of the population was German around the middle of the nineteenth century,[126] German breweries began appearing in the late 1840s. Like other new businesses, they went through financial difficulties at first, but by 1860, there were a number of successful German breweries in Milwaukee, bearing such names as Pabst, Schlitz, Blatz, and Miller.[127] The heavy concentration of Germans in and around St. Louis likewise provided a market for the establishment of a German brewery there by Anheuser-Busch, producers of Budweiser beer.

Although the most successful mid-nineteenth-century German-American businesses tended to be those serving the special tastes of German immigrant communities,[128] with the passage of time numerous other German firms arose, serving the larger American society. Sometimes this was because the product itself spread into the larger society—frankfurters and beer being classic examples—but more often because Germans had the technical skills and managerial abilities to produce something that was in general demand. For example, in 1849 a German immigrant optician named John Jacob Bausch and a German immigrant businessman named Henry Lomb established the optical firm of Bausch and Lomb, which eventually became the world's largest lens manufacturer—producing lenses for eyeglasses, cameras, microscopes, binoculars, and other optical devices.[129] Another German immigrant, John Augustus Roebling, brought engineering and architectural skills that enabled him to invent wire cable and to use it in building the first suspension bridges—including the Brooklyn Bridge.[130] Piano building was another area in which the skills the Germans brought to America are still reflected in such well-known German-American names as Steinway, Knabe, and Schnabel.[131]

Nineteenth-century German immigrants and their offspring were responsible for establishing leading businesses in many American industries. A German immigrant named Frederick Weyerhaeuser went from lumberyard worker to founder of his own lumber products firm, which remains today one of the largest in its industry. A second generation German American named Henry J. Heinz began marketing food products that he grew in his garden while still in his teens. This developed into the H. J. Heinz Company, which sold even more than the "57 Varieties" of food products that became its advertising slogan. The wide range of industries that German skill and entrepreneurship helped develop is suggested by such names as Studebaker and Chrysler in the automobile industry, Wurlitzer Organs, Steuben glass, the Wanamaker department store chain, and Rockefeller in petroleum and other industries.[132] These were not German big businessmen who became American big businessmen. They were typically people from modest beginnings, whose skill found opportunities to flourish in America.

One of the most important social changes wrought by German immigrants was their promotion of numerous forms of innocent public family entertainment. Music, picnics, dancing, card playing, swimming, bowling, and other physical activities were among the American pastimes, now taken for granted, but introduced or promoted by Germans in the nineteenth century.[133] The Germans organized marching bands, symphony orchestras, and singing groups of all sorts.

Previous generations of Americans—including previous generations of German Americans—regarded organized recreation with puritan suspicion and participation in them on Sunday as sinful. The saloon, games, and other pastimes were relegated—in theory at least—to the sinners and the riffraff. But nineteenth-century German beer gardens, unlike American saloons, were places where the whole family went on Sunday to hear music and eat pretzels; and parades, plays, and gymnasium sports were considered good clean fun at any time. These German pastimes were viewed with shock and suspicion at first. But eventually, the Germans' "jovial, yet orderly" activities,[134] their "hearty and harmless diversions,"[135] made an impression on other Americans—leading to a growing acceptance and wider practice of a more relaxed attitude toward recreation, even on Sunday. As an observer noted in 1883:

The German notion that it is a good thing to have a good time has found a lodgment in the American mind. Except in isolated rural localities where the Teutonic immigration has not penetrated, there is no longer any such feeling about dancing, social games, and dramatic performances as was almost universal among respectable people thirty years ago.[136]

The German head start in such activities as music and gymnasium sports continued to be reflected in many ways, long after these became general American activities. It was perhaps significant that one of America's first Olympic swimming champions (in the 1920s) was of German ancestry—Johnny Weissmuller, later better known for playing Tarzan in the movies. The first woman to swim the English Channel was also a German American—Gertrude Ederle. While these were individual achievements of a later era, they were also products of a long tradition that Germans brought to the United States in the nineteenth century. German traditions also produced many prominent American musical figures. These included Walter Damrosch and Bruno Walter and the famous composer of march music, John Philip Sousa.[137] Germans were also prominent in the manufacture of musical instruments, especially the piano.

Education was another area in which Germans made contributions that helped shape American institutions. Both the kindergarten and the university originated among Germans in Europe. German immigrants created the first kindergartens in America. A kindergarten established in a small Wisconsin community in 1855 has been credited as being the first in the United States.[138] In 1873, the first American public school system to have kindergarten was in St. Louis—a center of German population—and nearly all the early kindergarten teachers were German.[139] Germans also actively promoted the introduction of physical education and vocational education into American schools.

Both German Lutherans and German Catholics established their own parochial schools in nineteenth-century America. Other Germans established their own private schools as well. These were pioneering efforts at a time when the idea of universal education was by no means universally accepted. Even after public schools emerged, the German schools were usually better.[140] Germans remained one of the most education-conscious ethnic groups, although German farmers— like farmers generally—sometimes had their doubts about "book learning."

A unique series of language schools was created in the nineteenth century by Professor Maximilian Berlitz. An immigrant who arrived in the United States in 1869 with little money, Berlitz opened his first language school in 1878. His method of teaching language was so successful that he was soon establishing Berlitz Schools throughout the United States and eventually hundreds around the world.[141]

The Germans were organizers—whether of lodges, bowling clubs, labor unions, businesses, singing groups, orchestras, schools, theater groups, or churches.[142] They organized gymnastic clubs called *Turnvereine*—or Turner Societies—throughout the United States, stressing athletic activity, patriotism, and mental development. Germans did little political organizing, however. Politics never became a consuming interest of German Americans. They were among the targets of nativist political attacks during the Know-Nothing era of the 1820s, but these attacks centered on the Irish, and the whole episode was relatively short-lived. Germans were also actively opposed to the laws and campaigns to outlaw drinking—being allied with the Irish on this issue—and were opposed to Sunday "blue laws" that forbade many innocent pastimes. But aside from such issues, Germans were not heavily involved in politics—certainly not on the scale of the Irish, nor with anywhere near the success of the Irish.

Earlier generations of Germans had been almost all Protestant,[143] partly because the British government turned back German Catholics trying to immigrate to the American colonies.[144] In the nineteenth century, Catholics and Protestants were about equally represented in the German immigration.[145] Most nineteenth-century German Americans were either Catholics or Lutherans.[146] The German Lutherans in the eastern seaboard states represented an earlier immigration that had, over the generations, adopted ideas and practices of other American religious denominations—practices that were considered unacceptable by the more orthodox Lutherans arriving from Saxony in the nineteenth century and settling in the midwestern German areas. These later arriving German Lutherans founded their own Missouri Synod, with more conservative religious doctrines.[147]

German Catholics often found themselves in conflict with Irish Catholics, who increasingly dominated the American hierarchy. The Irish considered themselves more Americanized than the Germans, and therefore rightfully in charge of the church's efforts to acculturate them. The Germans, however, considered themselves more educated than the Irish and resented having their parishes "run by Irish ignoramuses."[148] Ultimately, the pope himself had to intervene to restore peace.[149] Over the years, German, Polish, and other Catholics began to have churches and schools manned by priests and nuns of their own ethnicity.

Among the German immigrants of the nineteenth-century were many German Jews. They often settled among other Germans and considered themselves "Germans of the Hebrew faith," rather than a wholly separate group, as later eastern European Jews would. They spoke German, rather than either Hebrew or Yiddish, were proud of the German culture, and participated in the social life of educated Germans.[150] Although many immigrated to escape anti-Semitic policies instituted by the German aristocracy restored to power by the Congress of Vienna, the plight of Jews among Germans was far less dire than elsewhere. Indeed, this continued to be true up to the generation of Hitler and the Nazis. German-Jewish communities in the United States flourished within the German communities. The first rabbinical school in the United States was built in Cincinnati,[151] a center of German Americans. As late as World War I, American-Jewish newspapers were so pro-German that the U.S. government prosecuted them during the wartime anti-German feeling.

The German Americans of the eighteenth and nineteenth centuries were also noted for their ability to get along with the Indians they encountered in their frontier and near-frontier settlements. Relatively few Germans settled in the South, and fewer still became slaveowners. Those areas of the South where German Americans and the Scotch-Irish were heavily settled—notably the Piedmont region—were less repressive toward blacks than other parts of the South, both before and after emancipation. Moreover, the few antislavery publications in the South were concentrated in that same region.[152] In the North, Germans were strong opponents of slavery. While most German voters were Democrats into the 1840s, they switched to the newly formed Republican party in the 1850s, when slavery became a heated political issue. The large German element in Missouri has been credited with keeping that state from joining the Confederacy when the Civil War erupted.[153]

When the Civil War came, Germans fought on both sides, depending on where they lived, and most Germans were in the North. However, German support was more than a matter of geography and the military draft. Even before the draft was instituted, about 4,000 Germans in Pennsylvania volunteered for the Union Army, as did about 6,000 in New York State. Whole regiments of Germans were created, with their commands being given in the German language. An estimated 300,000 German Americans joined the Union Army. There were more than 500 German-born Union officers, including nine major generals and several brigadier generals.[154]

The most famous German American of the Civil War era was Carl Schurz. He was one of that small but prominent element known as the "Forty-Eighters"—liberal, radical, and democratic refugees from the abortive German Revolution of 1848, which had sought to unite Germany as a republic. They and their democratic ideas were controversial in mid-century America. Carl Schurz agitated against slavery before the Civil War, and he and other "Forty-Eighters" helped to rouse German Americans to the political support of Abraham Lincoln before the war and to join the military service after hostilities began. Schurz eventually became a general in the Union Army and after the war made a celebrated report on conditions in the South during Reconstruction. Although Schurz was sent to make his survey by President Andrew Johnson, by the time the report was completed, Johnson attempted to suppress the report, which he considered too favorable to blacks and too unfavorable to southern whites. But this attempt at suppression only guaranteed the report's place in history. Schurz's postwar activities included editing a German-language newspaper in St. Louis, serving as a United States Senator from Missouri and later Secretary of the Interior—where he urged more humane treatment of the Indians. Later, he became editor of the *New York Evening Post* and *Harper's Weekly*.[155]

Germans never became as well represented in politics as they were in industry, science, or music. Still there were some notable individuals of German ancestry in politics in the nineteenth century. Besides Carl Schurz, there was John Peter Altgeld, who was elected governor of Illinois—the first foreign-born person to hold that office.[156] Altgeld began in America as a laborer with little education, but educated himself in the law and became a judge, as well as writing a book that argued that the criminal law was unfair to the poor. Later, as governor, he was noted for being prolabor and for pardoning those convicted (wrongly, he thought) of the Haymarket bombings. This last act has been held responsible for ending his promising political career.

The leading political cartoonist of the nineteenth century was a German-American artist named Thomas Nast. He was praised by Lincoln for his pro-Union cartoons during the Civil War. It was Nast who originated the elephant and the donkey as symbols of the Democratic and the Republican parties and who first drew Santa Claus as the chubby, white-bearded figure known today. Nast's greatest fame came as caricaturer of Boss Tweed, head of the corrupt Tammany Hall political machine. Tweed considered these cartoons more dangerous than editorial attacks: "I don't care so much what the papers write about me—my constituents can't read; but, damn it, they can see pictures!"[157] Nast's cartoons about the Tweed machine were so widely known that the fleeing Tweed was captured in Spain because someone recognized him from these cartoons.

Germans continued prominent in American science, medicine, and invention. German pharmacists were unique because they were trained in chemistry. Germans founded the pharmaceutical company now known as Merck.[158] A German immigrant named Charles P. Steinmetz, a crippled man barely four feet tall, became famous for his scientific genius, which helped shape the history of electricity. The General Electric Corporation was built around this man and his many patented inventions.

The Germans

The Twentieth Century

By the beginning of the twentieth century, German Americans were in an enviable position. They were, by and large, a prosperous people and to some extent an accepted and respected people—becoming more Americanized and at the same time seeing much of their culture adopted by other Americans. Frankfurters, German chocolate cake, beer, kindergarten, gymnasiums, and universities were now all American institutions, and the German language was widely taught in American schools. These happy developments were rudely changed by the anti-German feelings that swept the United States when World War I began.

Even before America became directly involved as a combatant in 1917, the United States was flooded with anti-German propaganda, especially from Britain, which had the advantage of presenting its viewpoint in the language used by most Americans. Anti-German feeling among Americans was not confined to Germany, but extended quickly to the whole German culture and to German Americans, many of whom were sympathetic to their former homeland. German books were removed from the shelves of American libraries, German-language courses were canceled in the public schools, readers and advertisers boycotted German-American newspapers. Wedding marches by Mendelssohn and Wagner were removed from marriage ceremonies. The term "Hun" was applied to all Germans (although the Huns were not in fact a Germanic people). President Woodrow Wilson spoke disparagingly of "hyphenated Americans" with supposedly divided loyalty—a cutting remark affecting many American ethnic groups and leaving a legacy of emotional response to the use of hyphens in designating them.

German Americans responded in many ways to these attacks. Some defended themselves and their loyalty to the United States. Some changed their names. Some German-American organizations dropped all reference to Germany in their titles. "German-American" banks became "North American" banks. The Germania Life Insurance Company of New York became the Guardian Life Insurance Company.[159] German-American newspapers began to die out.

When the United States entered World War I against Germany, German Americans evidenced no divided loyalties. Thousands fought in the American Army against Germany—armies led by General John J. Pershing, a German American whose family name had once been spelled Pfoerschin.[160]

Socially, German Americans slowly assimilated in the early twentieth century, and more rapidly later on. Most Germans married other Germans in the 1920s, according to data from various parts of the country. In the period from 1908 to 1912, more than two-thirds of all Germans in New York City married other Germans, and in Wisconsin during the same year, just over four-fifths of Germans married other Germans, as was the case also in Nebraska at about the same time.[161] Nor was this a matter of a lack of other ethnic groups. In New York City, Germans were less than 10 percent of the population. By the 1920s, intermarriage had increased so that only about three-fifths of Germans still married other Germans in Nebraska, Wisconsin, and New York State. The same was true of New Haven by 1930, but in other places, most Germans continued to marry other Germans on into the 1960s.[162] Nationally, by 1969 only about one-third of German husbands were married to German wives.[163]

One of the most famous German Americans of the twentieth century was seldom identified ethnically, although he grew up in a home where German was the primary language spoken. He begin inauspiciously as a delinquent whose parents committed him to a Catholic home for orphans and incorrigibles, from which he emerged several years later as a professional baseball player—still so young and naive that his teammates called him "the babe." His name was George Herman Ruth. As a young pitcher with the Boston Red Sox, Babe Ruth set an American League record for shutouts in a season by a lefthanded pitcher—a record that still stands. His greatest fame came later with the New York Yankees, where he teamed up with another German-American player, Lou Gehrig, to form the most feared pair of hitters ever seen in the same lineup. Of the ten highest slugging averages ever achieved in a season, seven are by Babe Ruth and Lou Gehrig.[164] Of the ten highest totals of runs scored by a player in a season, six are by Babe Ruth and Lou Gehrig—the top six. Over a lifetime, the two players with the most runs batted in, in proportion to their times at bat, were Babe Ruth and Lou Gehrig.[165] They were the heart of the great Yankee dynasties of the 1920s and 1930s. The Yankees had never won a pennant before Babe Ruth joined the team.

Among other German-American baseball stars, Honus Wagner was the best known. Generally considered the greatest shortstop in history, Wagner retired in 1917 with more hits, runs, and stolen bases than anyone else had ever made at that time.[166] Numerically, however, Germans never dominated baseball as the Irish did in one era or blacks in

The Germans

another. Germans made their marks in gymnastic sports, notably swimming.

Individual Americans of German ancestry continued to reach notable positions in politics, but not on a large scale, nor as ethnic representatives. Herbert Hoover was the first president of German ancestry, and Dwight D. Eisenhower was the most recent. Senator William E. Borah became famous as an opponent of Woodrow Wilson's postwar foreign policy, and Senator Robert F. Wagner, Sr., put his name on the basic labor relations law—the Wagner Act—in 1935. His son, Robert F. Wagner, Jr., was best known for being mayor of New York.

With the rise of Hitler and Nazis in Germany in the 1930s, a new migration of Germans to the United States began—including some of the world's leading scholars, artists, scientists, and men of letters. Most were Jews—Albert Einstein being the most illustrious—but there were also such other outstanding non-Jewish Germans as Thomas Mann and Paul Tillich. Among those destined for later prominence in America was a German-Jewish refugee named Henry Kissinger. It may have been one of the largest transfers of intellectual talent from one nation to another in human history. The transfer of Einstein alone was historic, for it made the United States the first nation to achieve nuclear power.

Like the German refugees after the abortive Revolution of 1848, these 1930s refugees tended to be of a liberal and democratic persuasion—which had its impact on both the German Americans and the American society in general. Unlike the German immigrants of the pre-World War I period, these Germans did not come with feelings of identification with Germany, but with fierce anti-Nazi feelings. Whether for these or other reasons, German Americans on the eve of World War II showed no such strong pro-Germany feelings as in the early years of World War I. A small pro-Nazi group—the German-American Bund—existed, largely in New York City, but it hardly spoke for German Americans as a whole.

World War II saw another wave of anti-German feelings in the United States, but with nothing of the magnitude that had existed during World War I. No one questioned the loyalties of German Americans in the insensitive manner of Woodrow Wilson. Again, the American Army that landed in Europe to help defeat Germany was commanded by a general of German ancestry—Dwight D. Eisenhower, a descendant of the Pennsylvania Dutch. Many other top American military men of World War II were also of German ancestry, including

Admiral Chester Nimitz and General Carl Spaatz of the American Air Force, whose duties included bombing German cities to rubble.

GERMAN AMERICANS TODAY

After decades of assimilation, those Americans who still identify themselves to the Census Bureau as being of German ethnic origin may or may not be typical of the descendants of those people whose ancestors originated in Germany. In any event, individuals who considered themselves German Americans in 1972 constituted about 13 percent of the American population, and had incomes 11 percent above the national average.[167] Only about 8 percent of German males were still farmers or farm laborers, as so many of their ancestors had been.[168] The average ages and education of German Americans were virtually identical to the national average.

The real story of the German Americans is not so much what they have achieved for themselves as what they have contributed to the development of the United States—in industry, science, culture, military strength, and recreation. Americans of all racial and ethnic origins are a different people—and a more prosperous people—because of the many contributions of German Americans.

Chapter 4

THE JEWS

JEWS came to America not from one country or culture but from many. The first Jews who arrived in colonial America were Sephardic Jews, who had lived for centuries in Spain and Portugal, under very different conditions from those in Germany, Russia, or eastern Europe, from which later generations of Jewish Americans came. Culturally, these were all different groups, however much they might be lumped together by outsiders. They have not entirely blended together to this day.

The great majority of Jews in America are descended from the millions who emigrated from Russia, Poland, and other eastern European countries in the last two decades of the nineteenth century and the first two decades of the twentieth century. In that period, one-third of all the Jews in eastern Europe migrated to America.

Although divided by national cultures, and even internal differences of religious theory and practice, Jews shared not only their ancestral origins in ancient Israel and a core of common religious beliefs and traditions but also centuries of history as a minority subjected to varying degrees of hostility wherever they went. Other groups became "minorities" in America. Jews had centuries of experience living as a minority in countries throughout Europe.

HOMELANDS

The ancient Jews were forced from their ancestral homeland in 70 AD, when the armies of the Roman Empire conquered Palestine. Thus began the diaspora—the long centuries of their dispersion throughout Europe and eventually the world.

After Christianity replaced paganism throughout Europe, the Jews were the only non-Christian people on the Continent—the universal "outsiders." This was a particularly vulnerable position during periods of Christian religious fervor—such as the Crusades—or periods of great religious fear, as during the plagues that sporadically decimated whole regions during the Middle Ages. As the Crusaders moved through Europe to go fight the Moslems, they often paused to massacre the Jews in places along the way, joined by local mobs. When the devastating plagues struck Europe, many saw them as a sign of God's anger, which they hoped to placate by getting rid of the Jews living in their midst. In addition to these more or less straightforward motives of bigotry and fear, there were also many who stood to gain materially from eliminating a people who were seen as economic or religious competitors, or holders of debts that would be liquidated with their deaths and the deaths of their heirs. The profound ignorance of the masses of people during this era made them readily manipulable by more shrewd political, economic, or religious leaders, who directed their passions against the Jews. For centuries, Jews were periodically persecuted, massacred, or expelled en masse from various countries in Europe.

In between these dramatic historic events, Jews sought whatever unobtrusive safety they could find as an interstitial element in different cultures, societies, and economies. Jewish resistance by force would have been suicidal, as they were hopelessly outnumbered everywhere. The oppressed Irish or Italians were a majority in their respective lands, and could at least conduct sporadic uprisings or underground terrorism against their conquerors. But while oppression bred fighting

70

qualities in the Irish and the Italians, in the very different situation of the Jews it produced an emphasis on the futility of the use of force and violence and reliance instead on their wits, resourcefulness, and perseverance in the face of adversity. When the Jews were a people living in their own homeland in Palestine, they were a fighting people—as they would be once again in modern Israel—but not so in the long centuries of their dispersion.

The position of the Jews was in many ways better during the early centuries of the Roman Empire than in its later decline or in the emergence of medieval Europe. The early Roman Empire was pagan and pluralistic. The Jews were simply one of many diverse racial and religious groups accommodated within a relatively tolerant empire. Ironically, it was the Judeo-Christian theology that introduced a major element of intolerance into the Roman Empire and into Western civilization in general. Neither Jews nor Christians would engage in the rites or observances of mutual respect that were common among the many religions in ancient Rome. To do so would be "idolatry." Both were punished by the authorities of the Roman Empire for their politically disruptive attitudes and practices, but this was not religious persecution in the sense later to become all too familiar in medieval and modern Europe.

With the eventual triumph of Christianity as the state religion of the Roman Empire, religious intolerance emerged in the sense of forced conversions and punishment of heretics or infidels not accepting the one true faith. The number of Christians killed by other Christians in religious controversies in the later Roman Empire far exceeded the number ever put to death by the Romans in pagan times. Jews were among the many victims of this religious militancy. With the eventual triumph of one unified doctrine in the West—Roman Catholicism— Jews were left isolated as the only major religious minority. The same theological concept—"idolatry"—that made the Christians unwilling to compromise with the pagans made the Jews unwilling to compromise with the Christians, or vice versa.

The Jews were not simply religious dissenters, serious as that would have been in that era. Because of their dispersion after their own homeland was conquered, they were also an alien people in country after country, bearing an alien culture, speaking a different language, wearing different clothes, and generally living in separate communities or sections of towns. They were, in short, a marked people—natural targets for whatever passions or fears might sweep over an ignorant and superstitious population around them. Moreover, the Jews, who were typically excluded from landownership and many other economic endeavors, often worked as middlemen—notably small tradesmen and money lenders—and those who perform such economic functions are almost universally unpopular around the world.[1] Where middlemen are an ethnically distinct group—the Chinese in Southeast Asia, the East Indians in Uganda, and the Ibos in Nigeria—that ethnic group is hated by the masses who deal with them. The Jews are the classic example of such a group in such occupations.

It was the elite—the nobility, the kings, and the popes—who offered the Jews what small protection they received. This often had less to do with either humanitarianism or justice than with self-interest. The Jews had useful skills, and sometimes wealth. In many places, they simply had to pay the authorities for the privilege of living in the latter's domain. A change in political climate or personal caprice among the rulers could end their dearly purchased toleration at any time. The Jews were seldom an integral part of the community, even when they had lived in the same place for generations, or even centuries. Intermarriage remained very rare.

The Jews typically lived together, and with the passing of the centuries and the rise of militant Christianity, they were forced to do so. In Poland in 1266, it was decreed that Jews "shall not live among the Christians, but should have their homes near or next to one another in some sequestered part of the state or town," and this separate section "separated from the common dwelling place of the Christians by a hedge, a wall, or a ditch."[2] This and similar provisions in various countries evolved into the classic Jewish ghetto—walled in and with gates that were locked at night.[3] This institution lasted for about four centuries.[4]

In many parts of Europe, Jews were not safe outside the ghetto. Depending upon local circumstances, they might work outside during the day, sometimes at profitable or occasionally prestigious tasks, but all their personal lives and social relationships were within the ghetto. The Jewish community was a separate, self-governing entity, with its own culture, courts, and tax collections. The Jewish culture and its values were a pervasive influence on the individual, whose identity was that of a Jew, whether he lived in Italy, Poland, or France. Among the genetic consequences of these small, in-bred societies, was an unusual amount of physical and mental defects.[5]

The Jews

The ghetto precluded an agricultural life for most European Jews. They were urbanized centuries before reaching New York and other American cities. In those parts of Europe where Jews were most isolated, the modern intellectual currents of post-Renaissance Europe largely passed them by, and their culture remained a folk culture of an earlier era. The Jews who emigrated en masse from eastern Europe to America were from such a folk background.

The many isolated Jewish communities in Europe kept in intermittent contact with one another. Each kept alive the Jewish traditions, but largely separately. Inevitably, the slow modifications of Judaism and the Jewish culture took different forms in different places—setting the stage for internal religious differences and controversies when the different groups came together later in America. Refugees from various kinds of persecution brought international contact among the Jews of Europe. In this way arose Yiddish, a German dialect with Hebrew and Polish modifications.[6]

One of the classic features of European Jewish culture was respect and reverence for learning. This was primarily religious learning, knowledge of the Talmud, and careful, minute analysis of its meanings or implications. Mothers wanted their daughters to marry learned men, even if they were poor. Most of the Jewish immigrants who moved to the United States did not have much education, and many were illiterate, but their affinity for education was extremely high.

The Jews were also skilled workers, and many were small tradesmen, money lenders, and a few large merchants and bankers. In some countries, Jews became tax collectors and other government officials and advisors. Association with political power holders brought some individual or group protection, but it also made Jews hated by enemies of the regime and especially likely to become targets in the event of its overthrow.

Among the Jewish patterns in Europe that were later to become important in America were cleanliness, philanthropy, and a very low rate of alcoholism. Public baths were an institution among Jews at a time when individual indoor plumbing was virtually unknown. Charity was also a long-established religious tradition among the Jews of Europe, even in their poverty, and large-scale philanthropy was destined to become a Jewish tradition under more prosperous conditions in America—ironically so, in view of the stereotype of Jewish miserliness. In much of Europe for much of history, dangers of popular resentment made it highly inadvisable for Jews to display any wealth or even evidence of prosperity, and the need to be ready to flee if necessary made it inadvisable to keep whatever they accumulated in immobile forms such as clothes or home furnishings, and more sensible to have it in gold or jewelry. Like the Italians, Jews served wine with meals but seldom became drunkards. Drunkenness, boisterousness, or recklessness induced by drink could easily have become fatal in the precarious situation of most European Jews.

After the passage of many centuries, some of the many restrictions against Jews began to be relaxed or eliminated in the modern world. A wider development of commerce, industry, and banking made the Jew less anachronistic than in feudal society, as well as making his skills and experience in these areas more valuable. The eighteenth century saw political rights extended to Jews in England, France, and Holland,[7] and in the early nineteenth century, other Euopean nations began to remove legal disabilities. The spread of the French pattern with the Napoleonic conquests emancipated Jews in various parts of Europe, but the eventual defeat of Napoleon marked a retrogression for them in many places. Massacres and expulsions erupted again.[8] Still, the political emancipation of Jews progressed across Europe in an uneven pattern from country to country. The first Jew sat in the British Parliament in 1858, but the last ghetto was not destroyed in Italy until 1885.[9]

Where the restrictions on Jews were most relaxed—in western Europe—more cultural and even biological assimilation occurred. Distinctions of dress and hairstyles tended to disappear. The Jews began to speak the language of their respective countries and to become acquainted with its literature and philosophy. Judaism itself adapted more to the outward rituals of Christianity, with such things as organs in the house of worship, mixed choirs, stained-glass windows, and services on Sunday instead of Saturday.[10] This Reform Judaism originated in Germany, one of the more liberal countries in its policies toward Jews. Orthodox Judaism remained dominant in Russia and eastern Europe, where the Jews remained a more separate and still restricted people.

In the West, individuals of known Jewish ancestry, could live as non-Jews in a Gentile world. Among the notable nineteenth-century examples were Benjamin Disraeli, David Ricardo, and Karl Marx. While the first professed Jew entered the British Parliament in 1858, Ricardo had sat in Parliament in 1819, and Disraeli entered it in 1837. Neither was "passing" in the sense of concealing his ancestry, but both lived as Christians among other Christians. Similarly, Karl Marx, although descended from rabbis on both sides of his family, was the son of a convert to Christianity and was baptized a Lutheran. Marx never considered himself a Jew, and always spoke of Jews in the 'third person.

Even for those who remained in the Judaic religion, in the more liberal Western nations this did not imply a separate existence or a denationalization. They could be seen as Frenchmen, Germans, or Hollanders of the Jewish faith. In Eastern Europe, being a Jew was much more of a total, separate identity, with different forms of worship and dress. In short, there were profound social and even religious differences between the Jews of Western Europe and those of Eastern Europe in the nineteenth century, when immigration to America began on a large scale.

JEWISH IMMIGRANTS TO AMERICA

Sephardic Jews

The first group of Jews who arrived in colonial America were Sephardic Jews, with their own religious rites (distinguished from those of the Ashkenazic Jews of the rest of Europe) and a social history in Spain and Portugal that was generally more favorable than elsewhere. In Spain and Portugal, Jews were not confined to ghettos, and some were even major landowners, political figures, bankers, and industrialists, and they dominated the liberal professions—although most were craftsmen, small shopkeepers, money lenders, and the like.[11] The history of Jews in the Iberian Peninsula was not, however, wholly free of the persecutions and sporadic massacres that marked their history elsewhere. During the rule of the Visigoths, from the sixth to the eighth century, the position of Jews changed back and forth under successive kings—sometimes accepted and prospering at the highest levels of government and at other times expelled from the government and even forced to flee the country.[12] However, later Spanish monarchies provided protection for Jews while utilizing their skills in the governmental apparatus and benefiting from their economic activity in general.

The first Jews to come to colonial America did so as a result of events set in motion in the very year Columbus discovered the hemisphere. After centuries of living under much more tolerant and prosperous conditions than Jews in other parts of Euope, the Jews in Spain were suddenly expelled from the country by royal decree in 1492. Complex internal political considerations were behind this massive expulsion,[13] and the Jews who left sought many destinations. Some were on boats in the harbor at Seville when Columbus sailed past them out to sea to find a new route to India. Some who became converts to Christianity to escape persecution were among the crews of Columbus' ships. Indeed, part of the voyage was financed with money confiscated by the government from the expelled Jews.[14] After having been forced to help pay for the discovery of America, it was perhaps fitting that more Jews were later settled in the United States than in any other country in the world, more even than in Israel.

Many of the expelled Jews settled first in nearby Portugal, but others went to Holland or other places of refuge. The large Sephardic community in Amsterdam helped to make little Holland a major international commercial and financial power. Portugal eventually forced many Jews out, after taking much of their wealth by various devices. Changing political forces elsewhere—for example, the change in Brazil's status from a Dutch colony to a Portuguese colony—forced the Sephardic Jews to continue moving.[15]

By the seventeenth century, British policy in the American colonies permitted Jews greater freedom than in most of the rest of the world. The first synagogue in North America was established in New York in 1695.[16] Although the wealth of the Sephardic Jews was often exhausted (or confiscated) by the time they had reached colonial America, the skills that had produced this wealth recreated it in America. All in all, there were about 2,000 Jews in the colonies at the time of the American Revolution.[17] Most were Sephardic and by now prosperous, and they maintained "an attitude of exclusiveness and hauteur" toward other American Jews who were Ashkenazic. A Sephardic Jew who married an Ashkenazic Jew risked being disowned by his family.[18] The two groups of Jews were also "rigidly separate" in Holland and in England, although their religious rites differed only in details.[19] Centuries of separation in different countries had made them socially different, although adherents of the same religion. In modern times, in both the United States and Israel, Sephardic Jews do not average as high IQs as Ashkenazic Jews.[20] Historically, Sephardic Jews were never as oriented toward scholarship as other Jews but were highly successful in business. They were more worldly in a world that offered them more opportunities than other contemporary Jews had in other countries.

German Jews

German Jews entered colonial America shortly after the Sephardic Jews. When they were only a trickle, German Jews tended to enter the existing Jewish communities and adapt to the Sephardic rites. As the German-Jewish element grew larger, they separated to form their own communities and built their own temples of the Ashkenazic rites, and particularly Reform Judaism.

The later arriving German Jews, especially in the nineteenth century, were not merely newer immigrants, but poorer and less acculturated and from a more provincial background in the smaller towns of Germany.[21] They were socially very different from the older Sephardic Jews, who were by now very well established and prosperous in America.

The emigration of Jews from Germany greatly changed the size of the American-Jewish community, as well as its internal composition. There had been less than 3,000 Jews in the American colonies in 1776, but this increased between four and five times by 1820. By 1850, there were estimated to be about ten times that number. By 1880, the Jewish population had increased another ten times to over half a million.[22] The bulk of this was due to emigration from Germany.

Unlike the Sephardic Jews before them or the Eastern European Jews after them the German Jews did not concentrate in a few communities. They spread out through the young American nation, working as small tradesmen and professionals scattered among their non-Jewish clientele.[23] Some settled among German farmers in Pennsylvania. Some settled in the Midwest, often among other Germans.[24] Others followed the wagons to the western frontier. The heavy denim trousers called Levis were named after one of these German-Jewish peddlers, Levi Strauss.[25]

In the desperate loneliness of many rural and frontier areas, the Jewish peddler was a welcome visitor. It was one of many contrasts with Jewish experience in Europe. Yankee peddlers had gone before them, so Americans were accustomed to such itinerant merchants with their miscellaneous combs, scissors, needles, and threads.

Among the early German-Jewish peddlers, it was common to travel with a peddler's pack on one's back, and only later did the more successful move up to horse and buggy. Some peddlers eventually settled down and opened local stores.[26] Many of the great wealthy Jewish families began in America as peddlers—the Guggenheims, the Gimbels, and the Altmans, for example.[27]

By the middle of the nineteenth century, Jews were an accepted part of American life, and most were German Jews. By the time of the Civil War, there were more than fifty synagogues in New York alone.[28] There were also numerous Jewish civic and philanthropic organizations. The German Jews were active not only in their own communities but also in American society at large as businessmen and bankers. The large credit-rating agency of R. G. Dunn found 374 Jewish firms worthy of a commercial rating in 1860 and 1,714 by 1870.[29] Many Jews were destined to play important roles in developing such major American institutions as Macy's Department Store chain, Sears Roebuck, and *The New York Times.* As of 1880, 40 percent of all the German-Jewish families had at least one servant. Only 1 percent of the heads of Jewish families were still peddlers, and fewer than 1 percent worked as laborers or domestic servants.[30]

In a sense, American Jews had "arrived." In another sense—numerically—they had not yet begun to arrive. The great, massive immigration of eastern European Jews began in the 1880s—the coming of the ancestors of most Jewish-Americans today.

Eastern European Jews

During the thirteenth and fourteenth centuries, the Polish royalty encouraged Jews to settle in their country and issued charters to protect them. The Jews were vehicles by which skills and knowledge from the more advanced parts of Europe could be brought into Poland. Jews in Poland were allowed more freedom and community autonomy than most contemporary Jews elsewhere and were not locked in ghettos, although they typically lived together under Talmudic law. As the artisans and merchants progressed over the centuries among the poor, illiterate peasants, they were resented and hated by them and by their church religious leaders. The fact that Jews worked as tax collectors for the government and collected rents for landlords brought more hatred against them. Depending on changing political fortunes, Jews were protected or persecuted by the authorities.[31]

Much of the area where Jews lived in Europe was taken over by Russia in the eighteenth century. There had been very few Jews in Russia before this, and the Russians confined the Jews to their former place of settlement in the lands newly acquired from Poland. Catherine the Great in 1791 established an area called the Jewish Pale of

The Jews

Settlement. Few Jews were permitted to move "beyond the Pale." Many of the rights formerly enjoyed by the Jews in Poland were taken away by the Russians. Successive czars followed changing policies toward the Jews, some recognizing the value of their skills, others being more concerned with their religious and social differences from the other Russians. In the nineteenth century, brutal attempts were made to "Russify" the Jews—taking their boys away at age twelve (or earlier) for six years of training in Greek Orthodox schools, followed by the twenty-five years of military service to which all Russian males were subject. Desperate evasions were used by the Jews—including even maiming their children. Equally drastic methods were used by the Russians, including sending kidnappers at large to capture children they might chance upon.[32] Eventually, the law was changed under Czar Nicholas II, who also freed the serfs. But with the assassination of the czar in 1881, a new round of violently anti-Jewish laws was issued by his son.

Compounding the anti-Semitic policies of the new czar were widespread riots and peasant massacres of Jews throughout the region of the Pale. Mobs rampaged through Jewish areas—destroying, looting, raping, and murdering. Even children and infants were not spared.

With these tragic events began one of the great human migrations in history. Over the next four decades, 2 million people—one-third of all the Jews in eastern Europe—moved to the United States.[33] During those years, three quarters of all the people who left Russia for the United States were Jews, and three quarters of the Jews who arrived in the United States were from Russia.[34] In addition to those who emigrated directly from Russia, there were many Jews who escaped to become refugees in other European countries and only later moved to America, often with the help of Jewish philanthropic organizations or relatives in America.

The overwhelming majority of these Jewish immigrants came to stay. The rate of return migration was lower among Jews than among any other large group of immigrants.

About half the Jews in nineteenth-century Russia were literate— roughly two-thirds of the men and one-third of the women.[35] This was much higher than for the Russian population as a whole. Jews were also far more urbanized. Less than 3 percent were in agricultural occupations, while more than 30 percent were in commerce, nearly 40 percent in mining and manufacturing, and 5 percent in professional occupations.[36] Almost half of all Russian Jews worked in some aspect of clothes production.[37]

THE MASS IMMIGRATION ERA

The eastern European Jews began arriving in the United States in huge numbers in the 1880s. In that decade, more than 200,000 immigrated to America, followed by 300,000 in the 1890s, and about a million and a half from the turn of the century to the beginning of World War I.[38]

The size of the eastern European Jewish immigration swamped the existing American Jewish community of largely German origin. The eastern European Jews were also heavily concentrated in New York City and, in fact, were even more localized on the lower east side of Manhattan, which contained the largest number of Jews ever assembled in one place on earth in thousands of years. The German Jews already established in America were appalled not only by the numbers but also by the way of life of the eastern European Jews. The eastern Jews were not only poorer—most arrived destitute, with less money than any other immigrant group[39]—but were also far less educated (a 50 percent illiteracy rate), and with rougher manners than the more sophisticated and Americanized German Jews. Eastern European Jews had lived a provincial life, outside the mainstream of the general European culture in which German Jews were immersed. Eastern Europeans even looked different—earlocks, skull caps, beards, old-fashioned Russian-style clothing, scarves about the women's heads, and a general demeanor reminiscent of a painful past that German Jews had long ago left behind.[40] The Orthodox Jewish religious services were full of traditions and practices long abandoned by the modern Reform Judaism of Germans. The very language of the eastern European Jews—Yiddish—was a folk dialect disdained by more educated Jews, who used either the language of the country or classical Hebrew.

In short, the eastern European Jews were an acute embarrassment to the German Jews in America. Their numbers, ways, and concentration made them highly visible, alarming other Americans and threatening an anti-Semitic reaction that would harm the German Jews, who had quietly gained acceptance before.[41] The Jewish press, controlled by German Jews, was openly critical of the new immigrants, whom they described as representing "Oriental antiquity," speaking a "piggish jargon,"[42] and "slovenly in dress, loud in manners, and vulgar in discourse."[43] Their religion was referred to as "medieval Orthodoxy."[44] The vicissitudes of the eastern European Jews were seen by the German Jews as filling the newspapers with "daily records of misdemeanors, marital miseries, and petty quarrels."[45] It was the German Jews who coined the epithet "kike" to apply to eastern European Jews.[46]

Overriding all of these antipathies, however, was the Jewish philanthropic tradition. German-Jewish organizations made strenuous efforts to aid, and especially to Americanize, the eastern European Jewish immigrants.[47] Schools, libraries, hospitals, and community centers were established to serve "downtown" Jews, financed by "uptown" Jews. Yet even these humanitarian endeavors carried over some of the intergroup tensions. For example, even after 90 percent of the patients at New York's Mt. Sinai Hospital were eastern Europeans, no eastern European physicians were admitted to the hospital staff.[48] Religious services at People's Synagogue were conducted wholly in Hebrew and German, and Yiddish was taboo.[49] As a contemporary wrote:

In the philanthropic institutions of our aristocratic German Jews, you see beautiful offices, desks, all decorated, but strict and angry faces. Every poor man is questioned like a criminal, is looked down upon; every unfortunate suffers self-degradation and shivers like a leaf, just as if he was standing before a Russian official.[50]

As soon as their financial condition permitted, eastern European Jews began to establish their own philanthropic organizations. These began to arise by the late 1880s. One of these organizations proclaimed: "In dispensing money and matzos to the poor, all are recognized as the children of one Father, and no lines are drawn between natives of different countries."[51]

Although the terms "uptown" (German) Jews and "downtown" (Russian) Jews were peculiar to New York City, the divisions they symbolized were not. In mid-nineteenth-century Chicago, the German Jews regarded the Polish Jews "as an inferior caste."[52] A Chicago rabbi, in appealing for funds for the United Hebrew Relief Association, lamented that the Jews in Chicago were "divided by pecuniary, intellectual, and social distinctions, provincial jealousies, and even religious distinctions and differences," and asked of the new immigrants, "are they less poor, are they less Israelites because Poland or Russia is the land in which they first saw the light, or rather the darkness, of this world?"[53] While the appeal was successful in financial terms, still the German Jews who contributed "looked down with pity—benevolently, to be sure, but with a certain condescension—upon their Russian and Polish co-religionists."[54] As in New York, the German Jews in Chicago ran philanthropic organizations whose clienteles were eastern

European Jews. As in New York, the eastern European Jews resented the way they were treated and began setting up their own charitable organizations.[55]

The Jewish immigrants "brought with them the hunted look of the Pale" and seldom ventured beyond their own streets. They "lacked self-confidence and presence" in dealing with others, and were often unable to communicate with strangers—even American Jews who did not speak Yiddish.[56] Walking with bent heads—"the ghetto crouch"— and obviously fearful and unresisting, they were natural targets for street bullies who insulted and harassed them or casually pulled their beards.[57] Their passivity under provocation only increased the German Jews' resentment of them, for letting Gentiles think that Jews were cowards.[58] But the German Jews, who had been safely prospering in America, had never experienced anything like the horrors still vivid to the eastern European immigrants.

Between the eastern European Jews and German Jews, there long remained "caste-like divisions." For example, in Philadelphia in 1940, the Jewish upper class was "still almost entirely German in ethnic origins."[59] In New York, "uptown" Jews seldom married "downtown" Jews.[60] In Chicago, Russian Jews built up "their own separate community life,"[61] and intermarriage among the various nationalities of Jews long remained "almost as rare as intermarriage between ghetto Jews and Gentiles."[62]

The so-called overprotective Jewish mother came out of the eastern European background.[63] Her desire to always have her children around her, within her sight, is all too understandable in view of the Jewish experience in eastern Europe, where Jewish children who wandered off might never be seen again. In eastern Europe, even Jewish children who lived near the woods seldom went swimming or fishing or walked in the forest.[64] The life pattern of centuries was not readily broken in America.

Anti-Semitism in the United States assumed growing and unprecedented proportions in the last quarter of the nineteenth century, with the mass arrival of the eastern European Jews. German Jews were hard hit by this, as many were financially in a position to be eligible for exclusive social clubs, posh hotels, and other benefits and honors denied them by reason of their religon—and the immigration of their newly arrived co-religionists.[65] At less Olympian levels, help wanted ads began to specify "Christians,"[66] as they had once specified "Protestant" to exclude the Irish.

The Jews

Economic Conditions

The immigrant generation of Jews flooded into the lower east side of Manhattan at the same time as the massive influx of Italian immigrants, helping create one of the most crowded communities on the face of the earth. In a pattern repeated many times with many groups in American history, the initial middle-class inhabitants (German and Irish at this time) began to withdraw as the poverty-stricken newcomers moved in.[67] Eventually, one-sixth of New York's total population lived here, on one-eighty-second of its land.[68] By the turn of the century, the lower east side averaged more than 700 people per acre— more than in the worst slums of Bombay.[69] A contemporary described the lower east side as "the eyesore of New York . . . the filthiest place in the Western continent."[70] Not only were families crowded into small quarters; they often took in roomers and boarders to help them pay the rent.[71] Even so, large-scale evictions for nonpayment of rent were common—more than 10,000 in one year in just two judicial districts on the lower east side.[72] One indication of the economic condition of eastern European immigrant Jews at this time was that a proposal to require each new immigrant to have twenty-five dollars in cash with him before being admitted to the United States sent alarm and anger throughout the lower east side Jewish community.[73] Most of them had not had one-third of this much when they arrived in America.[74]

The immigrant Jews typically worked in manual occupations—ranging from casual laborers who gathered on street corners early each morning hoping to be hired by somebody for a day's work[75] to skilled craftsmen working at their respective trades. The occupational range of the immigrants was limited by their own religious and social constraints. Unlike the German Jews before them, the eastern European immigrant Jews could not readily spread out across the nation—or even across the city. Their religious orthodoxy restricted their ability to work in factories at a time when factories often worked on Saturdays, the Sabbath observed by Orthodox Jews. Their language differences also made it difficult for them to work or live among other Americans, as did their need for kosher food and a synagogue. In short, they needed to live and work among other Jews, to a far greater extent than German Jews had at a similar stage. The German Jews had been less religiously and culturally self-restricted and had never had an enduring all-Jewish neighborhood in New York, such as now existed in a large area of the lower east side.[76]

For all their poverty, Jews seldom became servants. In New York City in 1880, about half of all Irish and Italians were working in personal service, and even 21 percent of the Germans, but less than 4 percent of the Jews. Yet Jewish women did not simply remain home as housewives. Home was the site of much work contracted from businessmen and performed by all members of the family, including small children. These were the famous "sweatshops" of the lower east side tenements, where "whirring sewing machines behind closed doors" could be heard on every floor.[77]

Jews had been concentrated in clothing production in eastern Europe, and in America, they arrived just as the mass production ready-made clothing industry was developing. As late as 1880, less than half of the men's clothing in the United States was ready-to-wear clothing.[78] Homemade or tailor-made clothing was the rule, and a large market existed for secondhand clothing. Isaac M. Singer's perfection and promotion of the sewing machine changed that almost overnight.[79] By 1885, there were 241 garment factories in New York City— 234 of which were owned by Jews.[80] These were mostly German Jews, with eastern European Jews as their employees. In a familiar pattern of group succession, a generation later the eastern European Jews would be employers in the garment industry, with Italians and others as their employees. New York was destined to remain the center of the American clothing industry, and Jews predominated among its businessmen. As of 1890, about half of all Jews working in American industry were clothing workers.[81]

While the nineteenth-century home sweatshop was the bane of reformers then and historians later, it provided a way for Jewish women to work without leaving their chidlren unattended and a way for people with no knowledge of English and a reluctance to leave their own neighborhoods to earn a living nevertheless. It had its costs—long hours in cramped quarters, often sacrifice of opportunities for their children to get schooling—and all for wages that were below even the standards of the time. The frequent charge of "exploitation," however, overlooks the fact that the subcontractor or "sweater" for whom the immigrants worked frequently worked long hours himself for a relatively small profit.[82] It was essentially a system by which the mass of Americans obtained brand-new clothing at a price they could afford. The Jewish sweatshop workers were, by contemporary accounts, able to save a substantial portion of their earnings,[83] providing for the future economic rise of themselves and their children. In view of their later success, it would be arrogant of others to claim that they were not making the best of their meager opportunities.

Over half of all the Jewish immigrants worked in manual occupations, and even the "white-collar" occupations included many push-cart peddlers.[84] Between 1880 and 1905, the number of peddlers in New York City increased by 75 percent, largely due to Jewish immigrants, about 10 percent of whom were peddlers at one time,[85] although many more passed through that stage during their adjustment to American life.[86] Other "white-collar" occupations included butcher, baker, and grocer. Only about 5 percent of the immigrant Jews worked in "high white-collar" occupations, and as late as the turn of the century, only about 1 percent of the Jewish immigrants were professionals. Two-thirds of all Jews were *skilled* workers, however.[87]

Social Conditions

While the Jews experienced poverty and slum living, their own peculiar culture and values enabled them to escape some of the long-run consequences. They lived in overcrowded firetraps, and were struck hard by tuberculosis, but alcoholism never became a serious problem among them, and their traditional concern for cleanliness spared them some of the other diseases that struck some other slum dwellers.

Physically, the eastern European Jewish immigrants were small and were described by contemporaries as "physical wrecks" and among "the most stunted of the Europeans."[88] Part of this may have been a result of their poverty and of traditional Jewish de-emphasis of the physical in favor of the mental. It may also have been a genetic result of centuries of inbreeding in small enclaves—which would also explain its disappearance among later generations, born in the much larger Jewish communities in America.

Yet for all their apparent physical disadvantages, Jews had lower death rates than others—often lower than those in more prosperous neighborhoods. One factor was their traditional emphasis on cleanliness, whether religiously based or evolved from centuries of urban living in Europe. Public bathhouses were a tradition among eastern European Jews and were recreated in New York. By 1897, over half the bathhouses in New York City were Jewish.[89] Individual home bathtubs were virtually unknown on the east side at this time. An indoor water faucet or water toilet, to be shared by many tenants, was a recent improvement and by no means universal. There were still thousands of outdoor toilets in the backyards.

Within these severe limits, immigrant Jews tried to maintain traditions of cleanliness. Their success must be measured within this context and compared to other slum dwellers, although they were faulted on this score by their middle-class contemporaries. The Jews did not suffer the cholera epidemics that had decimated Irish neighborhoods in various cities, decades earlier. But there were obvious limits to cleanliness in an area with about 300 bathtubs among a quarter of a million hard-working people.[90]

Religious rules regulating the handling and preparation of kosher food also had sanitary effects.[91] Neither the people nor the food always fulfilled the highest standards of cleanliness[92]—German Jews pointedly included lessons on soap and water in their programs for eastern European Jews[93]—but everything is relative. Health and cleanliness were more characteristic of Jews than of other city slum dwellers.

Similarly, such scourges as tuberculosis, venereal disease, and desertions of families by fathers appeared among the lower east side Jews in alarming amounts compared to what they had been used to in the more stable communities they knew in Europe but usually were well below the levels of other slum dwellers. Alcohol was never the problem among Jews that it was among other groups. Their rates of alcoholism have remained among the lowest in America.

While the lower east side contained less than 20 percent of New York's population, it suffered almost 40 percent of its deaths from fire.[94] Closely packed tenements readily communicated fire, and the overcrowding of people and furniture—often even in the halls and on fire escapes—made escape or rescue difficult in an emergency.[95] A 1908 survey showed that less than one-tenth of the east side families slept less than two in a room. About half slept three or four to a room, and more than a third slept five or more to a room.[96]

What has been most striking about the Jews has been their attitude toward education. Although very few of the eastern European Jews were well educated—about half were not even literate on arrival—they came from a culture where learning had been revered for centuries.[97] The learned man—or even a well-schooled child—earned respect in the community. Free schools and free public libraries in New York were seized upon by children and adults alike. A survey of public libraries in the Russian-Jewish tenement neighborhoods in New York in 1912 showed that 53 percent of the books borrowed were nonfiction and that the bulk of the fictional works were by such authors as Tolstoy, Dumas, and Dickens. Frothy best-sellers "remained dusty on the shelves."[98]

The Jews

Most of the people in these neighborhoods were manual workers—skilled, but manual—and even those statistically categorized as "white collar" were often pushcart peddlers, butchers, grocers, or in other occupations where book learning was of no economic value. Yet they not only read but went to all sorts of public lectures on topics far from relevant to their daily lives. As one contemporary later observed, "You can imagine how badly we needed Herbert Spencer on Delancey Street in those days!"[99]

Jewish immigrant children worked in the sweatshops and elsewhere, but seldom full time, because of their parents' desire for them to go to school.[100] In the schools, the teachers were usually Irish[101]—seldom Jewish—and the classrooms were overcrowded. In the late 1880s, it was estimated that there were eighty-seven pupils per teacher in the lowest primary grade—and even so, thousands of children were refused admission due to lack of space.[102] Even around the turn of the century, "classes of 60, sitting three to a seat" were not unusual.[103] Earlier figures for pupils per teacher, in mid-century New York, were even higher during the period of Irish immigration.[104] A number of lower east side schools were over 90 percent Jewish.[105] Attempts to relieve overcrowding in these schools by busing these children to west side schools in Irish neighborhoods provoked protest meetings and irate editorials in the Jewish newspapers.[106] The plans were abandoned.

While some teachers spoke glowingly of the lower east side Jewish children, others found teaching them to be "unusually tedious"[107] and observed that "many come from families in which English is seldom spoken at all, and where good manners and cleanliness are decidedly at a discount."[108] Much may depend on whether the east side Jews were being compared with other slum dwellers or with middle-class contemporaries. A sympathetic Irish schoolteacher from the lower east side wrote fictional stories about the area in which both pictures of Jewish schoolchildren appear—at times eager to please and at other times "a howling mob of little savages." The teacher-heroine of the stories delivered daily lectures on personal grooming and hygiene, in which her discussions of soap and water "became almost personal in tone."[109]

The remarkable achievements—especially intellectual achievements—of later generations of Jews cannot simply be read back into the immigrant generation. These children often had serious educational problems. A 1910 survey of a dozen cities found two-thirds of the children of Polish Jews to be below the normal grade for their age.[110]

This was an era when it was common to avoid promoting children until their scholastic performance merited it, but even so, the record of Polish Jews was worse than others. A 1911 study showed that 41 percent of the 5,431 Russian-Jewish children surveyed were behind the "normal" grade level. Partly this may be because so many entered school late due to overcrowded New York schools that annually turned many away. However, even among the Russian-Jewish children who entered at age six, 23 percent were behind their normal grade level[111]—about the same as for the New York City school system as a whole,[112] where most were presumably enrolled. As late as World War I, soldiers of Russian—mostly Jewish—origin averaged among the lowest mental test scores of any of the ethnic groups tested by the U.S. Army.[113] These results led a leading contemporary authority on tests to declare that this disproved "the popular belief that the Jew is highly intelligent."[114] Like so many confident "expert" conclusions, this one failed to stand the test of time.

LATER GENERATIONS

The upward movement of American Jews—across broad economic, intellectual, social, and political areas—was unprecedented and unparalleled. Between 1897 and 1907, the number of Jewish physicians in Manhattan rose from 450 to 1,000, pharmacists from 45 to 115, and dentists from 59 to 350.[115] These were still small proportions of the hundreds of thousands of Jews on the lower east side of New York. However, it indicates something of a general trend. A broader picture shows the proportion of New York Jews in "high white-collar" occupations rising from 5 percent in 1880 to 15 percent in 1905.[116] Peddling declined by 75 percent.[117] Even among those Jews who began as manual laborers in Boston, only about half were still manual laborers at the end of their careers. Their upward mobility was double that among other groups.[118] By the middle of the twentieth century, 20 percent of Jewish males were professionals (double the national average), and 35 percent more were proprietors (compared to 13 percent for the U.S. population as a whole). Most Jews were white collar workers, while most other Americans were still blue collar workers at that time.[119]

The Jews

As the Jews rose economically, they also spread out residentially. The younger generation was English-speaking (often bilingual) and so was less tied to the lower east side by Old World language and culture. The building of the New York subway system in the early twentieth century made uptown—notably Harlem and the Bronx—more accessible to work places than before. Both became heavily settled with Jews. The more Americanized Jews also found other parts of the United States more accessible than their immigrant parents had. New York, however, still remained the center of the eastern European settlement. But whereas three quarters of the city's Jews had lived on the lower east side in 1892, this proportion had dropped to half by 1903 and to only 23 percent by 1916.[120]

By 1930, there were more Jews living in Brooklyn than in Manhattan, and by 1940, both Brooklyn and the Bronx had at least twice as many Jews as Manhattan. By mid-century, among the five boroughs of New York, only Staten Island had fewer Jews than Manhattan, their original stronghold.[121] Similar residential changes occurred in Chicago. The west side of Chicago was the original settlement area of eastern European Jews.[122] The portion of the west side slum that was Jewish differed from the rest of that section of Chicago only in having far fewer saloons.[123] In 1931, almost half of the Jews in Chicago still lived on the west side, but by 1958, only 6 percent were still there, while most were living in the more prosperous north side of Chicago.[124]

Nationally, more than half of all American Jews continued to live in the northeastern United States, on past the mid-century mark. New York City alone contained 40 percent of all the Jews in the United States.[125] The proportion of Jews living in the Midwest and South declined, while the proportion of all Jews who lived in the West more than doubled, and those living specifically on the Pacific Coast quadrupled between 1900 and 1968—from 3 percent to 12 percent.[126]

Jews rose to have not only higher incomes than other Americans[127] but also more education and higher IQs. By the middle of the twentieth century, more than one-fourth of all Jewish males had four or more years of college, while less than 10 percent of the U.S. population as a whole had that much education.[128] The incomes of Jewish males were 36 percent higher than those of American males in general.[129] Various studies show Jews now have higher IQs than other Americans.[130] More than one-fourth of all Nobel prizes won by all Americans have been won by Jewish Americans, who are only 3 percent of the population.[131] Jews became prominent among American writers, scientists, motion picture producers, and millionaires. The

Jewish lower east side of New York also produced notable boxers, entertainers, union leaders, journalists, and criminals, as such neighborhoods have typically done with other groups. Fanny Brice, Jack Benny, the Marx Brothers, Milton Berle, and Danny Kaye have been among the many comedians who are Jewish. Among the Jewish movie moguls were Samuel Goldwyn and Louis B. Mayer, whose names were incorporated into the initials for MGM Studios. David O. Selznick, the Warner Brothers, and William Fox were others.[132]

Two of the most distinguished newspapers in New York history—in very different ways—were founded or developed by Jews. *The Jewish Daily Forward* was the first daily newspaper written in the long-disdained Yiddish dialect and was a major influence in the lives of eastern European Jews in New York. Its circulation grew to 20,000 in 1900 and to more than 130,000 by 1918.[133] It was and remained for decades the largest Yiddish-language newspaper in the world.[134] *The New York Times* became an internationally famous institution after being bought by Adolph Ochs in 1896. Joseph Pulitzer, who was half-Jewish, developed the *St. Louis Dispatch* and *The New York World* and established the Pulitzer prize.[135]

In the arts, Jascha Heifetz and Nathan Milstein became leading American violinists of their time, and Artur Rubinstein was one of the leading classical pianists. George Gershwin created a unique musical idiom out of his classical training and the music of the Negroes whom he lived near as he grew up. Irving Berlin and Eddie Cantor came out of New York's lower east side.

In science and medicine, Albert Einstein, J. Robert Oppenheimer, and Jonas Salk are perhaps the best known of the many Jewish Americans who achieved distinction in these fields. In economics, Milton Friedman, Paul Samuelson, and Simon Kuznets were Nobel prize winners. Among the literary figures, Lillian Hellman, Arthur Miller, J. D. Salinger, and Saul Bellow are part of a very long list of Jewish contributors to American letters. In the legal profession, such names as Brandeis, Frankfurter, and Cardozo are part of a larger Jewish pattern that has been characterized as "from rags to robes."[136]

While the Jewish passion for education has been evident and a factor in the rise of many leading individuals and crucial for whole professions, it can be overemphasized as a factor in their initial rise from the slums. The initial stages of the rise of the eastern European Jews were apparent by the turn of the century[137]—at a time when no Jewish child had graduated from a public high school in New York City. The first graduating class from a New York City public high school was in

The Jews

1902.[138] As of 1908, 16 percent of Jewish youngsters graduated from high school, and although that was well in excess of such groups as the Irish or the Italians,[139] it could hardly explain the rise of the other 84 percent of Jews. Public schools and public libraries were undoubtedly very important in the Americanization of the eastern European Jews, and this in turn opened the doors that would have otherwise remained closed, but it was not as scholars or intellectuals that most of the immigrant Jews rose in America. Even among the millionaire movie moguls, theirs was by no means the life of cultured intellectuals. Instead, they have often been described as "vulgar, crude, and overbearing."[140]

After the first generation of Jews rose out of the immigrant slums, they could afford to send their children off to college, and did so to a greater extent than other Americans. But higher education was the consequence of an already achieved prosperity, not the cause of it for most Jews. Free municipal colleges in New York were a godsend to a people with the Jewish intellectual tradition and not yet wealthy enough to afford comparable other colleges. But these municipal colleges became predominantly Jewish only *after* upward mobility was underway. The most famous of these schools—City College in New York—had only 11 percent eastern European Jews among its alumni for classes graduating in the early 1920s. It was not until the 1930s that the eastern European element became one-half of City College's graduates. Among the Jewish graduates in the early part of the century, most were German Jews.[141] Similarly, at New York's Hunter College in 1906, only about a fourth of the graduates were Jews, and most of these were German Jews, with less than 10 percent of the Hunter graduates being eastern European Jews.[142]

Many Jewish youngsters were working, even before reaching college age. In 1880, 38 percent of the clothing workers in New York City were teenage Jews. In 1914–15, 37 percent of all working papers issued to teenagers in New York City went to Jewish teenagers.[143]

The patterns of Jewish success in America to a large extent followed patterns of skills, habits, and orientation that had existed in eastern Europe. The prevalence of occupational skills among the Jewish immigrants ultimately meant more than their almost total lack of money. The industry in which their skills were concentrated—clothing manufacturing—absorbed a substantial part of all Jewish labor and provided the basis for many Jews to move up to become owners of their own businesses. The long Jewish tradition of respect for education influenced Jewish youngsters to continue in school, and this helped not only those few who went on to higher education but also those for whom eight years of schooling was a ticket to white-collar jobs at the time and still others who were simply enabled to move more easily in an American society that still remained foreign to their parents.

The few areas of lesser success—or actual failure—also reflect the Jewish tradition and experience before reaching America. This most successful of all American ethnic groups was repeatedly a failure in agricultural ventures in various parts of the United States.[144] Like other immigrants, Jews were often encouraged by reformers to move out of the crowded city on to the land. Often it was the urban German Jews who thought that rural life was better for the eastern European Jews. Among those few Jews who did settle on the land, their total lack of experience in agriculture became painfully apparent as their ventures all failed financially. Centuries of urban life in Europe lay behind their failure as well as behind their many successes.

In the early years especially, eastern European Jews were slow to have an impact in the worlds of politics and sports, areas in which they had had virtually no experience in Europe. German Jews had had some political experience in America as early as the middle of the nineteenth century, but only a few eastern European Jews were in politics in the early twentieth century—usually in positions wholly subordinate to Irish politicians.[145] The eastern European Jews "lacked the necessary experience, the self-assurance, and, most of all, out-goingness."[146] The Irish were well ahead of them in all of these qualities (as a result of *their* history in Ireland) and remained in control of New York City politics until at least World War II, even though New York had the largest Jewish population of any city in the world. The Jewish political thinking tended to be ideological or programmatic—socialism in its early period, and liberalism later[147]—whereas the Irish were preoccupied with getting into power, which they did very successfully. Even after the Jews managed to make a major impact in politics, it was typically through men known primarily for their substantive programs or administrative expertise, rather than their charismatic personalities.

Another area into which Jews moved slowly was sports. This, too, reflected long traditions of de-emphasizing physical activity for recreation in favor of reading, chess, or playing music. Sholom Aleichem may not have been absolutely correct when he said, "The best fiddlers have always been Jews,"[148] but clearly, they have been much overrepresented among the great violinists. They have been comparatively underrepresented among great athletes. Whereas the Irish quickly rose to domination in boxing and baseball, and remained dominant for decades, the first outstanding Jewish boxers appeared only around World War I, and Jewish baseball players reached the major leagues only in the 1920s, with Hank Greenburg still considered a curiosity when he appeared with the Detroit Tigers in 1933. There have been other Jewish baseball stars of the first magnitude—Al Rosen and Sandy Koufax, for example—but the total number of Jewish players remained very small compared to either the Irish or Germans before them or the blacks or Latin Americans after them.

The rise of the Jews in America was by no means unopposed. While American anti-Semitism never reached the levels seen in Europe, it was still a factor in barring Jews from many positions, including the leading banks and law firms, and from the executive ranks of many large corporations. Here, too, their centuries of experience as a minority in Europe helped them. They were long familiar with barriers and knew that they could be overcome or circumvented. Rather than surrender to despair or exhaust themselves in trying to reform others, the Jews found or made their own opportunities. They largely *created* the American clothing production industry, replacing both homemade clothes and tailor-made clothes. To a large extent, they developed the motion picture industry and created the Yiddish theater and the "borscht circuit," where Jewish entertainers could get a start before heading out into a wider world. They established their own law firms and banks. Barred from many leading universities until after World War II, they pursued scholarly careers where they could, worked in government, and created such a pool of highly educated people that it ultimately became too costly for universities to keep them off their faculties. Today, Jews are overrepresented among college and university faculty.

Understanding the spectacular rise of the Jews may be useful for understanding social progress in general. It was not that they began with such presumed prerequisites as money or education—they were more destitute and illiterate than other immigrants—nor were they politically adroit. Nor did the larger society "accept" them socially or open opportunities for them economically. Yet the internal values and traditions of the Jews were almost tailor-made for success in the American economy. The Jews came not only with specific skills but also with a way of life adapted to centuries of urban life and commercial and industrial activity. Even when the Jews were apparently just workers like other workers, they were often workers who were the sons and grandsons of merchants and scholars[149]—from families whose livelihoods had been destroyed by anti-Semitic policies in Russia but who retained the experience, initiative, and confidence engendered by the earlier success. Even when the Jews lived in slums, they were slums with a difference—lower alcoholism, homicide, accidental death rates than other slums, or even the city as a whole. Their children had lower truancy rates, lower juvenile delinquency rates, and (by the 1930s) higher IQs than other children. The Jews had lower infant mortalities and more organizations than other low-income people. There was also more voting for congressmen by low-income Jews than even by higher income Protestants or Catholics.[150] In short, the Jews had the social patterns and values of the middle class, even when they lived in slums. Despite a voluminous literature claiming that slums shape people's values, the Jews had their own values, and they took those values into and out of the slums.

In short, with Jews as well as with many other ethnic groups, neither their successes nor their handicaps can be understood solely in terms of the American context. Many of the reasons for both reached far back into history.

Social Conditions

The special importance of the family has been characteristic of the Jews in the United States, although the size of the family has been reduced more drastically among Jews than among other Americans. Jews are more likely to marry at some point in their lives than others and much less likely to divorce.[151] The rate of intermarriage of Jews with non-Jews ranged between 5 and 9 percent during the 1930s.[152] By the 1950s and 1960s, intermarriage rates for Jews ranged between about 8 percent in New York City to 37 percent in Marin County, California, to more than half in Iowa.[153] Although the Jewish intermarriage rate rose, it is still well below those of other groups. In general, Jewish intermarriage rates have tended to be higher where the Jewish community has been very small and surrounded by a much larger Gentile group. But even in as large a Jewish community as existed in New York, intermarriage rates rose. Still, these rates are not high compared to the intermarriage rates of other European origin groups.

The size of the Jewish family has undergone dramatic changes over the years. Back around the turn of the century, Jewish families were larger than those of most other ethnic groups,[154] but by mid-century, Jewish families were among the smallest. As of 1910, the average number of children per women in their mid-thirties and mid-forties was 5.3 for Jews, compared to 3.4 children for the United States as a whole.

94

The Jews

Jews had more children than blacks, the Irish, or the Italians, and the same as Mexican Americans, a perennially high fertility group. By 1969, the number of children per woman had fallen by more than one-half among Jews—2.4—compared to a national average of 3.4.[155] The large generation of older Jews and the small generation of younger Jews has meant an average older age for Jews than for any other ethnic group. The average age of American Jews is forty-six, more than double the average age of blacks, Indians, Puerto Ricans, or Mexican Americans.[156] This has helped contribute to the overrepresentation of Jews in high-level occupations requiring experience as well as education.

Despite low rates of intermarriage with other groups, Jews have historically had peaceful and even cooperative relations with other ethnic groups. This, too, is a pattern carried over from Europe, where needless hostilities would have been dangerous to Jewish survival. In the United States, Jews had historically peaceful relations with Germans and Italians, and have cooperated with and partially financed black civil rights organizations. While the Irish had conflicts with the Jews, as they did with other groups, Jewish employers hired Irish workers when other employers would not, although Irish employers generally did not reciprocate by hiring Jewish employees.[157] Jews have historically offered less resistance when blacks moved into their neighborhoods.[158] Harlem was a predominantly Jewish community in the early twentieth century.

Politically, Jews have historically tended to adopt, or at least to be responsive to, the viewpoint of the "underdog"—long after that ceased to be their own position economically. Socialism and liberalism have been dominant political themes among American Jews. The early socialism, anarchism, and unionism of Jewish immigrants gave way to a generalized liberalism as Jews moved up out of the working class and into the middle class, although Jews continued to be overrepresented among radicals. Back in the nineteenth century, when the Republican party was considered to be more liberal than the Democratic party, Jews were Republicans—supporters of Lincoln, for example.[159] Jews continued to vote Republican into the 1920s, although Woodrow Wilson had captured their vote in 1916.[160] In 1920, there were eleven Jewish congressmen—ten Republicans and one Socialist. But in 1922, for the first time in the twentieth century, there were more Jewish Democrats than Republicans elected to Congress. By 1940, 90 percent of American Jews voted for the Democratic presidential candidate, Franklin D. Roosevelt, and did so again in 1944 and again in 1948, when Truman ran. The lowest that the Jewish vote for the Democratic presidential candidates has been over the next twenty years was 60 percent in 1956.[161] The party switch of the Jews largely coincided with a change in the parties themselves in regard to liberalism and conservatism. Blacks made a similar switch at about the same time. A survey of Jews in New York found three quarters to be registered Democrats, and half described themselves as "liberal" and just over a quarter described themselves as "moderate."[162] Other Americans in the Jews' income brackets tended to be more conservative and Republican. This would be difficult to explain purely on the basis of the Jewish experience in America—in particular, their spectacular economic rise—but much more understandable against the background of centuries of Jewish religious tradition of taking care of their own poor and their general role as a persecuted minority throughout Europe.

Jewish candidates often do well with Jewish voters, but usually both are liberal, and non-Jewish liberals also do well among these voters. Hubert Humphrey won a higher percentage of the Jewish vote than Arthur Goldberg in 1968.[163] In 1962, Republican Jacob Javits lost the Jewish vote to an Irish Democrat.[164]

One of the highly uncharacteristic Jewish phenomena of the first half of the twentieth century was the Jewish gangster. Violence of any kind became abhorrent to Jews of the Diaspora, although ancient Israel had its great warriors. Even boxers were denied burial in holy ground by Sephardic Jews when that sport first began in England.[165] By and large, the Jewish neighborhoods on the lower east side of New York were peaceful, and few Jews were in prison or other penal institutions.[166] Jews were more typically victims of crime rather than its perpetrators.[167] But among the second generation—as among other immigrant groups—there arose a tough criminal element. In 1909, 3,000 Jewish youngsters were brought before the Juvenile Court in New York, and afterward, Jewish adult gangsters became famous hoodlums.[168] Prostitution appeared, to the alarm of the Jewish east side community, one not used to such phenomena among Jews in Europe or America.[169] But pimps, thieves, hoodlums, and gangland mobsters emerged among the second generation of east side Jews. By the 1920s, Arnold Rothstein was "absolute boss of the New York underworld." The notorious "Murder Incorporated" killers-for-hire organization was headed by Jewish gangsters. In the largely Jewish garment industry in New York, gangsters were used by both labor and management during strikes, and some even became officials of both companies and unions.[170]

The Jews

Another uncharacteristic occupation for the children of Jewish immigrants was that of boxer. Benny Leonard and Barney Ross were among the best known of the Jewish boxers in the early decades of the twentieth century. Many fought professionally under Irish names, because of the great reputation that Irish boxers had already established. With the general economic rise of Jews, Jewish boxers tended to disappear, along with Jewish mobsters. Both of these were dangerous occupations, and have usually been avoided by groups that have worthwhile options elsewhere.

One of the most traumatic events for later generations of American Jews occurred outside the United States—the rise of the Nazis in Germany and the subsequent Holocaust in which 6 million Jews were brutally killed. Not only was this catastrophe horrifying in its methods and magnitude; it was especially shocking in Germany—an advanced, modern nation, in which Jews had historically been more accepted and better treated than in many other parts of Europe. Only a generation earlier, during World War I, American-Jewish publications had been so favorably disposed toward Germany that they were investigated and prosecuted by the U.S. government for writing favorably about an enemy nation in wartime. Oliver Wendell Holmes's "clear and present danger" doctrine arose in these cases during World War I involving Jewish writers—*Abram* v. *United States* and *Schenk* v. *United States.*

If even Germany could turn on Jews in this savage, genocidal fashion, could the Jews ever relax and quietly blend into the rest of the population? Being a Jew was no longer an incidental feature of one's life. The attempts of assimilationist Jews to be simply "Germans of the Hebrew faith" became a tragic and horrifying mockery and made Jewish identity and Jewish cohesion a more urgent issue for Jews everywhere. The Nazi extermination of Jews, while unique in itself, emphasized a long historic pattern of alternating rapprochement and rejection, protection and expulsion, prosperity and massacre, which had also marked the history of Jews in Spain, Poland, and Russia.

A very different event—also abroad—strengthened Jewish identity in America in a much happier way: the establishment of the modern state of Israel. After centuries as a scattered people, living on the uncertain sufferance of others, Jews once again had a homeland. The fighting spirit that established and defended the new Israel countered the image of Jews as helpless, fearful people, as they had been in the era of the ghettos and the Pale. Jewish philanthropy, which had supported many civic and groupwide activities in America, also heavily supported the new state of Israel. Some American Jews even went to Israel to play important roles there. Golda Meir from Milwaukee was one of these.

The sense of identity of American Jews today is not the Old World religious sense of Jewishness. Most American Jews today do not observe the traditional Jewish Sabbath, nor are they active in the temple or synagogue. Their identity as Jews is an ethnic or racial identity, even though historically derived from a particular religion.

JEWISH AMERICANS TODAY

Jewish family incomes are the highest of any large ethnic group in the United States—72 percent above the national average.[171] While Jews are both older and better educated than other Americans, these factors alone do not account for all the differences. Even where neither education nor age is a factor, Jews earn more. Among families headed by males with four or more years of college and aged thirty-five to forty-four, Jews still earn 75 percent higher incomes.[172] Part of the reason is that Jews have not only more education but also better education— from higher quality colleges and in more demanding and remunerative fields, such as law, medicine, and science.[173] Among families headed by males with less than nine years of school and aged thirty-five to forty-four, Jews still earn higher incomes than others with the same characteristics.[174] In short, there are other qualitative and cultural differences not captured in the statistics, which obviously have a major impact on the outcome. The work of women and children, which helped support Jewish immigrant families, today is no longer characteristic of Jewish families. A smaller proportion of Jewish families today have multiple earners than is true of American families in general.[175] Even Jewish families with no one working have higher incomes than other families with no one working. Earnings from investments of one sort or another are apparently greater among Jews, as are other advantages built up in the past.

In a sense, Jews are the classic American success story—from rags to riches against all opposition. Moreover, like other groups that have found in the United States opportunities denied them in their homelands, Jews have been proud and patriotic Americans. Yet the history of Jews is longer and larger than the history of the United States. At other times and other places, Jews have risen to heights of prosperity and influence, only to have it all destroyed in unpredictable outbursts of anti-Semitic fury. Jews could not readily become complacent members of the establishment, however much they might possess all of its visible signs. Jews have tended to remain on the political left, despite their affluence. Jews also remain over-represented among radicals— although most Jews are not radical. As a distinguished scholar has observed, "Out of one hundred Jews, five may be radicals. Out of ten radicals, five are likely to be Jewish."[176]

Jews have contributed heavily to the support of liberal candidates, whether or not the candidates were themselves Jewish. Even when George McGovern was spurned by the general electorate in the 1972 presidential election, receiving only 38 percent of the popular vote, he still received 65 percent of the Jewish vote.[177] Father Drinan, a liberal Roman Catholic, received 64 percent of the Jewish vote when he ran for Congress in 1970.[178] By contrast, only 2 percent of the Jewish voters supported the 1972 presidential candidacy of George Wallace, who received more support than that (3 percent) even among nonwhites.[179]

The rise of "affirmative action" programs in the 1970s has split some Jewish groups from their traditional liberal and radical allies, including black civil rights organizations. The numerical "goals and timetables" for employment, promotion, or college admissions under such programs are reminiscent of quota systems used to restrict the opportunities of Jews in the past in the United States, and still more so in Europe. Moreover, Jews have struggled upward over the generations to a position where they are now overrepresented on university faculties, in high-level government positions, and in various industries and labor unions. The doctrine of demographic "representation" is necessarily detrimental to their current interests, regardless of its intent.

Rare as the success of the Jews has been, it is not absolutely unique. Episcopalians, for example, have had higher incomes than Jews.[180] It is the social and economic distance covered in a relatively short period of history that makes the story of Jewish Americans so remarkable.

Chapter 5

THE ITALIANS

Most Italian Americans today are descendants of people who immigrated to the United States from the southern part of Italy. Regional differences in culture, values, and traditions are very pronounced in Italy, as are differences between the economy and geography of the more industrialized north and the more agrarian, poverty-stricken south.

The people who came to America lived largely in villages and small towns in southern Italy, and were generally either peasants or agricultural laborers. They began to immigrate to the United States in substantial numbers in the late nineteenth and early twentieth centuries. Annual immigration from Italy passed the 10,000 mark for the first time in 1880, was over 50,000 by 1890, and over 100,000 in 1900. In peak years in the early twentieth century, more than a quarter of a million people a year immigrated to the United States from Italy.[1] Immigration fell sharply during World War I, but went back over 200,000 per year in 1921, before the new American immigration laws stopped the massive inflow of people from around the world. Even today, however, a substantial number of immigrants—between 25,000 and

30,000 annually—continue to arrive from Italy,[2] more than from any other country in Europe. The number of people emigrating across the Atlantic from Italy to the Western Hemisphere was nearly equaled by the number immigrating to other countries in Europe.[3] Altogether, it was the largest exodus of people ever recorded from a single nation.

ITALY

Although the Italian peninsula has had a rich history that goes back before Christ, to the Roman Republic and the Roman Empire, Italy as a nation is relatively new, dating only from 1861, when the many provinces were united under one government for the first time in centuries. The people who left this relatively new country for the United States left as Neapolitans, Syracusans, or Calabrians; they became "Italians" only after reaching America. Italy was fragmented both linguistically and geographically. The many local dialects were often incomprehensible to people from other regions.[4] "Not only each region, but each town, feels itself a self-contained, unique culture, its people feeling no kinship with those even a few miles away."[5] Villages only a mile or two apart have linguistic and cultural differences.[6] Geographically, the country is split by mountains (the Apennines) running down its center, creating many isolated valleys, and Sicily and Sardinia are islands.

The Country

Arable land is both scarce and scattered in southern Italy, leading to many isolated settlements—contributing in turn to the linguistic and other cultural differences. Moreover, there are very few long navigable rivers to facilitate trade and communication. Such modern means of travel or communication as broadcasting, railroads, and airlines were of course not yet in existence, or were not yet significant in southern Italy, when the massive immigration to America was taking place. Even in the middle of the twentieth century, however, geographical isolation was still extreme in some southern Italian villages.[7]

As in the case of the Irish and others, conditions in their original homeland continued to affect Italian Americans after generations of living in America. The effect of the localism and regionalism of Italy can still be seen in the residential patterns, fragmented organizations, and even voting patterns of Italian Americans in the twentieth century.

The climate and terrain of southern Italy contributed to its poverty. While the temperatures are relatively mild, rainfall is both low and concentrated in only a few months. The growing season is dry— "drought may endure for six months or more."[8] When the rains finally come, they are torrential, causing erosion.[9] The dryness during the growing season in turn limits the use of fertilizers.[10] The impermeability of much of the hilly soil facilitates rapid water runoff when it does rain, and the deforestation of southern Italy's once heavily wooded areas adds to both erosion and the collection of water in stagnant pools, breeding malaria.[11] Italy has been the most malarial country in Europe, and southern Italy more so than the rest of the country.[12] In addition to the direct suffering and death caused by malaria, disease also exacted an economic toll. Because the most fertile lowlands were also the most malarial, peasants and agricultural workers lived up on hillsides in order to be away from the malaria-bearing mosquitoes at night, when they bite. This in turn meant that much of the day was spent going to and from home and work—often miles apart—instead of actually working.[13]

While much of southern Italy is hilly and mountainous, the highlands are at just the wrong height for agricultural purposes. They are too high and rugged to be good cropland and too low to collect snow, which would melt and give a slow, steady runoff of water during the spring. In addition to lacking these advantages common in some other European countries, Italy also does not have its sod broken up by nature through successive freezes and thaws during the winter. The southern Italian farmer must perform the vital function of breaking up the soil entirely by his own efforts and that of his animals pulling the plow.

Italy's natural deficiencies are both agricultural and industrial. About three quarters of the land area of Italy consists of mountains and hills. Only about half of the land is arable,[14] and most of that is in northern Italy.[15] In the south, the mountains "reach so close to the sea that arable land is limited to mountain villages, high plateaus, or coastal plains"—the latter being generally "very narrow."[16] Italy is also lacking in both the quantity and quality of coal and iron ore needed for producing iron and steel[17]—a mainstay of modern industry.

History has added to the problems created by nature. Southern Italy was long a battleground for contending empires and dynasties, which fought back and forth across the Italian peninsula for centuries, going back at least as far as the Roman Empire. For two centuries during the Middle Ages, invasions were "frequent and almost annual."[18] At various times, southern Italy was conquered by a variety of foreigners,[19] including the Lombards, the Arabs, and the Normans.[20] Massacres, pillage, rape, and enslavement were the common fate of the population.[21] In Italy, "the blood of nations was mingled in a thousand channels,"[22] just as the Italian language grew out of a mixture of the languages of the many foreigners who passed through the peninsula at various times in history.[23]

The great accomplishments of the Italian Renaissance were of northern Italian origins, and had little effect in the south. Columbus, Dante, Michelangelo, and Rossini were all northern Italians.[24] The history of the Roman Empire—"the glory that was Rome"—likewise meant nothing to the southern Italian peasants, whose ancestors had been slaves during much of that glory. Spartacus' rebellion of 90,000 slaves took place in southern Italy. So did numerous other uprisings and rebellions over the centuries—all brutally crushed, there being no sufficient unity among the oppressed peoples of the region to achieve a coordinated, regionwide movement.

Northern Italy has been better treated by both nature and man. The rain falls in the spring and summer, when it is needed for agriculture. It has "several rivers, whose waters are kept at a relatively steady level by melting Alpine snows," and those "provide considerable water and power for agriculture and industry."[25] In addition, northern Italy has "a system of irrigation that has been nowhere excelled and rarely approached"[26]—at least during the era of massive immigration to America. Northern Italian agriculture has been described as "luxuriant under cultivation," yielding "a notable variety of crops."[27] Deforestation and other natural and man-made evils of the south were less prevalent in the north.

In the middle of the twentieth century, southern Italy, with about 40 percent of the land and people of Italy, produced only about 20 percent of the country's output.[28] Per capita income in the north was about two-thirds to four-fifths higher than in the south.[29] Back in the nineteenth century, while illiteracy was high in both regions, it was higher in the south (where 84 percent of the people were illiterate) than in the north (where 59 percent were illiterate).[30]

Geographic and economic differences between the regions were paralleled by differences between the peoples of northern and southern Italy.

The People

The people of southern Italy have had not only a distinct and tragic history but also a level of poverty seldom equaled in the Western world[31] and a distinctive set of values and behavior patterns—many of which persisted among Italian-American immigrants and their descendants.

The subjugation and ravaging of southern Italy were not simply a matter of unjust or oppressive laws being imposed. Because of the lack of a strong central government, local nobles and overlords dominated the people directly, in their own arbitrary and capricious ways. For the people, it was not simply a matter of obeying general laws but of directly placating people with enormous power. The aftermath of this tradition could be observed in southern Italian villages, even in the middle of the twentieth century:

When a gentleman of Montegrano buys a melon or a basket of tomatoes in the public square, he hands it wordlessly to the nearest peasant boy, woman, or man, who carries it to his home as a matter of course. He hands his burden to any peasant with whom he is acquainted, and there is no thought on either side of payment for the specific service. The peasant wants to be polite and amiable (*civile*) and he knows that a time will come when the gentleman can give or withhold a favor or an injury.[32]

The southern Italian peasant was not simply poor and powerless, but despised. A novelist from this region had one of his characters say:

At the head of everything is God, Lord of Heaven.
After Him, comes Prince Torlonia, lord of the earth.
Then come Prince Torlonia's armed guards.
Then come Prince Torlonia's armed guards' dogs.
Then, nothing at all. Then nothing at all. Then nothing at all.
Then come the peasants.
And that's all.[33]

Even peasants themselves took it for granted that they were "a different breed" from other people.[34] In a highly stratified society like that of southern Italy, *initiative* was considered completely out of place for a peasant or a laborer, whether in working, self-improvement, or seeking a voice in public or political affairs. Initiative was unlikely to be rewarded and more likely to be resented by people further up in the hierarchy[35]—people whom peasants could not afford to antagonize. The peasant was expected to work hard and faithfully, but always following orders and never going beyond them. It was a characteristic of Italian immigrant workers later noted with dismay by American employers.[36]

As of the time of mass immigration to America, the bulk of the population consisted of agricultural workers—a few of whom owned small plots of land and most of whom either leased or worked on someone else's land.[37] Of those who immigrated to the United States around the turn of the century, 77 percent were agricultural laborers, and less than one-half of one percent were in the professions.[38]

While the historic traumas and desperate poverty of the southern Italians were comparable to those of the Irish, they were also quite different in certain key specifics, leading to very different responses and cultural adaptations to cope with them. Whereas the Irish were oppressed by an alien race with a different religion, and responded with an intense group consciousness, the Italian peasants had long been oppressed by people of the same race (or mixture of races) and the same religion. Instead of leading to group solidarity, their situation led to desperate, every-man-for-himself measures—relying only on other members of the immediate family. In both countries, the constituted authorities were seen as illegitimate, but the elaborate series of organizations that grew up in Ireland never developed in southern Italy, where the circle of those to be trusted seldom extended beyond the closest kin. The southern Italian ways of striking back—the vendetta and the Mafia—were both centered on the family.

Southern Italians have long had extremely strong ties to the family, as the only social institution on which they could depend. By the norms of most of the rest of the Western world, the southern Italian's attachment to his family was extreme—transcending competing claims of country, religion, and morality. Sentiment, loyalty, and morality virtually began and ended with the family. Italian nationalism for example, was significant only among northern Italians, who unified the country in the nineteenth century and who were Mussolini's main followers in the twentieth century. Religious institutions were viewed distantly and even cynically by southern Italians, in contrast to the devotion of the Irish, whose church suffered from oppression with them over the centuries. Even in the twentieth century, the southern Italian philosophy has been called "amoral familism"—maximizing the immediate well-being of the nuclear family[39] and preserving its honor, both at all costs.

One of the perceived threats to this family, and to the southern Italian way of life, was education—as introduced and controlled by northern Italians after the unification of Italy. The first compulsory school attendance law was passed in 1877. It met with resistance, noncompliance, and even rioting and the burning of schoolhouses.[40] Education was not seen as an opportunity for upward mobility by the peasants—as in fact it was not in such a castelike society. Rather, it was seen as an intrusion into the sanctity of the family, singling out the child as an individual and teaching values at variance with those of the home. To desperately poor people, the loss of a child's work or outside earnings was also a painful sacrifice.

Attempts at spreading education in southern Italy met with only slow and partial success. As late as 1900, the illiteracy rate for southern Italy was 70 percent, more than ten times that of England, France, or Germany at the same time.[41] Whereas the Irish lacked an educational tradition and tended to be apathetic about it, the southern Italians were actively hostile to education and openly disparaged it in the home. These attitudes would persist among Italian-American immigrants and to some extent their descendants.

The defense of the family honor included protecting the chastity of the young women. Girls were kept at home as much as possible, chaperoned when out, and male relatives were protective and—if need be—vengeful. Public flirtation, common in Rome, was considered offensive by southern Italians. Around the turn of the century, the rates of illegitimacy in southern Italy were less than half of what they were in many northern provinces. The illegitimacy rate in the region around Naples was about one-fifth what it was in the region around Rome.[42]

Attitudes toward life in general reflected the realities of southern Italy. Southern Italian peasants and farm laborers tended to be fatalistic and believers in luck, like agricultural peoples elsewhere, whose fate is at the mercy of the weather. Psychological studies in the mid-twentieth century showed attitudes in a southern Italian village to be drastically different from those in northern Italy, and both to be different from attitudes in the United States. A sense of impending calamity was much more common among the southern Italian villagers, as was the feeling that any possible benefits derived from either luck or the favor of the powerful, not from personal initiative or long-range planning.[43] The speech patterns of southern Italian peasants showed virtually no use of the future tense.[44] Spiritual or religious attitudes reflect similar influences. Religion or spirituality as con-

ceived of by the southern Italian was not in terms of following prescribed rules for ultimate salvation, but in terms of immediately
placating capricious powers—saints, Satan, and such non-Christian
powers as "the evil eye" or the magic of numbers.[45] Spiritual powers
that failed—as during the devastation caused by an eruption of Vesu-
vius—were likely to be cast aside, in this same personalized, short-run
perspective.[46]

That so much was beyond one's control did not mean an irresponsi-
ble attitude toward what was within one's control. On the contrary,
there was a pattern of hard work, frugality, zealous guarding of the
family's well-being and honor, and numerous religious and magical
practices designed to ward off evil and seek favors. The cultural values
of southern Italians emphasized the heavy responsibilities of men and
women, in a family setting. To be manly was not to be "macho" in the
individualistic style of courting needless dangers.[47] Casual brawling,
for example, was to be avoided, but a serious fight was to be pursued
implacably. In complete contrast to the Irish style of quick-to-anger
and quick-to-forgive, the southern Italian pattern was one of very polite but firm warnings to head off trouble—and implacable vengeance
if the other party persisted in the offensive acts.[48]

Alcohol consumption was viewed in the same serious way. While
wine consumption was widespread, losing control to the point of getting drunk was very uncommon and remained so among Italian-American immigrants and their descendants. This pattern may have been
facilitated by the fact that the climate and soil of Italy were suited to
producing wine, a relatively slow-acting drink, while the climate and
soil of Ireland were suited to producing the ingredients of hard liquor.

The attitudes and values of northern Italians have been much more
like the attitudes and values of other Europeans or of Americans. To
them, the attitudes of southern Italians have seemed variously quaint,
backward, savage, or incomprehensible. The condescension—or even
bigotry—of northern Italians toward their compatriots in the south
goes far back in Italian history and persisted when they both reached
America. Like the hierarchical social caste system, the regional peck-
ing order was finely graduated, with Tuscans at the top and Sicilians
at the bottom: "Neapolitans who scorned the condescending attitudes
and actions directed against them by their northern brethren were
just as quick in denigrating their countrymen further south," and even
after reaching America, "the Sicilians were ostracized by other
Italians."[49]

THE ITALIANS IN AMERICA

There is a history of Italian immigration into the more prosperous adjoining countries of Europe—France, Germany, and Switzerland—and into South America (notably Brazil and Argentina) even before the massive movement of southern Italians to the United States.[50] In the nineteenth century, more Italians immigrated to South America than to North America, although this pattern was reversed in the twentieth century.[51] The origins and character of the immigration varied substantially over time, as well as in numbers and destinations.

From 1820 to 1850, a grand total of less than 5,000 Italians moved to the United States. About 9,000 arrived in the decade of the 1850s and another 12,000 in the decade of the 1860s. These were mostly *northern* Italians, and their numbers were too small to attract much public attention, even in an era of nativism.[52] Only about one-seventh of them were laborers, and many were craftsmen or small tradesmen.[53] They were also somewhat scattered around the country[54]—they were prominent among fruitsellers in New York and winegrowers in California[55]—unlike the later southern Italians who were to be concentrated en masse in a few port cities. These earlier Italian immigrants had gained a measure of acceptance and prosperity by the time massive waves of southern Italians arrived.

Internal Differences

The relationship between the earlier arriving members of a group and those arriving later is an important factor in the history of most American ethnic groups. Generally, the earlier arriving members have acquired advantages in the form of understanding the laws, organizations, norms, and culture of the larger society and have some acceptance in and access to that society, in addition to their material advantages. The extent to which these advantages are used to ease the transition for the later arrivals varies greatly from one group to another, and at different periods in history. The spectrum ranges from proudly embracing the later arrivals as brothers to trying discreetly to get them to conform to American norms, to openly repudiating them in order to avoid the larger society's condemnation of the whole group for the behavior of the less acculturated. The northern Italians openly repudiated the southern Italians—perhaps more forcefully than any other American ethnic group has repudiated others of the same nationality. Many northern Italians "preferred to pass for Americans"[56]

The Italians

rather than face the nativist reaction to the southern Italian immigrants.[57] They were so insistent that they were two different races of people that the U.S. government was persuaded to keep separate statistics on the two groups.[58] These data show great disparities between them.

Around the turn of the century, only about 12 percent of the northern Italians in the United States were illiterate, compared to 54 percent of the southern Italian immigrants.[59] Forty percent of the northern Italian workers were unionized, as were only 11 percent of the southern Italians.[60] Although northern Italians were only about 15 percent of the 5 million people to immigrate to the United States from Italy before mass immigration ended,[61] most Italian Americans who achieved professional status were either northern Italians or nonpeasant southern Italians, on into the 1930s and 1940s.[62] Even among Italian-American workers in factories and mines, the few northern Italians earned more than the southern Italians and had higher literacy rates.[63]

Return Migration

The southern Italian immigrants brought an entirely different pattern with them. The southern Italian immigration was the first great migration of a people who went back to their native land from the United States in large numbers. Although this was at the time unique in American history, it was not unique in Italian history. There were more temporary than permanent emigrants from Italy to the rest of the world in the last quarter of the nineteenth century and into the early twentieth century.[64] About 90 percent of the Italians who immigrated to other parts of Europe in this era returned home.[65] Returning home from the United States was a more formidable task, but the steamship made it more feasible for the Italians, whereas even one ocean crossing had been hazardous for the Irish in the era of wind-driven ships. The proportion of Italians returning from the United States fluctuated between 11 percent and 73 percent.[66] Most of those who returned did so within five years of arriving in the United States.[67]

While it is not possible to directly know how many of those returning to Italy had intended from the outset to stay only temporarily, and how many returned because of disappointment, there are many indications. The proportion of males in a migration—internal or external—is one clue to whether it is intended to be permanent or is transient or exploratory. Groups making a permanent move tend to have an equal balance of the sexes, and substantial numbers of children with them, as in the case of the Irish and the Jews. But in the early years of the Italian immigration to many countries, nearly 90 percent of the immigrants were male, and afterward about 80 percent. The proportion of children coming to the United States from Italy was lower than from any other country.[68] About two-thirds of those returning to Italy from the United States were unaccompanied by members of their family. The evidence is substantial that the movement was intended from the outset to be either transient or exploratory, and returning was neither a sign of failure nor disappointment. Many who returned did so with enough money earned in America to buy land or otherwise become substantial citizens back in Italy.

The large return migration had important effects on the Italian Americans who remained, as well as on Italy. Those from America took back to Italy not only material wealth but also different views of the world—including more appreciation of education.[69] In the United States, the expectation of returning to Italy reduced incentives toward Americanization—a permanent handicap to many who came for a sojourn but eventually ended up extending their stay and finally settling permanently. Italian immigrants who became eligible for citizenship actually became citizens far less than members of other immigrant groups,[70] and also fewer learned the English language.[71] This is a pattern also found in other groups with large back-and-forth migration patterns—French Canadians living in the American Northeast and Mexican Americans living in the Southwest, for example.

One of the peculiarities of Italian-American speech was the creation of hybrid words—part English and part Italian. Sometimes this was done simply because no word had existed in the Italian peasant's vocabulary for such things as cars, factories, or refrigerators, which the Italian Americans called *"carru," "fattoria,"* and *"frigidaira."*[72]

Residential Patterns

The residential patterns of Italian-American immigrants reflected their regionalism in Italy. People from the same village or province in Italy tended to cluster near each other and to limit their social or community life to fellow villagers or fellow provincials.[73] A given American city would have hundreds of mutual aid organizations among Italians—each for people from a particular locality in Italy—and these did not consolidate into organizations for "Italians" in general. This was not a pattern peculiar to America. In the large Italian immigrant population of Argentina at the same time, people from one region of

The Italians

Italy were not admissible to mutual aid societies for people from other parts of Italy.[74] In the United States, Italian-American mutual aid societies were often named for the Italian village where its members originated or for the patron saint of that village.[75] American employers learned from experience that mixing people from different Italian villages in the same work crew was an invitation to violence.[76]

While particular streets might have a concentration of former Neapolitans or former Sicilians, Italians seldom made up a majority in any large-sized neighborhood in American cities.[77] Other immigrant groups—the Irish, Germans, Jews—typically shared the same neighborhood. The Italian immigrants were segregated from the larger American society in the same sense that their contemporary immigrants were—that immigrant neighborhoods seldom contained any native American families. Italians were, however, far from being randomly distributed. Italians in 1880 and 1910 were more "segregated" (in the statistical sense of deviation from a theoretically random distribution) than other immigrants and more segregated than blacks in the same years.[78]

The closeness of family and even Italian village ties limited the meaningful social contacts of Italian immigrants. Conversely, the absence of strong groupwide identity muted intergroup friction. Italian Americans peacefully coexisted with highly diverse groups (in contrast to the history of the Irish, for example). Jews and Italians arriving in New York at about the same time in the late nineteenth century have historically avoided any serious violence or even strong political strife.[79] In Boston as well, "Jews and Italians get along with each other better than either does with the Irish."[80] The same was true of Italian American relations with other European ethnic groups in various cities around the country. Even racial differences did not disturb this pattern of peaceful coexistence. Italians have long shared the Chinatown section of New York with Chinese Americans, with little friction and no significant violence. In the American South, Italian immigrants were so unconcerned about maintaining traditional southern racial distinctions that they themselves became targets of native southern whites for undermining "white supremacy."[81] Italian Americans in New York continue to coexist with the avant-garde and deviant culture of Greenwich Village, in which they themselves take little or no part.

The coexistence of Italians with others did not mean assimilation with them. For example, Italian immigrants almost invariably married within their own group, and this remained the dominant pattern even within the second generation.[82] At first, Italian immigrants usually married people from the same province—or even village—in Italy.[83] Almost always marriage for the Italian immigrants was with another person of Italian extraction, and almost never a north-south Italian marriage. Moreover, when intermarriage occurred, it was not so much a step toward amalgamation of groups as an isolated event in the lives of upwardly mobile individuals who had already drifted away from the ethnic community.[84] The Italian-American community was left largely unaffected by such subsequent intermarriages.

Work

Half of the Italians who came to the United States at the beginning of mass immigration in the late nineteenth century were laborers—as compared to one-seventh of the Germans and one-third of the Irish at that period of history.[85] Few followed the agricultural occupations from which they came in Italy—there being little agriculture in the American port cities in which they settled. To a large extent, the early Italian immigrants followed the occupational paths of the Irish immigrants before them.[86] They were factory hands, miners, or pick-and-shovel workers on construction projects, including the building of railroads and subways. In New York, many Italians were ragpickers, whose jobs involved going through the city's garbage to find salvageable items, and others were bootblacks—more than 90 percent of all bootblacks in New York State.[87] Less than one half of one percent of the southern Italian immigrants were in professional occupations.[88] Small businessmen were somewhat more common among Italians than among the Irish but were not prominent among either group.

The effects of their southern Italian background showed in their American work patterns in various ways. Few of the immigrants from deforested southern Italy went into lumbering occupations in the United States, but many went into work involving the use of stone, which was a more common building material in Italy because of its lack of wood.[89] Italian immigrants were also prominent in fishing, as they had been in Italy.[90]

While thousands of southern Italian immigrants worked as sailors, masons, tailors, shoemakers, and barbers at the turn of the century—and more than 100,000 as laborers—doctors, lawyers, and schoolteachers among them put together added up to less than one hundred.[91]

While Italian immigrant women often worked in America, unlike in southern Italy, they almost never worked as domestic servants, contrary to the pattern among the Irish or blacks, who were otherwise in comparable unskilled work. Being live-in maids, as the Irish had often been in the nineteenth century,[92] would have been incompatible with southern Italian traditions of sheltering young women from even the possibility or appearance of sexual laxity and incompatible with southern Italian views of the total commitment of a mother to her own family. The home sweatshop was one way of reconciling conflicting needs for work and keeping the family together. It also facilitated the early introduction of children to work[93]—another feature of life in southern Italy transplanted to America. More than any other immigrant group, the Italians were noted for pulling their children out of school to go to work,[94] whether in the home or elsewhere.

The low rates of alcoholism they brought with them caused American employers to compare the Italians favorably with the Irish as regards sobriety, regularity in reporting to work, and dependability on the job. However, American employers also cited an absence of initiative among Italian immigrant workers and a consequent need for costly supervision of them. The lack of initiative among Italian immigrants also reflected their southern Italian backgrounds, where initiative would have been resented rather than rewarded. All in all, American employers did not regard Italian immigrant labor as particularly desirable, primarily because of the greater amount of supervision they required.[95] Their daily output was found to be less than that of other groups[96]—including contemporary Irish and black workers—and they were accordingly paid less. Everything is relative, however. In Argentina, Italian immigrant workers were considered much more productive than native Argentineans.[97] This might reflect the large proportion of northern Italians among the emigrants from Italy to America or simply the difference between U.S. and Argentinean work standards.

In America in 1910, Italian males earned less annually than either native white or black males.[98]

One of the curious observations of the early immigrant era was the lack of size or strength among Italian workers.[99] The prevalence of such observations then, but not later, raises a question as to whether the physiques of Italian Americans actually altered with time. Better nutrition might be one explanation, but Italian workers were no poorer than the Irish workers whom they replaced in railroad building, construction work, or other unskilled occupations, and the Irish had never been considered scrawny or weak. Another explanation seems more likely. Among other peoples living for generations in isolated little communities, stunted development has also been common—as have later increases in size, once they began marrying outside of the little communities where many inhabitants would necessarily be related, even if only too distantly for them to be aware of it. It is a genetic phenomenon. While the immigrant generation of Italians tended to marry disproportionately descendants from the same village or province in Italy, with time they began to marry more widely within the Italian community.[100] There would, therefore, be a genetic basis for increasing size among later generations of Italian Americans, even without intermarriage with other groups. The Irish Americans had never been so internally fragmented and so geographically confined in their choice of marriage partners.

Another peculiarity of the Italian immigrant generation was the *padrone*. The *padroni* were recruiters, organizers, and supervisors of Italian work crews. The *padrone's* lines of communication often reached into several American cities and even back to Italy.[101] The *padrone* supplied the railroads, construction firms, or other users of unskilled labor with large numbers of Italian immigrants and acted as interpreter and supervisor, making their labor more valuable to the American employer than if the latter had to perform these functions himself, with people whose ways were unfamiliar. For the worker, the *padrone* provided contacts with employers; transportation through an unfamiliar country; food of a kind the worker was used to; and miscellaneous credit, banking, and other services that immigrants would have had difficulty in finding or understanding in a new country. The employer paid the *padrone*, and the *padrone* paid the workers—after deducting his fees, expenses, advances, rent, and credit charge.

The *padrone* system was in widespread use from the beginning of the massive immigration of southern Italians in the 1880s to about World War I.[102] It was not confined solely to Italian Americans but was in use to some extent among other southern and eastern Europeans as well.[103] At the end of the nineteenth century, *padroni* controlled two-thirds of the entire labor in New York City.[104] In Chicago, at about the same time, a little more than one-fifth of all Italians were working for a *padrone*.[105] In the farming areas around Philadelphia, *padroni* supplied Italian seasonal workers recruited in the city.[106] Under the *padrone* system, Italian immigrants with no initial capital could spread across the country, living and working with compatriots in a familiar culture and typically returning with what were considered sizable savings at the time.[107] Many settled in places they first saw as contract laborers, establishing Italian-American communities that still exist in such places as Omaha, Syracuse, Newark, and Detroit.[108]

Some Italian immigrant parents apprenticed their children to *padroni*, who sent them out to work in agricultural fields or into such urban occupations as peddlers, newsboys, or street musicians.[109]

The *padrone* often grew very prosperous from the various operations conducted with little or no scrutiny from employers or legal authorities and with workers unfamiliar with prevailing American rents, transportation, or interest charges that were being deducted from their pay. The *padrone* was typically a tough and demanding leader, often armed and perhaps backed up by other armed men, protecting his investment in the workers to whom he had advanced expenses. Some used corporal punishment with workers—adults or children—who were not performing up to expectations. Being of southern Italian backgrounds themselves (often from the same provinces as their workers), the *padroni* knew that the workers would be very unlikely to go to the authorities to report any frauds or abuses or even to organize against it. Nevertheless, the system came to the attention of social reformers, who became aroused and conducted a determined campaign to eradicate it,[110] joined by the Italian government and American authorities. These efforts largely failed. Although laws were passed against labor contractors, Italian immigrants would seldom admit that they had paid a fee for their jobs.[111] Their balance of the net advantages and disadvantages of the *padrone* system was apparently quite different from that of the reformers. Although reform efforts failed to stop the *padrone* system, the passage of time eroded it away. As Italian Americans became more familiar with the language and culture of the country, better able to find their own jobs, better adjusted to working in an American setting, the need for the *padrone*'s services declined. The system died out rapidly after the turn of the century, but vestiges remained even in the 1930s—significantly, among older workers.[112]

Social Institutions

In America as in southern Italy, the family was the central, overriding institution for Italians—indeed, virtually the only institution that could demand allegiance.

Religion was not a strong competitor for their loyalty. While most Italian immigrants were Catholics, the church had no strong hold over them in Italy, where anticlericalism was prevalent, and the Irish-dominated American Catholic Church was even more remote from them. In southern Italy, church services typically had low attendance, except at Christmas, Easter, and other holidays.[113] In America, Italian-American Catholics contributed only about 5 to 10 percent as much per capita to the church as American Catholics of Polish, Irish, or German ancestry.[114] The Irish conception of Catholicism often clashed with that of the southern Italians—the latter being less rigid, more festive, and centering more on patron saints and the Virgin Mary, rather than on ideological orthodoxy, communion, or the rosary.[115]

Religion, like other aspects of southern Italian culture, was highly personalized. Very few Italian men became priests, and in the Irish-dominated American Catholic Church, very few of these priests were promoted in the hierarchy.[116] In the immigrant generation, very few Italian children were sent to parochial schools, which were dominated by Irish nuns even in Italian neighborhoods, just as the church in general was run by the Irish.[117] In Chicago, for example, less than 5 percent of the Italian children of schoolage were in parochial school,[118] and in New York, more than seven times as many Italian children were enrolled in the public schools as in the parochial schools, in contrast to the Irish, whose children were about equally divided between the two school systems.[119] Italian-language newspapers openly encouraged this nonenrollment in parochial schools on the grounds that religion should be taught in the home.[120]

Some of the Irish clergy even expressed antipathy to Italians as a group. One declared: "Italians are not a sensitive people like our own."[121] Others called the Italians "dagoes" from the pulpit and made them sit in the back of the church with the Negroes.[122] Italian immigrants remained remote also from many public and private charity organizations. This too reflected southern Italian values. A sense of self-reliance made Italians reluctant to turn to others for aid, whether to the police or other legal authorities to avenge wrongs or to charity to sustain oneself. In both cases, the southern Italians preferred to take care of matters themselves. Italian immigrant men, when alone, continued to work "at any work they could find," even when starving. Only after the family was with them would they turn to charity in desperation, to prevent the women and children from suffering. When Italian immigrant families were forced to accept charity, it was only when they had "exhausted or starved bodies, stricken with illness."[123] This extreme resistance to accepting charity eroded somewhat with time, especially during the massive relief programs of the Great Depression of the 1930s,[124] but it remains even today a distinct feature of Italian Americans.[125]

116

The Italians

To shield themselves from the misfortunes to which they were subject in a new economy and society, Italian immigrants organized mutual aid societies. Mutual aid societies were numerous and fragmented, according to the Italian village or provincial origins of the Italian Americans.[126] This was a pattern also found among Italian immigrants in Argentina, where in the late nineteenth century there were twenty different mutual aid organizations in Buenos Aires alone.[127] In Chicago, there were 400 mutual aid societies among Italians in 1910.[128] In New York at the same time, there were 2,000 mutual aid societies among Italians.[129] They never combined into a general mutual aid society for all Italian Americans. Even so, such societies were a form of cooperation going beyond what had existed in southern Italy,[130] where such commitments outside the family were virtually unheard of. A noted student of Italian societies pointed out: "It would be hard to find in southern Italy a synonym for the English word 'community.'"[131] Even the southern Italian crime syndicates, and later on their American counterparts, were centered on the family.

The Italian-American mutual aid societies, like the *padrone* system, was a step toward organization in the modern sense—a social structure formed by strangers brought together for a purpose defined by the structure itself. General Motors, the Red Cross, political movements, labor unions, or sports leagues are all organizations in this sense. Southern Italians have usually not created organizations in this sense. Their own groupings have been based on people previously known to each other—generally related to each other by blood or godparenthood, or (in America) sharing the same cultural origins from an Italian province. But creating a large-scale activity based on the cooperation of strangers has been difficult among southern Italians, whether in Italy or in the United States. In southern Italy, formal organizations are generally established from the outside—usually by the Italian government or the Roman Catholic Church. Groupwide organizations for Italian Americans generally emerged much later than among other groups, and have generally not been nearly as effective as B'nai B'rith for Jews or the NAACP for blacks.

The Italian immigrants were active in labor unions established by others, and played a role in the formation of the American Clothing Workers,[132] but by and large, they created few organizations. Even joint endeavors for a common purpose have been conceived in personalized terms, and with little trust in people not already familiar from the family or locality. This pattern has been found among Italians both in southern Italy and in modern America.[133]

Crime and Violence

Italian immigrants had lower crime rates than immigrants as a group,[134] and the crimes they committed were typically gambling, fighting, and the like, rather than professional criminal activities, such as burglary, fraud, or armed robbery. The nineteenth-century Italian immigrant was described as being "as honest as he is hot-headed"[135]— generally inoffensive if not provoked, and less inclined to "make trouble" than others.[136] The casual Irish approach to brawling was foreign to southern Italians, to whom fighting was a very serious matter. The Italian immigrant was often armed with a knife or a gun, and an attack on him was a deadly risk. The arrival of large numbers of such people in immigrant neighborhoods in the nineteenth century has been credited with reducing the amount of fighting there.[137] Picking fights with strangers or attempting petty robberies against passersby were common occurrences when the Irish were the dominant group in the immigrant slums,[138] but such activities became far more dangerous when the stranger minding his own business could turn out to be a knife-carrying Italian.

Professional criminal activities had become a well-developed art in southern Italy, and especially Sicily, home of the Mafia. Most Italian immigrants took no part in these activities, although they suffered the stigma of it, in addition to being themselves the principal victims.[139] Organized crime in the United States had not yet reached the dimensions it achieved later, in the Prohibition era and after. Moreover, during the Italian immigrant period, the leaders of American organized crime were predominantly Irish and Jewish.[140] The pattern of ethnic succession found in other occupations and neighborhoods was later to occur in organized crime as well.[141]

With Italians as with other immigrant groups, it was typically not the first generation that had high rates of crime or delinquency, but the second generation. Among Italian Americans in New York City, the crime rate almost doubled between generations.[142]

One particular crime was especially notable by its absence among Italian immigrants. An 1890 survey found "hardly any Italian prostitutes" in either New York or Philadelphia.[143] Like so much else in Italian-American life, this too reflected the social patterns and values of southern Italy.

The Italians

LATER GENERATIONS

With the passage of time, many of the values and patterns of Italians were modified in an American setting, but others persisted. As with other immigrant groups, American values and ways were introduced in the schools, the children becoming both bilingual and bicultural as a result of growing up in two different worlds. This facilitated upward movement in American society, but it also fostered intergenerational conflict in the family and often conflict within the individual himself.

The family remained by far the dominant influence and the dominant loyalty. Divorce, separation, or desertion remained rare among Italians,[144] in contrast to the Irish immigrants before them or urban blacks in the twentieth century. Simple living without ostentation also remained the pattern among Italian Americans.[145] Moreover, the Italian family remained largely patriarchal, although the mothers made most of the day-to-day decisions, including budgeting the bulk of the fathers' earnings.[146]

In recounting the rise of Italian Americans, it is easy to forget the cost of that rise—as Joseph Lopreato eloquently expressed it, their encounters with "the indignant Irish, the superior and alarmed 'Americans,' the avaricious and scheming *padroni,* the uncertain employment, the inevitable job accidents, the long hours spent bending over pick and shovel listening to the snarling voice of the boss, the ethnic jokes and curses, the putrid air of the ghetto cells, the sick children, the children returning home from schools wishing to know why it was bad to be a 'Guinea'...."[147]

Education

Formal education was slow to gain acceptance among Italian Americans, and continued to be seen as a competitive threat to the values of the family, as well as costly in terms of lost opportunities for the children to work and contribute to the pressing economic requirements of the family. Practical understanding was highly valued by Italians, in the United States and in Italy, but formal schooling was not seen as practical.[148] In southern Italy it clearly was not, for the class of people who immigrated to the United States, nor was it obviously so in the kinds of jobs held by the first generation of Italian Americans. The opportunities available in the United States were simply beyond their experience or conception at that point. Mario Puzo, author of *The Godfather,* was a second-generation son from such a background:

My mother wanted me to be a railroad clerk. And that was her highest ambition; she would have settled for less. . . . She was illiterate and her peasant life in Italy made her believe that only the son of the nobility could possibly be a writer.[149]

The lack of family support for formal schooling was shown in many ways, including high rates of truancy, work after school, and withdrawal from school at the earliest legal age[150]—if not sooner. This pattern reflected not only the parents' desires but also the uneasiness of the children, whose speech, dress, and other cultural traits made them targets of ridicule in American schools,[151] and where teachers viewed their entrance "with regret and alarm," as a contemporary put it.[152] However, the lure of earnings can be seen in the fact that American-born Italian children in Chicago left school even more so than the foreign-born, who were not as employable.[153]

Under the scheme of values among early Italian Americans, "it was the 'bad' son who wanted to go to school instead of to work, the 'bad' daughter who wanted to remain in school instead of helping her mother."[154] Education meant estrangement from the family. Those individuals who nevertheless pursued their education did so with ambivalence and guilt, handicaps in competing with others whose educational advancement was being supported and abetted by family and friends. Against this background, it is understandable why Italian youngsters were often behind their normal grade in school, more so than most other large immigrant groups. A study published in 1911 showed 63 percent of the children of southern Italian immigrants to be behind the "normal" grade for their age. Partly this was due to more than half of them entering school at age seven or older, but even among those who entered at age six, nearly half were behind the normal grade level at the time of the survey.[155]

School attrition was common among immigrant children in general but was especially pronounced among the Italian children. In New York City in 1908, there were only about one-third as many children in the eighth grade as in the third grade. Among Italian children, there were only one-tenth as many.[156] Partly this reflected attrition, partly educational deficiencies. Students were not promoted until they met the standards of a given grade, and "overage" students or "laggards" were common—again, more so among Italian children than among those of other immigrant backgrounds.[157] While 16 percent of the Russian Jews and 15 percent of the Germans completed high school in that era, less than 1 percent of the Irish did so and no Italian

120

youngsters at all in New York City.[158] By 1931, about 42 percent of all high school students in New York graduated, but only 11 percent of the Italian-American high school students did so.[159]

The notorious failures of Italian children in the public schools led many "experts" of the time to contend that they were genetically mentally inferior. Italian adults and children of that period both scored very low on mental tests[160]—no higher than among blacks today—but Italian IQ scores rose over the decades as their social and economic assimilation progressed.[161] Italian-American IQs have fluctuated around the national average since the 1950s.[162]

Along with socioeconomic progress has come internal class differentiation. Among the less upwardly mobile Italian Americans, education continued suspect even in the mid-1950s, with student disinterest and parent-approved truancy a major problem.[163] College attendance remains less common among Italian Americans today than among Americans in general,[164] although the differences are no longer so great as in the past. But even among those Italian Americans going on to college, the older traditions leave their mark in various ways—for example, poorer reading habits[165] or emotional ambivalence about somehow "betraying" the family by moving outside its orbit.[166] The traditional utilitarian approach to education is seen in Italian Americans' choices of specialization—typically "practical" or applied fields, such as engineering for men and teaching for women.[167]

Work

While first-generation Italian immigrants were overwhelmingly unskilled laborers, the next generation moved up the occupational ladder, diversifying its jobs and fields of work. There was also upward movement within the lives of the first-generation immigrants themselves.

Among first-generation Italian immigrants in New York in 1905, the proportions doing white-collar work varied with their length of residence in the United States. However, about 40 percent were unskilled, regardless of years in the United States. The proportion in high-level white-collar jobs was negligible (less than 2 percent) up to twenty-five years of residence. About 14 percent of those with more than twenty-five years in the United States were in high-level white-collar positions, but this would reflect not only the effect of time but also the fact that most Italians from a quarter of a century earlier were northern Italians. For those with up to twenty-five years of residence, the proportions in white-collar work in general ranged from about 9 percent

121

for those who had been in the United States less than seven years to about 24 percent for those with fifteen to twenty-five years in the country.[168] Among Italian immigrants in Boston, almost two-thirds were low-level manual workers in 1910, but this was down to 38 percent for the same individuals later in their careers. While only 12 percent were white-collar workers in 1910, 37 percent reached that level before the end of their careers.[169]

Occupational changes from generation to generation also reflected the rise of Italian Americans. In New York, half of all Italian workers were laborers in 1916, but this was down to 31 percent by 1931.[170] Italians were diversifying into such occupations as electricians, painters, plumbers, contractors, and foremen. By the 1920s, Italians were replacing Jewish workers in the needle trades, as the latter moved farther up the ladder.[171]

Italians also moved into jobs as municipal employees, initially on a small scale and at the bottom of the occupational ladder. In Chicago in the 1890s, there were over a hundred Italian streetsweepers, as well as others who worked as sewer diggers, as garbage collectors, and on various construction and maintenance jobs. Three Italians became policemen before the turn of the century, a handful became firemen a little later, and these numbers rose modestly but steadily into the dozens over the next two decades.[172] There were less than a dozen Italian schoolteachers in Chicago at the turn of the century, but this too increased slowly but steadily to forty-two by the early 1920s.[173] In New York, with a much larger Italian population, there were just over 200 Italian teachers in 1905 and just over 400 in 1915.[174] By contrast, there were about 8,000 Italian municipal employees laboring on public works in New York, even in the late nineteenth century.[175] In San Francisco as well, Italian municipal employees were concentrated in such jobs as streetsweepers (where they were said to "enjoy a virtual monopoly"), diggers of sewers and water and gas pipes, as well as construction and maintenance workers on bridges, canals, and the harbor.[176] Similar patterns existed in other cities around the country.[177]

Like other groups concentrated in urban slums, Italian Americans were subjected to repeated urgings by social reformers to move out into the country. And like the Jews, the Irish, and others, Italians largely ignored these campaigns. Most had no money to buy a farm, many were planning to return to Italy, and few wanted utter isolation in scattered farms, especially when even a distant "neighbor" probably could not understand their language—much less their way of life. However, some Italian Americans did go out into the countryside, in groups, mostly as seasonal agricultural laborers and some as agricultural entrepreneurs.

In California, many northern Italians became entrepreneurs in the production of fruits, vegetables, and wine. At the turn of the century, half of all Italians in the state were in agriculture—a sharp contrast with the highly urbanized occupations of Italians in the country as a whole.[178] By helping finance these investments, A. P. Giannini built up what was to become the largest bank in the world—the Bank of America. Another agricultural colony of northern Italians was established in Wisconsin as early as 1860. They too were highly successful and were accepted into the social life of the local community.[179] There were also small Italian agricultural communities in other states, notably Texas, Arkansas, Louisiana, and upstate New York.[180] Many of these settlers were of southern Italian origin, and became successful less quickly and encountered more resistance from local natives. However, their experiences farming poor quality soil in Italy enabled them to cheaply purchase poor quality land regarded as "useless" by native Americans and make it productive.[181] Many initially very poor southern Italians were thus able to become landowners and to add to the output of the country, as well as advancing themselves economically. Eventually, they too became an accepted part of business communities in these areas.[182]

A key ingredient in their success, in these as in other fields, was their willingness to work longer and harder than others. Many of the early Italian agriculturalists began as farm laborers or sharecroppers. Given their lack of money, even the low prices for wasteland, muck, cut over timberland, etc., often required long hours of work, extra jobs, the whole family working, and much saving and borrowing for years before it finally paid off. In some areas, such as Oswego County in upstate New York, Italians eventually became predominant among fruit- and vegetable-growing entrepreneurs.[183]

Occupationally, the Italians caught up to the Irish and in business ownership overtook them. In 1909, 22 percent of the Italians in Boston were in business, compared to only 5 percent of the Irish.[184] By 1950, the two groups had virtually identical occupational distributions.[185] By the late 1960s and early 1970s, Italian-American incomes were a shade ahead of those of the Irish,[186] who had come to the United States more than a generation before them.

The channels through which the Italians advanced over the years were generally not those requiring formal education. Italian-American workers became more skilled over time, and their earnings rose to levels above what might be expected on the basis of their formal schooling alone. Sheer willingness to work remained a potent force in their economic rise,[187] and unusually low rates of alcoholism made them dependable and desirable employees. Paradoxically, there were (and are) very few Italians who do not drink at all, and wine is commonly served with their meals (sometimes even to children), but excessive drinking remains taboo.

A willingness to work hard should not be confused with a strong "career" orientation in the larger American sense. A career involves a long-term progression through predetermined stages, often beginning in college, and a level of emotional commitment that often competes with family commitments. This kind of orientation has been slow to take hold among Italian Americans. Working long and hard for the sake of the family has been part of the Italian-American pattern, but working at the expense of the family has not.[188] Civil service jobs, with regular hours and rewards for steady, conscientious work, have remained popular with successive generations of Italian Americans.[189] More absorbing or all-consuming jobs—executives, scholars—have not been.[190]

Social Institutions

With the rise of the Italian Americans has come not only economic differentiation but also social differences. Even the family no longer has the same meaning across social classes. Middle-class people of Italian ancestry visit their relatives only slightly more than other middle-class Americans. But working-class Italians visit their relatives twice as often as other working-class Americans.[191] Middle-class Italians began to emphasize education and in post-World War II America even began to send increasing numbers of their children to parochial schools. With more Italian priests and nuns, parents no longer had to fear, like earlier generations of Italian parents, that their children who went to parochial school would "become Irish."[192]

The size of the family also changed over the years—both relatively and absolutely. Whereas in 1910 the average Italian-American family was larger than the national average, by the late 1960s Italian Americans had fewer children than other Americans and less than half as many as their forebears in the earlier period. In 1910, American women in their mid-thirties to mid-forties had an average of 3.4 children. Italian-American women of the same age averaged 5.5 children. By 1960, the national average had fallen to 3.0 children and the Italian-American average to 2.4. After having one of the largest size families among American ethnic groups, Italians now were tied with Jews for one of the smallest.[193]

Along with the rise of Italian Americans in the general economy and society came their rise in organized crime—to a position of pre-eminence in that field. Organized crime had existed in the United States before Italians became part of it. The leading gangsters were Irish or Jewish, on into the 1920s.[194] The introduction of Prohibition greatly increased the scope of organized crime in the United States, at about the same time that Italians were entering it in force. The boot-legging of liquor and the operation of illicit drinking places (often in conjunction with gambling or prostitution) became big business—and a highly competitive business. The Italian gangsters had two decisive advantages in this violent and deadly competition: (1) they could traffic in liquor without themselves becoming alcoholics and (2) family loyalties were as central to Italian crime as to Italian life in general. Sobriety and loyalty were particularly important in a life-and-death business.

Italian organized crime was also highly regionalized, like the rest of Italian life. The great bulk of Italian-American crime families were (and are) Sicilian in origin.

The tradition of the Mafia in Sicily provided a framework for Italian-American crime syndicates, but the Mafia in the United States was neither a branch nor a transplant of the Sicilian Mafia. Organized crime was an existing American institution, and the Italian Americans had to literally fight their way into it. The highly regionalized origin of Mafia personnel was underscored by the fact that, even in the 1920s, Italian Americans as a whole had lower crime rates than other Americans.

Along with crime, sports, entertainment, and politics have provided important avenues of upward movement for Italian Americans, as for other ethnic groups without the initial capital or educational traditions to rise as readily in business or intellectual careers. Italian Americans entered sports later than the Irish and never achieved the same overwhelming dominance. But such names as Joe DiMaggio, Rocky Graziano, Vince Lombardi, Yogi Berra, and Rocky Marciano indicate major contributions. In music—both classical and popular—Italian Americans have been unexcelled in the United States, as Italians have been in Europe. Italian-American figures in classical music have included Enrico Caruso, Arturo Toscanini, Anna Moffo, and Gian-Carlo Menotti. Among popular singers, Frank Sinatra, Perry Como, Dean Martin, and Tony Bennett are only the best known of a long list of Italian-American singers, including many with anglicized names like Connie Francis or Bobby Darin.

Italian Americans rose slowly in politics but ultimately produced well-known municipal, state, and national figures. The first major Italian-American political figure was Fiorello H. La Guardia, one of the very few "reform" politicians with a grass-roots understanding of the people and a mass appeal. Lack of political experience and lack of ethnic cohesiveness handicapped Italian political efforts. Irish politicians represented Italian districts on into the early twentieth century—unchallenged at first and then skillfully dividing and conquering when Italian challenges arose. Only after decades of struggle were Italian politicians able to compete successfully with the Irish and other more politically experienced groups. It was 1949 before Carmine DeSapio became the first Italian leader of New York's Tammany Hall, although the Italians had long been one of the largest ethnic groups in the city.[195] Italian candidates did not carry the Italian vote as regularly as other ethnic candidates carried the votes of their respective groups. Even the popular Mayor La Guardia failed to carry the Italian vote in New York in his 1941 reelection campaign against an Irish opponent (William O'Dwyer).[196] Even in the 1970s, a Jewish candidate for mayor of New York (Abe Beame) carried the Italian vote against an Italian opponent.

ITALIAN AMERICANS TODAY

In income, education, IQ scores, and other indices, Italian Americans are very much like other Americans today. Recent census studies show slightly higher than average family incomes for people of Italian ancestry, but such people are disproportionately urban, and higher incomes (and living costs) are common in large cities. That Italian family incomes have averaged about 12 percent above those of other Americans in recent years[197] may reflect only regional or urban-rural differences, but even to have reached the national average is no small accomplishment for a group that earned only 45 percent of the national average in the first decade of the twentieth century.[198]

What is also remarkable is that this rise was not primarily through the supposedly classic channels of education and the jobs associated with education. As late as 1969, Italian Americans over thirty-five years of age were almost two years behind other Americans of the same age in years of schooling, and less than two-thirds as many completed college.[199] They were underrepresented in professional and other high-level positions requiring education.[200] In New York City, a smaller proportion of Italians than of blacks were in professional occupations.[201] Italian Americans remain underrepresented on the faculties of New York's city colleges and universities.[202] By 1972, the younger Italians (twenty-five to thirty-four years old) had reached the national average in years of schooling, and were close to the national average in completion of college.[203] Much of this may have been a consequence of the economic rise of Italians—their parents could now afford to send their children on to higher education—but was clearly not the cause for the rise that had already taken place. Italian incomes were already above the national average in 1968.[204]

Italian Americans did not merely work; they also saved. Among the early immigrants—mostly men preparing to bring families over or to return to Italy with money to establish themselves—saving over half their income was not uncommon.[205] A de-emphasis on conspicuous consumption remained a trait of later generations.[206] So did self-reliance, which took many forms, including refusal to take government benefits to which they were legally entitled,[207] maintaining good credit ratings even when on low incomes,[208] and taking little interest in politics or elective endeavors.

Against this background, it may be possible to understand the paradoxical change in relations between Italians and blacks over the generations. Whereas the immigrant generation of Italians evidenced less hostility to blacks than did other whites (especially in the South), currently Italian-American opinion is more unfavorable to blacks than is that among other whites.[209] The paths to group advancement emphasized by black leaders have been precisely those paths rejected by Italian Americans as inconsistent with the latter's values—government aid and special treatment.[210] The life-styles of the two groups also clash.[211] Words and body language are often taken as calculated insults by each side, when in fact they have entirely different meanings in the two very different cultures. These conflicts are exacerbated by the fact that Italian Americans have been reluctant to abandon their neighborhoods,[212] in the familiar pattern of white flight (there is still an Italian-American community in Harlem), and so have more contacts and opportunities for conflict with blacks than do many other groups. Italian Americans have similar problems with Puerto Ricans,[213] but not with the Chinese, whose values and life-style do not clash with theirs, even though they are a different race. The Italians got along with the Chinese far better than with the Irish, whose life-style—especially in the nineteenth century—was a forerunner of the black urban life-style of the twentieth century. In short, the blanket "racism" explanation does not capture the key ingredients in these intergroup hostilities.

As much as Italian immigrants and their descendants cling to many cultural traits from their homeland, there was no correspondingly strong sense of Italian-American groupwide identity, and still less nationalistic feeling for Italy. With Americanization came more of a sense of being a single Italian-American ethnic group and some concern for Italy as a country, though with nothing like the preoccupation of Irish Americans with Ireland or Jewish Americans with Israel. For a brief time, Italian Americans were captivated by the rise of Benito Mussolini, but so were many non-Italian Americans in the 1920s and 1930s, as demonstrated by the favorable press treatment of him in that era.[214] No serious attempt was ever made to transfer his ideology to America. Italian Americans readily participated in the invasion of Italy by the U.S. Army in World War II with no sense of conflict of loyalties. Their presence may have contributed to the friendly reception of the American Army by the Italian populace.

The new sense of group identity among Italian Americans has still not meant anything like the groupwide cohesion or political bloc voting of some other ethnic groups. Italian political candidates still cannot count on the Italian vote, as other candidates can in other groups. In the 1965 primary election for nomination as comptroller, Mario Procaccino lost the Italian vote to his Jewish opponent and received the nomination only because he (Procaccino) carried the Jewish precincts![215] In a later election, Procaccino carried the Italian vote but apparently more because of his stand on issues that were important to Italian voters than because of his Italian name.[216] In the 1962 gubernatorial race in Massachusetts, Italian candidate John Volpe won only 51 percent of the Italian vote against an old-line Anglo-Saxon named Endicott Peabody.[217]

Italian political success has come relatively late. The first Italian senator was elected in 1950, and the first Italian cabinet member was appointed in 1962. Some Italian candidates have carried large shares of the Italian vote, but so have some of the Jewish candidates, and John F. Kennedy carried 85 percent of the Italian vote in Massachusetts in the 1960 presidential election.[218] Generally, Democrats run better than Republicans with Italian voters, but extremely liberal candidates of ei-

The Italians

ther party—such as Mayor John Lindsay of New York in the 1960s— have lost heavily.[219]

Despite much publicized black-versus-Italian political (and other) confrontations in such cities as Newark and Philadelphia, these racial-ethnic conflicts are also strong issues conflicts (over such things as police powers and crime control) that are difficult to separate from intergroup hostility as such. Still, anticivil rights presidential candidate George Wallace carried 21 percent of the Italian vote in Newark in 1968, 29 percent of the Italian vote in Cleveland, and about 10 percent of the Italian vote nationwide, compared to 8 percent with other nonsouthern voters.[220] But in the same year, a black Republican candidate for U.S. Senator from Massachusetts, Edward Brooke, carried more than 40 percent of the Italian vote, higher than his party's presidential candidate, Richard M. Nixon.[221] In New York in 1970, a black candidate for statewide office received a majority of the Italian vote in upstate New York but not in New York City, where blacks and Italians were often on opposite sides of local issues.[222] Unlike the 1928 anti-Catholic vote against Al Smith in the South—where there were very few Catholics—Italian political clashes with blacks seemed to occur primarily where an actual on-the-spot conflict of interest and values puts them in opposition, rather than primarily because of generalized racism, which would apply whether or not blacks were nearby.

While Italian Americans long resented and resisted prescribed programs of "Americanization" by schools, settlement houses, and other outsiders,[223] they became, at their own pace and in their own way, confirmed Americans, notable for their patriotism.[224] In World War I, when soldiers were classified by ethnicity, Italian Americans were found to enlist more than others and ultimately sacrificed more than others. Italian Americans were 10 percent of the war casualties, although only 4 percent of the population.[225]

In the long run, America proved to be a land of opportunity for those who came here from Italy. But it was an opportunity turned into the reality of progress only by great toil and persistence. Some early Italian Americans may have summarized it best when they held up the hands with which they earned their living and said, "America is here—this is America."[226]

III

Americans from Asia

Chapter 6

THE CHINESE

CHINESE AMERICANS are part of a larger worldwide phenomenon of "overseas Chinese," who are spread from southeast Asia to the Caribbean. By 1930, more than 8 million Chinese had left China to settle around the world.[1] These overseas Chinese have often become successful tradesmen, merchants, and bankers in societies where the native populations were desperately poor—arousing the same kind of resentment, political persecution, and sporadic violence to which Jews were long subjected in Europe. The Chinese have often been called "the Jews of Asia." The overseas Chinese have worked in very similar occupations to those of the Jews and have lived their own separate cultural and social existence in a variety of host countries, also like the Jews. The skills and organizational abilities of the Chinese have made them valuable additions to many poor countries, while their affluence has made them political targets.[2] The result has been an ambivalence toward them by the governments of such countries. Various Latin-American nations have alternately encouraged and restricted Chinese immigration. As late as 1966, the government of the Solomon Islands debated deporting them all.[3] There have been massacres of Chinese in

133

Indonesia and Mexico.[4] Currently, a quota system in Malaysia is restricting the access of the Chinese minority to desirable jobs or other economic opportunities, in favor of native Malaysians.[5] Many of the "boat people" forced out of Vietnam after the Communist takeover have been overseas Chinese.

Chinese Americans have always been a tiny part of the worldwide phenomenon of the overseas Chinese. Their story shows a distinctive interaction between the culture they brought and the circumstances they found in the United States.

CHINA

China has a long history as a nation and a culture, going back thousands of years before Christ.[6] For much of that period, China was economically, technologically, and organizationally the most advanced nation in the world. China in the eleventh century had achieved a level of economic development not reached by any European nation until the eighteenth century.[7] The oldest printed book in existence was printed in China in the ninth century.[8] Cast iron existed in China a thousand years before it existed in Europe.[9] An iron and steel industry existed in China, producing over 100,000 tons of pig iron annually during the Sung Dynasty, which lasted from the tenth to the twelfth centuries.[10] Marco Polo found a city of 2 million inhabitants in China, at a time when the largest cities in Europe had no more than 50,000.[11] As late as the sixteenth century, China had the highest standard of living in the world.[12]

The creation of the overseas Chinese was related to the decline of this great civilization. Both date from the Ming Dynasty (1368–1644). Governments dominated by reform-minded intellectuals assumed pervasive control of the economy and society, especially of large-scale business.[13] In the last century of the Ming Dynasty, there began an exodus that created the first large overseas Chinese communities.[14] The skills and organizational abilities carried by these Chinese emigrants sustained their own prosperity and contributed to the decline and poverty of China itself. Much of modern history has seen the paradox of Chinese people prospering in countries throughout the world, but desperately poor in China itself.

The Chinese

The Chinese who immigrated to the United States before World War II came overwhelmingly from one province—Kwantung—in southern China.[15] Indeed, they were even more localized in origin, coming from just one of the seven districts of that province, Toishan. This was very important in a highly regionalized country like China. The language of the original Chinese Americans was a Toishan dialect similar to Cantonese, but so different from the dominant Mandarin Chinese language as to make the two dialects mutually incomprehensible.[16] While China has long had a common *written* language,[17] its spoken language has varied so greatly as to have many mutally unintelligible dialects.[18] The post-World War II Chinese immigrants to the United States have typically spoken Mandarin Chinese, creating a language barrier between themselves and existing Chinese Americans.

The regionalism of China, like that of Italy, derives from its topography. Mountains and hills fragment the country, and the basins of its two great rivers—the Yellow River in the north and the Yangtze in the south—are very different.[19] The racial homogeneity of the Chinese has not prevented them from seeing themselves as radically different groups of people, according to their respective regional, linguistic, and cultural backgrounds. Their turbulent and often brutal history has left a legacy of local clan loyalties and an enormous emphasis on the family as the individual's only dependable refuge. Implacable revenge against enemies of the family was a long-standing and deep tradition in China[20]—again, as in Italy.

In modern China, weak and ineffective governments at local and national levels have led to autonomous centers of force and violence— clans, warlords, and secret societies.[21] The modern Chinese secret societies, or tongs, like the Mafia in southern Italy, were at one time popularly supported forces of resistance and revenge under oppressive alien overlords, and they too became criminals specializing in extortion.[22] These secret societies, or tongs, became a common feature of overseas Chinese communities, including those in the United States.[23]

Another characteristic of the Chinese culture that was to follow the Chinese to the United States was respect for learning. Imperial China had for centuries chosen its civil servants according to their education and performance on examinations, and learned men were accorded great respect. It would be generations before Chinese Americans could obtain and utilize higher education in the United States, but they were prepared before the opportunity arose.[24] Although China as a whole was (and is) predominantly agricultural, the Toishan District of Kwantung Province is a rocky and almost barren plateau with little agriculture. Its people often turned to trade, acting as middlemen, salesmen, and merchants.[25] Many of them traveled to the port of Hong Kong, where they became familiar with Europeans and where they heard the fateful news of the discovery of gold in California in 1849.[26] Thus began the Chinese immigration to America.

THE IMMIGRANT GENERATION

Many of the Chinese came to the United States as contract laborers or on money borrowed from Chinese-American organizations that assumed a supervisory role toward them in the United States.[27] Like other immigrants wholly unfamiliar with the language and culture of the United States, the Chinese laborers often worked in gangs under the supervision of a fellow countryman. The Chinese, although physically smaller than Americans, were hard workers in agriculture, railroad building, and other taxing physical labor. They also worked cheaply and lived frugally, saving money out of what would be considered a pittance by Americans. These very virtues, however, made the Chinese feared and hated as competitors by white workers.

By 1851, there were 25,000 Chinese in California.[28] By 1870, there were 63,000 in the United States, almost all on the West Coast. Almost 6,000 Chinese entered the United States in 1880, twice as many in 1881, and then five times as many in 1882.[29] An exclusionary immigration law directed against the Chinese reduced the inflow to less than 1,000 until 1890, when 1,716 entered.

The initial Chinese immigration was almost exclusively male. As in other cases, this indicated a tentative rather than a permanent move to the United States. Many were sojourners rather than immigrants. About half of the early Chinese who came to the United States did not stay.[30] In the 1880s, the number of Chinese leaving the United States was greater than the number coming in.[31] Partly this was a result of initial intentions to return to China after making money in the United States. Partly it was a result of unhappy experiences in this country.

The reception of the Chinese immigrant in the United States was harsh and often violent. The Chinese were both nonwhite and non-Christian, at a time when either trait alone was a serious handicap. They looked different, dressed differently, ate differently, and followed customs wholly unfamiliar to Americans. They were considered incapable of being assimilated, culturally or biologically. They were feared as competitors whose harder work and longer hours for cheap pay would drive down the standard of living of American labor. Labor unions were in the forefront of decades-long efforts to exclude Chinese immigrants and to expel Chinese residents from the United States. In 1885, Chinese workers employed as strikebreakers were massacred at a Wyoming coal mine.[32] Only the hardest, dirtiest, most menial jobs were open to them. Most of the laborers who laid the Central Pacific Railroad tracks through California and across the Sierra Mountains into Utah to drive the golden spike were Chinese.[33] Chinese who tried to work as independent gold miners were forcibly driven from the mining camps by white miners in camps throughout the West.[34] In 1885, the entire Chinese population of one California community was forced to leave by the threat of mob violence.[35] At about the same time, Seattle and Tacoma, Washington, expelled their Chinese populations. Similar events occurred in Vancouver and Alaska.[36]

Casual harassment was a common occurrence in between these more dramatic assaults. Cutting off the long pigtail, or queue, worn by Chinese men was a popular prank,[37] although one with serious consequences to the men, who could not return to China without it under the laws of the Manchu Dynasty.[38] Chinese immigrants arriving in San Francisco were "escorted" to Chinatown by street hoodlums with "taunts, beatings, brick-bats and hurling of overripened fruit in an atmosphere of drunken Irish hilarity."[39] But behind these harassments was the ever-present threat of more serious violence, which could erupt at any time. Mobs of whites sporadically burned and sacked Chinatowns on the West Coast and in the Rocky Mountain region, killing inhabitants as they went. In Los Angeles in 1871, a mob of whites shot, hanged, and otherwise killed about twenty Chinese in one night.[40]

In addition to attacks by hoodlum elements or mobs, the Chinese came under a different kind of attack by the more "respectable" classes. The Chinese Exclusion Act of 1882 severely curtailed their immigration, and new laws first prevented Chinese already here from becoming naturalized American citizens—and then made citizenship a prerequisite for entering many occupations or even owning land. From 1854 to 1874, a law was in force preventing Chinese from testifying in court against white men[41]—in effect, declaring open season on the Chinese, who had no legal recourse when robbed, vandalized, or assaulted.

The almost total exclusion of Chinese immigration had devastating long-run effects on Chinese Americans. Because the early Chinese immigration was almost exclusively male, all hope of a normal social or family life was destroyed for the great majority of the Chinese population of the United States. Many of these Chinese men had wives and children back in China, whom they would not see again for decades, if at all. The severe restrictions on economic opportunity meant that many could not even afford to return to China to resume a normal life. Passage to the United States could be arranged in exchange for labor to be performed here. Passage in the other direction—more than twice as far as to Europe—was a much more difficult obstacle. Many of those who came as sojourners were permanently stranded in the United States. Others who had thought of settling here with their families were prevented from bringing them over and were themselves prevented from becoming citizens.

The smuggling of Chinese into the United States became a major activity after the imposition of severe immigration restrictions. Some were smuggled in for the usual reasons for immigration, but many were women—some as voluntary or forced prostitutes.

The phrase "not a Chinaman's chance" arose during this era[42] to describe hopeless odds.

The Chinese experience in Hawaii was much better than on the mainland of the United States. An early history of amicable relations between Polynesians and whites had created a climate of more relaxed interracial relations, including many people of mixed ancestry.[43] The tremendous excess of single men among the Chinese immigrants led to marriage with Hawaiian women,[44] while on the mainland marriage with white women was both socially and legally forbidden. The Chinese reached a high of 22 percent of the Hawaiian population in 1884. The influx of other groups to Hawaii reduced the Chinese proportion in later years. When Hawaii was annexed by the United States in 1898, the Chinese Exclusion Act was extended to that territory.

Economic Conditions

Where the Chinese were tolerated, it was in occupations urgently needed and that white men were reluctant to fill—cooks and laundrymen in the mining camps, for example, or as domestic servants in the cities. The early Chinese were also agricultural field laborers, working long hours for low pay. In 1870, about one-tenth of all farm labor in California was Chinese, and by the mid-1880s, more than half were Chinese.[45] The Chinese proved to be more diligent and conscientious than whites in such work. The Chinese were also found to be industrious and persevering working in gangs laying railroad tracks. Ten thousand Chinese workers helped to build the Central Pacific Railroad.[46]

The Chinese in the United States were quite different from the overseas Chinese elsewhere. The merchants, bankers, and educated Chinese did not come to the United States to face insults, discrimination, and violence. The poorer, less educated, often younger, and less experienced Chinese came.[47]

With the passage of time, the Chinese either left or were driven out of mining camps, agricultural field labor, and railroad gangs. They typically settled in cities in California, and some dispersed eastward. Those American employers who hired Chinese were subjected to harassment and threats, so the Chinese were left with little more than self-employment or work as domestic servants. For several decades, their principal occupation was as laundrymen. Chinese restaurants were another major source of jobs. These were usually located in Chinese communities, or Chinatowns, to minimize the appearance of competing with whites. Even as late as 1920, more than half of all employed Chinese in the United States worked either in laundries or restaurants.[48] Laundries were far more numerous than restaurants because laundries require very little capital to start and require less knowledge of English to conduct. Although severely restricted to two main kinds of work, Chinese succeeded in those areas. The Chinese hand laundry became an American institution. So too did the food created in Chinese restaurants for Americans—chop suey, chow mein, and fried rice, none of them authentic dishes from China.[49] In addition, Chinese grocery stores opened in Chinatowns to supply the kinds of food preferred by the Chinese themselves.

Even in their constricted world, the Chinese continued to be harassed by legal impositions. Special taxes and fees were applied to the kinds of businesses conducted by Chinese or conducted in the Chinese manner. For example, license fees in nineteenth-century San Francisco were higher for laundries that did not deliver by horse-and-buggy, and it was made a misdemeanor to carry baskets suspended on a pole across the shoulder—the way the Chinese delivered.[50]

The Chinese reaction to pervasive discrimination was withdrawal and inconspicuousness,[51] much like the European Jews in the ghetto or the Pale. Chinatowns developed their own community organizations and leaders to conduct their own internal affairs with an absolute minimum of recourse to the institutions of the larger society around them. This was a common pattern also among overseas Chinese in Asia and elsewhere. In the United States, the Chinese leaders deliberately kept out of the courts and out of the political arena. This was possible in part because the Chinese in America lived in tight-knit communities of people from one district of one province in China. In those enclaves, they kept alive and intact a culture, a set of traditions and values, that was eroding in China itself.[52]

The source of power for the leaders of American Chinatowns was not political popularity but wealth and access to the use of force. The Chinese employers who dominated civic organizations could purge either political radicals or trade unionists by the simple expedient of denying jobs or credit, at a time when the larger society offered very few economic opportunities to Chinese and even fewer social opportunities. The internal Chinese organizations could determine who could work where, and who could open a business where, and with what financing. Economic and social pressure was supplemented by physical force. The secret societies, or tongs, that existed in China and in other overseas Chinese communities also existed in American Chinatowns. Their use of the hatchet as a weapon in the nineteenth century led to the term "hatchet man,"[53] now applied to a wide variety of other activities. The tong's hatchet men, however, graduated to revolvers and machine guns as part of their assimilation to American society.

The tongs divided territory for the prostitution, gambling, and opium use that were common activities among the homeless and womanless men who made up the bulk of early Chinatown inhabitants. These tongs had sporadic outbreaks of violence. There were particularly bloody "tong wars" in Chinatowns in the nineteenth century, and new outbreaks from time to time in the twentieth century, as late as 1931.[54] Despite these sensational tong wars that made newspaper headlines, most Chinese Americans remained quiet and nonviolent.

Social Conditions

Perhaps the greatest tragedy of the early Chinese immigrants was that a people so dedicated to the family were denied the possibility of having families in America. After immigration from China was unilaterally curtailed by the United States in 1882, the result was a greater imbalance between the sexes than in any other ethnic group. In 1860, there were almost twenty Chinese men for every Chinese woman in the United States. By 1890, there were about twenty-seven Chinese men for every Chinese woman. As late as 1930, the ratio was still four to one.[55] Many of the early Chinese were obviously unable to produce children under these circumstances. This meant that the cultural assimilation of the group as a whole was retarded. The virtual absence of an American-born second generation not only statistically left most of the Chinese population foreign born until about 1940,[56] but it also meant that the absorption of the English language and American customs via the school was delayed and that the usual role of second-generation children in helping their parents become acculturated was aborted. The Chinese men were often trapped in the United States without the possibility of normal family life and at the same time unable—because of poverty—to get passage back to China. Many thousands of these intended sojourners lived out lonely lives as permanent residents in a country where they neither were wanted nor wanted to be.

Clans remained strong among the Chinese in America as in China. Clan leaders were both economic and social powers. A Chinese merchant "usually assumed leadership of his clan, established a hostelry about the store for his kinsman, and provided aid, advice, contact and shelter."[57] Because of the relatively small number of Chinese in the United States, some clans combined to act as one clan. Clans kept trade secrets and limited the entry of new stores, laundries, or restaurants. Different clans dominated the Chinatowns of different cities.[58]

In addition to clans, various mutual aid organizations arose to act as employment agencies, rotating credit associations, mediators, and social organizations. Because of its many functions, it could command the respect or acquiescence of individual Chinese, who would be bereft of many needed services and comforts in a foreign land without it. Various Chinese-American mutual aid organizations have consolidated to ultimately form the Chinese Consolidated Benevolent Association, popularly known as the Six Companies, acting as a unified voice for Chinatown and speaking also for Chinese Americans generally.[59]

The moral, economic, and social pressures of the clan, the Six Companies, and the tongs (both independently and as enforcers for the other groups) made American Chinatowns very self-enclosed communities.

Chinatowns in the last quarter of the nineteenth century were centers of vice, not only for the Chinese but for whites seeking prostitution, drugs, and gambling. The Chinese introduced opium into the United States. The white clientele of Chinatown vice districts were often ruffians and hoodlums, who added to the dangerousness of an area where tong violence might break out at any time. The shabby-looking, vice-infested, and violence-prone Chinatowns of this era were used by anti-Chinese elements as arguments for continued immigration restrictions, although in fact existing immigration restrictions were a major part of the reason for such conditions.

LATER GENERATIONS

With the passage of years, the few Chinese women in the United States produced a small second generation of children, and these children grew up to slightly ease the serious sex imbalance that remained characteristic of Chinese Americans on up through World War II. There were also an unknown number of Chinese women smuggled into the United States—some for the explicit purpose of prostitution[60]—among a large but unknown number of other Chinese smuggled in during the long era of immigration restrictions. It is known that, as recently as 1960, many Chinatown residents deliberately avoided the census takers for fear of discovery of their illegal immigrant status.[61] Some well-to-do merchants had wives who were elaborately secluded from view, much less contact, with the many Chinese males.[62] A very small percentage of the Chinese men married. In New York, into the early decades of the twentieth century, just over half of the few Chinese men who married, married non-Chinese women.[63] This percentage tended to decline over the next decades as more Chinese females became available. As the total number of Chinese males who married increased, the proportion of intermarriages dropped to about one-fourth in the 1920s and 1930s. Most of the non-Chinese women they married were white.[64]

Although most Chinese males lived alone, they were usually not in fact single. As of 1910, there were more married than single Chinese men living in the United States, but the great bulk of their wives were living abroad.[65]

Despite the prevalence of prostitution, opium dens, and gambling in Chinatowns, the Chinese men also sent substantial remittances to their families in China. With the great majority of Chinese Americans being from one district of one province, the remittances from America were concentrated in one place, and this place—Toishan—became one of the most prosperous districts in China.[66] Its streets were paved and lit by electric lights. It continued to have the best educational facilities in the province, on into the time of the Chinese Communist government in the middle of the twentieth century.[67] These schools had been built and maintained by remittances from Chinese in America. Civic projects in Toishan were financed by canvassing Chinese in America, collecting small sums from the laundrymen, restaurant workers, and other workers whose poverty by American standards nevertheless represented prosperity by Chinese standards.[68] From 1938 to 1947, for example, an average of $7 million a year was sent from the United States to China.[69]

The subculture of the stranded sojourner in Chinatown slowly eroded away as these men grew old and died off or, in more fortunate cases, amassed enough money to return to China. The crime rates fell in Chinatowns with the decline of the stranded sojourner element. Between 1900 and 1927, two-thirds of all arrests of Chinese in the United States were for the three crimes most associated with the sojourners: prostitution, drugs, and gambling.[70] In the late 1950s and early 1960s, more than 70 percent of the Chinese patients at the drug treatment center in Lexington, Kentucky, had been born in China, over 90 percent worked in laundries or restaurants in the United States, and more than 60 percent were over fifty years old.[71] During the same period, the suicide rate among Chinese in San Francisco was three times the national average—and almost all among men born in China.[72] This was all part of the tragic price of laws and practices that made it nearly impossible for the first generation of Chinese in America either to prosper here or to return home to their families.

Modification of the immigration laws in 1930 permitted some small numbers of wives from China to join their husbands in the United States. The repeal of the Chinese Exclusion Act of 1882 in 1943 and new legislation permitting limited immigration from China in 1945 helped ease the sex imbalance and permitted more normal family life to develop among this very family-oriented people. The bulk of the new Chinese immigration was female,[73] and the female preponderance was concentrated among young people of marriageable years.[74] More than 8,000 Chinese men brought their wives to the United States within a few years.[75] Some of them were reunited after decades of separation—sometimes with mutual shock on seeing each other again.[76] Many men went back to China to get married, often using the traditional services of a matchmaker.[77] Even among Chinese marrying within the United States in this era, a substantial proportion were marrying mates chosen by parents and/or matchmakers, with varying degrees of assent by the parties themselves.[78]

Economic Conditions

Despite the highly restricted economic opportunities for early Chinese Americans, the Chinatown communities took care of their own indigents. Even such disasters as the San Francisco earthquake of 1906 and the Great Depression of the 1930s did not force the Chinese to resort to public assistance. Although San Francisco's Chinatown was burned out by the fires that followed the great earthquake of 1906, leaving many homeless, the Chinese in San Francisco received far less aid than in proportion to their numbers, and few even applied for public assistance. Instead, internal Chinese-American community organizations collected money from Chinese in other cities to provide relief and rehabilitation.[79]

Even when the Great Depression was at its worst in the early 1930s, few Chinese received federal unemployment relief. Whereas 10 percent of the whites in Chicago received federal employment relief in 1933, only 4 percent of the Chinese did so. In New York, 9 percent of the whites but only 1 percent of the Chinese received this aid. Similar patterns were found in other cities.[80] During this period, some Chinese family associations made a practice of keeping a barrel of rice open in the foyer so that a hungry member visiting could privately remove what he needed for himself or his family and privately return it when his circumstances permitted.[81]

The ferocious anti-Chinese feelings of the nineteenth century, when Chinese competed directly with white workers, could not be maintained indefinitely at the same fever pitch after the Chinese withdrew into their own enclaves and offered neither competition nor resistance to whites. Chinatowns became tourist attractions. Their image was carefully controlled by their own internal organizations, which took care of its poverty and other problems themselves as much as possible and which raised virtually no political protests.[82]

Isolated individual Chinese, especially of the younger generation who were American born and therefore citizens, were sent to college and made their way unobtrusively into a few professional occupations. These pioneers provided examples and arguments against the stereotype of the Chinese as unassimilable aliens and in favor of more acceptance.[83] These unspectacular tactics, combined with a lessening of American racism in general[84] and of anti-Chinese feeling in particular,[85] resulted in an increase in Chinese professionals, both relatively and absolutely. As of 1940, only 3 percent of Chinese Americans in California were in the professions, while 8 percent of whites were. By 1950, the Chinese percentage had approximately doubled to 6 percent,

144

and the white percentage had risen to 10 percent. In the next decade, however, the proportion of Chinese who were professionals tripled to 18 percent, passing the whites at 15 percent.[86] Paradoxically, in Hawaii, where there had always been less hostility to the Chinese than on the mainland, the advance of the Chinese was not quite so great, absolutely or relative to whites. Some indication of how far the Chinese had come is that, as of 1900, the proportion of Chinese and Japanese in the professions was lower than that of blacks, and more than twice as high a percentage of Orientals as of blacks were domestic servants.[87]

The initial "entering wedge" of college-educated Chinese in the United States was very small—less than 2 percent of all Chinese over twenty-five years of age in 1940. But of this tiny group, more than 80 percent entered the professions—mostly scientific professions.[88] As the number of college-educated Chinese youth increased over the next twenty years—to 20 percent of all workers—the fields of work remained relatively stable. As of 1960, just over half of all Chinese Americans in the professions were in science, accounting, engineering, drafting, and college teaching—and more than half the college teachers were teaching engineering or the natural sciences.[89]

Much of the initial economic rise of the Chinese, however, was not in professions in the larger society but in businesses in Chinatown itself. Lack of access to banks and other financial institutions in the larger society could not prevent Chinese businesses from being established. Rotating credit associations were an old institution among the southern Chinese,[90] by which money could be pooled and used for investment. The device itself was quite simple—each member in his turn had access to the pooled resources of all—but what made it successful was that default on repayment was extremely rare. A strong sense of individual and family honor made it unlikely that anyone would fail to repay the pool, and his family would probably make restitution if he did. The device was not unique to the Chinese. What was crucial was that the whole constellation of Chinese values—particularly the honor of the family—made it viable, whereas defaults would have ruined the whole scheme. The rotating credit associations remained the primary instrument for raising capital in Chinatowns on into the 1950s.[91]

The labor shortages of World War II opened many new job opportunities for the Chinese, as it did for other ethnic groups and for women. Many Chinese abandoned traditional Chinatown occupations to move into these new jobs.[92] The diligent work habits and the lack of need for supervision, which had marked the Chinese workers from the first generation in America, now proved to be decisive advantages in the labor market, once the discriminatory barriers came down. By 1960, there were fewer Chinese Americans in manual occupations than in the professions and business.[93] The average income of Chinese Americans in 1959 was higher than that of other Americans.[94]

Along with this spectacular economic rise came more residential dispersion of Chinese Americans. Most Chinese Americans no longer live in Chinatowns,[95] which are occupied by the aging sojourners left stranded from an earlier immigration and by new refugees repeating much of the poverty experience of earlier generations of Chinese Americans—working long hours at low pay in Chinese restaurants or light industry. The aged sojourners and the new refugees are behind the paradoxes that (1) Chinatowns have more than their share of low-income people, despite the above-average incomes of Chinese Americans as a group and that (2) the illiteracy rate among Chinese Americans is much higher than the national average (several times that among blacks), even though Chinese Americans as a group have above-average levels (and qualities) of education.

Social Conditions

Unlike other immigrant groups, the Chinese population in the United States decreased over the decades. There were 107,000 Chinese in 1890 but only 61,000 in 1920.[96] Chinese were dying and leaving the country, but few were coming in to replace them. However, the downward trend eventually reversed, as the proportion of women rose and more Chinese children were born in the United States. The Chinese-American population rose to 75,000 in 1930, and by 1950 was higher than it had been at the previous peak in 1890.[97]

The shabby and sordid Chinatowns of the late nineteenth and early twentieth centuries began to change with changes in the demographic composition of Chinese Americans. The aging, death, or repatriation of sojourners reduced the demand for Chinatown vice industries. The beginnings of the Chinatown restaurant and tourism industries created economic incentives for the suppression of the violence and sordidness that reduced the tourist appeal of the Chinese community. In addition, the slow but steady growth of family formation among the Chinese created another element opposed to crime and violence in Chinatowns—a small but ever-growing part of the Chinese-American population.

In the early decades of the twentieth century, the balance of power

The Chinese

within Chinatowns tipped against the criminal tongs. The Six Companies ordered their member merchants to refuse to pay any more "protection" money to the tongs. Chinatown residents began to cooperate with police in apprehending and prosecuting criminals and the corrupt policemen who had long protected tong activities. All of this would have been unheard of in an earlier era. Where vice could not be stamped out—gambling being an old custom among Cantonese—it was driven underground. Under pressure from Chinese businessmen trying to attract tourists, remaining gambling dens were kept hidden away from tourists' view and were no longer open to people from outside the Chinese community.

The physical rehabilitation of Chinatowns was also undertaken by Chinese leaders, who decorated these areas with the famous pagoda-like designs typical of Chinatowns today. Tourism flourished in the new Chinatowns. Chinese festivals and parades received police protection and became civic events attracting large crowds of non-Chinese.

The declining profitability of vice and the rising profitability of tourism caused some of the tongs themselves to abandon crime in favor of restaurants and shops serving the new tourist trade. Many dropped the name "tong" and substituted "merchant association."

Although sophisticated organized crime existed in Chinatowns, the average Chinese American was very law-abiding—a parallel to the situation among Italian Americans. The decline of organized crime in Chinatowns therefore meant a declining incidence in crime in general there. A survey in 1946 showed only one arrest for alcoholism over an eight-year period in New York's Chinatown, and no arrest at all for murder or any other major crime during that period.[98]

The new generations of Chinese children born in America encountered many of the language difficulties of other immigrant children and sometimes attended schools explicitly segregated (as in San Francisco at the turn of the century) or with a concentration of Chinese children due to residential concentration. The Chinese children did equally well in school whether concentrated in all-Chinese schools or scattered among other ethnic groups.[99] Some early studies of Chinese IQs showed them below the national average, but by the 1930s, Chinese youngsters' IQs were at or above the national average—and remained so.[100] Teachers in New York's Chinatown rated the Chinese children "better behaved, more obedient, and more self-reliant" than their white classmates.[101] American-born Chinese youngsters automatically escaped the anti-Chinese laws that forbad noncitizens to enter various occupations or to exercise various rights. The new generation of Chinese Americans entered a different world from that faced by their parents, and were well-equipped to advance in that world.

With the belated appearance of a substantial second generation of Chinese Americans, the intergenerational tensions common to immigrant groups began. The traditional parent-arranged marriage was a special point of contention with American-bred offspring.[102] But compromises kept Chinese-American families close knit, and by American standards, "strong parental authority" remained the rule,[103] with the parents emotionally more distant from their children than among other Americans.[104] There has long been a very low incidence of juvenile delinquency among Chinese-American youth,[105] although in earlier times, when Chinatowns were crime-ridden, the few Chinese youths there were also heavily involved.[106]

The general sympathy of Americans for China, especially after its invasion by Japan, helped the acceptance of Chinese Americans—now seen as a quiet, orderly group living in a problem-free community, or at least one whose problems seldom came to the attention of the larger society.

The traditional role of women has been very subordinate in Chinese culture, at least outwardly. Yet even in China itself, Chinese men have for centuries had the reputation of being among the most henpecked in the world.[107] Among Chinese Americans, the lopsided sex ratio alone gave women considerable leverage. While Chinese-American husbands are to all outward appearances rulers of their families, it is not uncommon for the wife to make most of the major family decisions—and not confined to domestic concerns.[108]

Although Chinese families are traditionally larger, including those in America until recent times, by 1970 the average number of children per Chinese-American woman was only two.[109] Among women aged thirty-five to forty-four, those with less than nine years of schooling averaged three and a half children, while those with a college education averaged just under three.[110]

The "Hong Kong Chinese"

After the Communists took control of China in 1949, hordes of refugees from all over the country poured into the British colony of Hong Kong. Many eventually found their way to the United States. As a result of changing American immigration laws, the Chinese population of the United States almost doubled—from 237,000 to 435,000—in the decade of the 1960s.[111] Many of the new arrivals settled in the Chinatowns that most Chinese Americans had left or were leaving. In the largest Chinese-American community, in San Francisco, the population density per square mile was three times the citywide average in 1960 and six times the citywide average just three years later.[112] The Chinese populations of New York, Los Angeles, Boston, and Chicago all more than doubled during the decade of the 1960s.[113] About 20,000 Chinese legally entered the United States annually from Hong Kong and Taiwan, and it is estimated that an equal number also entered illegally.[114]

This new immigration has been very different from the old. The traditional Chinese-American community consisted of people from one regional culture—a culture carefully preserved in the United States, even as it changed in China. Chinatowns had not only strong nuclear families but also were crisscrossed with community organizations—such as clans, tongs, and the Six Companies. The Hong Kong refugees were not part of this culture and usually neither spoke nor understood the Toishanese dialect that dominated American Chinatowns. Yet they also did not speak English and could not readily disperse through American society. Although embarking for the United States from Hong Kong, their regional origins in China were diverse.

For many decades, Chinese Americans had escaped the devisive regionalism of China because of their own highly localized origins in one district of one province. Now they began to experience the devisiveness that had long been a problem among emigrants from a similarly regionalized country, Italy. The new immigrants and their many problems were resented by established Chinese Americans—not only for the problems they directly caused, but also for the disgrace they were felt to bring on Chinese Americans in general.[115]

The Hong Kong Chinese were not only from different regions of China; they were also partly Westernized in Hong Kong. The traditional Chinese values and constraints—especially the family—were no longer so dominant among them as among Chinese Americans. The difference between youths from Hong Kong Chinese families and those from traditional Chinese-American families was particularly dramatic. Traditional Chinese-American youths were kept busy with schoolwork, sometimes supplemented with Chinese school after the public school day was over, or by work helping in the family business. Despite inevitable generational conflicts as Americanization proceeded, the traditional Chinese-American youngsters seldom had occasion to deal with police or judges.[116] The new Hong Kong Chinese youths, however, were often problems in the schools and on the streets. They disdained the "menial" jobs open to unskilled people in Chinese restaurants or shops,[117] and instead hung out on street corners and engaged in gang activities.

Crime and violence have increased dramatically in Chinatowns across the United States—from New York to Honolulu. Hong Kong Chinese youth gangs have insulted and harassed the tourists on whom the Chinatown economy is dependent. They have also engaged in vandalism, violence, extortion, theft, terrorism, and murder.[118] Like youth gang members of other groups, they can be seen in Chinatowns "strutting down the street in bright peacock colors."[119] They can also be found dead in the street when gang warfare erupts. There were about 200 youth gang murders in New York's Chinatown in 1973[120]—a community in which such activities were unheard of just a generation ago. In San Francisco's Chinatown, one youth gang alone has 400 members.[121] Some Chinese youth gangs have branches in various cities.[122]

The adult Hong Kong Chinese typically are hardworking—and hard-pressed. As recent, unskilled, unacculturated, and often illegal arrivals, they work long hours at low pay and live in overcrowded and dilapidated housing, infested with rats and roaches.[123] Some are paying off debts incurred in making large bribes to Hong Kong officials for permission to immigrate to the United States—or are paying off smugglers who got them into the United States illegally.[124]

Many of the Hong Kong Chinese are vulnerable to illegally low wages and illegally long hours of work, and to illegally bad housing conditions, because either they or some member of their family is living in the United States illegally—and would be deported if the authorities were to learn of it. Over 6,000 illegal Chinese immigrants have been deported annually.[125]

Just over half the men in New York's Chinatown work in restaurants.[126] Three quarters of the women operate sewing machines in the Chinatown garment district.[127] The proportion of families living in poverty in New York's Chinatown is more than twice the citywide average.[128] Because of long hours, especially in restaurants that do most of their business at night, many of the immigrant Chinese families can have only a few meals together all week.[129] The children are often left to grow up on the street. The Hong Kong Chinese in other cities live under similar conditions.

While the adult Hong Kong Chinese fled the oppression of Communist China and sought better economic opportunities in the United States than in Hong Kong, the Hong Kong Chinese youth compared their lot not with China or Hong Kong but with the lot of other American youths—including better educated and more prosperous traditional Chinese-American youths. The Hong Kong Chinese have also seen the traditional Chinese Americans as landlords and employers of their parents, who earn less and pay more than other Americans. The Hong Kong Chinese youth have tended to be bitterly resentful of Americans and—the supreme irony—favorable toward Maoism, which caused their families to flee China in the first place. This has created an additional source of friction within the Chinese-American community, which has steadfastly supported the Nationalist government on Taiwan.

The leaders of the Chinatown communities have faced a dilemma in dealing with the Hong Kong Chinese. Because Chinatowns are so dependent on tourism, open discussion of the poverty, crime, and violence there could reduce tourism and therewith the livelihoods of many of its inhabitants and the profitable businesses of the Chinese leaders. They have been very reluctant to apply for federal antipoverty programs of various sorts or to invite government presence in a community where so many are so vulnerable to any exposure of illegal conditions—notably immigration, housing, and working conditions. Internal accommodation has been sought, by either buying off or scaring off Hong Kong Chinese youth gangs. Many Chinese restaurants in New York serve gang members free meals. Some Chinatown businesses pay them "protection" money.[130] Some tongs in San Francisco employ youth gang members as lookouts in the gambling dens or to curb other gangs.[131]

The Hong Kong youth gangs in Chinatowns are threats not so much to traditional Chinese Americans—most of whom do not live in Chinatowns—but to tourists and their much-needed spending. Hoodlums on the streets discourage tourism, especially when they call the tourists "honkeys" or otherwise harass or rob them. But even when gang activities are not specifically directed against tourists, they affect tourism. Some tongs in San Francisco's Chinatown have themselves retaliated against youth gang members. They issued a public warning to those who engage in "unruly behavior harmful to the commercial and social life of our community." The bound bodies of five Hong Kong Chinese youths were shortly thereafter found floating in San Francisco Bay.[132] More conservative Chinese leaders have encouraged more vigorous police action in Chinatowns, including the liberal use of billy clubs on the heads of young hoodlums. Far from complaining about "police brutality," Chinatown leaders have encouraged the police to administer "curbstone justice." They have been concerned only to minimize public discussions of this or any other negative news from Chinatown. Sometimes they have appealed to newspapers to downplay news that could hurt the vulnerable tourist industry on which Chinatowns depend, and at other times, they have simply bribed reporters.[133]

CHINESE AMERICANS TODAY

Chinese Americans today have higher incomes than Americans in general and higher occupational status. One-fourth of all employed Chinese Americans are working in scientific and professional fields.[134] The Chinese have risen to this position despite some of the harshest discrimination and violence faced by any immigrants to the United States in the history of this country. Long confined to a narrow range of occupations, they succeeded in those occupations and then spread out into other areas in later years, when opportunities finally opened up for them. Today, much of the Chinese prosperity is due to the simple fact that they work more and have more (and usually better) education than others. Almost one out of five Chinese families has three or more income earners—compared to one out of thirteen for Puerto Ricans, one out of ten among American Indians, and one out of eight among whites.[135] When the Chinese advantages in working and education are held constant, they have no advantage over other Americans. That is, in a Chinese family with a given number of people working and with a given amount of education by the head of the family, the income is only about average for such families, and often a little less than average:

Family Earnings of Chinese-American Male-Headed Families
(Chinese Income as Percentage of U.S. Income in the Same Categories)

Education of Family Head	One-Income Families	Two-Income Families	Three or More Incomes
Less than high school	98%	98%	97%
High school	92	105	100
College (1–3 years)	80	94	106
College (4 years)	82	99	106
Postgraduate (1 year)	75	86	148
Postgraduate (2 years or more)	93	96	107

SOURCE: 1970 U.S. Census, Public Use Sample.

The Chinese

Oriental academics, scientists, and engineers typically have significantly higher qualifications than either blacks or whites—that is, a higher proportion of the Orientals (Japanese and Chinese in this case) have Ph.D.s, and especially Ph.D.s from the higher ranked universities.[136] Among academics, Orientals publish more than either blacks or whites.[137]

Among notable Chinese Americans have been three Nobel prize winners—all in physics. Another Chinese-American physicist—a woman—helped develop America's first atomic bomb during World War II.[138] In architecture, I. M. Pei's striking designs have become famous. His well-known buildings include the Hancock Tower and the John F. Kennedy Library in Boston and the spectacular annex to the National Gallery of Art in Washington, D.C.

Many Chinese Americans have become prosperous in business. As early as 1939, a Chinese immigrant workman named Joe Shoong had built up a chain of stores that gave him the second highest income in the state of California.[139] Gerald Tsai, Jr., is today president of a Wall Street firm with more than $400 million in assets.[140] Another Chinese American, C. Y. Tung, is one of the largest individual shipowners in the world, and spent more than $3 million for a single ship.

In politics, the Chinese have only recently made an appearance. Among the first Chinese Americans to hold political office was Wing F. Ong, elected to the Arizona State Legislature in 1946 by a predominantly white electorate, which contained only thirteen Chinese.[141] The most famous Chinese-American political figure has been Hiram Fong, U.S. senator from Hawaii from 1959 to 1976, after having first served for fourteen years in Hawaii's territorial legislature.[142]

While Chinese Americans as a group are prosperous and well educated, Chinatowns are pockets of poverty, and illiteracy is much higher among the Chinese than among Americans in general. These paradoxes are due to sharp internal differences. Descendants of the Chinese Americans who immigrated long ago from Toishan Province have maintained Chinese values and have added acculturation to American society with remarkable success. More recent Hong Kong Chinese are from more diverse cultural origins, and acquired Western values and styles in Hong Kong, without having acquired the skills to prosper and support those aspirations in the American economy. Foreign-born Chinese men in the United States earn one-fourth lower incomes than native-born Chinese-American men with the same education and other advantages, even though the foreign born have been in the United States an average of seventeen years.[143] While the older

Hong Kong Chinese work tenaciously to sustain and advance themselves, the Hong Kong Chinese youths often react with resentment and antisocial behavior, including terrorism and murder. The need to maintain tourism in Chinatowns causes the Chinese leaders to mute or downplay these problems as much as possible.

There are today only about 11 percent more Chinese men than Chinese women in the United States,[144] and much of the remaining sex imbalance is among older Chinese who came to the United States in an earlier era. Among Chinese Americans of marriageable ages, the sexes are more or less evenly balanced.[145] In this, as in so many other areas, there has been great progress. Families remain strong among Chinese Americans. Almost 90 percent of all Chinese-American families have both husband and wife present.[146] Nearly 80 percent of Chinese-American males in their mid-thirties to mid-forties are married and living with their wives.[147] In contrast to the high rates of intermarriage during the era of great sex imbalance, 87 percent of Chinese men today are married to Chinese women. Less than 10 percent of Chinese Americans are divorced.[148]

As a group, Chinese Americans have, in one sense, integrated into American society occupationally and residentially, while retaining their own values and ethnic identity. It is no small achievement, against great odds.

Chapter 7

THE JAPANESE

T HE HISTORY of Japanese Americans is a story of tragedy and triumph. Few people ever came to America more predisposed and determined to be good Americans. Few met such repeated rebuffs and
barriers—including barriers of mass internment camps—or more completely triumphed over it all, across a broad spectrum of economic,
social, and political success.

Much of the history of Japanese Americans was shaped by attitudes,
prejudices, and discrimination against Chinese Americans, who preceded them to the United States by a generation. Both groups were
lumped together in the popular mind as Orientals or as "the yellow
peril," although in fact they have been and remained separate and
distinct groups. International relations between Japan and the United
States also influenced the history of Japanese Americans. But in the
end, the unusual history of Japanese Americans was shaped by the
unusual qualities these people brought with them across the Pacific.

155

JAPAN

Emigration from Japan to the United States began in the late nineteenth century, at a crucial stage in the history of Japan. In 1868, the ruling shoguns of the Tokugawa clan were overthrown, to be replaced not only by a new set of political rulers but also by a whole new set of values and national aspirations. The Meiji Restoration of 1868 marked the beginning of modern Japan, emerging from centuries of feudalism and isolation into modern industrialism and into international commerce, cultural exchange, and war.

Japan had long been one of the world's most isolated nations. When the first *Encyclopaedia Britannica* was published, in the eighteenth century, it covered all that was known about Japan in the West in one sentence, giving its latitude and longitude.[1] As late as the middle of the nineteenth century, very restricted access to Japan was permitted in only one port, Nagasaki. Japan's isolation was forcibly ended in 1854, when Commodore Perry brought a fleet of U.S. Navy fighting ships into Tokyo Bay and induced the Japanese government to sign a treaty giving broader access to the country by Americans. This action not only brought Japan into contact with Western ideas and technology. It also made it painfully clear how far behind the West Japan was at that point in its history, and how costly its total isolation had been. In a sense, it set the agenda for Japanese political developments for the next hundred years—equaling and surpassing the West. Resentment of the West for its arrogance was combined, or alternated with, admiration for its accomplishments that made such power possible. Japan of the Meiji Restoration was a nation all but obsessed with the West. It was the Japanese of that era who immigrated to America. It was the culture and values of that period that remained dominant in Japanese-American communities in the United States, long after Japan itself had evolved further. Japanese immigrants to other countries at other times carried a very different culture with them. As a twentieth-century writer in Japan observed: "If you want to see Japan of the Taisho Era (1912–1926), go to Brazil; if you want to see Japan of the Meiji Era (1868–1912), go to America."[2]

Japanese Attitudes Toward the West

Meiji Japan introduced the study of English in its secondary schools in 1876,[3] permitted the establishment of Christian churches and schools,[4] and its leaders and intellectuals publicly expressed strong admiration for the United States and the American way of life. The United States was described as "an earthly paradise,"[5] a "benefactor" to Japan by ending its isolation,[6] and American freedom was extolled as something to be both envied and emulated.[7] Government-issued textbooks in the schools held up Benjamin Franklin and Abraham Lincoln as models to be followed by Japanese children, even more so than Japanese heroes.[8] Perhaps never before has a foreign people been so indoctrinated with the American way of life as those of Meiji Japan. The desire to win the acceptance and respect of Americans was to become and remain a major theme in the later history of Japanese Americans, descendants of those who emigrated from Japan in the Meiji Era.

The perception of the West in Meiji Japan induced both self-denigration and ultranationalistic self-assertion—the latter sometimes viewed by the Japanese themselves as a psychological defense overcompensation.[9] Both assertions of inferiority of the Japanese people and denials of it were frequent in Japanese publications of the Meiji Era.[10] For example, in the 1880s, a Japanese writer bluntly asserted that the Japanese people "do not have ability," and another Japanese writer spoke of the "slow comprehension power and weak physique of our people."[11] Ultranationalism, traditionalism, and militarism were among the reactions to such feelings. The worship of the emperor as the divine leader of the Japanese race was an innovation of the later Meiji period—not yet the pervasive influence that it was to become in Japan. Immigrants to the United States were already adults by the time emperor worship reached its zenith and were so critical of it and other aspects of Japanese ultranationalism that many publications by Japanese Americans were banned in Japan.

Some indication of Japan's internal ambivalence was the emotional reaction in Japan to its successful war against China (1895) and then against Russia (1905)—the first time an Asian nation had defeated a Western nation. Because Japan "has defeated the ancient and great country of China," one Japanese newspaper editorialized, the "diffident Japanese people" were now convinced that "they are not inferior" to other races.[12] Before this, the Japanese had viewed "the civilized nations of the West as the penniless do the extremely rich. . . ." That is, "outwardly they talk big, saying they are people and we are people, but if their innermost thoughts are probed they fear Western capability, power and knowledge and are resigned to the thought that they possibly cannot ever win in competition with them. . . ."[13] By 1899,

Japan was confident enough to end the extraterritoriality that it had granted Westerners, and in the early twentieth century, it was ready to challenge and defeat czarist Russia.

Economic Conditions

Internally, Meiji Japan wrestled with the problem of maintaining traditional control while dismantling feudalism and selectively adopting Western ideas, including capitalism and modern technology. This involved many social dislocations and political stresses. Modern conceptions of property and contracts gave farmers freedom of movement and occupation[14] but also enabled landowners to oust tenant farmers from the land whenever this proved economically expedient.[15] The old samurai warriors were pensioned off and declined economically and socially,[16] pulling down with them the merchants and craftsmen who had served their needs.[17] New export markets brought prosperity to some industries, such as silk and tea production. But competition from imports brought declines to other Japanese industries, such as cotton cloth. Farmers, who were 80 percent of the population, suffered from heavy taxes continued from the previous (Tokugawa) regime—and engaged in numerous riots, also continued from the previous regime.[18]

Population and Migration

Overlaying these economic and political developments was the rapid growth of Japanese population. The Japanese population grew 30 percent in just over a quarter of a century, reaching 44 million in 1900.[19] This was due to both declining death rates, with improvements in sanitation, and to rising birthrates.[20] The additional population flowed from the countryside into the cities. The population in agriculture continued at the same level as before, while city populations swelled. The average standard of living of the middle class rose, but the dislocations were severe for many, as indicated by such things as rising unemployment and family suicide rates.[21]

Meiji Japan was a country in which people could no longer simply follow ready-made patterns of work and life, as in feudal times, but now had to look for work and seek to make a place for themselves in the world. Many sought opportunities overseas, where standards of living were much higher than in Japan. Contemporary American workers were earning five to ten times what Japanese workers were receiving in Japan.[22] Although the Japanese had long been a village-bound people, the new economic conditions of the Meiji Era had made internal migration a familiar pattern, both to those who relocated to

The Japanese

the city and those who became migratory workers moving from one end of the country to the other.[23] The tension between village-consciousness and migratory work patterns was resolved by leaving and returning. Many traveled to seek economic benefits, within Japan and beyond, and yet came back to live among family and neighborhoods and to be buried with their ancestors. Leaving for a foreign land was not seen as emigration but as a sojourn, as in the manner of the Italians or the Chinese. But while many Japanese carried out their plans for return migration, many others did not—also like the Italians and the Chinese.

The decision to migrate, even temporarily, was not a random individual decision. Neither was the destination chosen. In Japan, as in other countries, the particular destinations and experiences of the initial emigrants strongly affected the later migration patterns of those from their respective localities in Japan. This continued to be true even in post-World-War II Japan. For example, 90 percent of those who emigrated from Miho Village in postwar Japan settled in one specific area of Canada.[24] More than 90 percent of Okinawan immigrants to the United States went to Hawaii, while 8 percent reached the continental United States.[25] In an earlier era, over half of all Okinawans from one district went to the Philippines.[26] Ironically, one of the Japanese prefectures that sent a concentration of people to the United States during the initial immigration period and in the twentieth century was Hiroshima.[27]

Part of the reason for such patterns were human ties based on family, friends, or local acquaintances. Partly it was the result of the activities of commercial recruitment organizations that found it economical to concentrate in a limited area in soliciting people to work overseas.[28]

Emigration began in the first year of the Meiji Era, 1868, when 148 contract laborers sailed from Japan to Hawaii. Mutual dissatisfaction of Hawaiians and Japanese led the Japanese government to intervene, repatriating some workers immediately and allowing no others to go to Hawaii for many years. Japan's interest in Japanese overseas, and its possession of the national power and prestige to intervene in their behalf, were factors distinguishing Japan from contemporary China, which was too weak to prevent itself from being dismembered, much less effectively act on behalf of overseas Chinese. The general effectiveness of Japan's control of working conditions abroad need not be exaggerated, however, but it was there and was an influence to be reckoned with.

Dire economic conditions in Japan in 1885[29] forced the Japanese government to reconsider its ban on immigration to Hawaii. In 1886, an informal agreement between Hawaii and Japan permitted the resumption of Japanese migration, which supplied the growing sugar plantations with much-needed workers.[30] Japan controlled the selection of these temporary emigrants. Whereas the first Japanese emigrants had been urbanized workers from the prefectures of Hiroshima and Yamaguchi, the later contract laborers were from a farming and fishing community in the latter prefecture,[31] avoiding the mismatching of workers and work that had contributed to the early mutual disappointments of the Japanese and the Hawaiians. Almost all the Japanese who went to Hawaii in this era became plantation workers in the sugarcane fields. They were overwhelmingly young males.

Japanese migration to the United States began in the same era as their movement to Hawaii, which did not become an American possession until 1898. Japanese migration to the mainland of the United States was just over 200 in the decade of the 1860s, less than 200 in the decade of the 1870s, but rose rapidly thereafter. More than 2,000 Japanese moved to the mainland of the United States during the 1880s, then tripled this during the 1890s and reached a peak of more than 100,000 in the first decade of the twentieth century.[32] After the restrictive American immigration laws of the 1920s, very few Japanese entered the United States. The Japanese migration was predominantly male—seven times as many males as females in 1890 and twenty-four times as many in 1900[33]—and involved much return migration.

Many stayed, however. Less than half the passports issued by Japan for travel to the United States in the 1880s and 1890s were ever returned, whereas most Japanese who went to Russia or China did return their passports.[34] The sex imbalance among Japanese in Hawaii was less, although still substantial. There were three and a half males to every female among the Japanese in Hawaii in 1900, about two to one in 1910, and only 16 percent more males than females by 1930.[35] The migration of Japanese to the United States thus had the classic characteristics of a temporary or tentative migration. The Japanese government in fact designated the emigrants as temporary, and American laws growing out of anti-Chinese feelings made Asians ineligible for American citizenship. Nevertheless, many who came chose to stay.

The people who left Japan were usually neither the lowest nor the highest classes. Although the Japanese are justly known for their hard work and careful saving, such traits were by no means universal across the class structure. In Meiji Japan, there were lower classes in which "the money earned by the right hand is quickly spent by the left hand" and in which absenteeism from work was common right after payday.[36] Such people did not go to America. Neither did the nobility. The Japanese who migrated to Hawaii or to the United States were the ambitious young men of limited means, from farming backgrounds, who could get family and village notables to vouch for them and to agree to be responsible for their passage expenses.

They more than repaid their debts. The average amount of money sent back annually by migrants from the Hiroshima prefecture in the early twentieth century was more than two years' average earnings in Japan.[37] Similar patterns were found in other prefectures. The average savings brought back to Japan by migrants from one district of Hiroshima were greater than the average annual income of the top one percent of the Japanese population.[38] Such results reflected the great differences in economic conditions between Japan and the United States, as well as the frugality of Japanese migrants.

Many of those who returned to Japan could not only pay off obligations incurred for passage money but had enough left to buy substantial amounts of farmland or to go into business.[39] Japanese villages that had many emigrants in the United States or migrants returning from the United States tended to be visibly more prosperous—even if they had been poverty-stricken before.[40] Homes were more expensive and often of Western design. Nationally, the sums of money were significant alongside Japan's international balance of payments.[41] Locally, as in Hiroshima prefecture, the remittances and sums brought back amounted to more than half as much as the whole prefecture government spent.[42] In short, the importance of Japanese migrants in America was substantial in Japan. It may even be that the money earned in America helped build Hiroshima into such an industrial center that it became a prime military target in World War II.

THE JAPANESE IN AMERICA

The Japanese were initially welcomed, both in Hawaii and in the United States. They were a preselected group of healthy young men of good reputation, ambitious enough to venture thousands of miles from their homeland. They made excellent workers in the hard labor of Hawaiian sugarcane plantations. On the mainland of the United States, about 40 percent began as agricultural laborers,[43] and the rest worked in a variety of other strenuous laboring tasks on railroads and in mines, lumber mills, canneries, meat-packing plants, and similar arduous occupations.[44] Some became personal servants to affluent Americans. In all these occupations, the Japanese accepted low pay, long hours, and difficult working conditions without complaint. One indication of their diligence is that, when they were paid on a piece-work basis in agriculture, they earned up to twice as much as other laborers.[45]

When the Japanese worked as assistants to whites, they willingly carried out not only the responsibilities of their own jobs but often many of the duties belonging to the white workers. In this way, they acquired higher skills and experience that could later be useful to themselves.[46]

Like some others speaking a foreign language and having special diets, the Japanese often worked together, supervised by a labor con-tractor of their own nationality.[47] The Japanese migrants were marvels of thrift as well as industry, steadily saving small amounts from wages that were low by American standards but high by the standards of Japan.[48] When the Japanese were paid by the hour, instead of by piece-work, they were initially paid less than whites (about 14 percent less),[49] but about half the Japanese were either contract laborers or pieceworkers and in these cases earned more than whites doing the same work.[50]

The very virtues of the Japanese eventually turned others against them. While Japanese migrants made excellent employees, that made them rivals feared and hated by American workers and American la-bor unions. AFL President Samuel Gompers denounced Asian workers and refused to allow them into unions, even in segregated locals.[51] The thrift, diligence, and ambitions of the Japanese meant that increasing numbers of them began to move up from the ranks of labor to become small farmers or small businessmen. With that, the American farmers and businessmen who had welcomed the Japanese as employees turned bitterly against them as rivals. Moreover, the occupational and geographical concentration of the Japanese in a relatively few special-ties in a few communities in California made them far more visible targets than otherwise. As the Japanese in California moved up from the ranks of agricultural laborers to tenant farmers or (more rarely) landowners,[52] the hostility against them as competitors rose from the

162

white agricultural laborers to the white farmers. The additional hostility—now including a more influential class—was enough to launch a
wave of anti-Japanese legislation and practices that continued for decades in California. Chief among these was the Alien Land Law of 1913,
which forbade the owning of California land by aliens ineligible for
citizenship—that is, Asians in general and Japanese in particular. At
the national level, California led the political drive to stop Japanese
immigrants from being admitted to the United States.

Because Japan was emerging as a major world power around the
turn of the century—having defeated China in war in 1895 and Russia
in 1905—the ending of Japanese immigration to the United States
could not be done in the same abrupt, unilateral, and contemptuous
manner in which Chinese immigration had been stopped a generation
earlier. A face-saving device was worked out between the American
and Japanese governments, known as the Gentlemen's Agreement of
1908. Under the terms of this agreement, Japan itself severely limited
the number of immigrants to the United States, and the American government allowed the wives of existing Japanese in the United States to
join their husbands and for parents and children to be reunited here.
In this way, the extreme sex imbalance that accompanied the cutoff of
Chinese immigration was not quite so severe among Japanese Americans. Much of the reduced emigration from Japan after the Gentlemen's Agreement consisted of women. While initially the sex
imbalance among the Japanese on the mainland of the United States
was comparable to that among the first generation of Chinese—about
twenty-four Japanese men to every Japanese woman in 1900—the imbalance was reduced substantially over the years. By 1910, there were
"only" seven Japanese men to every Japanese woman and by 1920 less
than two to one.[53] Some of the women who came were wives joining
their husbands, and some were women married in Japan by proxy so
that they could be legally brought to America. These latter were so-
called "picture brides" chosen by the family in Japan and accepted by
the Japanese male in America after having seen a photograph. Arranged marriages were common in Japan, and these transpacific couples were typically matched by regional and social backgrounds,[54] but
the practice was shocking to Americans and added to anti-Japanese
feeling. Nevertheless, the forming of a family on American soil
marked a putting down of roots. With this act, the Japanese were no
longer migrants or sojourners. They became Japanese Americans.
Many continued to return to Japan—including some of the females

sent from Japan.[55] Those who stayed were, however, the first generation of Japanese-American immigrants—the *Issei*, as distinguished from the *Nisei* (second generation) and *Sansei* (third generation).

The Immigrant Generation

Unlike other nations, Japan did not send America its tired, its poor, its huddled masses. The Japanese were perhaps unique among immigrants to America in the extent to which they were a highly selected sample of their homeland population. They were not usually from wealthy or affluent families, however. The average sum of money brought by Japanese immigrants to America ranged from about eleven dollars in 1896 to a high of twenty-six dollars in 1904—more like the poverty-stricken eastern and southern European immigrants than like the emigrants from northern and western Europe.[56] Their selectivity was not financial but in terms of human potential.

The male *Issei* were a group preselected in Japan by the government for their health, character, and willingness to work.[57] They also grew up in an era when the people of Japan were predisposed to accept and emulate the American way of life. The women who sailed across the Pacific to join them in America were sufficiently traditional and dutiful to go halfway around the world to marry men selected for them, sight unseen, by their parents in Japan. Both the males and the females were an uncommon generation, in terms of their values and self-discipline. The rising role of Japan on the world scene made it easy for them to maintain their pride in being Japanese, while following American ideals that were already part of the culture in Meiji Japan.

The *Issei* were an educated people who valued reading, although their occupations were overwhelmingly manual (in either agriculture or industry). Almost all could read and write Japanese, and numerous Japanese-language newspapers flourished among them.[58] While literacy in Japanese was of no immediate economic value to American employers, it was indicative of their cultural level—and literacy even in a foreign language has long been associated with economic progress in America for many races and nationalities.[59] In short, education is generally a symptom of other social characteristics, such as local, class or family aspirations and the inculcation of individual values and traits likely to help realize such aspirations. Among Japanese males born in Japan, the general level of education in the prefecture from which they originated was more highly correlated with their later success in America than was their own individual education.[60] The ambitions and

164

character traits of their locality may have been more fundamental factors in their level of success.

Quantitatively, the Japanese immigration to the United States was quite small, despite widespread cries of "yellow hordes" or a "yellow peril" in California in the early twentieth century.[61] The largest immigration recorded for any year was about 30,000 Japanese in 1907 and 40,000 Chinese in 1882.[62] Even if unrecorded illegal immigration was enough to double these figures, they would still amount to a tiny fraction of the immigration from Europe. At its peak in 1907, Japanese immigration was less than 3 percent of the total immigration to the United States.[63] Moreover, the return migration to Japan was high. From the time of the Gentlemen's Agreement of 1908 to the complete cutoff of immigration from Japan (and other countries) in 1924, about 160,000 Japanese arrived and about 70,000 departed.[64] Their concentration in parts of California created an impression of a much larger Japanese "invasion" than in fact existed, and even in California, the Japanese were never more than 3 percent of the total population.[65] As a noted economic historian observed: "Seldom have so few innocuous people inspired so much irrational hatred and apprehension."[66]

In Hawaii, where the Japanese were a larger proportion—more than 20 percent—of the population,[67] the alarm was not nearly so great. However, even in Hawaii, there was pay discrimination against the Japanese and efforts to block their rise into skilled occupations.[68] A strike of Japanese agricultural laborers in 1909 exacerbated relations between the whites and the Japanese, although it produced some benefits to the Japanese fieldhands.[69]

Discrimination in pay against the first Japanese immigrants eroded as Japanese Americans became farmers and employers of Japanese farm laborers. Initially, white farm laborers were paid more by the hour than were the Japanese but received less when both were paid on a piecework basis because the Japanese workers produced more output.[70] However, Japanese farmers paid Japanese farm workers higher wages than the white farmers paid them and so forced the white farmers to increase the pay of Japanese employees. After 1909, the discrimination against Japanese farm workers had virtually disappeared. A decade later, Japanese farm workers actually received higher wages than white farm workers due to the greater efficiency of the Japanese, which was now widely recognized.[71]

The Japanese tenant farmers also prospered, even though they paid higher rents than whites for the same land. This economic discrimination against the Japanese had its political offset, however. The higher rents paid by Japanese tenant farmers meant that an influential class—large, white landowners—had an incentive to resist attempts to force the Japanese off the land altogether, as the original version of the Alien Land Bill attempted to do.[72] The political compromise that went into law allowed the Japanese to *lease* land, even if they could not own it. These laws passed both houses of the California Legislature by nearly unanimous votes[73]—an indication of the strong anti-Japanese feeling in California, which would lead to many other laws and practices directed against *Issei.*

The actual effectiveness of the Alien Land Law in stopping the economic rise of the Japanese is much more questionable. World War I followed almost immediately after the Alien Land Law of 1913, and because many white farm workers left agriculture for better paying jobs in the factories, the Japanese were in great demand as tenants. Moreover, loopholes in the law allowed many of the more prosperous tenant farmers to become de facto landowners. With the birth of children of the *Nisei* generation, there were now Japanese who were native-born American citizens—able to own land and exercise many other rights denied their parents. Much land was owned by Japanese families in the names of children. Sometimes sympathetic whites held legal title to land actually farmed as their own by Japanese farmers who bought it. Some dummy corporations were also formed to evade the Alien Land Law.[74] By 1920, these evasions had become so widespread and so well known that these loopholes were plugged by a new law, passed as an initiative by a three-to-one vote of the electorate.[75] The Alien Land Law of 1920 now forbade the leasing of land by aliens "ineligible for citizenship" (Asians), as well as ownership, and sought to outlaw the holding of land in the name of native-born children. But court decisions and new evasive devices enabled the Japanese to hang on in California agriculture.[76] A majority of employed Japanese males were farmers as late as 1940.[77] The law was not wholly ineffective in reducing the acreage owned by the Japanese[78] or in creating costly obstacles to their economic rise; it simply did not completely stop them. One reason was that—almost inevitably—a growing proportion of the Japanese-American population consisted of people born in the United States and therefore not covered by the laws against "aliens ineligible for citizenship." The Fourteenth Amendment prevented the law from specifying the Japanese as its intended victims. By 1930, about half of all Japanese Americans in the continental United States were native-born.[79] By 1940, about a third of the value of all commercial truck crops grown in California was produced by Japanese Americans.[80]

In addition to their success in agriculture, Japanese Americans became celebrated in California for their skillful work in the related fields of entrepreneurial or contract gardening. The "Japanese gardener" became an institution among the white middle-class homeowners whose lawns and yards he tended on weekly visits. It was a small business that required little capital and yet offered independence, for the gardener who collected fees from many homeowners was not the servant of any. As early as 1928, there were 1,300 Japanese gardeners in southern California alone.[81] Another offshoot of the Japanese success in agriculture was the produce market, usually marketing the output of Japanese farms. In 1929, there were more than 700 Japanese-owned produce markets in Los Angeles alone.[82]

The Japanese also moved into entrepreneurial ventures not associated with the soil, and were highly successful there as well. By 1919, almost half of the hotels and one quarter of the grocery stores in Seattle were owned by Japanese.[83] In Los Angeles, *Issei* owned dry cleaners, lunch counters, and fisheries, as well as cheap hotels.[84] Some of the Japanese-owned businesses began as enterprises serving the needs of their own immediate ethnic community, especially in meeting the special food preferences of the Japanese. However, the number and volume of business of many Japanese American enterprises went far beyond what could be supported by the ethnic community alone. Moreover, some of the Japanese-owned businesses, such as gardening and produce markets, were known to have served an almost exclusively *non*-Japanese clientele.

The ability of the Japanese to move up from manual labor to small-business ownership was only partly a result of their own individual thriftiness. They, like the Chinese, made use of revolving credit associations to pool funds to finance new businesses. But this simple institution depended for its success on a whole complex of relationships of trust, based on family and community ties and concepts of honor, which would have made defaults virtually impossible. Equally important—and for some businesses more important—was the sheer willingness to undertake the risks of entrepreneurship and the diligence and persistence to make a success of a new business. The amount of capital needed to become a gardener was only a small truck, a lawn mower, some shears, rakes, and other similar tools. The personal equipment was much more decisive. The reputation that the Japanese had earned as diligent and trustworthy workers in such occupations as farm laborers and houseboys made many homeowners willing to trust them in the new field of contract gardening, which involved to some extent exposing their homes and valuables to them.

The principal occupations of more than 90 percent of *Issei* men were in farming, business, and blue-collar work. All the professional and clerical workers of that generation put together added up to less than 10 percent of the *Issei*.[85] In short, the initial economic rise of Japanese Americans was *not* due to education nor was it in occupations requiring education. *After* the *Issei* had achieved a measure of economic success, they were able to send their children—the *Nisei*—on to higher education and from there into the professions and other occupations requiring formal training.

The Japanese, like the Chinese, studiously avoided political agitation for their rights, although they did fight numerous court cases. As in the case of the Chinese, the fever pitch of anti-Oriental feeling could not be maintained over decades, as the Japanese quietly went their way and prospered. Moreover, the Japanese-American community did not provide the sensationalist press with a stream of lurid stories about tong wars, opium dens, and vice districts, such as came out of contemporary Chinatowns. The quiet and often rural life of Japanese Americans did not make news.

Japanese families of the first generation were larger than American families in general. The birthrate of Japanese Americans was four times that of whites,[86] lending credence to the fears of those afraid of "inundation" by this very small group of people. However, one reason for high birthrate statistics was that a disproportionate number of Japanese Americans were young adults in the prime of life. Very few elderly people or children had immigrated. Moreover, the young men and women were from a rural culture, where fertility rates are usually high around the world.

Japanese families were extremely stable; very few divorces ever occurred. The children were controlled strictly, but their well-being was paramount to the parents, who often sacrificed greatly for the children's current and future well-being. Strong family obligations were reciprocal. One sign of the parental care among Japanese Americans is that their children had far fewer accidents than either white or black children.[87]

Japanese children in the public schools were notable for their obedience, politeness, and hard work and were welcomed by their teachers. The schools attended were almost always integrated because of the

The Japanese

small number of Japanese children at any given place, and they were typically treated well by their teachers.[88] These children's school achievements were equal to those of white children and so were their IQ scores, despite the fact that they came from homes where English was not spoken and where parents' occupations—and their own occupational prospects, in light of contemporary discrimination—made formal education of little apparent value.[89] It was simply regarded as a matter of honor that they do well. Upholding the honor of the family and the honor of the Japanese people in America were values constantly taught by the *Issei* to their children. Strong family control, pressure, and influence were supplemented by that of community organizations and by the informal but pervasive gossip in the small, close-knit Japanese-American communities. Such social controls extended well beyond children. These American communities were notable for their lack of crime, juvenile delinquency, or other forms of social pathology. From the earliest period of immigration, the Japanese-American community had far fewer crimes than other Americans, and the crimes they did commit were less serious. This was true both on the mainland of the United States and in Hawaii.[90] Deviant behavior brought forth pressure not only from the individual's family but also from other relatives, neighbors, and members of the Japanese-American community at large. Few individuals could stand up to such pressures. The rare individual who continued to defy community norms could find himself being shipped back to Japan, rather than being allowed to tarnish the image of Japanese Americans in the larger society. Unbridled individualism was not part of the Japanese system of values, in which the well-being of the community was paramount. There is no Japanese word for "privacy."[91]

The Japanese Association was founded soon after the arrival of the *Issei* on American soil. Its branches in various cities served both as internal community control organizations and as liaisons with the outside world. The Japanese Association helped to curtail prostitution, gambling, and other activities that would reflect adversely on Japanese Americans in the eyes of the larger society. It sponsored recreational and civic activities. It also reported crimes or grievances of individual Japanese to the police, other American authorities, or—because the *Issei* were legally citizens of Japan—to the Japanese consulate.[92] It was, in short, the organized voice of the first generation of Japanese Americans.

Smaller organizations also crisscrossed the Japanese-American communities. People from particular regions of Japan belonged to their own respective prefecture organizations in America. These provided recreational and social outlets and aid to those in distress. This aid was accepted only in dire need because of the disgrace that was felt in accepting charity. However, between family aid and aid from internal Japanese-American community organizations, almost no Japanese American went on public relief. Even after the San Francisco earthquake of 1906, when 10,000 Japanese were left homeless, virtually none applied for relief because their prefecture organizations organized massive aid for them.[93] During the Great Depression of the 1930s, almost no Japanese went on relief.[94]

The Nisei

The "generation gap" between first and second generations of Japanese Americans was in some respects greater than that in other immigrant groups. The belated formation of families, due to the initial sex imbalance among the *Issei*, meant that the age gap between parents and children was larger than usual. As of 1942, the average age of *Issei* males was fifty-five, while that of *Nisei* was only seventeen.[95] Most of the *Issei* spoke Japanese and little English, while most of the *Nisei* spoke English and very little Japanese.[96] In the 1930s, three quarters of the *Issei* were Buddhists while half the *Nisei* were Christians.[97] Moreover, the values that the *Nisei* learned at school and from the American culture were often in conflict with the values of the *Issei*, especially on such things as dating and arranged marriages.

Attempts were made to strengthen the hold of traditional Japanese values on the *Nisei* by sending them to Japanese-language schools after public school hours or on weekends. These schools, often taught by instructors imported from Japan, sometimes taught the ultranationalism that had become increasingly strident in Japan. To some of the *Nisei*, these schools were seen as social institutions in which to meet other Japanese-American youths. To others, the indoctrination was offensive and another cause of friction between generations. As a high school student in 1939, Daniel Inouye was thrown bodily out of such a school in Hawaii when he objected to what was being said. However, these schools were diverse in politics and religion, and the *Nisei* were diverse in the extent to which they attended—virtually all going to the schools in Honolulu and virtually none in some areas of the continental United States.[98]

As the *Nisei* came of age, they formed their own separate organizations, finally consolidated into the Japanese American Citizens' League (JACL), which eventually supplanted the Japanese Association of the *Issei* as the voice of Japanese Americans. The JACL promoted Americanism in culture and politics.[99] The *Nisei* were not subject to the legal discriminations their parents had suffered. Their efforts were bent toward gaining more acceptance in the larger American society, to which they were qualified by virtue of their education and acculturation.

One sign of the internal generational stresses within the Japanese-American community were the bilingual newspapers that circulated there. These papers not only covered the same stories in both languages—to reach both *Issei* and *Nisei*—but often covered their political stories from different editorial points of view.[100] While organizations composed of *Issei* tended to either support or rationalize Japan's aggressions in the 1930s,[101] the JACL creed of the *Nisei* began "I am proud to be an American citizen of Japanese ancestry" and expressed a willingness to defend the United States "against all enemies."[102] That was written in 1940. Just one year later, that loyalty would be put to the acid test.

Wartime Internment

On December 7, 1941, Japan launched a massive surprise attack on the American fleet at Pearl Harbor, Hawaii—inflicting the most catastrophic defeat ever suffered by Americans. The shock was compounded by the facts that (1) the sneak attack was launched in the midst of a peace mission by Japanese diplomats in Washington and that (2) a simultaneous military offensive launched by Japan in the western Pacific inflicted a series of devastating defeats on the United States and other Western powers over the next several months. Fears were rampant that the West Coast of the United States would be the next target of military attack or even invasion.

American anger and apprehensions about Japan turned also against Japanese Americans. This was sometimes expressed sporadically in verbal abuse or outbreaks of physical violence, more officially in FBI roundups of about 1,500 Japanese Americans as potential threats to American security—a roundup publicly supported by *Nisei* leaders, who saw the pro-Japanese position of their elders as disloyalty to the United States and as a threat to Japanese Americans in general.[103] However, the scope of the hysteria and the roundups expanded at unpredictable intervals, and in February 1942, President Roosevelt signed an Executive Order giving the army authority to evacuate "any and all persons" from "military areas" as designated by the army and to provide "accommodations" for them elsewhere.[104] The Executive Order did not mention Japanese Americans, but it was they alone who were rounded up en masse on the West Coast. Between March and November 1942, more than 100,000 men, women, and children were shipped off to huge internment camps in isolated, barren regions scattered from California to Arkansas.[105] These locations were "places where nobody had lived before and no one has lived since."[106]

Ironically, no such roundup was made of the 150,000 Japanese Americans in Hawaii, where the attack on Pearl Harbor occurred. The virulent anti-Japanese feelings in the continental United States and the personality of the general in charge of the Western Defense Command apparently had more to do with the internment policy than the "military necessity" used to justify it. General J. L. DeWitt was an elderly career bureaucrat with experience primarily in supply units rather than in combat units and was held in low esteem by other generals.[107] The internment camps for Japanese Americans represented a vast expansion of his bureaucratic empire and public importance. But what made that possible was the pervasive hysteria and hostility toward Japanese, whether in Japan or in America. General DeWitt echoed a widespread opinion in the post-Pearl Harbor days when he declared publicly, "A Jap's a Jap, and it makes no difference whether he is a citizen or not."[108] The public support for the internment of Japanese Americans stretched across the spectrum, from the Hearst newspapers and racist bigots like columnist Westbrook Pegler on the Right to outstanding liberals like Earl Warren[109] and Walter Lippmann,[110] Leftists like Carey McWilliams,[111] Vito Marcantonio,[112] and the editors of the Communist *Daily Worker* and *People's World*.[113] The Executive Order authorizing internment was accepted as legitimate by the American Civil Liberties Union[114] and by a unanimous Supreme Court. But despite the virtually unanimous fears of the times, not a single Japanese American was ever convicted of a single act of sabotage during all of World War II.

The impact of the mass internment on the Japanese Americans was devastating. The financial impact alone was massive. There were forced, hasty sales of homes, furniture, and other belongings before being shipped off to internment. Businesses built over a lifetime of hard work had to be liquidated in a few weeks. The financial losses of the Japanese Americans were estimated by the government itself at about $400,000,000—at 1942 price levels.[115] Added to the financial losses were the many personal traumas of forced uprooting and internment and the body blow to the leadership of the Japanese American Citizens' League, representing the *Nisei* efforts to become, and be

172

accepted as, good Americans. The JACL's official position was one of cooperation with the internment, realizing the futility of resistance and the implication of disloyalty to America if they were to attempt to resist. But this position made the JACL vulnerable to the anger and scorn of those Japanese Americans who saw the internment as a racist slap in the face, despite all their previous efforts to be good, productive citizens. Sometimes bitter internal dissension erupted among the interned Japanese. A few of the more militant objectors renounced their American citizenship and even used force and threats to get other internees to do the same.[116]

By and large, however, Japanese Americans accepted the internment as a grim fact of life and put their efforts into making the best of a bad situation. The camps typically had mass, primitive facilities—for eating in mess halls or using communal bathing and toilet facilities. Families were crowded into small quarters inside an area surrounded by barbed-wire fences and patroled by armed sentries.[117] The Japanese tried to "humanize" their environment by doing such things as planting gardens and building furniture out of scraps of wood.[118] But there were limits to beautification possible with "long rows of tar paper-covered wooden barracks" and rooms containing "a stove, a droplight, an iron cot and mattress."[119]

Life within the internment camps considerably altered traditional Japanese roles and patterns of life. The very low wages paid for performing various tasks in camp were the same for women as for men, for young or old, and so the role of the father as primary breadwinner was completely undermined. Moreover, those positions of responsibility in the camp administration available to Japanese Americans were available only to American citizens—that is, the younger generations, who were elevated above their elders. The tiny quarters packed together destroyed the privacy of the family. Family-centered activities such as meals were taken out of the home.

The manpower needs of wartime America began to erode the internment program, even before all the Japanese Americans had been put behind barbed wire. In the spring of 1942, some seasonal agricultural laborers were allowed furloughs to help ease farm labor shortages.[120] These furloughs were later changed to permanent relocations outside the camps, provided that the work was located outside the restricted military area and that the individuals had passed loyalty tests. In the summer of 1942, hundreds of *Issei* railroad workers were allowed to return to their jobs in eastern Oregon.[121] More than 4,000 *Nisei* college students were allowed to leave to resume their studies—in the East or

Midwest,[122] so as to circumvent rather than challenge the "military necessity" rationale for the Western Defense Command's roundup. The civilian authorities in charge of the internment camps were generally more sympathetic to the Japanese, and their various plans for releasing special groups were repeatedly denounced by the military.[123] Finally, however, even the military high command began to tap the manpower of Japanese Americans. In January 1943, the U.S. Army began to recruit *Nisei*,[124] who had previously been classified as ineligible for military service as "enemy aliens." Despite the anomaly of the situation, and the bitterness of some interned Japanese youth, most of those eligible seized the opportunity to prove their loyalty in combat.

More than 300,000 Japanese Americans fought in World War II. Separate Japanese-American units fought in the European theater of the war. They were sent into some of the bloodiest fighting of the war in 1943, and their 442nd Regimental Combat Unit emerged the most decorated combat unit in World War II, or in American history.[125] They suffered more than 9,000 casualties in action against Nazi troops[126] and earned fifty-two Distinguished Service Crosses and a Congressional Medal of Honor.[127] In the Pacific, several thousand Japanese Americans served as interpreters—a valuable military role, for the military forces of Japan often failed to code their messages, assuming that Americans could not understand Japanese. But there were "Nisei on every battlefront reading captured documents and passing information on to allied commanders."[128]

The tragic wartime experiences of the Japanese Americans proved ultimately to be a turning point in their history in the United States. Never had a group so proved their loyalty under impossible conditions. Gradually, more and more American officials advocated their cause—some within the government and others publicly. Eventually, even the Western Defense Command announced an end to the "military necessity" used to justify the roundup, and the civilian authorities announced that the camps would be closed down. President Roosevelt, whose Executive Order in 1942 had authorized the rounding up of Japanese Americans, was by mid-1944 publicly defending their loyalty.[129] By the end of 1944, the Supreme Court declared unconstitutional the internment of those Japanese who were American citizens.

Despite the large and irreparable losses suffered by the *Issei*, for the *Nisei* the internment camps marked the beginning of a new movement into American society and a rapid rise up the social and economic ladder. The old bonds of a narrow ethnic world were broken. No longer need they follow the few occupations in which their fathers had worked. In the internment camps, Japanese Americans worked at a wider range of jobs than in civilian life, where occupational licenses and other restrictive devices and practices constricted their occupational choices. The *Nisei*, as citizens, were privileged among the internees in the camps and were disproportionately represented among those first released from the camps. Their resettlement in eastern and midwestern locations opened up new opportunities. Their own dedicated work—whether as college students or as soldiers—won acceptance and support from other Americans.

Bigots were not completely silenced, and isolated "incidents" of varying degrees of seriousness occurred, particularly in California, as the interned Japanese made their way back from the camps in postwar America.[130] But a new trend was clearly marked in 1946, when, for the first time in California history, an anti-Japanese initiative was defeated by the voters—overwhelmingly.[131]

Postwar Nisei and Sansei

The prewar progress of Japanese Americans could not be simply resumed in the same patterns. Thousands of farms and businesses were irrevocably lost. Many of the *Issei* were simply too old to start them all over again, and lacked the education and acculturation to move into new fields with any great success. Contract gardening, however, could be readily resumed, and as late as 1958, about three quarters of all Japanese-owned businesses in Los Angeles were in this field. These are by no means inconsequential jobs. A 1963 survey found that a significant portion of the upper-income Japanese Americans as of that date were contract gardeners.[132]

The *Nisei* were, however, well educated and English speaking, free of the occupational constrictions based on citizenship requirements, and able to take on the informal barriers of bias among employers. As early as 1940, Japanese Americans had more education than whites, and the gap widened over the next decade.[133] The college degrees were almost never in liberal arts but were instead in applied areas such as engineering, optometry, or business administration.

By 1959, Japanese-American males on the mainland of the United States earned 99 percent of the income of whites.[134] For the total Japanese-American male population (including those in Hawaii), Japanese-American income was 98 percent of white income in the same age bracket.[135] By 1969, the average personal income of Japanese Americans was 11 percent above the national average, and average family income was 32 percent above.[136] The rise of Japanese Americans on the mainland was more rapid than in Hawaii—suggesting that the wartime internment need not have had a permanently negative effect. Perhaps it even had a positive effect—in narrowly economic terms—by freeing the *Nisei* from the restrictive bonds of parental expectations, particularly as regards taking over the family business rather than pursuing new fields. In this regard, many Japanese Americans themselves—including Senator S. I. Hayakawa—have credited the internment experience with improving their long-run mobility.[137]

Whatever the reasons, there was not only an economic rise but also a striking change in occupational distribution among Japanese Americans. In 1940, the proportion of Japanese Americans working in professional occupations was less than half that of whites, both in California and in Hawaii. By 1950, the Japanese Americans in California had narrowed the gap and by 1960 had slightly more representation than whites in professional occupations. In Hawaii, the Japanese still lagged behind whites in professional occupations.[138]

Along with a general socioeconomic rise of Japanese Americans, and a general decline in racism in postwar America,[139] has come a new pattern of residential dispersion and intermarriage. *Nisei* who worked in high-level white-collar jobs tended to live in predominantly white neighborhoods, and were less likely to belong to Japanese ethnic organizations. Indeed, in the continental United States, all-Japanese neighborhoods became unusual.[140] Intermarriage has increased over the decades, as the Japanese Americans dispersed occupationally and residentially. In the 1920s, only about 2 percent of all Japanese-American marriages in Los Angeles were with non-Japanese partners. In the immediate postwar period, this rose to 11–12 percent. By the late 1950s, the proportion had climbed to over 20 percent.[141] A similar pattern existed in Hawaii.[142]

The third generation of Japanese Americans—the *Sansei*—was born early in the wartime internment camps or in postwar America. A remarkable 88 percent of the *Sansei* have attended college, and 92 percent intend to become professionals.[143] Most of their elders consider them "too American,"[144] but they themselves—94 percent—say that they would like to be able to speak Japanese (meaning that they do not). Moreover, they are among the most vocal about the wartime internment,[145] of which they have no personal memory. Political militancy has been a phenomenon confined largely to the *Sansei*.[146] It has been a widespread phenomenon among many ethnic groups to find heightened or more militant group consciousness among the third generation[147]—that is, among those who have suffered least and have retained the least of the cultural characteristics of the group.

JAPANESE AMERICANS TODAY

There are today about 600,000 Japanese Americans.[148] About a third of them live in Hawaii, another third in California, and less than one-fifth live in the Northeast, Midwest, and South combined. Although they began in the United States as agricultural laborers and tenant farmers, today about 90 percent of Japanese Americans live in urban areas, and even among those in rural areas, most are not on farms.[149]

About 88 percent are native-born Americans, but nearly 70 percent of the working-age males (twenty-five to sixty-four years old) are only second-generation Americans.[150] The geographic location and urbanization of Japanese Americans are important factors in their above-average incomes. Less than 5 percent live in the low-income South, and most live in the high-income states of California and Hawaii. While their median family incomes are 32 percent above the national average, in California Japanese-American family income is only 15 percent above the statewide average,[151] and among urbanized California families, the Japanese Americans earn only 11 percent more than urbanized whites.[152] Still, this is a remarkable achievement for a group that has advanced in the face of decades of descriminatory laws and practices—and that had to start all over again after losing virtually everything during their internment in World War II. And this is only the second generation! The third generation (*Sansei*) is just entering adulthood, and the fourth generation (*Yonsei*) are still children.

The economic achievements of Japanese Americans today are due primarily to (1) their working more—a higher than average percentage are in the labor force,[153] a lower than average percentage are unemployed,[154] and a higher proportion of Japanese-American families have multiple income earners[155]—and to (2) higher than average levels of education, combined with a concentration in higher paying scientific and applied fields.[156] Historically, the Japanese Americans' rise came in occupations requiring little or no education—farming, contract gardening, small-business ownership—and only *after* the *Issei* had suc-

177

ceeded in these fields were they able to send the *Nisei* off to college to pursue professional careers. Education was not the cause of the Japanese Americans' initial rise, just as it was not the cause of the Jews' initial rise, although both groups consolidated and further enhanced their economic positions in later generations with formal schooling.

Family Earnings of Japanese-American Male-Headed Families
(Japanese Income as a Percentage of U.S. Income
in the Same Categories)

Education of Family Head	One-Income Families	Two-Income Families	Three or More Income Earners
Less than high school	107%	120%	140%
High school	105	120	118
College (1–3 years)	101	112	104
College (4 years)	84	104	123
Postgraduate (1 year)	90	108	111
Postgraduate (2 years or more)	83	100	106

SOURCE: 1970 U.S. Census, Public Use Sample.

The Japanese have no consistent income advantage in families with one breadwinner (see above), and in almost no category do they have an economic advantage as large as their 32 percent higher family incomes—which results from their different distribution among these categories. More Japanese are working, and more are in higher educational brackets.

The economic and social positions of Japanese-American families are enhanced by their smaller families. While the average American woman in the thirty-five to forty-four-year-old bracket has three children,[157] the average Japanese-American woman in the same age bracket has 2.2 children.[158] With fewer children to support and higher incomes, the Japanese-American family has not only a higher standard of living but also can more readily afford to send its children to college to perpetuate its advantages. But again, it is necessary to distinguish the situation of the current generation from the factors that led to the initial rise of Japanese Americans. The *Issei* had *larger* than average families, just as the Jewish immigrants had larger than average families. In neither case did the larger family imply neglected children or disruptive behavior in school. Later generations had smaller families to fit a new life-style and college aspirations for children.

By any index, Japanese Americans are assimilating. Nationally, about 12 percent of married Japanese-American men and about a third of married Japanese-American women had spouses of a different race in 1970.[159] In Los Angeles County in the early 1970s, about half of all new Japanese-American marriages were intermarriages.[160] The same was true of Hawaii.[161] Among the youth, the high grade point average of earlier generations of Japanese-American students was found to be gradually declining toward the norm, while social problems among them were rising.[162]

Japanese Americans have made notable contributions in many aspects of American life. The beautiful and imaginative designs of architect Minoru Yamasaki can be seen in buildings and structures from coast to coast, including the Woodrow Wilson School at Princeton, the Oberlin Conservatory of Music, the St. Louis Airport, and the Seattle World's Fair.[163] In the field of semantics, S. I. Hayakawa established a renowned scholarly reputation long before he became known to the general public as president of San Francisco State College and then United States senator. Japanese Americans have been relatively late participants in politics on the mainland but have been more active in Hawaii, where they have constituted a larger proportion of the population. In 1959, Daniel K. Inouye, a hero of World War II who lost an arm in battle and received a battlefield commission, was elected to the U.S. House of Representatives and later (1962) was elected to the U.S. Senate, where he still serves. In 1976, Hawaii also sent Masayuki Matsunaga to the U.S. Senate as the third Japanese-American senator[164]—3 percent of the Senate from less than half of 1 percent of the population. It was symbolic of the remarkable achievements of Japanese Americans.

IV

Americans from Africa

Chapter 8

THE BLACKS

BLACK AMERICANS were the only racial or ethnic group brought to America against their will. They came from a vast continent—larger than Europe—and initially spoke a great variety of languages and represented many very different cultures. In more than two centuries of bondage, their many ancestral languages and cultures faded away, and their genetic differences were amalgamated (together with a substantial mixture of Caucasian genes) to produce the American Negro—a cultural and biological product of the New World, rather than a direct descendant of any given African nation or culture.

Black Americans are thus among the oldest Americans, and their cultural heritage is one formed almost exclusively on American soil. In another sense, blacks are among the newer Americans—entering the larger society as a free people with an independent existence of their own only in 1863, with the abolition of slavery. Their arrival in urban America, after massive internal migrations, came even later, so that many (perhaps most) blacks today are only the second generation in the urban world in which they live. In that sense, blacks are about where the Irish were one hundred years earlier. In short, marking the

183

starting point from which to measure the progress of black people in the United States is not easy, and may vary with the particular issue.

While Africans were amalgamated in America, Afro-Americans were also differentiated—not according to ancestral cultures, as among other groups, but according to different histories in the United States. The time of acquiring freedom was a crucial differentiation. Although most American Negroes were freed by the Emancipation Proclamation of 1863, half a million were already free before then. These "free persons of color" had a history, a culture, and a set of values that continued to distinguish their descendants from other Negroes, well into the twentieth century. A third small but important segment of the black population consists of emigrants from the West Indies. They too have had a very different economic and social history from that of other blacks.

AFRICA

Although little or no African culture survives among American Negroes, the history of Africa is not without relevance to how and why masses of Africans came to be captured and sent to the Western Hemisphere as slaves. While the continent of Africa is larger than Europe, its coastline is not as long as that of Europe because Africa has few natural harbors indenting its coast. Africa's rivers are only intermittently navigable, according to terrain and season of the year. Dense jungles and vast deserts add to the difficulty of internal transportation and communication. Narrow coastal plains bounded by cliffs and mountains limited the size of coastal settlements. The net result has been a continent of highly fragmented and isolated peoples—speaking more than 800 languages and divided into myriad tribes. The political and military vulnerability of people in such conditions provided the opportunity for their mass enslavement by foreigners.

The great civilizations on the African continent arose where these geographic barriers were not so formidable. The 4,000-mile-long Nile River—mostly navigable—provided the economic and social basis for the ancient civilization of Egypt. Mediterranean ports and land routes to Asia also enabled the northern part of Africa to develop larger and more complex nations than Africa south of the Sahara. The more

The Blacks

united and powerful peoples of that region—the Arabs—became the first mass enslavers of African Negroes.

Slavery had long existed among the African tribes,[1] as it had existed for centuries among Europeans, going back to ancient Greece and Rome.[2] But massive commercial sales of Negro slaves began after the conquest of northern Africa by the Arabs in the eighth century. Arab slave traders penetrated down into the center of Africa and on the east coast as far south as Mozambique. In cooperation with local tribes, they captured or purchased slaves to take back with them across the Sahara Desert, which eventually became strewn with the skeletons of Negroes who died on the long march across the burning sands. The Arabs were notable as the most cruel of all slave masters.[3] As late as the nineteenth century, British explorer David Livingstone had nightmares for weeks after witnessing the treatment of slaves by Arabs.[4] Slavery was not completely abolished in the Arab world until after the middle of the twentieth century.[5]

Slavery in Europe had died out over the centuries, when Africans were brought to Spain by Arab slave traders. The Spanish and Portuguese eventually ventured to sub-Sahara Africa to capture their own slaves. By the time Columbus discovered America, Spain and Portugal already contained small but significant numbers of Negro slaves.[6] When the Spanish began to colonize the Western Hemisphere, they transported masses of slaves there from Africa to do the hard work. As the British, French, and Portuguese followed suit in exploring and colonizing, they also began to buy or seize masses of Africans to ship to the New World.

By the middle of the seventeenth century, 10,000 slaves per year were being transported across the Atlantic.[7] By the eighteenth century, the slave trade had reached a peak of 60,000 per year.[8] Over the centuries, nearly 10 million African slaves were shipped to the Western Hemisphere.[9] More than half came in the century ending in 1820. More than 80 percent came between the beginning of the eighteenth and the middle of the nineteenth centuries.[10] Many of the slaves came from a region of West Africa east of the River Niger—as many as from all the rest of Africa put together.[11] The Ashanti tribe alone sold thousands of other Africans into slavery.[12]

In addition to the millions actually transported across the Atlantic, many uncounted others died along the way—some fighting to defend their freedom in Africa, some killed trying to escape, some by suicide in captivity, and many by death at sea, during the hazards and horrors of the voyage to America. The loss of life at sea alone ranged from

185

about 9 to 16 percent of all African slaves shipped by the British, French, and Spanish in the eighteenth and nineteenth centuries[13] and ranged even higher in the seventeenth century and among Dutch slave ships.[14] A rough, conservative estimate would be that a million slaves died en route. This does not count the Africans killed by European diseases for which they lacked biological immunity,[15] just as many Europeans died from African diseases to which they were vulnerable.[16]

Out of a grand total of about 10 million African slaves who arrived in the Western Hemisphere, about 400,000 were shipped to the American colonies.

SLAVERY IN AMERICA

The United States held the largest number of slaves of any country in the Western Hemisphere—more than one-third of all the slaves in the hemisphere—in 1825. Yet other countries actually imported more slaves, and Brazil six times as many. The difference was that the United States was the only country in which the slave population reproduced itself and grew by natural increase. In the rest of the hemisphere, the death rate was so high and the birthrate so low that continuous replacements were imported from Africa. The conditions under which slaves were held were generally more brutal in other countries.[17] However, they were brutal in the United States as well. Whippings were common.[18] The sale of children away from their parents happened often enough to be a danger to be constantly feared.[19] The forcible separation of husbands and wives also occurred with considerable frequency—about one out of six couples.[20] Other cruelties and atrocities,[21] although sporadic, were inherent features in the institution of slavery and the caprice of slave owners.

In narrowly material terms, slaves in the United States were usually amply fed with low-quality food,[22] and their housing—although primitive by today's standards—was comparable to (or better than) that of contemporary European peasants or workers.[23] The average life span of nineteenth-century American slaves was slightly below that of whites in the United States, but the same as the life span in Holland and France and greater than that in Italy or Austria.[24] Slaves in the

The Blacks

United States lived an average of thirty-six years; peasants in Ireland, nineteen years. To the slave owner, slaves were an investment, and one to be safeguarded. For example, slave owners usually hired white workers—typically Irish immigrants—to do work considered too dangerous for slaves.[25]

The central feature of any slave system—preventing escape—was accomplished in the antebellum South, not by fences or guards, but by keeping the slave ignorant, dependent, and in fear. The overwhelming majority of slaves could neither read nor write, and most southern states made it a crime to teach them. Because slaves were kept in captivity by ignorance rather than by physical restraints, it was easy to escape a slave plantation temporarily[26] but very difficult to escape permanently. Patrols manned by local whites recaptured runaways and regulated or punished other slaves who were off their plantations for whatever reason.

The slaves were kept dependent on the slave owners for rations of food or clothing and for the organization of their daily lives and living conditions. A leading slave owner advised, "create in him a habit of perfect dependence on you. . . ."[27] This philosophy in practice was observed during the celebrated travels of Frederick Law Olmsted through the South. Olmsted concluded that the southern strategy was to try to train the slave to work and yet "prevent him from learning to take care of himself."[28]

With many generations of discouragement of initiative and with little incentive to work any more than necessary to escape punishment, slaves developed foot-dragging, work-evading patterns[29] that were to remain as a cultural legacy long after slavery itself disappeared. Duplicity[30] and theft[31] were also pervasive patterns among antebellum slaves, and these too remained long after slavery ended.

Among themselves, slaves had to evolve some pattern for living. Racial solidarity was basic and betrayal to whites unforgivable.[32] Even the slave driver—a slave immediately in charge of other slaves and authorized to mete out punishment—had to make his compromises within that framework.[33] On large plantations, some house servants might form personal attachments to members of the white household, but they too had to respect the line between internal differences among blacks and outright betrayal to whites.

The black world was ultimately the only world in which slaves could find emotional fulfillment and close attachments, and to become a pariah there meant personal devastation. The norms of the slave community therefore carried weight, even without official sanction or institutions to enforce them. Incest taboos, for example, were more widely observed among slaves than among contemporary whites. Marriages between first cousins were common among white slave owners, but very rare among black slaves, in keeping with differences in incest taboos between Europe and Africa.[34] In short, the slave community had its own norms, which were not mere copies of the whites' patterns. Even slave owners found it expedient to accommodate the wider incest taboos of blacks by allowing marriages between their slaves and slaves who lived on other farms and plantations, even when there were eligible mates (by white standards) in the slave plantation community. In one rare case of nuclear family incest, the slave owner was forced to sell a father who had made his daughter pregnant, for other slaves had threatened to kill him.[35]

There were manners and mores among slaves. The young addressed their elders as "uncle" and "aunt" (whites forbad blacks to use titles such as "Mr." or "Mrs." to one another)[36] and took their hats off when approaching them.[37] When a slave couple was caught off the plantation without permission by a patrol, the man was expected to volunteer to take the woman's whipping as well as his own.[38]

The slave community evolved its own culture as well as its own mores. Its most notable cultural product was the Negro spiritual, which later had such offshoots as the blues and jazz, setting the framework for the whole development of American popular music.[39] Some of the folk music of the Negro was also incorporated into Dvorak's New World Symphony. The banjo was invented by a free Negro during the era of slavery.[40] The fables and folklore of the slaves also provided a basis for such adaptations as the Br'er Rabbit stories by a white Southerner, Joel Chandler Harris. Unlike the moral fables of an ancient slave, Aesop, the stories of the Negro slaves in America generally featured the weak and humble triumphing over the powerful, arrogant, and blind.

The most important human relationships among the slaves centered on the family. Slave marriages and slave family relations had no legal standing, but usually lasted for decades,[41] if not for a lifetime.[42] This pattern existed throughout slave society—in all geographic regions, in both rural and urban settings, among field hands as well as house servants. A local study of ex-slave couples in 1866 showed that more than half of those in their forties had been together for twenty or more years.[43] While premarital sex and premarital pregnancy existed among slaves, marriage itself was taken very seriously[44] and was not lightly terminated. Sometimes slave marriages were forcibly terminated, usually by the sale of one of the partners. Most of these forcibly terminated marriages had also lasted many years.[45] The testimony of many former slaves told of the anguish these partings caused, and many slave owners were reluctant to part slave couples for fear that the remaining partner would try to escape. Still, nearly one-sixth of Mississippi blacks in 1864–65 had been forcibly separated from a spouse.[46] After emancipation, many separated couples searched for each other for years.[47] During slavery, there were instances of suicide after separation,[48] and of murder of whites for raping a slave wife,[49] although that meant sure death for the man who killed the rapist. That there were hundreds of documented instances of slaves murdering whites—for a variety of reasons—also suggests that the enslaved people were not lacking in values that were deeply felt. In addition to the documented instances of murder, there were many poisonings and arson not traceable to anyone, although it was known that these were among the favorite weapons of slaves.

Most of the children of slaves grew up in two-parent families,[50] with the father as head, and (secretly) bore his surname. Because of premarital relationships, some families contained children fathered by someone else, but a local study of nineteenth-century slave families indicated that, in three-fourths of the families, all the children had the same father and mother.[51] In short, slave families were stable, insofar as slaves could keep them so. The offspring could at any time be sold away from the family and never seen again. Most sales of slaves were of teenagers and young single adults[52] so that the relative stability of slave marriages did not mean a stability of the slave family.

Slave owners found marriage and family relations among slaves a stabilizing force, reducing the incidence of fighting over women and inhibiting escape attempts. However, the strength of family ties among slaves was also seen as inappropriate to their status, a threat to master-slave relationships, and a source of difficulty when individual slaves were sold. Slave owners tried to keep family ties from becoming so strong as to interfere with slavery itself. They forbad the slaves to use family names,[53] and slaves were liable to punishment even for using such expressions as "my sister" or "my mother."[54] This only drove such expressions underground. Surnames were passed down for generations in black families, although all knew better than to use them around whites, and even after emancipation, many ex-slaves remained reluctant to tell whites their surnames because the habit of concealing them had become so engrained.[55] The surnames of slaves were usually *not* the surnames of their owners.[56] More often, it was a name whose origins were lost in generations past—sometimes the name of an owner of a previous generation of the family or simply a name chosen by African ancestors when they arrived in America. Its purpose was not to connect the black family with the white person from whom the name was taken but to give the black family an enduring mark of identification for itself. The same was true of the given names of slaves. About one-fourth of the boys were named for their fathers,[57] and many children were named for uncles or aunts[58] or for siblings who had died[59] or had been taken away and sold.[60] Significantly, daughters were usually not named for mothers, although that was a common pattern among contemporary whites.[61] Here again, the slave community had its own customs.

Slavery as an institution was not the same everywhere or at all times. It varied considerably over time, from one place to another, and from one kind of occupation to another. Three quarters of all white families in the South owned no slaves at all.[62] Of those who did, most were on farms rather than on plantations,[63] and few plantations ever reached the size or magnificence of the fictional antebellum southern estates such as those depicted in *Gone with the Wind*.

Regional Differences

As a result of the invention of the cotton gin in 1793, the growing of cotton ultimately became the work of 60 percent of all slaves in the United States.[64] Slaves were increasingly concentrated in those parts of the South where soil and climate were most suitable for the growing of cotton. The states of the Deep South—Alabama, Mississippi, Texas, and Louisiana—had rapidly increasing numbers of slaves, while Upper South states, like Virginia, Maryland, and the Carolinas, had declining numbers of slaves. The geographic center of the black population moved steadily southwestward at an average of about fifty miles per decade.[65] Between 1830 and 1860, well over half a million slaves were moved from the Upper South to the Deep South.[66] Most of this massive movement of slaves—aptly called "one of the great forced migrations in world history"[67]—occurred by the relocation of slave owners with their work forces, rather than by the sale of individual slaves.[68] But the latter also occurred often enough to spread fear among the slaves—fear of being sold away from family and friends—and to leave as an historical residue in the language the phrase "sold down

190

the river." Yet even when a whole plantation moved together, this often severed family ties because some family members (particularly husbands and fathers) were often owned by someone else and lived on a different farm or plantation.[69]

Some parts of the country were more suitable than others for growing the kinds of crops that were economically feasible to produce with slave labor.[70] Crops requiring routine, mass-production labor that could be easily monitored by overseers were particularly suitable to slave labor.[71] Cotton growing was the classic example in the United States, but sugar production in Louisiana and in much of Latin America also fit that pattern. Other staple crops such as rice, wheat, and corn were also grown with mass-production slave labor.[72] Climate and soil largely determined where such crops could be grown and therefore determined the geographic distribution of slaves.

Relatively few slaves were ever used in the North, where the climate was unsuitable for plantation crops, and parts of the South likewise had little plantation slavery. One such southern area was the Piedmont, or foothill, region running through western Virginia, western North Carolina, eastern Kentucky, and eastern Tennessee. It is an erosion-prone region[73] with "lean soil,"[74] unsuitable for plantation slave crops. Neither the slave plantation nor the racial ideology that justified it took as deep roots here as in the fertile Mississippi delta and the rich land of the "black belt" stretching across Arkansas, Louisiana, Mississippi, Alabama, and Georgia. These Deep South states have historically been the most extreme and intransigent on racial issues—first slavery and later civil rights—while the liberal elements in the South came largely from the Piedmont region.

Antislavery newspapers were concentrated in Kentucky and western Virginia, which later broke away to form a separate state rather than join the Confederacy along with the rest of Virginia.[75] John Brown operated in this region. So did the underground railroad, which helped slaves escape to free states. The first periodical in the United States devoted exclusively to the abolition of slavery was published in eastern Tennessee.[76] In North Carolina, a Manumission Society existed in the 1820s,[77] which would have been unheard of in the Deep South. Free Negroes in North Carolina were permitted to vote until 1835, and their disenfranchisement that year was opposed by almost all the *western* counties of the Piedmont region[78]—where the Germans and the Scotch-Irish lived. Racism and pro-slavery sentiment existed in all these states, but the mixture and intensity of feeling varied substantially. The moderate Whig political party was able to contend with the pro-slavery Democrats only in those parts of the South that were in the Piedmont region.[79]

The raw facts of geography not only reduced the incidence of plantation slavery in the Piedmont; the absence of a slave economy and society attracted to such areas people who did not want to compete with the labor of slaves or to be part of such a society. These included people of Scotch-Irish and German ancestry,[80] who poured down from western Pennsylvania through the Cumberland Gap and into the Piedmont region. This region also attracted many Quakers, whose religion forbad the holding of slaves and who were prominent in antislavery activity, especially in North Carolina. In short, the effect of geographic differences within the South were accentuated by differences in the people attracted to these different regions.

Changes Over Time

The first Africans brought in captivity to colonial Virginia in 1619 became indentured servants, like the white indentured servants who were common at that time.[81] Both were released as free people after some years of bondage. Precisely when and how this situation changed to perpetual slavery for blacks remain unclear, but by the 1640s, Africans brought into Virginia no longer had indenture contracts, although as late as 1651 some Negroes whose period of indenture expired were still being assigned land for themselves, like the white indentured servants at the end of their terms of service.[82] The first explicit law passed in America that recognized slavery as a perpetual condition, extending to future offspring, appeared in 1661 in Virginia.[83] By the time Africans began to be brought to other colonies, the precedent of Virginia law was followed, and slavery was their fate from the outset.

Slavery has existed for thousands of years in virtually every part of the world. But slavery as it evolved in America had unique features. Whereas slavery was politically and morally accepted without question for centuries in many nations—even by the leading moralists of the times[84] —the bringing of African captives to America was embroiled in controversy from the beginning. Some colonies passed laws to prevent it, but these laws were nullified by the British government.[85] Opposition to slavery did not necessarily imply either moral scruples or human concern for Negroes. There are economic, social, and military problems created by the presence of a large number of racially distinct people held in bondage, and many Americans wanted to spare themselves such problems. This, in fact, continued to be a major element in later antislavery efforts, which often included schemes to send Negroes back to Africa.[86] Once the decision had been made—in London—to institute slavery in America, the options facing all subsequent generations of Americans were radically changed. The issue of the wisdom or justice of slavery now had to compete with the issue of whether the new American nation could absorb an alien people with no experience of free, self-supporting existence in this society—a people constituting about 20 percent of the total population in 1800.[87]

Slavery in a free society raised heated issues that kept political controversy alive throughout the history of the institution in the United States. It forced ideological justifications that other slave societies had not found necessary. Essential to these justifications was the assertion that the enslaved peoples were so different that the principles and ideals of the country did not apply to them—that they were inferior in intellect and lacked the feelings that would cause them suffering from degradation, hard work, or the destruction of family ties. The intense racism that developed as a defense of slavery in the American setting meant that merely freeing individuals or even abolishing the institution of slavery itself would not be the end of the problem. Indeed, the intensity of racism made even antislavery advocates—including de Tocqueville and Lincoln—fearful of the effects of emancipation.[88] Such problems are not inherent in slavery as an institution. No such enduring stigma attached to ex-slaves and their descendants in the Roman Empire, where one of the emperors—Diocletian—was the son of ex-slaves.[89] What was peculiar about American slavery was that (1) the slaves and masters were physically different; (2) slavery in a free society required extreme ideological justification; and (3) the moral quandary of slavery as an institution here finally emerged and became heated in both England and America, leading eventually to an agreement between the two nations to ban the international slave trade in 1808.

The American Revolution and its ideals made the moral issues of slavery more prominent and central. During and after the Revolutionary War, northern states began banning slavery, and southern states began passing laws to ameliorate the treatment of slaves. In Virginia, Thomas Jefferson, George Washington, Patrick Henry, and James Madison all publicly advocated the abolition of slavery[90] —as did many other people throughout the South.[91] Any hope of success was destroyed when Eli Whitney invented the cotton gin, in 1793, making the South "the cotton kingdom"—not only of the United States, but of the world. The dilemma of slavery and emancipation was now localized. Northern states had avoided the problems of emancipation by announcing a future ban on slavery, causing northern slaves to be sold to the South. The question of what to do with millions of people who had been denied a normal development was now no longer a national question but a regional one.

Slave uprisings and massacres of whites in the Caribbean spread fear throughout the South toward the end of the eighteenth century. Rumors of plots for similar slave uprisings in the United States periodically revived these fears. In 1831, such an uprising materialized in Virginia, led by Nat Turner, and killed 60 whites before it was crushed. On the political front, the rise of militant abolitionist movements in the North in the 1830s added to the South's sense of being beleaguered. All of these events heightened southern regionalism. This was expressed externally in bitter political attacks on its enemies and in widespread violence in new territories such as Kansas—known as "bleeding Kansas"—where Southerners and northern settlers bitterly fought for control to determine whether the state would enter the Union as a state permitting or forbidding slavery. Internally, the South tightened its "black codes"—laws regulating the conduct of both slaves and free blacks. It stamped censorship on abolitionist literature—even censoring the U. S. mails[92]—and made life intolerable for those who opposed, or even questioned, the institution of slavery. These repressions in turn led many with different views to migrate out of the South. Their departure left behind a more conformist and intolerant southern population.

The Legacy of Slavery

Numerous genetic, linguistic, and cultural distinctions among Africans were obliterated in more than two centuries of slavery. But the black population became differentiated in a new pattern based on occupational roles under slavery, on the date of family emergence into freedom, and on proportion of white ancestry.

There were significant differences in the work performed by slaves. Domestic servants or "house slaves" had more opportunities to acquire American culture (including literacy in a few cases) and values than did "field hands." Urban slaves—most of whom were domestic servants—had still wider exposure, extending well beyond the slave-owning family. About 30 percent of urban slaves worked as employees, paid part of their earnings to their respective slave owners, but often lived separately in housing they rented for themselves, and otherwise lived daily lives not very different from those of ordinary free working people. Even on the farms and plantations, where the great majority of slaves lived, there were privileges and pride developed among drivers, slaves in skilled occupations, and other isolated individuals.

Finally, there were the "free persons of color"—nearly half a million in 1860—who had somehow escaped the fate of the 5 million blacks who were enslaved. The first "free persons of color" were the captured Africans who were brought to Virginia in 1619 and who became free at the end of the traditional indenture period. But even after perpetual slavery became an established institution in the American colonies, individual slaves continued to acquire freedom by one means or another. In 1790, there were about 60,000 "free persons of color." Many northern states abolished slavery, and many individuals (and the whole Quaker community) manumitted their slaves in the ideological aftermath of the American Revolution. The number of "free persons of color" grew to more than 300,000 by 1830.[93] Another reason for blacks achieving freedom may be suggested by the facts that (1) 37 percent of the "free persons of color" were mulattoes, compared to only 8 percent of the slaves[94] and that (2) there were always more women than men among free Negroes—a pattern common throughout the Western Hemisphere.[95] Some of those freed were simply the children of slave owners and their mothers. This was often openly acknowledged in Latin America but not in Anglo-Saxon countries.[96]

The lives of most "free persons of color" were narrowly circumscribed, economically, politically, and legally. They were usually poor, unskilled workers, lacked basic civil rights in most of the South and much of the North, and had little or no legal protection against fraud or even violence by whites. Nevertheless, they were years—or even generations—ahead of the slaves in their acculturation to American society. Most "free persons of color" could read and write in 1850, although only 1 or 2 percent of the slaves could do so.[97] It would be 1900 before the literacy rate of the black population as a whole rose to a level reached by the "free persons of color" in the middle of the nineteenth century.[98] It would be 1940 before the black population as a whole became as urbanized as the "free persons of color" were in 1850.[99] In short, "free persons of color" had a large head start over the rest of the black population in their adjustment to American society.

There were enduring consequences to this head start. The descendants of "free persons of color" remained prominent among Negro leadership in many fields, on into the twentieth century. They were among the founders, supporters, and early leaders of the NAACP. W. E. B. Du Bois, Thomas Fortune, and Charles Waddell Chestnutt were all descendants of the "free persons of color," as was Thurgood Marshall in a later era. So apparently were most black holders of doctoral degrees in the middle of the twentieth century, and most Negroes working in the professions in the nation's capital.[100] "Free persons of color" and their descendants were responsible for the founding and running of the first and most outstanding black public high school—Dunbar High School in Washington, D.C.—which turned out the first black general, the first black federal judge, the first black Cabinet member, the discoverer of blood plasma, the first popularly elected black senator, the first black professor at a major university, and a long list of other "firsts" in many fields.[101]

Because white ancestry was more common among "free persons of color" than among slaves, lighter complexioned Negroes were long overrepresented among high-achieving members of the race, leading both whites and blacks to attribute their success to a genetic superiority based on their white ancestry.[102] Color consciousness mixed with class consciousness in the black elite, which long remained remote and aloof from the black population, although speaking publicly in their name.[103] As with other groups, initial historic advantages among blacks produced enduring internal differences.

FROM EMANCIPATION TO JIM CROW

The Civil War was not only the turning point in the history of black Americans. It was itself a final trauma in the story of slavery. As this bloody and desperate war dragged on for four years, the southern economy was drained and disrupted, and blacks and whites alike suffered as both armies confiscated food and committed other depredations and sometimes atrocities.

Blacks were also more directly part of the war. More than 186,000 black soldiers were in the Union Army,[104] constituting about 10 percent of all federal troops. Twenty-one blacks won the Congressional Medal of Honor during the Civil War.[105] Desertion—a major problem

The Blacks

during the war—was more common among white soldiers than among black soldiers.[106]

Ambivalence marked the relations between blacks and whites in the South during the Civil War. Even across the barriers of slavery, emotional ties had formed, as well as bitter resentments and domineering cruelties. Some slaves remained loyal and even protective toward the slave-owning family while the man was away fighting for the Confederacy. Other slaves escaped to freedom as the northern armies approached. Often the same individual behaved ambivalently, like the slave who carried his wounded master back from the battlefield to a safe hiding place—and then himself escaped in the opposite direction to join the Union Army.[107] Whites were equally ambivalent—praising and damning blacks, laughing at them and crying with them, giving the slave paternalistic solicitude and individual generosity, and yet whipping them and selling them like cattle. The emotional shock of slave owners was apparent in numerous postwar expressions of disappointment or despair at what the whites considered the "desertion" or "ingratitude" of many slaves who refused to stay on, even as paid employees of their former masters.

The emotional resentment of whites toward blacks was not confined to former slave owners. Beaten, weary, and hungry Confederate soldiers, returning home to a disrupted and sometimes destroyed and starving South, vented their bitterness in atrocities against helpless blacks.[108] Slave owners sometimes took revenge against the women and children of black men who escaped from slavery to join the Union Army.[109]

After two centuries of slavery, in which Negroes were conceived to have no rights, white Southerners resented not only emancipation but also any behavior, words, or attitudes by blacks implying common humanity or common rights. The general attitude of white Southerners toward blacks was aptly summed up by a colonel in the Union Army in the South in 1865: "To kill a negro they do not deem murder; to debauch a negro woman they do not think fornication; to take property away from a negro they do not consider robbery."[110] It was an attitude summarized earlier by the Supreme Court in the Dred Scott decision, which declared that blacks "had no rights which the white man was bound to respect."[111] In short, the freedom of American Negroes began in an atmosphere that was as unpromising emotionally as it was economically and politically.

Although blacks suffered in body and mind under slavery, they did not emerge as a spiritually crushed people. Great numbers of black men fought ably during the Civil War. During the northern occupation of the South, black soldiers controlled and disciplined whites.[112] The position of newly freed blacks was made precarious by the undependable protection of the Union Army and the rampant terrorism of white mobs and vigilantes. Racial violence and terrorism used against blacks to try to keep them "in their place" were evidence that they were not wholly submissive.

Freedom was for blacks both a deliverance and an uprooting. Many took to the roads, carrying their meager belongings in bundles, often "hungry, sick, and barely clad,"[113] either looking for a new life somewhere or trying to locate family members long separated by sales on the slave market. As a contemporary Freedman's Bureau official observed, "every mother's son among them seemed to be in search of his mother; every mother in search of her children."[114] A contemporary journalist reported meeting black men walking along the roads of Virginia and North Carolina, many of whom had walked across the state—or across more than one state—looking for their families.[115] Many parents made what a contemporary federal official characterized as "superhuman efforts" to find their chidlren.[116] After several months, the mass migrations subsided, but the search for lost family members continued through newspaper advertisements that filled the newly established black newspapers on into the 1880s.[117]

Occupations

One of the great fears of white Southerners, and then of the federal military occupation officials, was that the newly freed slaves would not settle down and work, but would continue to live off emergency government rations (given to both blacks and whites in the war-torn South) and private charity, supplemented by thefts. Local governments, often with the support of federal authority, imposed stringent vagrancy laws, applied to black adults, compulsory apprentice laws for black children, and numerous other statutes and regulations severely restricting the freedom of choice of the newly freed slaves as to where and for whom to work.[118] The abuses under these laws sometimes amounted to a virtual reenslavement of blacks.

Most blacks continued to do the same kind of work after emancipation as under slavery. As late as 1890, more than half of all Negroes worked in agriculture, and more than 30 percent worked as domestic servants.[119] In the Deep South, the proportion in agriculture was even higher.[120] Among those few Negroes living outside the South, domestic service employed more than 60 percent.[121] Professionals were rare—only 1 percent of black workers.[122]

In one respect, however, work patterns did change. Many black women who were married now stayed home to raise their children, instead of working in the fields or in white people's homes.[123] The consternation and resentment this produced among southern whites who lost a portion of their house servants[124] were indicative of the whites' underestimates of the importance of family life to blacks.

Most blacks who worked in agriculture were agricultural laborers, although there were also sizable proportions of tenant farmers who paid their rent either in money or in a share of the crop.

Negroes as they emerged from slavery were largely destitute of cash—and certainly lacked such sums as would be necessary to support themselves through a whole crop-growing season until harvest time. They were therefore dependent on white employers, landowners, and storekeepers (sometimes all the same person) to advance them the provisions needed to live until the crop was harvested. For some postbellum Negroes, this meant being perpetually in debt and in a state of virtual peonage. This situation, which has been widespread among other very poor agricultural peoples, was accentuated among blacks by their lack of experience in budgeting or in managing their own daily lives under slavery and by the habits of carelessness, little foresight, and dependence on whites engendered by that system. Slaves had long been careless and wasteful with food, firewood, clothing, and other necessities issued to them by slave owners[125] and had cherished such small luxuries as they may have acquired, often as cast-off items from slave owners' family members. The economic weighing of necessities against luxuries, which was common and taken for granted among other peoples of the world, was something that slaves in the United States had not experienced for centuries. The initial habits, values, and behavior patterns of American Negroes as they emerged from slavery slowly changed over the years and generations, as they acquired new experience and changed perspectives. But, as with other groups, they did not all instantly adapt to the new realities; over the years, different elements adapted to varying extents. For generations, on into the twentieth century, black leaders themselves repeatedly complained about the wastefulness, extravagance, or improvidence of their own people.[126]

In the immediate post-Civil War era, blacks were kept in poverty not only by their own difficulties in learning to manage their own lives but also by their pervasive illiteracy, which enabled white employers and storekeepers to cheat them while keeping the books on months of advances of food, clothing, and other items purchased on credit.[127] In the immediate aftermath of the war, the newly freed Negroes were so inexperienced and vulnerable that some whites even continued to hold them as slaves, by keeping the Emancipation Proclamation secret from them.[128]

However outrageous the frauds and deceptions of an employer or storekeeper might be, such people afterward found themselves deserted by their black workers or consumers. As a black man observed in 1866: "They may cheat the poor negro out of a year's work, but in spite of them he has acquired a year's experience. . . ."[129] Even without being able to read, write, or count, blacks could tell when relatives or friends elsewhere were doing better. Whites quickly acquired good or bad reputations among blacks,[130] and the whites in turn quickly became aware that their reputations were a capital asset that had to be maintained for the sake of continuing profit.[131] With many stores located within a short distance of each other,[132] and many landowners needing labor, even illiterate people exercised their options. The mobility of blacks was supplemented by the mobility of white landowners, who rode on horseback from place to place recruiting black workers.[133]

The changing character of the American Negro in the decades after the Civil War was reflected in changing economic relations between blacks and whites. As workers, blacks had acquired little sense of personal responsibility under slavery. Lack of initiative, evasion of work, half-done work, unpredictable absenteeism, and abuse of tools and equipment were pervasive under slavery,[134] and these patterns did not suddenly disappear with emancipation. The immediate post-Civil War work patterns attempted to cope with these work habits. Some white landowners of the immediate postbellum period even insisted on the right to continue corporal punishment of their black laborers or sharecroppers, but this quickly subsided under the pressure of economic competition among landowners for laborers and sharecroppers—and because of active physical resistance by blacks themselves.[135] Gang labor under white overseers was tried, as under slavery, but blacks preferred other systems whenever available. By 1880, the gang system was dying out.[136]

The work of black tenant farmers was at first closely supervised by white landowners[137] and even kept under surveillance by white store owners who advanced credit.[138] But as blacks acquired more experience in managing their own farms, they began to acquire discretion and independence. The share of the crops going to black tenants tended to increase over time.[139] By 1880, share-rent systems began giving way to fixed-rent systems, which bound the farmer to pay a fixed amount in cash or crops, no longer sharing the management or the risks with whites.[140] By 1910, about one-fourth of all black farmers were owners (or buyers) rather than renters.[141] None of these things happened automatically. They reflected a growing (although modest) level of responsibility and skill among blacks in agriculture and a consequent rise in the demand for their labor.

The auxiliary benefits rose along with the wages and crop shares. Immediately after the Civil War, most blacks lived in the same log cabins with dirt floors that they had lived in as slaves. Windowpanes were almost unknown. Gradually, log cabins were replaced by frame houses, dirt floors by planks, and by the turn of the century, glass windowpanes began to appear.[142] The houses at this juncture were still usually lacking in plumbing, small, crowded, and—almost inevitably—dirty.[143] Urban blacks were housed on the average with three rooms per family in 1896[144]—crowded in that era of large families, but less so than the Jews or Italians of New York at the same time.

In the post-Civil War era, southern white employers and landowners sought to band together to restrict the money and discretion they had to give to blacks.[145] Yet, despite the economic strength, political power, and organizational advantages of the whites, these restrictive agreements failed repeatedly in the face of competition for laborers and sharecroppers.[146] Black income grew at a higher percentage rate than white income during the last third of the nineteenth century.[147]

Job discrimination against blacks usually took the form of refusal to hire Negroes for various desirable jobs, rather than wage differentials for doing the same work. In money-wage terms alone, wages paid whites in southern states averaged 8 percent higher than wages paid to blacks doing the same work, at the turn of the century,[148] but black workers often received pay in kind as well.[149] When both races were paid entirely in cash, there was in general no racial differential.[150]

Politics

The Reconstruction era in the South under federal military occupation saw the emergence of civil rights and political power for blacks, despite bitter opposition by southern whites, often in the form of extralegal intimidation and terror by various vigilante groups, of which the Ku Klux Klan became the most notorious. With the withdrawal of federal troops and the return of local government in the South after the political compromise of 1877, the political participation and civil rights of blacks declined sharply. An uneven retrogression for blacks continued for decades in the South, culminating in the pervasive segregation laws and discriminatory practices around the turn of the century summarized as Jim Crow. The U.S. Supreme Court's 1896 ruling that "separate but equal" facilities were constitutional set the stage for massive and rigid racial segregation in public facilities that were usually far from equal.

Along with the political and legal repression of southern Negroes rose the number of lynchings of blacks, to a peak of 161 per year in 1892.[151] Lynching had long been a southern practice, but only after 1886 were there more blacks than whites lynched.[152] With the passage of time, lynching became primarily a matter of whites killing blacks.

Education

Virtually all slaves were illiterate, and slaves constituted about 90 percent of the black population in 1860. Public schools were a relatively new idea, still fighting for a foothold outside the South, and even rarer within the South. Under slavery, the law forbad teaching a slave to read or write in most southern states, and even in many northern communities, blacks were not admitted to the public schools. Moreover, some states in the Deep South made it illegal for "free persons of color" to send their children to schools—even to private schools at their own expense.[153]

Despite this formidable array of barriers, black education has a long history in America. In the late eighteenth century, various philanthropic individuals and groups in the North either established schools for black children or enrolled black children in schools attended by whites.[154] Blacks also took the initiative in creating schools for their own children. As early as 1807, the 500 "free persons of color" in Washington, D.C., built that city's first school for black children—the first of many private schools that free black children attended for decades, before finally being admitted to the city's public schools in 1862.[155] Among the prosperous "free persons of color" in New Orleans, education was widespread, and extended for some all the way to the university level—for those able to send their offspring to Europe for an education.[156] Similarly, in Baltimore, there were schools for the children of free Negroes by 1830.[157] New York, Philadelphia, and other cities also had schools for black youngsters. Various white religious groups—notably the Quakers and the Catholics—also educated free

The Blacks

black children, often in defiance of the law.[158] So did some of the Scotch-Irish of the Piedmont region.[159]

After the Nat Turner insurrection of 1831 and the rise of abolitionism, the southern states imposed ever-tighter restrictions on the actions of all blacks, slave or free. It was in that period—roughly from 1830 to 1860—that many southern states outlawed the teaching of black children by anyone. These laws led to widespread clandestine schools for free black children. About three-fifths of all "free persons of color" were literate in the census of 1850.[160] In the cities, the literacy rate was higher—even in states with laws against educating black children.[161]

The eagerness with which newly freed Negroes sought education in the postbellum South was both dramatic and pathetic.[162] Contemporary observers were surprised at the number of black adults, as well as children, who enrolled whenever an opportunity was presented to acquire literacy. This desire for education was not, however, based on any experience with the work that it entailed nor on any realistic basis for assessing its actual contributions to their well-being. The conviction that education was a good thing to have was no substitute for the disciplined work or intellectual values that make it possible or effective. Educating a people lacking these prerequisites was to prove a sore trial to generations of teachers of both races.[163] Still, in one way or another, American Negroes went from a state of being nearly 100 percent illiterate to almost 75 percent literate in the fifty years after emancipation—a remarkable achievement.

After the Civil War, northern whites, largely from the American Missionary Association, moved into the South to establish schools to educate the chidlren of the recently freed slaves. In less than a decade, they established more than a thousand schools and sent more than two thousand teachers into the South.[164] In the half-century following the Civil War, northern sources contributed an estimated $57 million to Negro education, and blacks themselves contributed an additional $24 million.[165] In the early postwar years, the Freedman's Bureau was the major contributor to black education, spending about $3.5 million in the period from 1865 to 1870.[166] By contrast, public schooling for blacks was slow to get under way in the South, especially so at the secondary and higher levels. The first black public high school in the United States was established in 1870 in Washington, D.C. The first public high school for blacks in Baltimore was established in 1892, in New Orleans in 1916, and in Atlanta in 1924.[167] Rural schooling for blacks remained far behind. As late as 1911, there were so many rural areas with no schools at all for black children that philanthropist Julius Rosenwald established a fund to contribute to the building of black schools in the South. Over the next twenty years, more than 50,000 such public schools were built with contributions of more than $4 million from the Julius Rosenwald fund.[168] When Julius Rosenwald died in 1932, more than one-fourth of all black children in the United States were being taught in schools whose construction he subsidized.[169]

It was 1916 before there were as many black youngsters attending public high schools as there were attending private high schools.[170] Even after southern states began building public schools for Negroes, from 1913 to 1932 about one-third of their construction costs were shared equally by the Julius Rosenwald fund and by small voluntary contributions from blacks themselves.[171] In general, the sums spent by southern states for educating blacks were some small fraction of the sums spent educating white students.[172] Nor was this necessarily improving with time. The difference between expenditures per capita on blacks and whites in the public schools was greater in 1910 than in 1900, in every southern state.[173]

In the schools set up by the American Missionary Association after the Civil War, three quarters of the teachers were women, and three quarters of the women were unmarried.[174] These were the "New England school marms" described in such terms as "prim" and "forbidding," but dedicated. These white teachers with black students faced certain hostility and ostracism from the southern whites, and some were threatened, beaten, or murdered.[175] Their black pupils not only lacked any educational preparation or values, but were often guilty of absenteeism, tardiness, unreliability, lying, and theft.[176] In the early postwar years, the average teacher lasted three years.[177] Yet from this foundation was built the education that generations of blacks looked back on with gratitude and reverence. Later black leaders, from W. E. B. Du Bois to Booker T. Washington, praised the selfless work of these missionary schoolteachers who helped create an educated class of black Americans. Du Bois called it "the finest thing in American history,"[178] and Mary McLeod Bethune spoke of "those beloved, consecrated teachers who took so much time and patience with me when patience and tolerance were so needed."[179]

In higher education, the first black man to receive a college degree was a graduate of Bowdoin College in 1828.[180] The first black woman to receive a college degree graduated from Oberlin in 1862. The first black man to recieve a degree from Harvard graduated in 1870, and the first Harvard Ph.D. awarded to a black man went to W. E. B. Du Bois in 1896. Throughout the whole nineteenth century, less than two thousand Negroes received college or university degrees.[181]

A number of black colleges and universities were founded shortly after the Civil War by the American Missionary Association and by black religious groups, as well as Howard University by the federal government. But most of the black "colleges" actually taught precollege material for many years before the major portion of their work was actually at the college level. Initially, they were essentially white-run colleges for black students, due to the scarcity of blacks with sufficient education to teach on a college faculty.

Leadership

The antebellum "free persons of color" were the most educated and acculturated element among American Negroes in the post-Civil War era. They (and their descendants) provided much of the leadership of the race on into the twentieth century, with the notable exception of Booker T. Washington. As with other groups with internal cultural differences, continuing ambivalence marked the relationship between black leaders and the people in whose name they spoke.

Where the cultural differences were greatest—between the affluent Creole "free persons of color" in New Orleans and the recently freed blacks—so was the ambivalence. As of 1860, nearly 85 percent of "free colored" males in New Orleans were artisans, professionals, or owners of businesses.[182] About a third of the antebellum "free colored" families of New Orleans owned slaves,[183] and 3,000 of these free Creoles had joined the Confederate Army.[184] Much of their immediate postwar effort went into differentiating themselves from the newly freed Negroes. They resisted efforts to "relegate us to the rank of the brutalized slaves" and denounced those who "confused the newly freed people with our intelligent population."[185] Nevertheless, being relegated to legal and social inferiority to whites gave the Creoles an incentive to fight for full political equality—but focusing on those aspects of life that were most important to themselves, whether or not they were the most urgent for the black masses. For example, the Creoles opposed the founding of Southern University, which provided desperately needed education for blacks, because it represented a principle of racial separateness that was repugnant to the mulatto elite.[186] The clash between ideological and pragmatic goals was to become an enduring source of internal struggles among black leaders, classically between

W. E. B. Du Bois and Booker T. Washington. Socially, the Creoles remained separate from other Negroes on into the twentieth century. The great jazz pianist, Jelly Roll Morton, was disowned by his Creole grandmother for associating with ordinary Negroes.[187]

New Orleans was the extreme example of a tendency that was far more widespread. Its history as a Latin slave society before becoming part of the United States with the Louisiana Purchase of 1803 explains many social patterns there (including slave-owning Negroes) that were uncommon or unheard of in Anglo-Saxon slave societies.[188] What was more general, however, was the division of the American Negro population into the black masses and the lighter-complexioned elite, from whom the political, economic, and social leadership came. The folk culture of the black masses—spirituals, jazz, dialect—was rejected by the elite in favor of the more aristocratic elements of white American culture.[189] Color differences within the Negro population became social barriers,[190] erected by many of the same people who first led the NAACP's fight against color barriers erected by whites.[191] This apparent inconsistency was, however, quite consistent when seen as an attempt by the Negro elite to join the larger American elite from which it was excluded solely because of race. But the moral and political claims that might enable them to do so had to rest on democratic rhetoric and on their role as spokesmen for the whole race.[192]

The first of the nationally recognized black leaders was Frederick Douglass. An escaped slave, and free many years before the Civil War, he combined the experiences that were to divide Negro leadership in later years. He was a tireless writer, lecturer, and political leader in both the antebellum and postwar eras. Douglass was an imposing man of bitter eloquence who fought for both pragmatic goals and goals of principle—for abolition of slavery, full civil rights, and for self-help among blacks. The Reconstruction era in the South seemed to promise the equality and progress for which Douglass had fought so long, but the Compromise of 1877 and the rise of Jim Crow and lynchings brought the black race in America to one of its lowest ebbs by the time of Douglass' death in February 1895.

In the year of Douglass' death, there suddenly emerged a new black leader, Booker T. Washington. Born a slave and freed as a child by the Emancipation Proclamation, Washington had painfully acquired an education and had then become a teacher. In 1881, he headed up the newly founded Tuskegee Institute in Alabama. In September 1895, he delivered a speech at the Atlanta Exposition that brought him national recognition and launched his career as a Negro leader. Washington urged southern Negroes to work out their destiny in the South—"cast down your buckets where you are"—and appealed to more moderate white Southerners to cooperate in pragmatic mutual concerns, however separate the races might remain socially. He said: "In all things that are social we can be as separate as the fingers, yet one as the hand in all things essential to mutual progress."[193] His speech was welcomed by blacks and whites alike. W. E. B. Du Bois—his later rival—was among those who sent congratulations to Washington on his Atlanta Exposition speech.[194]

In this desperate era of Jim Crow, white vigilante terrorism, and lynchings, what Booker T. Washington offered was not a new set of goals but a new order of priority in the existing goals. The political struggles that still preoccupied much of the black elite nationally seemed to him futile for the disfranchised and vulnerable black masses in the Deep South. Washington's top priority was to meet "the real needs and conditions of our people"[195] with basic skills and discipline—not only job skills, but "how to bathe, how to care for their teeth and clothing."[196] Tuskegee Institute concentrated on the most basic, pragmatic concerns—work habits, hygiene, character. Its aim, in the words of one of its teachers, was "the promotion of progress among the many, and not the special culture of the few."[197] This was the thrust of Washington's general social and political philosophy as well. He declared that "political activity alone" could not save the Negroes, for "back of the ballot he must have property, industry, skill, economy, intelligence and character. . . ."[198]

From the outset, Washington expressed his desire that "all privileges of the law be ours,"[199] that there be "universal free suffrage,"[200] and that the law be applied "with absolute honesty . . . to both races alike."[201] But his public utterances seldom dwelled on these things. Privately, he aided and financed federal court challenges to Jim Crow laws and sought to favorably influence political decisions affecting blacks from behind the scenes.[202] But the major thrust of Washington's public utterances and educational activity was toward economic advancement and character development among the black masses. Although consumed by this goal, he did not consider it the ultimate limit of black aspirations, but as a necessary historical stage that would "prepare the way for successful lawyers, Congressmen, and music teachers."[203]

While Booker T. Washington's approach was primarily adapted to the situation of the black masses, W. E. B. Du Bois emerged in the early twentieth century as a spokesman for what he called "the talented tenth." Du Bois, a descendant of free mulattoes, grew up among educated whites in Massachusetts and received a Ph.D. from Harvard. Du Bois' educational emphasis was on liberal arts, rather than on the vocationalism of Washington, and his political emphasis was on unrelenting public pressure for full civil rights as soon as possible. He was one of the founders of the National Association for the Advancement of Colored People.

These were differences of emphasis rather than of principle.[204] Both men recognized the need of the great mass of blacks—only the second generation out of slavery—to acquire the skills and discipline to succeed in a complex modern economy.[205] Both also recognized the need for higher levels of education for that small part of the race already prepared and able to acquire it.[206] The bitterness that ultimately developed between the followers of these two men is much more difficult to explain by their small differences in emphasis than by their personality differences and by their social differences. The black elite regarded Booker T. Washington as a spokesman for the black lower classes—the descendants of slave field hands.[207] The NAACP, which Du Bois founded, was, initially at least, the preserve of the elite, and some lower-class blacks referred to it as "the National Association for the Advancement of *Certain* People."[208]

Despite a divided black leadership, much was accomplished by both camps. There was more than enough work for both to do.

THE GREAT MIGRATIONS

The migration of the rural southern Negro toward the cities and toward the North began long before the Civil War. The antebellum "free persons of color" were by 1860 more urbanized than the white population,[209] and the general direction of their population shifts was toward the Northeast, while slaves were moving toward the Southwest. At least 90 percent of all American Negroes lived in the South until the turn of the twentieth century,[210] but the antebellum "free persons of color" were evenly divided between North and South, and within the South, they tended to gravitate toward its more liberal regions, such as the Piedmont area.[211]

The movement of blacks toward the cities and toward the North continued in the post-Civil War period, although on a relatively modest scale. The black population of a number of southern cities increased somewhat between 1850 and 1900,[212] but there was little migration of blacks out of the South in the immediate post-Civil War period.[213] Then began the great migrations.

Black migration to the Northeast and the Midwest in the 1890s was more than double what it had been in the 1880s. A similar level of migration out of the South continued into the first decade of the twentieth century—then doubled in the second decade and again almost doubled in the 1920s.[214] This mass movement of people compared in size with the great international migrations in history. More than three-quarters of a million blacks left the South in the decade of the 1920s[215]—more people than migrated from Ireland to the United States during the famine decade of the 1840s.[216] There were many reasons for the size and timing of this mass exodus from the South—worsening race relations in the South toward the end of the nineteenth century,[217] improving race relations in the North during the same period,[218] the economic distress in the South caused by the boll weevil,[219] and increasing job opportunities caused by the World War I mobilization combined with a reduction of competitors as immigration fell sharply because of the war.[220] Like most great migrations—internal or international—this was primarily a movement of those in the prime of life. Almost half of all black males from fifteen to thirty-four years of age in Georgia *left* Georgia during the 1920s.[221] The much higher birthrate in the South kept the *number* of southern blacks increasing through 1960, even though the *proportion* of all blacks living in the South was declining.[222]

The consequences of the mass exodus of blacks out of the rural South were as historic as the magnitude of this migration. The massive northern black ghettos began during the era of these great relocations of population. Harlem, the first and most famous of these ghettos, was still predominantly white as late as 1910.[223] More important, the lives of those living in most northern urban Negro communities prior to the great migrations were quite different from what they became afterward.

There were small numbers of free Negroes living in a number of northern cities long before the Civil War and even before the Revolutionary War. While there were some notable and financially successful individuals among them,[224] most were working-class people with no special skills or status. As emancipation in the North and escaped slaves from the South added to their numbers, there was growing awareness of them, and hostility to them, by the white population in general and the lawmakers in particular. Discriminatory laws and practices arose, barring black children from schools and black adults from equal access to public accommodations.[225] However, with the passage of time and a growing acculturation of these small Negro communities, such restrictions tended to relax, and there was even some modest upward mobility in occupations toward the end of the nineteenth century.[226]

As of 1860, blacks in Boston were not quite as badly off occupationally as the Irish,[227] and in New York, black waiters in the 1880s were paid more than Irish waiters.[228] As late as 1895, black laborers working on the Croton reservoir in New York were paid more than Italian workers.[229] New York blacks generally held modest but respectable jobs as barbers, waiters, or skilled craftsmen. Few were unskilled manual laborers, and most were "better off than the mass of recent white immigrants to the city."[230] Their general improvement was noted by Jacob Riis in his study of New York and by W. E. B. Du Bois in his study of Philadelphia.[231]

Toward the end of the nineteenth century, residential segregation was no longer of the magnitude that it had been before or would become again. In New York City, Negroes were more numerous in some neighborhoods than in others, but no neighborhood was all black.[232] In Detroit as early as 1860, no neighborhood was even 50 percent black,[233] and in Chicago as late as 1910, more than two-thirds of the black population lived in neighborhoods where the majority of residents were white.[234] Similarly, in Philadelphia and Washington, D.C., there was not yet racial segregation in housing of the sort that would become common later on.[235] Northern urban blacks also acquired greater access to public accommodations, to the voting booth, and to a wider social role. Blacks were among the leading caterers in Philadelphia.[236] In Detroit, black physicians and dentists had clienteles that were predominantly white.[237] Black politicians were elected to public office in Michigan by a predominantly white electorate.[238] In Chicago, social as well as business relations between blacks and whites were accepted, and even intermarriage was not unknown.[239] In short, the last quarter of the nineteenth century represented "an unprecedented period of racial amity and integration" in northern urban communities.[240]

The beginning of the twentieth century saw the beginning of a sharp reversal of these trends. The masses of unacculturated, ill-educated, rural southern Negroes who flooded into the northern cities were bitterly resented by blacks and whites alike. The Negro middle

The Blacks

class and the northern Negro press denounced them as crude, vulgar, unwashed, rowdy, and criminal[241] and as a menace to the standing of the whole race in the eyes of the larger white community.[242] These southern migrants soon became in fact the bulk of the northern black communities. Whites reacted to them by raising racial barriers against Negroes as a group. Now attempts by blacks to live in the same neighborhoods as whites brought forth violence. The Ku Klux Klan began to appear for the first time in northern cities. In 1911, Baltimore passed the first residential segregation law, copied by a number of other cities.[243] Rigid job barriers, residential barriers, and social barriers arose—many to last for decades or generations.

There was a pause in the migrations to the North during the Great Depression of the 1930s, when massive unemployment became pervasive in the big northern cities. But beginning in 1940, a new and even larger migration from the South resumed. Well over 1 million blacks moved out of the South in the decade of the 1940s and again in the 1950s.[244] More than 4 million blacks migrated from the South between 1940 and 1970—a number comparable to the great international migrations in all of history.

This was not simply a geographic movement. It was a mass uprooting from a rural southern way of life and a transformation into a modern industrial and urban way of life. It was, in short, the kind of traumatic social change that took other ethnic groups generations to adjust to. The social pathology that other groups experienced—violence, alcoholism, crime, delinquency—all reappeared in the transplanted black populations of the cities. Not only whites withdrew from contact with them; the older and more stable, settled, and financially secure black middle-class families tended to separate themselves from the newer arrivals socially[245] and to lead an expansion of the ghetto into the surrounding white community, braving social barriers, restrictive covenants, and outright violence. They eventually won a legal battle against restrictive covenants when those were declared illegal in 1948. This was hailed as a great victory for the Negro race as a whole, although it made little or no difference in the residential patterns of most blacks, and was impelled by a desire of the black elite to escape the black masses.

Social Conditions

The black migrants to the northern cities in the early twentieth century represented a second massive uprooting of people in just two generations. After two centuries of slavery, 5 million Negroes were abruptly thrown into the midst of a war-ravaged and disorganized southern economy and society, amid embittered, defeated, and often hungry whites, steeped in the racial ideology used for centuries to sustain slavery. The blacks began destitute, illiterate, and unfamiliar with even the basics of hygiene, social behavior, or responsibility.

As late as 1890, three-fifths of all black wage earners could neither read nor write.[246] This was symptomatic of more general disadvantages and deficiencies that extended to the preservation of health and life itself. In 1896, Du Bois pointed out that "personal cleanliness" was "woefully deficient" among blacks[247] and that this—combined with bad eating habits and carelessness about their health in general—contributed to their rising mortality rates.[248] The historical pattern of black mortality rates supports Du Bois' contention. In the decades immediately after emancipation, when blacks first became responsible for their own health, death rates among Negroes rose from what they had been under slavery.[249] But as later generations of blacks became more experienced and acculturated, their death rates declined absolutely, and the large gap between black and white death rates also narrowed.[250] The racial differential continued most acute in deaths from infectious diseases—syphilis, tuberculosis, pneumonia[251]—rather than from degenerative diseases, such as heart or kidney disease or cancer,[252] which were less likely to reflect hygienic practices or crowded living conditions. Poverty and less access to medical care were also obvious factors, but factors that applied to degenerative as well as to infectious diseases.

After decades of worsening oppression and terrorism in the South, the next generation of blacks began to move North, where life was economically and socially better for Negroes. But the conditions of northern Negroes at that time were no indication of what southern Negroes could expect in the North. The rural southern migrants were still generations behind the northern urban Negroes in acculturation. One index of this was that southern black schoolchildren continued for decades to be automatically put back a full year when they entered schools in Harlem or other northern ghettos,[253] even though such schools might be substandard compared to white schools in the same cities. High rates of disease, alcoholism, and homicide so ravaged the black communities that many contemporary observers around the turn of the century predicted the eventual extinction of the race.

Most of the migrants were young (more males than females), unmarried, and unskilled.[254] With the passage of time, there was some modest upward movement, but as late as 1925, 72 percent of the black

The Blacks

males in New York were either unskilled laborers or service workers—compared to 86 percent in 1905.[255] The great bulk of black women were domestic servants. The percentage declined from 80 to 72 percent in New York City from 1910 to 1920, and by similar amounts in Chicago and Cleveland.[256] About half of all black males were also domestic servants in 1910, but this declined below 40 percent by 1920, as more black men moved into factories and other urban manual labor.[257] Few blacks worked in professional occupations—only about 2 percent by 1920.[258]

Black family life in the early decades of the twentieth century was typically one featuring two-parent households. More than four out of five Negro families in New York in 1905 were headed by the father.[259] As late as 1925, only 3 percent of black families in New York were headed by a woman under twenty.[260] The unwed teenage welfare mother emerged in a later era.

While blacks were migrating from the South to the North, they were also migrating within the South—from the farms to the cities and from one part of the South to another. Only about a fifth of southern Negroes lived in metropolitan areas in 1900, but almost half did by 1960.[261] This combination of interregional and intraregional migration was a major reason why black income rose relative to white income during the period from 1940 to 1960.[262]

Birthrates among blacks have historically been higher than among whites[263] but have by no means been unique. As of 1910, for example, the number of children per woman among blacks was exceeded by the number among American women of Jewish, Polish, Italian, and Mexican ancestry.[264] Over the years, the birthrates of black women have followed the national trends—generally falling from the 1920s to a low in the mid-1930s, rising again to new highs in the late 1950s, and now declining again. Birthrates among blacks in 1950 were about what they were in 1920.[265]

The internal distribution of children among blacks has made the upward movement of the race as a whole more difficult. The general tendency of poor people to have more children than middle-class people has been accentuated among American Negroes. Better educated and higher income blacks have even fewer children than their white counterparts, while low-income blacks have even more children than equally low income whites.[266] Much of the struggle that brought some blacks up from poverty has had to be repeated in successive generations because successful blacks did not have enough children to reproduce themselves.[267]

Education and Culture

At the turn of the century, nearly half of the black population in the United States was still illiterate. By 1920, less than a quarter of all Negroes were still illiterate, and that figure was cut in half again over the next twenty years.[268] It was 1930 before the average American Negro had six years of schooling, compared to ten years of schooling for contemporary whites.[269] The educational differences were even greater than the years of schooling would indicate. Black children in parts of the South spent only two-thirds as many days in school per year as white children.[270] For the South as a whole, expenditures per black pupil in 1912 were less than one-third the expenditures per white pupil, and in the Deep South, the disparity was even greater.[271] Black teachers had less training and taught larger classes.[272]

The great migrations to the northern cities brought both quantitative and qualitative improvements in the education of Negro children. So too did the migration from the rural South, where discrimination was greatest, into the southern cities. Segregation of the races in the schools facilitated discriminatory treatment and remained pervasive throughout the South until after the 1954 Supreme Court desegregation decision in *Brown v. Board of Education*. As late as 1910, there were no public high schools at all for black children in the states of Alabama, Georgia, or Louisiana, and about half of the elementary schools in these states were in makeshift quarters (homes, churches, etc.) rather than in school buildings.[273]

As late as the 1930s, only 14 percent of black children in the South reached high school. But a few high-quality black high schools were created during this era—in Washington in 1870, Baltimore in 1892, New Orleans in 1916—and—after a bitter political struggle by blacks—the first and only black high school in the state of Georgia was built in Atlanta in 1924.[274] These early high schools contributed a disproportionate share of the black pioneers of later years. Their alumni were graduating from Ivy League colleges while a majority of blacks in school were still in the first four grades.[275] It was one measure of the large internal social differences among Negroes.

Higher education showed these internal class differences even more clearly. The light-complexioned descendants of the Negro elite continued dominant as both students and faculty at the black colleges, well into the twentieth century. It was only after World War II that the children of the black masses became the predominant element in the Negro colleges,[276] many as a result of the G.I. bill. As for educational quality, most Negro colleges and universities began after the Civil

The Blacks

War teaching elementary and secondary school material to most of their students, and as late as World War I, the great bulk of their "college" students were still studying precollege material, with only three black colleges teaching predominantly college material.[277] In the 1920s, these institutions began to become colleges in fact as well as in name. But even the best of the black colleges remained well below the level of high-quality national institutions, by almost any index.[278]

As the children of the black masses flooded into the colleges, their lack of preparation, reading habits, or intellectual discipline made top quality education difficult to achieve.[279] The slow but steady opening of opportunities for black students in leading American universities led more and more of the better prepared black students to go elsewhere. In the 1960s, more black students went to white colleges than to black colleges.[280]

Although the black masses made slow and painful progress in formal education during the period of the great migrations, they were nevertheless developing a new cultural style in the urban ghettos of the North. They spoke, dressed, and lived differently. Their music was no longer the old southern spiritual but modern jazz.

Many prominent blacks began to emerge into the national limelight during the same era—notably in music, with great jazz musicians like Louis Armstrong and Duke Ellington, composers like W. C. Handy ("St. Louis Blues") and Scott Joplin, singers like Roland Hayes and Marian Anderson, and in popular music, Ella Fitzgerald, Billie Holliday, and many others emerged in fields from vaudeville to the fine arts. Paul Robeson became famous first as an all-American football player, then as a singer, and finally as a radical political figure. In boxing, Jack Johnson became the first black heavyweight champion, and then—decades later—Joe Louis won a new respect for black Americans in general, both as champion and as a man of great dignity and sportsmanship. The cultural and psychic changes during the 1920s caused many to speak of a New Negro. Confidence and assertiveness appeared in the music and literature of blacks, as well as in their politics and demeanor. The Great Depression dampened many of the optimistic hopes for further progress, but the momentum resumed when that decade passed.

Along with the slow, steady economic rise of blacks in general came a new middle class, risen from the black masses rather than descended from the mulatto elite. They displaced or merged with the old elite in many northern cities. A few of the newly arrived blacks had substantial fortunes: Madame C. J. Walker became the first black woman millionaire with her cosmetics firm.[281] John Johnson rose from shoeshine boy in Chicago to become owner of the multimillion dollar Johnson publishing enterprises (*Ebony, Jet*, etc.).[282] Other blacks became millionaires in life insurance, sports, and entertainment.

WEST INDIANS[283]

Not all of the black migration into the northern cities was from the rural South. Beginning in the early twentieth century, a stream of black immigrants moved to New York's Harlem from the islands of Jamaica, Barbados, Trinidad and from other parts of the British West Indies. By the 1920s, one-fourth of Harlem's population was West Indian.[284] Nationally, West Indians have been about 1 percent of the black population but have been disproportionately overrepresented among black professionals, businessmen, and public figures. Prominent blacks of West Indian ancestry have included Marcus Garvey, James Weldon Johnson, Claude McKay, Shirley Chisholm, Malcolm X, Kenneth B. Clark, W. Arthur Lewis, Sidney Poitier, and Harry Belafonte.

While not racially distinct from American Negroes, West Indians have had a different cultural background and have remained socially distinct from the other blacks around them.[285] Intermarriage rates between the two groups have historically been extremely low. The overwhelming majority of West Indians in America marry other West Indians, even though living in communitites of American blacks or even when attending colleges where the great bulk of other students are American Negroes.[286]

Differences between the two groups go back into history, and are still reflected today in substantial socioeconomic differences. These differences provide some clues as to how much of the situation of American Negroes in general can be attributed to color prejudice by whites and how much to cultural patterns among blacks.

History

During the era of slavery, the British West Indies, like the North American colonies, received a mixture of Negroes representing many

African tribes. There is no evidence of any initial difference in the mixture of people brought to the West Indies and to America.[287] In fact, the West Indian islands were an interim stop for many African slaves who later ended up in the American colonies.[288]

For those who remained in bondage in the West Indies, slavery was usually even harsher than in the American South. The cost of raising slaves in the West Indies was considered higher than the cost of importing replacements from Africa,[289] and the slaves were treated accordingly. The black population of the islands was never able to fully reproduce itself, but had to be constantly supplemented by continuous importations from Africa. Jamaica alone imported over 800,000 slaves between 1690 and 1820, but its total black population from 1820 was less than half the number imported. Barbados had a declining black population in the seventeenth and eighteenth centuries, despite continued imports.[290] By contrast, the United States never imported as many slaves as Jamaica, but the American Negro population grew to about 5 million people by 1860, through natural increase.

Slavery in the West Indies was usually large-scale plantation slavery—much larger than in the United States.[291] These huge commercial operations (usually sugar growing) typically had absentee owners living in London.[292] Complete control was in the hands of local white attorneys and overseers, whose financial incentives were to maximize current production (on which they received a percentage[293]) at all costs, without regard to the long-run cost in terms of worn-out slaves or worn-out land.[294] Slave owners in the United States usually lived on their own farms or plantations, and were thus able to impose a longer run view of how the slaves and the land should be treated. One of the differences was that infant mortality among slaves in the West Indies was several times what it was among slaves in the United States.[295]

The sexual exploitation of black women by white men, which was episodic in the United States, was more systematic, pervasive, and even commercial in the West Indies.[296] West Indian overseers and much of the small white population of the islands were usually sojourning bachelors,[297] while in the United States slave owners preferred to hire married overseers, precisely to avoid problems brought on by overseers who had sexual relations with slave women.[298]

The paternalistic relations that sometimes mitigated the worst features of slavery in the United States had little place in the mass-production commercial plantation slavery of the West Indies. A contemporary observer in the eighteenth century noted that the Britons in the West Indies were never familiar with their slaves, "never smile upon them,"[299] and had little to say to them. The Briton "sees that they are well fed" but also exercises "those cruelties at which human nature no less recoils."[300]

Because the West Indian population was overwhelmingly black, while the American population was predominantly white, the British to some extent followed the Latin policy of divide-and-rule by making distinctions among free Negroes on the basis of color.[301] Gradations of color continued to fragment the West Indian Negro population down through history, more so than it did the black population of the United States.[302]

In short, the most bitterly criticized features of slavery—callous overwork, sexual exploitation, Negro fragmentation, and self-denigration of blackness—were worse in the West Indies than in the United States. However, several other features of West Indian slavery that have received less attention may help explain the greater success of West Indians in the United States. Unlike slaves in the United States, who were issued food rations and were often fed from the common kitchen, West Indian slaves were assigned land and time to raise their own food. They sold surplus food in the market to buy amenities for themselves.[303] In short, West Indian Negroes had centuries of experience in taking care of themselves in a significant part of their lives, even under slavery, as well as experience with buying and selling. Contemporary observers noted that the slaves in the West Indies worked perceptibly more energetically on their own plots of ground than on the land they worked for slave owners.[304] They had the kind of incentives and experience common in a market economy but denied American slaves for two centuries.

West Indian slaves were emancipated on August 1, 1838—a generation earlier than blacks in the United States. Moreover, there was a period of preparation of slaves for freedom in the West Indies, rather than the literally overnight sudden emancipation in the United States.

Much of the immediate postemancipation history of blacks in the West Indies paralleled that of American Negroes in the South. Peonage virtually reenslaved West Indian blacks. A disastrous decline in the sugar market spread economic distress through the West Indies, as wartime disruptions likewise plunged the postbellum South into economic distress. Poverty was pervasive among West Indian Negroes. Many immigrated to various parts of the world—some permanently and many as sojourners. Most of those who came to the United States settled in New York City.

The Blacks

West Indians in the United States

There was some trickle of emigration from the West Indies to the United States as far back as the eighteenth century. But significant numbers of black West Indians began to arrive in the United States—and principally in New York City—in the twentieth century. About 30,000 arrived in the first decade of the century, more than twice as many in the second decade, and about 40,000 during the 1920s.[305] By 1930, foreign-born blacks (mostly West Indians[306]) were about 1 percent of the American Negro population.[307] There were more males than females in the early years, but the sex ratio was almost balanced by 1930.[308] As in the case of native black migrants, most West Indian immigrants were young. More than half were under 30 years of age.[309]

About 40 percent of those who arrived in the first quarter of the century had been laborers or servants in the islands, and another 10 to 20 percent had worked in agriculture. Only about 4 percent had worked in the professions.[310] In short, the occupational level of the early West Indian immigrants was not very different from that of the southern black migrants who arrived in the urban Northeast at about the same time. The West Indian immigrants were not quite so predominantly from an agricultural background, however, and more were from industrial or comemercial occupations. Unlike the southern rural migrants, 80 percent of the West Indian immigrants were from cities.[311] The contrast between the West Indians and American Negroes was not so much in their occupational backgrounds as in their behavior patterns. West Indians were much more frugal,[312] hard-working, and entrepreneurial. Their children worked harder and outperformed native black children in school.[313] West Indians in the United States had lower fertility rates and lower crime rates than either black or white Americans.[314] As early as 1901, West Indians owned 20 percent of all black businesses in Manhattan, although they were only 10 percent of the black population there.[315] American Negroes called them "black Jews."

Separation, hostility, and conflict have long marked the relationship between the two black groups.[316] This has not usually been so overt or violent as some other intraethnic conflicts. Still, the suspicions and recriminations between the two groups have extended from the man in the street[317] to the intellectual leaders of both groups.[318]

The restrictive immigration laws of the 1920s brought the West Indian movement to the United States to a sudden halt. Revisions of the immigration laws later led to a sharply increased inflow of West Indians in the 1960s and 1970s—about 90,000 people in each decade.

About 15 percent of them were professionals and another 12 percent white collar.[319]

West Indians in the United States have continued to hold sizable advantages over American Negroes in incomes and occupations. As of 1969, West Indian incomes were 28 percent higher than the incomes of other blacks in New York City,[320] and 52 percent higher nationally.[321] Second-generation West Indians have higher incomes than whites.[322] While native blacks were substantially underrepresented in the professions, a slightly higher than average percentage of West Indians were professionals.[323] While native blacks had an unemployment rate above the national average, West Indian blacks had an unemployment rate below the national average.[324] As of 1970, the highest ranking blacks in New York's Police Department were all West Indians, as were all black federal judges in the city.[325] For many years, successive borough presidents of Manhattan were all West Indians.

Paradoxically, the very success and prominence of West Indian individuals have contributed to their "invisibility" as a group. West Indians, as such, are too small a group to have any political power, so West Indian individuals in public office hold their positions as "representatives" of the black population as a whole. To stress their specifically West Indian background would undermine their positions with blacks and whites alike. Moreover, the many West Indians in civil rights movements must attribute black poverty and unemployment almost solely to white racism, although the West Indian experience itself seriously undermines the proposition that color is a fatal handicap in the American economy.

Even those West Indians in the private sector of the economy may be dependent on the large black population for their prosperity. Many are businessmen, doctors, lawyers, publishers, and others whose customers or clienteles are American Negroes. West Indian immigrants in England are not nearly as successful there, perhaps because of the absence of a large non-West Indian black population to provide them with a constituency.[326]

BLACK AMERICANS TODAY

Along with the rising educational and skill level of the black population have come changes in the white population and in political and legal institutions. The period since World War II has been a turning point in the history of American racial and ethnic groups in general.[327] Shortages of manpower—civilian and military—during World War II broke down many barriers. The first black marines in history were trained in 1942.[328] Two black air combat units fought in Europe under the command of Benjamin O. Davis, the first black general.[329] In civilian life, many wartime jobs opened up to applicants without regard to race, sex, or other such criteria. In the postwar era, President Harry Truman made "civil rights" a major part of his election platform of 1948, even at the cost of splitting his party, losing southern states for the first time in decades, and jeopardizing his own election. Courts began to strike down discriminatory laws and practices as unconstitutional. Professional sports that once excluded black athletes began to be dominated by black athletes. Many retrogressions and violence on both sides marred these advances, but the advances continued nevertheless.

The steady rise in black incomes, occupations, and education and declines in disease and mortality occurred while the rest of the American population was improving in all these respects as well. "Gaps" remained and ratios showed no great change, despite widespread progress. The income of nonwhite families was 53 percent of the income of white families in 1948 and was the same percentage fifteen years later, although both incomes had risen more than 50 percent in real terms, even allowing for inflation.[330] Infant mortality rates declined by about a third, for both blacks and whites, from 1950 to 1970,[331] but the black-white ratio or "gap" did not change greatly.

Beginning in the mid-1960s, however, there were a number of areas in which blacks not only rose, but rose at a faster rate than whites. Between 1961 and 1971, white family income rose by 31 percent, while black family income rose by 55 percent.[332] The proportion of college-age young people who actually enrolled in college remained the same for whites between 1965 and 1972, but the proportion among blacks nearly doubled.[333] The number of whites in professional-level occupations increased by about one-fifth between 1960 and 1972, while the number of blacks in such occupations nearly doubled.[334] The number of black foremen, craftsmen, and policemen more than doubled, and the number of black engineers tripled.[335] The number of blacks in Congress doubled between 1964 and 1972. So did the number of blacks in state legislatures across the country. In the South, the number of blacks in state legislatures more than quadrupled.[336]

The geographic distribution of blacks distorts national statistical comparisons. Despite more than half a century of massive migration, just over one-half of all American Negroes still live in the South—a region of generally lower money income and lower living costs for both blacks and whites. Less than a third of whites live in the South.[337] Black families living outside the South earn more than 40 percent higher incomes than black families within the South.[338] Blacks in New York State earn more than twice as much as blacks in Mississippi.[339] The geographic distribution of the population affects both black-white comparisons and comparisons with other ethnic groups. Age differences between groups add further distortions. While gross differences between blacks and whites remain large nationally, differences between blacks and whites of the same age have narrowed remarkably, especially outside the South. Among young married couples (under 35) living outside the South, blacks had 78 percent of white income in 1959 and 93 percent in 1971. When both husband and wife worked in both races, black couples earned 5 percent *more* than white couples in 1971.[340] Nationally, Puerto Rican families earned slightly more than black families in 1969,[341] but black families living outside the South earned more than Puerto Rican families, almost all of whom live outside the South.[342] Even the substantial income advantage of Mexican Americans over blacks is a geographic phenomenon. Although Mexican-American families earned higher incomes than black families nationally in 1970,[343] black families in all regions other than the South had incomes above the national average for Mexican-American families.[344]

Along with general progress, blacks have experienced retrogression in particular areas. The proportion of one-parent, female-headed black families increased from 18 percent in 1950 to 33 percent in 1973—from double the white percentage in 1950 to more than triple the white percentage in 1973.[345] Despite attempts to depict this as a "legacy of slavery,"[346] one-parent, female-headed black families were a rare phenomenon in earlier times, even under slavery.[347] The proportion of blacks on welfare also rose during the 1960s and 1970s, as the proportion in poverty declined.[348] The proportion of the black population that is working has been declining both absolutely and relative to whites. Unemployment among blacks has risen, also absolutely and relative to whites.[349] Black teenage unemployment in 1978 was more than five times what it had been thirty years earlier. Among the factors responsible, a number of government programs—notably the minimum wage laws—have made it more difficult for blacks to find jobs,[350] and other government programs—notably welfare—have made it less necessary.

A number of governmental efforts have been made to advance blacks, but these efforts are difficult to disentangle from the effects of growing black education, skill, geographic redistribution, and changing racial attitudes by whites that made the civil rights laws and other government activities possible. The most controversial of the government programs has been "affirmative action," or racial quota hiring, established as "goals and timetables" in 1971. Economists have found these quota systems to have had little or no effect beyond what had already been achieved under "equal opportunity" policies in the 1960s.[351] The public perception of "affirmative action" has, however, engendered strong resentment among whites in general—resentment exploited by growing racist organizations such as the Ku Klux Klan and American Nazis, often in parts of the country where such organizations never flourished before. The historic alliance between Negro and Jewish organizations likewise broke up over the issue of quotas.

Blacks are now part of virtually every American institution, from the halls of Congress and the Supreme Court to the baseball diamond and the gridiron and the basketball court. No recital of American folk heroes would be complete without Joe Louis, Willie Mays, or O. J. Simpson. American music and American slang have been flavored from the music and speech of Negroes. Three blacks have won Nobel prizes—in peace (Ralph Bunche and Martin Luther King, Jr.) and in economics (W. Arthur Lewis). Part of this represents the lowering of barriers and the opening of opportunity. It also represents long and arduous efforts to raise a whole people to a level where their efforts would bear fruit. Both renowned and unsung heroes have been part of the struggle—from the clandestine schools of the antebellum South to the underground railroad, from those dead at Gettysburg and Antietam to those dedicated school marms who gave up their youth and tranquility to teach the children of slaves, from blacks who worked long hours in quiet obscurity to advance the race to others who put their lives on the line to gain justice.

Blacks in higher or more visible places continue to be disproportionately descendants of black elite families from generations past or West Indians. Supreme Court Justice Thurgood Marshall, U.N. Ambassador

Andrew Young, Secretary of the Army Clifford Alexander, and Julian Bond of Georgia represent the "old families."[352] Past and present CORE leaders James Farmer and Roy Innes are West Indians, as is Congresswoman Shirley Chisholm and California's former lieutenant governor Mervyn Dymally. Similar patterns exist among black academics, where descendants of the "free persons of color" include John Hope Franklin and Alvin Poussaint, and West Indians include W. Arthur Lewis, Nobel prize winner in economics, and Kenneth B. Clark, among many others.

The long history of black people in America has had many landmarks and many profound changes—slavery, emancipation, the great migrations, and the civil rights revolution of the mid-twentieth century, for example. Their rate of progress looks very different if measured from 1619, 1865, 1900, or 1954. Many of those living in the northern ghettos today are first- or second-generation migrants from the South—at the same stage where other blacks were fifty or one hundred years ago. The race as a whole has moved from a position of utter destitution—in money, knowledge, and rights—to a place alongside other groups emerging in the great struggles of life. None have had to come from so far back to join their fellow Americans.

V

Americans from Latin America

Chapter 9

THE
PUERTO RICANS

Puerto Ricans are both old and new Americans. Puerto Rico has been part of the United States since the end of the nineteenth century, and Puerto Ricans are born American citizens—and yet many migrate to an American society that remains foreign to them. Most are classified as white,[1] but they are as residentially segregated as blacks,[2] and have incomes and occupations that are very similar to those of blacks.[3] Puerto Ricans are repeating age-old patterns of other groups that migrated to New York and other eastern cities, and yet they are the originators of new migration patterns. They are the first airborne migration. They are a multicolored migration, and the first to arrive after the whole institutional array of the welfare state was already in place.

Puerto Rico first became part of the United States in 1898, as a result of the Spanish-American War. Puerto Ricans have legally become American citizens at birth since 1917, but the culture in which they grow up still reflects nearly four centuries of Spanish rule that went back to its discovery by Columbus. Although the island has been part of the United States for almost a century, its people have continued to live and develop separately from the United States, 1,000 miles from the Florida mainland—and even farther from New York City, where most Puerto Rican migrants have settled. Despite having been Americans for generations, Puerto Ricans are less assimilated than other groups (such as the Japanese) that came from farther away, and in some cases were racially more different from other Americans.

The rate of progress of Puerto Ricans depends on the point from which progress is measured—whether from Columbus' discovery of the island, annexation by the United States, or the mass migration to the American mainland made possible by the age of aviation. Much depends also on which Puerto Ricans are being considered—those who remain on the island or (as here) those who live on the mainland as part of the great mosaic of ethnic America.

PUERTO RICO

Puerto Rico is a tropical island several hundred miles south of the Bahamas and is the easternmost of a chain of large Caribbean islands called the Greater Antilles. Immediately to the west are the islands of Hispaniola (containing Haiti and the Dominican Republic), and then Cuba and Jamaica. Puerto Rico is about one hundred miles across and thirty-five miles from north to south. Puerto Rico is closer to South America than to the U.S. mainland. It is 550 miles north of Caracas, Venezuela, and 1,050 miles south of Miami.

The island of Puerto Rico has rich tropical vegetation, low mountain ranges, few navigable rivers, a warm climate, and periodically devastating hurricanes. The very word "hurricane" originated in Puerto Rico.[4] Puerto Rico was inhabited by about 40,000 peaceful Indians when Columbus discovered it during his second voyage to America.[5]

Although Columbus proclaimed Spanish possession of the island in 1493, it was 1508 before Spaniards returned under Ponce de León to establish a colony. The native Indians were enslaved and set to work on farms and mining gold. Many died of exhaustion, maltreatment, and diseases contracted from the Spaniards, for which the Indians had not developed biological immunity. An Indian rebellion in 1511 was

228

put down and 6,000 Indians killed. Many other Indians fled to the mountains or escaped to neighboring islands. African slaves were then imported to replace them—bringing with them a smallpox epidemic that killed over a third of the remaining Indian population, reducing the natives to only 4,000 people, or one-tenth their original number.[6]

The racial mixture of the Puerto Rican population included Spanish, African, and Indian strains. Few Spanish women came to Puerto Rico, so racial intermixtures and intermarriages became common centuries ago. However, Puerto Rico was one of the few islands of the Caribbean where the white population greatly outnumbered the black and Indian populations. Slaves were never more than 10 percent of the population of the island. In 1800, there were 150,000 people in Puerto Rico, half of whom were Spanish, 30 percent of "mixed blood," and the remainder Negro—half slaves and half free.[7] Upper-class Puerto Ricans continued through the generations to take pride in being—and remaining—white. However, race-consciousness in Puerto Rico never reached the dimensions in the United States, and color remained simply one of several indices of social class.[8]

Puerto Rico was first coveted by the Spaniards as a source of gold, but after the gold was quickly exhausted, it became a major producer of sugar and a fortified outpost guarding other Spanish possessions in the region. As a Spanish colony, it was ruled with absolute power by a government appointed from Spain and was allowed to trade only with Spain.

Puerto Rican aspirations for more freedom and autonomy began to be felt in 1810, when the first Puerto Rican representative in Spain argued against the Spanish policy of preventing the island from trading with other nations. In 1815, King Ferdinand VII issued a decree opening up trade between Puerto Rico and other nations.[9] An abortive armed uprising in 1868 and an equally abortive peaceful protest in 1887 were further milestones on the Puerto Rican quest for autonomy. In 1897, Puerto Rico was finally granted local autonomy by Spain. This lasted just one year, until the island became an American colony after the Spanish-American War.

The first American administration in Puerto Rico was a military government. In its two years on the island, the military government built schools, highways, railroads, hospitals, and sanitary facilities.[10] In 1900, the American Congress established civilian control over the island. The governor, cabinet, and one-half of the Puerto Rican legislature were to be appointed by the President of the United States. Puerto Ricans would vote for the other house of the legislature and for a Resident Commissioner who would represent their interests in Washington, with the right to address Congress but not to vote. Puerto Ricans were also exempted from U.S. taxes.

The first Puerto Rican Resident Commissioner in Washington, Luis Muñoz Rivera, pressed for more autonomy. In 1917, Congress passed a new act making Puerto Ricans citizens of the United States and giving them the right to elect both houses of their own legislature[11]—the most autonomy Puerto Rico had ever had in its history as part of the Western world.

The first quarter of the twentieth century saw Puerto Rican sugar production soar, along with its birthrate. In the last decade of Spanish rule, 57,000 tons of sugar were produced. This nearly quadrupled after ten years of American rule—and was to more than quadruple again over the next generation.[12] Puerto Rican population growth also rose dramatically. There were a million people in Puerto Rico in 1900 and two million by 1925,[13] turning a once sparsely populated island into one of the most densely crowded areas in the world.

The political struggle for greater autonomy continued, led by Luis Muñoz Marin, son of the first Puerto Rican Resident Commissioner. In 1947, Puerto Ricans were granted the right to elect their own governor, and in 1948, Luis Muñoz Marin became the first elected governor of the island. In 1952, Puerto Ricans achieved the right to make their own constitution.

Along with these political efforts toward local autonomy have appeared efforts toward statehood and outright independent nationhood. Not all who pursued these goals—especially nationhood—did so peacefully. In 1952, Puerto Rican nationalists tried to assassinate President Harry S Truman, and other Puerto Rican nationalists fired shots from the gallery of the U.S. House of Representatives, wounding several Congressmen. However, independent nationhood won less than 1 percent of the votes when a plebiscite was held in Puerto Rico in 1967. Most Puerto Ricans (60 percent) voted for continuation of the Commonwealth status (including tax exemption) and 39 percent for statehood.[14]

Economic development in Puerto Rico began even before political autonomy, and was accelerated under programs established by the new governor. Family incomes in Puerto Rico increased sixfold between 1940 and 1966. The number of automobiles on the island increased by more than ten times within the same span. The average life span in Puerto Rico was 32 years when the United States took control in 1898.[15] It more than doubled—to more than 70 years—by 1972.[16]

The economic development of Puerto Rico still left the island's standard of living far below that on the mainland of the United States. Unemployment also continued higher than American unemployment, partly as a result of minimum-wage-setting boards controlled by mainland economic interests (unions and businessmen), that had the power to price Puerto Rican labor at rates that would reduce competition with themselves.[17]

Migration to the U.S. mainland began very slowly. In 1910, there were less than 2,000 Puerto Ricans living in the continental United States. As late as the 1930s, the cost of a boat trip to the U.S. mainland was more than the average Puerto Rican earned in a year.[18] Still, by 1930, there were 53,000 Puerto Ricans living on the mainland, a more than sevenfold increase from the previous decade.[19] Most of these Puerto Ricans lived in New York City—a pattern that was to continue for decades.

The great migrations of Puerto Ricans began after World War II, when the cost of air travel came down within reach of working people. Thirteen thousand came over in 1945 alone, and this more than tripled in 1946. Part of this no doubt represented a pent-up backlog of potential migrants deterred from boat trips by submarine warfare. Over the next several years, migration fluctuated between 25,000 and 35,000. In 1951, migration to the mainland rose over 50,000, and in 1953, it reached its peak of 69,000. However, even these official figures greatly understate the massive movements of people, for these are *net* migrations—the number heading for the continent minus the number going back to the island. In 1955, for example, 343,720 Puerto Ricans arrived on the mainland and 297,706 departed—both figures being much larger than the 45,464 net migration. Some years—1961 and 1963, for example—more people left than came. While there was no net migration from the island, more than a million and a half people moved between Puerto Rico and the U.S. mainland in each of these years. By 1967, the total movement in both directions was more than three and a half million—but only about 26,000 net.[20]

By 1970, the Puerto Rican population of the United States was one and a half million people—about half as many as lived in Puerto Rico itself. There were more Puerto Ricans in New York than in San Juan.[21]

PUERTO RICANS ON THE MAINLAND

Since 1930, most Puerto Ricans in the continental United States have lived in New York City. When there were 53,000 Puerto Ricans on the mainland in 1930, more than 45,000 of them were in New York City. In 1955, when there were 675,000 Puerto Ricans on the continent, 500,000 were in New York City. With the passing decades, other Puerto Rican communities have developed, but two-thirds of the migrants from the island still lived in New York City in 1970.[22] There were a million Puerto Ricans in New York in 1970, with Chicago second with only 120,000, and Philadelphia and Newark the only other cities with 40,000 or more.[23] The east side of Harlem—"Spanish Harlem" or *el barrio*—was the first Puerto Rican community, but by 1970, there were more than twice as many Puerto Ricans in the Bronx or in Brooklyn as in Manhattan.[24]

The concentration of Puerto Ricans in New York City cannot be explained by geographic proximity since many parts of the United States are closer to Puerto Rico. Moreover, the predominantly airborne migration could easily have settled at any number of other places on the mainland. However, the basic pattern of Puerto Rican migration was established before World War II, in the era of boat travel, when New York was (and is) the leading port city. The vastly larger postwar migration simply went to where there was already an established Puerto Rican community.

Males were overrepresented in the early migration, as with other migrations in their tentative stages. Later, the sexes became balanced—the usual sign that an enduring community has emerged.

The timing of the migration—its ebbs and flows—has largely depended on the ups and downs of the American economy, compared with the progress or lack of progress in Puerto Rico.[25] The Great Depression reduced the migration, and the postwar boom accelerated it. As industrialization in Puerto Rico created more jobs and rising living standards during the 1960s, there were years when the return flow to the island exceeded the migration to the mainland.[26]

The growth of the Puerto Rican population in the continental United States is no longer simply a matter of migration flows from the island. Second and even third generations of Puerto Ricans have been born on the mainland. As of 1950, one-fourth of the Puerto Ricans in the continental United States had been born here. By 1960, this part of the Puerto Rican population had risen to a third,[27] and by 1969, it was more than 40 percent of all Puerto Ricans on the mainland.[28] However, because much of the second generation consists of children, more than 90 percent of adult, working Puerto Ricans in New York in 1960 were born in Puerto Rico.[29]

The People

When substantial migration began from Puerto Rico in the 1930s, it began from an island whose economy, society, and culture were much more like those of Latin American than the United States. Most of the people worked in agriculture under primitive conditions. They were usually barefoot. Malnutrition was widespread. Sewage disposal was primitive, and parasites infested the ground and the people. Illiteracy, which was 83 percent when the United States took over the island in 1898, was declining but was still 31 percent as late as 1940.[30]

Culturally, Puerto Ricans learned little English and retained little of the Spanish heritage other than the language and mores. Catholicism was the prevailing religion but was not a powerful force there as it was in Ireland and in some other European countries.[31] The priests in Puerto Rico were from Spain more often than from the island population.[32] The African traditions of the black population had eroded away much more so than among other black peoples in the Caribbean.[33] The family was important, and the numerous children loved and protected,[34] but there was also a high rate of family breakups and a succession of fathers.[35]

As in Italian and other Latin cultures, the chastity of female children was protected jealously by keeping them away from social contacts with males. Daughters escaped their isolation with early marriages. In the late 1940s, 6 percent of the married women in Puerto Rico had gotten married at age 14 or earlier. More than half were married by the time they were 18 years old.[36]

High fertility rates accompanied these early marriages. Among the Puerto Rican migrants to the mainland in 1946, one-third were from families with ten or more members. While more than half of all Americans at this time were from families of five or less people, about two-thirds of all Puerto Rican migrants were from families with six or more.[37] The people in the urban centers of the United States where Puerto Ricans concentrated were even more different in fertility patterns, as well as in other patterns.

Early marriages and high fertility rates were to remain a continuing

factor of major importance in the economic and social history of Puerto Ricans. The birthrate of Puerto Ricans in New York City in 1961
was one-third higher than among blacks and double that among
whites in the same city.[38]

Among the boys, machismo was a major preoccupation. In Spanish
cultures, this term covered a spectrum of daring behavior, from bull
fights to sexual exploits to an acute sense of personal dignity to a general defiance of rules and authorities. It identified manhood with
short-run daring rather than long-run accumulations of knowledge,
skill, or discipline, as in the Jewish or Japanese cultures. Within the
constricted confines of an urban community, machismo had few outlets other than disruptions in school and violence in the streets. Nor
was this simply a matter of clashing with Anglo-Saxon society. Even
in multiethnic Hawaii, Puerto Ricans in 1930 had the highest rate of
juvenile delinquency of any of the many groups on the island, as well
as the highest proportion on relief.[39]

Like other groups from a rural peasant background, Puerto Ricans
had little or no intellectual tradition. Together with their short-run
perspective,[40] fatalistic view of the future, and concern with immediate
individualistic machismo, this constituted a serious—and continuing—handicap in the schools. As of 1960, only 13 percent of Puerto
Rican youngsters finished high school—less than half the proportion
among blacks and less than a third of the proportion among whites.[41]
Moreover, Puerto Rican high school graduates were far more likely to
receive their diplomas from vocational high schools rather than from
academic high schools.[42] At the college level, the picture was even
more grim. Less than 1 percent of Puerto Rican young people graduated from college in 1960—less than one-fourth the proportion among
blacks and about one-tenth the proportion among whites.[43]

Language differences complicate the education of Puerto Ricans in
American schools. More than 70 percent of Puerto Ricans in the continental United States grow up in homes where Spanish is the language
spoken.[44] "Bilingual" programs have been created, but their effectiveness has been questionable. They have provided thousands of jobs for
Spanish-language teachers, but Spanish-language children in such
programs have done no better academically than those in regular
classes taught entirely in English, and many youngsters have been
kept in the special programs long after learning English.[45]

Political responses to the Puerto Ricans' educational programs, in
addition to "bilingual" programs, have included ending the distinc-

tion between academic and vocational high school diplomas in New York City,[46] "open admission" to the previously selective city colleges,[47] and an outlawing of IQ tests, on which Puerto Ricans and other minority children had low scores.[48] There has also been some attempt to "integrate" Puerto Ricans and other minorities in New York City with what are called "Anglo" children (although these latter include Celtic, Semitic, Slavic, and other non-Anglo-Saxon groups). But the combined Puerto Rican and black schoolchildren are a majority of all the children in the city's public schools and more than 70 percent of those in Manhattan and the Bronx,[49] so little integration with non-Hispanic whites was possible.

The language problems of Puerto Ricans are not unique. The persistence of a foreign language and a foreign culture has been characteristic of other groups with large and long continuing back and forth migrations—Italian Americans and French Canadians. living in New England, for example, and Mexican Americans on the West Coast.

Racial differences within the Puerto Rican population itself have been regarded less strongly than in the United States.[50] Individual color differences remain socially significant, however,[51] in a group that extends from pure Caucasian to pure Negro. The middle and upper classes in Puerto Rico have tended to be lighter colored or white,[52] and a similar pattern persists in the continental United States[53]—whether because of historical head starts or current mores. The migration from Puerto Rico to the continental United States has accentuated the importance of color differences among Puerto Ricans, as well as raising new issues of color differences between Puerto Ricans and the American population at large. The social and economic opportunities open to white Puerto Ricans provide an incentive for some of them to assimilate with the larger American society, while a desire to avoid being mistaken for American Negroes has provided incentives for darker Puerto Ricans to cling to the Spanish language and culture.[54] Color has become an additional complication in an already difficult situation.

Estimates of the proportion of the Puerto Rican population that is white have ranged from three quarters[55] to 90 percent,[56] and the 1950 census listed 80 percent of Puerto Ricans as white.[57] However, Latin racial designations have not been so stringent as those of Anglo-Saxons,[58] so the proportion that is white by American standards is probably lower than these figures suggest.

Between 80 and 90 percent of marriages among Puerto Ricans in New York City have been among people who classify themselves as white.[59] However, among Puerto Ricans whose color was classified by the American priests who married them, more than one-fifth were racial "intermarriages" by American standards.[60] Marriage outside the Puerto Rican group remains unusual, however. About 85 percent of all Puerto Rican married men have Puerto Rican wives. Of those who married outside the group, most married non-Hispanic women.[61] Among second-generation Puerto Ricans, however, between a fourth and a third of their marriages are to non-Puerto Ricans.[62]

Like other groups at a similar stage, Puerto Ricans have had high rates of crime, violence, and dependence on relief. Puerto Rican neighborhoods in New York City have unusually high rates of homicide, robbery, burglary, unemployment, and people on relief.[63] Although Puerto Ricans are only about 15 percent of the population of New York City and about 18 percent of the families below the poverty level, they are an estimated 40 percent of families on Aid to Families with Dependent Children.[64] Puerto Ricans arrived after the welfare institutions were widespread and welfare rights organizations helped to spread and legitimate receipt of public charity. Moreover, welfare benefits rose more than twice as fast as manufacturing wages in New York City during the mid-1960s.[65] About one-third of all Puerto Rican families were headed by women—a slightly higher proportion than among Negroes.[66]

Economic Conditions

The Puerto Rican migrants who arrived in New York City after World War II typically carried "cardboard suitcases that held everything they owned."[67] The middle class did not migrate from Puerto Rico. The migrants were generally youthful, unskilled, and with little education or experience. Just over half of those who migrated between 1957 and 1961 had never worked at all. About two-thirds were between fifteen and thirty-four years of age, and another one-fifth were children under fifteen.[68] Puerto Rican adults in New York City had an average of eight years of school.[69] With the passage of time, the migrants were drawn increasingly from rural and small town areas in Puerto Rico,[70] those more used to an urban existence having migrated earlier. In short, Puerto Rican migrants were not only ill-adapted to the American economy but also tended to become more so over time. Offsetting this is the tendency of a larger proportion of mainland Puerto Ricans to be born and grow up in the continental United States. As might be expected from these divergent trends, first- and second-generation Puerto Ricans on the mainland not only differ in occupations, but in addition, the differences are widening. In 1950, less than 10 percent of those born in Puerto Rico held clerical, sales, or similar white-collar jobs, while more than 20 percent of second-generation Puerto Rican males (and nearly 40 percent of the females) held such positions. Only 2 percent of the migrants from Puerto Rico worked in professional level occupations, but more than 5 percent of the second generation had reached that level. Among the women, just over 80 percent of the first generation were "operatives" or blue-collar workers, while only 40 percent of the second-generation Puerto Rican women worked in such jobs. Moreover, the decline in such work over the next decade was relatively small among first-generation women, but the proportions fell more sharply among second-generation women—only about one-fourth of whom were still doing such work in 1960.[71]

In general, Puerto Ricans continue to take predominantly unskilled and semiskilled jobs. They are a major part of the work force in New York's garment industry, in its hotels and restaurants (where they are typically bellboys, dishwashers, and busboys), and in its hospitals (where they are usually orderlies or in similar service jobs).[72] Puerto Ricans also worked in factories, on farms, and in civil service—again, usually in lower level jobs. In 1969, almost 80 percent of all Puerto Rican men were either blue-collar workers (63 percent) or service workers (16 percent). The same was true of more than 60 percent of the women.[73] Nationally, Puerto Ricans have about the same incomes as blacks.[74] However, the incomes of blacks located where Puerto Ricans are primarily located—in New York City—have been consistently higher than Puerto Rican incomes. For example, black family income in New York City was 16 percent higher than Puerto Rican family income in 1960.[75] Black family income in New York maintained this advantage over Puerto Rican family income in the 1970 census as well.[76] Puerto Ricans in New York City also had consistently higher unemployment rates than blacks there.[77]

Part of the reason for low incomes among Puerto Ricans is their youth. They are younger than either blacks or whites. The average age of Puerto Ricans in 1969 was eighteen years—four years younger than blacks and a decade younger than the American population as a whole. Age greatly affects income and especially occupations that require experience and education—as well as affecting unemployment rates, crime rates, and fertility rates.[78] For example, in 1969, a family headed by a Puerto Rican male in the twenty-five- to thirty-four-year-old bracket earned 96 percent of the income of families of other Americans of the same description.[79] Puerto Rican families headed by someone over twenty-five years old earned 16 percent higher incomes than black families of the same description in 1971,[80] despite the fact that black families in general earned 5 percent more than Puerto Rican families the same year.[81] There was simply a higher proportion of blacks over twenty-five years old.

One-fifth of all Puerto Rican families have no one earning an income.[82] Only 34 percent of Puerto Rican families have more than one income earner, compared to 51 percent of black families—and 61 percent of Japanese-American families.[83] While Puerto Rican men are in the labor force only slightly less than white or black men, Puerto Rican women are in the labor force much less than white or black women. The labor force participation rate of Puerto Rican women is just over one-half that for black women. In the prime earning years, from ages twenty-five to forty-four, Puerto Rican women are working less than half as often as white women and just over a third as often as black women.[84] This might be directly cultural—the husband's machismo or family values—or due to the large numbers of small children in Puerto Rican families, which keep their mothers out of the job market. Nationally, however, Puerto Rican women have no more children than black women in those age brackets.[85] An even higher percentage of Puerto Rican than black families are female-headed,[86] and Puerto Ricans are even more overrepresented on welfare.

How much of the Puerto Ricans' low income is due to discrimination because of color or Hispanic origin is difficult to determine. Other Hispanic and racially mixed groups, such as Mexican Americans, have consistently earned higher incomes than Puerto Ricans.[87] Black West Indian families earned 50 percent higher incomes than Puerto Ricans in 1969—partly because 60 percent of the West Indian families had more than one income earner.[88]

Where Puerto Ricans work as regularly as other groups, the income gap narrows, although educational, language, and other differences prevent its being wholly eliminated. While Puerto Rican families in 1971 had only 58 percent of the income of white families, those Puerto Rican families in which the family head worked full time, year-around had 73 percent of the income of white families that did the same—and 50 percent higher incomes than Puerto Rican families in general.[89] When education and number of income earners are both taken into account, a more mixed picture emerges:

The Puerto Ricans

Family Earnings of Puerto Rican Male-Headed Families
(Puerto Rican Income as Percentage of U.S. Income in the Same Category)

Education of Family Head	One-Income Family	Two-Income Family	Three or More Incomes
Less than high school	90%	91%	101%
High school	72	83	99
College (1–3 years)	82	96	87
College (4 years)	96	74	68
Postgraduate (1 year)	85	88	*
Postgraduate (2 or more years)	83	83	74

* No data

SOURCE: 1970 U.S. Census, Public Use Sample.

In general, the income gap narrows when the above factors are taken into account, even without taking into account the potent effects of age or the fact that Puerto Ricans do not work full time, year-around as often as others.

Politics

Because Puerto Ricans are all American citizens, they are eligible to vote in both national and local elections. However, most Puerto Ricans who are eligible to register do not do so, [90] and the proportion of registered voters who turn out has been lower among Puerto Ricans than among any other ethnic group in New York City.[91] Moreover, the proportion of Puerto Ricans who voted in New York in the 1968 presidential election was less than half what it had been four years earlier.[92]

Even where Puerto Ricans are a substantial part of the population—as in New York City—they are a smaller proportion of the adult population eligible to vote. A high percentage of the Puerto Rican population consists of children. More than half of all Puerto Ricans are either infants, children, or teenagers.

When Puerto Ricans vote at all, they vote overwhelmingly for the Democratic party. In 1960, John Kennedy received more than three quarters of the Puerto Rican vote.[93] In 1964, Lyndon Johnson received 86 percent. In 1968, Hubert Humphrey received 87 percent of the Puerto Rican vote, but reduced voter turnout lessened its significance in the outcome of that election.[94]

Puerto Ricans have gained few elective or appointive political offices. As of 1970, there were no Puerto Ricans serving in the New York City Council.[95] That same year, the first Puerto Rican was elected to Congress.[96]

Nonparticipation in American political life is a pattern common among groups that continue a large back-and-forth migration to their place of origin. A similar absence from politics was common among Italian Americans during their early period of continued returns to Italy, and the same pattern is found among Mexican Americans who maintain ties with Mexico.

Although Puerto Ricans in general have made little impact on American politics, a relative handful of Puerto Rican nationalists have gained sporadic public notice with acts of violence and terrorism. In addition to the attempted assassination of President Truman and the wounding of congressmen, at various times groups of Puerto Rican nationalists have claimed responsibility for bomb explosions in various offices in and around New York City. Their aim is independent nationhood for Puerto Rico—a goal rejected by 99 percent of the voters in Puerto Rico in a 1967 plebiscite.

While Puerto Ricans have had little influence on the course of American politics, they have been much affected by political decisions and institutions. Puerto Ricans are one of the few groups on the mainland to arrive in American society after the whole array of welfare institutions was in place. Many aspects of Puerto Ricans' lives are dealt with by government social service organizations—not only municipal, state, and national, but also by offices established by the government of Puerto Rico in New York City. Puerto Ricans have therefore not had to come together and establish their own grass-roots organization, as immigrant groups or blacks have had to do before them. There is no Puerto Rican equivalent of the NAACP or B'nai B'rith or the many other organizations that gave other groups cohesion.[97] The scarcity of community leadership institutions extends to other phases of Puerto Rican life. The leading Puerto Rican newspapers in New York were founded by an Italian and a Dominican. Puerto Ricans form substantial portions of the membership of the garment unions and the Catholic Church in New York, but have few leaders in either organization. Puerto Ricans are not isolated individuals, but the ties that exist tend to be family or personal friendship ties, not the wider cohesion made possible by organizations.

Most Puerto Ricans on the mainland have arrived—by migration or birth—after the rise of civil rights and protest movements. In some ways, these political institutions have eased the transition by providing economic and moral support and vehicles through which frustrations could be vented. In other ways, they have made adaptations seem less important, focusing instead on changing or eliminating existing standards in education, employment, or elsewhere. Courts have also facilitated such trends by eliminating language requirements for voting, mandating Spanish-language classes in schools, and generally supporting "representation" in jobs and schools based on demographic rather than skill-level criteria. The net economic effect of these political developments is unclear.[98] Certainly, there is little to support the view that Puerto Ricans are advancing faster than other impoverished groups (including native blacks or West Indian blacks) that arrived before these political trends had reached their present magnitude. The increased politicization of ethnicity has also pitted Puerto Ricans against the many other ethnic groups in New York City and elsewhere. Often these other groups have older, more established and experienced organizations that are better able to promote their goals politically, even over the opposition of Puerto Rican groups. Urban renewal programs have uprooted Puerto Ricans disproportionately.[99] Minimum wage laws, promoted by labor unions, have sharply reduced employment of the young and the unskilled,[100] which include many thousands of Puerto Ricans. Occupational licensing laws and many other government-created barriers make it difficult for new people to enter many fields.[101] In short, the impact of politics and the welfare state on Puerto Ricans cannot be estimated solely on the basis of the programs from which they benefit or the programs explicitly directed toward minorities.

PUERTO RICANS TODAY

Progress is difficult to measure in a population with a large turnover of people returning to their place of origin and being replaced by large numbers of newcomers. Still, the occupational advancement of second-generation Puerto Ricans in the continental United States demonstrates significant upward movement between 1960 and 1970 for those who chose to remain in the American economy.[102] In the schools as well, there is a high correlation between the number of years a Puerto Rican youngster has spent in mainland schools and his ability to score well on reading tests or IQ tests.[103] The rising intermarriage rate with non-Puerto Ricans—now about 30 percent of all second-generation Puerto Rican marriages[104]—suggests that social interaction with the American population is also increasing among those who choose to stay and become acculturated. The return migration, however, continues. From 1972 to 1977, there was a net flow of Puerto Ricans from the mainland back to Puerto Rico.[105]

A number of Puerto Ricans have made distinguished contributions in various areas of American life. The Academy Award-winning actor, Jose Ferrer, was born in Puerto Rico. Other Puerto Ricans in the entertainment field have included Jose Feliciano, Tony Orlando, Freddie Prinze, and Rita Moreno. Among Puerto Rican star performers in sports have been Roberto Clemente, Orlando Cepeda, and Luis Arroyo in baseball; boxing champions Sixto Escobar (1936), Jose Torres (1965), and Carlos Ortiz (1968); and golfer Chi Chi Rodriguez. Bestselling writer Piri Thomas became famous for his novel *Down These Mean Streets*, depicting life as he experienced it in a Puerto Rican neighborhood in New York. Among Puerto Rican businessmen, Manuel A. Casiano, Jr., and Nick Lugo both began at the bottom—a delivery boy and a dishwasher, respectively—and ended up as millionaires.[106] In politics, there have been two Puerto Rican congressmen, first Herman Badillo and then Robert Garcia, and the Puerto Rican mayor of Miami, Maurie Ferre.[107]

Upwardly mobile Puerto Ricans, like upwardly mobile blacks and Mexican Americans, tend to have drastically reduced family size. While Puerto Rican women as a group have more children than American women in general, this very high fertility is concentrated in those who never reached high school. More than half of all college-educated Puerto Rican women in their mid-thirties to mid-forties have had a total of two or less children. One-fourth have had no children at all.[108] Looked at in terms of money instead of education, among Puerto Rican women of that same age in families with incomes of $15,000 and above in 1969, half had two children or less.[109] Sterility operations have become relatively common among Puerto Ricans, both on the island and on the mainland.[110] However beneficial the restriction of children may be to those individuals struggling to rise out of poverty, for Puerto Ricans as a group it means that their most successful people leave less of their knowledge, affluence, and contacts to the next generation, which comes disproportionately from people whose parents have no such benefits to leave. More than half of all Puerto Rican women in their mid-thirties to mid-forties never reached high school. Overall, about half of all Puerto Rican children are born to women who never reached high school and less than 2 percent to those who finished college.

The Puerto Ricans

The Puerto Rican population in the United States remains one of the youngest of all ethnic groups. As of 1971, their average age was nineteen. This continues to have a significant economic impact. Even among Puerto Ricans who are working adults, they are younger—less experienced—than other working adults. The average Puerto Rican income earner in 1969 was thirty-four years old—seven years younger than blacks who were earning income.[111]

While younger Puerto Ricans necessarily lack experience, older Puerto Ricans generally lack education. Less than one out of five Puerto Ricans over the age of thirty have completed high school, in a society where most other people in their thirties and forties have at least that much education.[112] About half of all Puerto Ricans in their mid-fifties to mid-sixties have not even completed five years of school—a rarity among other Americans, 94 percent of whom have done so.[113] Even these quantitative measures of education do not tell the full story. Puerto Ricans are much more heavily represented among recipients of vocational high school education than among those taking academic high school courses. Those few who go on to college are much more likely to go to two-year community colleges than to full four-year institutions.[114]

When compared with people of the same age and education, Puerto Ricans earn comparable incomes. Increasingly, however, they are compared instead to a "national average" or to their "representation" in the population. In these terms, these statistical differences (often called "disparities" or "inequities") are large. Puerto Ricans continue to earn lower incomes and to have higher unemployment rates than the rest of the American population—or other Hispanics or blacks. In 1978, Puerto Rican family income was $8,282[115]—an increase of almost 40 percent over its level in 1970,[116] but only about three quarters of the income of black families, and less than half the income of families of Americans in general.[117] Unemployment among Puerto Ricans was 12 percent—which was higher than among blacks, Mexican Americans, Cubans, other Hispanics, or the U.S. population in general.[118] In Puerto Rico itself, over half the population of the island is on welfare.[119]

The rate of progress depends, as always, on the point from which progress is measured. Most Puerto Rican adults in the continental United States today are still the first generation where they are. Few groups in American history could claim more progress in as short a span, as history is measured.

243

Chapter 10

THE MEXICANS

SOME of the oldest and the newest Americans are from Mexico. The area that is now the southwestern United States had settlements of people from Mexico long before the Americans arrived. Most Mexican Americans, however, arrived in the United States in the twentieth century, and especially during and after World War II.[1]

There is no single name that adequately covers the various people of Mexican ancestry living in the United States: (1) descendants of the original Mexican settlers in the Southwest, before it was part of the United States; (2) illegal aliens from Mexico; (3) emigrants from Mexico who are here legally but are not citizens; (4) transients from Mexico staying in the United States for varying periods of time (from days to decades) on various kinds of official documents (visas, work permits, etc.); (5) naturalized American citizens from Mexico; and (6) American-born citizens descended from either legal or illegal immigrants, or from transients.

The U.S. Census estimates that there are about 5 million Mexican Americans—one of the largest ethnic groups in the United States[2] but one of the least publicized. An additional 2 million illegal aliens from

The Mexicans

Mexico are estimated to be living in the United States.[3] Together with a Census undercount of persons of Mexican ancestry (as well as other low-income individuals), this means that the true number of Mexican-origin people in the United States may be closer to 8 million.

The great majority of Mexican Americans live in five southwestern states, which have a combined Mexican-American population of more than 4 million people. About half of these live in California, where they substantially outnumber the black population and constitute about one-sixth of the people of that state.[4]

The culture of Mexican Americans goes back not only to Mexico but also to Spain, and thus to Western civilization in general. Yet their contemporary values and ways of life set them apart from other Americans. Racially, they are both Spanish and Indian in ancestry, to various degrees in a multicolored population.

The millions of people lumped together as "Mexicans," "Mexican Americans," or "Chicanos" represent a variety of historical experiences—many foreign-born, more native-born, and a handful of families that were here long before there was a United States. Their only common denominator is that, at some time or other, they originated in Mexico.

MEXICO

The Aztec civilization developed and spread through Central America before the European discovery of the Western Hemisphere. This warlike people conquered and ruled many other Indian tribes, including those in the region that would later become Mexico. Prisoners of war provided human sacrifices to the Aztec gods—the prisoners' hearts being torn out of their bodies in front of elaborate temples and their skulls later being stored on racks alongside. In other rituals, maidens were beheaded as they danced.

Aztec civilization lacked iron, coins, or the use of wheels for transportation or industrial purposes, such as gears. Their farming was primitive, lacking the use of plows. However, the Aztecs had writing, architecture, sculpture, and elaborate legal, social, political, and religious systems.

In 1519, Cortes arrived in Mexico, and was welcomed by the emperor, Montezuma. Believing Cortes and his men to be gods whose arrival was prophesized in Aztec religious doctrine, Montezuma showered them with gifts, including gold. Once the Spaniards realized that the Aztecs had gold, they determined to conquer them. The Spanish forces were joined by Indian tribes subjugated under the Aztecs. Another potent ally consisted of European diseases—notably smallpox, measles, and influenza—which the Aztecs had never known and to which they had little or no biological resistance. By 1607, European diseases had annihilated from 90 to 95 percent of the Indian population.[5]

In Mexico, as in Latin America generally, the Spanish conquerors were expeditions of men—not whole communities of men, women, and children, as in the British colonies in North America. Sexual liaisons—sometimes including marriage—with native women therefore produced mixed Spanish and Indian offspring soon after the Spaniards arrived. By 1800, the mixed offspring, or mestizos, clearly outnumbered the Spaniards born in Spain or the even smaller number of Negroes imported as slaves.[6] Ultimately, mestizos came to outnumber the Indian population as well.[7] Today, only a small percentage of Mexicans are either pure Caucasian or pure Indian.[8] An elaborate ranking of various racial mixtures existed in Mexico, as elsewhere in Latin America.[9] Similar elaborate gradations of color still exist in modern Mexican-American communities.[10] Both Latins and Anglo-Saxons equate whiteness with superiority, but the Latin emphasis on color gradation differs from the Anglo-Saxon emphasis on race as such—the stark dichotomy of black and white.

From Mexico, explorers, adventurers, and religious missionaries spread northward into what is now the southwestern United States. By the late eighteenth century, Spain had small isolated settlements scattered through California, New Mexico, and Texas. These included Laredo, San Antonio, El Paso, Santa Fe, Tucson, San Diego, Los Angeles, and San Jose.[11] These were typically small enclaves of civilian, military, and religious authorities who attempted to conquer local Indians and bring them into the Spanish culture and religion—at the bottom. Where this effort succeeded, the Indians were brought to live and work in the missions, in a state of tutelage and semibondage.[12] After the monarchy fell in Spain, as a result of the Napoleonic wars, Mexico struggled toward independence, which was proclaimed in 1821. Among the policies of the new Mexican government was one permitting the establishment of an American community on Mexican territories.

At first, the American immigrants adapted to the Mexican culture, learned the Spanish language, and some married Mexican women. But as the number of Americans rose rapidly during the 1820s, they retained their separate American communities, language, and customs. Increasingly hostile relations between the Americans and the Mexicans eventually led to the war for Texas independence. The United States sent troops in to aid the Americans, and in 1845, Texas was annexed as part of the United States. In 1847, American troops captured Mexico City, forced the resignation of the Mexican leader—General Santa Ana—and the following year signed a treaty with a new government, which transferred vast areas (one-third of Mexico) to the United States. From the territory acquired from Mexico were created the states of California, Nevada, Arizona, Utah, Texas, New Mexico, and parts of Colorado, Kansas, Oklahoma, and Wyoming. Before the war, Mexico had been larger than the United States.

The continuing influence of the Hispanic heritage on the southwestern states can be seen in the names of places—all the large cities of California have Spanish names—in the architectural styles of the region, as well as in the ranching patterns established by Mexicans and followed by Americans.

The Mexicans who remained in the new states became a minority—different in language, customs, and race from the growing American population in these areas. Substantial differences between American and Spanish property laws caused many of the Spanish or Mexican settlers to lose their lands, aided by fraud, corrupt officials, and violence. A few Mexican Americans struck back in armed outlaw bands. Most, however, found themselves powerless on the fringes of the new society. There were regional variations in the position of the small Spanish or Mexican populations left in the southwestern United States. In Texas, where the non-Hispanic population was the overwhelming majority at the time of annexation, the upper-class white Hispanic elite was accepted into the dominant American elite, but the multicolored masses of the Mexicans were rigidly excluded from social or political participation and were confined to the lowest economic positions. In California, a separate group of wealthy Hispanics—called *Californios*—remained socially, economically, and politically influential until the late nineteenth century. Other states tended to be somewhere in between. By and large, the indigenous Hispanic people and culture remained in a subordinate role throughout the Southwest. Few, however, returned to Mexico.[13]

In Mexico itself, there was a highly rigid social class system—about 1 percent upper class, 2 percent middle class, and 97 percent lower class. In the urban areas, there was a larger middle class, but still about three quarters of the people were in the lower class.[14] Virtually all the emigrants from Mexico were to come from the lower class. In nineteenth-century Mexico, debt peonage was so widespread as to be almost universal among the rural masses. Landowners as creditors held the peons in virtual bondage for debts that were rarely paid off and that were inherited from generation to generation, like slavery.[15] Illiteracy was widespread among the peons, who lived in extreme poverty and in social and political subjugation. As late as 1910, about 5 percent of Mexican families owned 90 percent of the land.[16]

Under the regime of General Porfirio Díaz (1876–1910), changing land laws turned the communal land of many peasant villages into private lands owned by speculators, throwing many peasants into peonage or into the stream of migrant labor. Advances in public health led to a great population increase—from about 9 million in 1876 to about 15 million in 1910. About 80 percent of the population in Mexico lived in rural areas.[17] Little of this growing and poverty-stricken population found its way into the United States in the nineteenth century. Some came to California during the mid-century gold rush, others to Arizona during the mining boom of the 1860s and the railroad construction period of the 1880s. Some also became migratory farm workers in Texas.[18] But by and large, relatively few Mexicans crossed the economic, social, and geographic barriers separating the two countries. For many Mexicans, getting free of debt peonage was no easy matter, and the great Southwest desert was a formidable barrier in the era before modern cheap transportation.

The construction of railroads in both the United States and Mexico opened the way for masses of poor Mexican villagers to find their way into the rapidly developing southwestern United States.[19] American employers began actively recruiting workers in Mexico, directly or through Mexican contract labor agents. In addition to the economic attraction of the American Southwest, Mexicans were moved by events in Mexico itself. The Mexican Revolution of 1909 set off more than a decade of internal political and military struggles, in which more than one million were killed.[20] Many fled to the United States, more as refugees than as immigrants.

The combination of "pushes" and "pulls" brought almost 10 percent of the total population of Mexico to the American Southwest after the turn of the century. The Mexican populations of Texas and New Mexico nearly doubled between 1900 and 1910. The Mexican population of Arizona more than doubled and that of California quadrupled. The

248

The Mexicans

Mexican population of these four states went from about 100,000 in 1900 to 200,000 in 1910. It doubled again in the next decade and tripled in the decade after that.[21] This was the first of three great waves of emigration from Mexico.

MEXICAN IMMIGRATION

The history of emigration from Mexico is that of three great waves of people moving into the United States, with two massive deportation periods separating them. The seeking and then expelling of Mexicans reflect counteracting tendencies among Americans in the Southwest. Employers of agricultural and other low-paid labor have pressed for a national policy of more open access to the United States from Mexico, while groups concerned with crime, welfare dependency, or other social problems among Mexican immigrants have pressed for more restrictive policies. Shifts in political strength among the contending groups of Americans are reflected in changing immigration policies and changing levels of enforcement. In more recent years, the growing political influence of Mexican Americans has also become a factor in American immigration policy.

The First Wave of Immigrants

The railroads that enabled masses of Mexicans to reach the United States also employed many of them after their arrival. Most Mexican immigrants in the early twentieth century worked for the railroad at some time or other—as construction workers, as watchmen, or as laborers maintaining the tracks. Many lived in boxcars or in shacks near the railroads—primitive settlements that were the beginnings of many Mexican-American communities today. Agriculture and mining employed most of the other Mexican Americans in the pre-World War I era.[22] These three dominant occupations all tended to isolate Mexican Americans in enclaves separate from the rest of the American population. Their children grew up in a separate, Spanish-speaking Mexican-American world. In agriculture, the children worked in the fields alongside their parents, often moving from place to place as the seasonal needs of different crops led the migratory labor gangs from one region to another. Education was either sporadic or nonexistent under such conditions. The separation of Mexicans from the larger society also contributed to their being an "invisible" minority as far as most Americans were concerned.

Throughout the Southwest, Mexican workers provided much of the "stoop labor" that did the hard work in the fields, working twelve to fourteen hours a day. Mexican-American agricultural workers did a wide variety of jobs, from growing cotton throughout the region to helping make California in this era become a major source of fruits and vegetables for the entire nation. The stereotypes of Mexicans as agricultural field hands were established in this era, and would persist for decades, long after most eventually became urbanized. Before 1930, however, more than half of all Mexicans in the United States lived in rural areas.[23] By and large, Mexicans in the United States settled close to the borders of Mexico during the early decades, although some seasonal migratory labor went north into the Rocky Mountain states or went deeper into California. During the 1930s, about 10 percent of the Mexican Americans found their way into factories and provided the nucleus of later Mexican-American urban communities.[24]

Agricultural laborers in this southwestern border region of the United States made double or triple the pay they made in Mexico in 1900, and the pay difference grew even wider over the next three decades. By 1930, the pay of agricultural laborers in the southwestern United States was about six times what it was in Mexico. Moreover, the pay in the interior regions of the United States was higher still, for the heavy supply of Mexican labor kept the pay from rising as much in the border regions as in the rest of the United States.[25] In railroads, mines, and factory occupations, the pay difference between the United States and Mexico was also very large. Mexicans working on American farms or in American factories were poor by American standards but were prosperous by Mexican standards. They returned home to Mexico able to afford farm animals, farm implements, radios, and some even automobiles.[26]

Attempts to control the flow of people across the border in the face of such disparities in pay between the United States and Mexico proved largely futile. American immigration policies and institutions were set up essentially to screen a population crossing the ocean from Europe and landing at a few large ports. Stopping people who could literally walk across a 2,000-mile border at any point and disappear into existing American communities in the desert Southwest was a far more difficult task. Great numbers of Mexicans who were unable to meet literacy requirements and other immigration standards simply entered the United States illegally.[27] Often they were aided and abetted by American employers and by labor contractors.

The massive movement of people from Mexico to the United States was not a permanent emigration. Many came to stay for a season or for a few years to accumulate money and return to Mexico with better prospects than they had before. Others came with the thought of returning but never did so. Some returned only to discover that they themselves had changed during the years in America, and were no longer content with the life and mores of their villages. The magnitudes of these movements are hard to establish, for the official statistics are more suggestive than definitive, given the massive illegal movements in both directions. It is known that more than a million Mexicans returned to Mexico during the period from 1910 to 1928.[28] This was more than the total *legal* immigration from Mexico during the first three decades of the century.[29] The term "wetback" was widely used to describe Mexican immigrants, for many simply waded across the Rio Grande River into the United States. Many border towns had large existing Mexican populations, and newcomers could easily blend in and be safe from the authorities.

Like other groups of transient, non-English-speaking agricultural laborers, Mexican Americans were often recruited by labor contractors and worked in gangs under the contractors' direction and almost total control. Problems of language, culture, and racial differences were solved by the expedient of contracts between an American employer and a Mexican or Mexican-American labor contractor, who assumed responsibility for collecting and supervising a Mexican work force and providing them with their food and other requirements. As in the case of the Italian *padrone*, the Mexican "coyote" protected his investment in his work crew by all means necessary, including the threat or use of force. In the early period, Mexican-American work crews were even marched through the streets of San Antonio under armed guards.[30]

The functions of the "coyote" included recruiting workers in Mexico; smuggling them into the United States; providing them with forged documents, transportation, and food; and acting as the intermediary between them and the contracting employer. The size of the work crews varied. Once an entire trainload of Mexican-American workers was shipped from Texas to Seattle.[31] Laws against labor contracting were widely evaded. As in the case of the Italian *padrone,* the "coyote" faded away only after the people themselves acquired enough knowledge of the language and the country to no longer require his services.

Mexicans living in the United States were poor and lived under primitive conditions that were shocking to other Americans. The shanties lacked not only amenities but also many things that Americans took for granted as necessities—running water and indoor toilets, electricity, and stoves.[32] These living conditions, as well as hard working conditions, were less shocking compared to conditions that the Mexicans had known in Mexico. The massive influx clearly revealed their preferences.

The Mexicans themselves were viewed with repugnance by Americans in the Southwest, especially Texas. Their poverty, illiteracy, folk culture, race, and work patterns set them apart. Laws reinforced their isolation. Segregated facilities were mandated by law in some parts of the Southwest—notably Texas—and maintained by custom elsewhere.[33] The Mexican immigrants were also viewed with repugnance by many Mexican Americans descended from families that had been in the United States longer—especially when those families were more acculturated, had higher incomes, and were lighter in skin color. Such people often called themselves "Spanish" or "Latin" to avoid being confused with the Mexican immigrants. They regarded the immigrants in much the same way as other middle-class people in other ethnic groups have regarded less acculturated newcomers—as dirty, ignorant, and lacking standards of appropriate behavior.[34] Partly, this reflected the familiar fear that the newcomers would undermine the acceptance of the whole ethnic group by the larger society. Partly also, it reflected the rigid class system in Mexico itself.

The more light-complexioned, acculturated, and middle-class portion of the existing Mexican-American population was readily accepted into the white society in many parts of the Southwest—although most of these Mexican Americans were of mixed Spanish and Indian ancestry, rather than white in the Anglo-Saxon sense. But the newcomers from Mexico were socially shunned by both the native whites and the more Americanized Hispanics. In this early period, more than 90 percent of all marriages among Mexican Americans were with other Mexican Americans.[35] Yet those do not reflect solidarity among Mexican Americans so much as social exclusion by others. The Mexican-American community was destined to remain internally fragmented for many more generations, with few leaders with any substantial recognition, much less following.

The early Mexican-American immigrants had very large families, even by the standards of the times in the United States. In 1910, there were 5.3 children born for every Mexican-American woman in her mid-thirties to mid-forties. This was substantially above the 3.4 children per woman of the same age among Americans in general at that time. However, Mexican-American families were not unique in high fertility. There were even more children per woman among Polish Americans (5.9) or Italian Americans (5.5), and the same number among Jewish Americans (5.3). These were all groups relatively recently arrived in America as of 1910. What was to be different about Mexican Americans was that their fertility rates did not decline with the years nearly so much as did the fertility rates of all these other groups. By 1969, the fertility rates of all these other groups had been more than cut in half, leaving Mexican Americans the most fertile of American ethnic groups, with 4.4 children per woman in the thirty-five to forty-four age bracket.[36]

Continuing high fertility rates were but one index of the slow acculturation of Mexican immigrants in the United States. High persistence of a foreign language as a native tongue was another. Low rates of application for citizenship was another indication of a very slow acculturation. Such patterns had been common among other ethnic groups with large return migrations, with continuing influxes of newcomers to keep the foreign culture alive, and with highly tentative or ambivalent plans as to permanent residence. But the drastic restrictions of the 1924 immigration laws cut off the new flow of immigrants from most European countries and made a large back-and-forth migration less sustainable, leading to the Americanization of the existing immigrant population. No such drastic restrictions applied to or were enforceable with Mexican immigrants, who continued the pattern of only partial or ambivalent acculturation in America and large return migrations to Mexico. They were not unique in 1910, but they remained in that pattern long after it had disappeared among other groups.

The first wave of immigrants from Mexico in the first three decades of the twentieth century came to an abrupt halt with the Great Depression of the 1930s. Massive unemployment in America reduced the attraction, and Americans' desire to be rid of Mexican immigrants led to large-scale deportations. Mexicans had long been overrepresented on the relief rolls, partly because an agricultural depression in the 1920s preceded the Great Depression of the 1930s and Mexican immigrants were disproportionately agricultural. In 1925, for example, 90 percent of the welfare budget in Riverside, California, was spent on Mexicans.[37] In this and other California cities, many Mexican farm workers regularly went on relief after the growing season ended. High rates of crime and disease among the Mexicans added to the public antipathy toward them. An influx of poverty-stricken Americans from the "dust bowl" in Oklahoma increased the desire to be rid of foreign labor while so many Americans were unemployed.

A systematic campaign to deport Mexicans got under way in the early 1930s, after it was discovered that the cost of shipping them to Mexico was less than the cost of supporting them for one week on relief. Mexicans who applied for relief were likely to be referred to an agency that would send them to Mexico instead.[38] Sometimes relief payments were withheld unless the Mexican recipient agreed "voluntarily" to leave the United States. By one means or another, tens of thousands of Mexican Americans were deported without formal hearings. The massive deportation included many who were American citizens. By 1930, there were more second-generation Mexican Americans in the United States than there were Mexican Americans born in Mexico.[39] The large illegal emigration from Mexico had led to thousands of deportations per year throughout the 1920s. Between four and five thousand Mexicans were expelled from the United States in 1927 for having entered illegally. This rose by another thousand in 1928, and then went over 8,000 in 1929. This more than doubled in 1930, when more than 18,000 were deported. Nearly 16,000 were deported in 1933, and throughout the later 1930s, about 9,000 Mexicans per year were sent to Mexico.[40] The Mexican population of the United States declined from more than 600,000 in 1930 to less than 400,000 in 1940.[41]

Some of the Mexicans were sent back home, but many others—especially the young—were going to a country they had never seen before. Even those who had come from Mexico had often become partially Americanized in their outlook. They were no longer satisfied with the way of life in Mexico nor were the indigenous Mexicans satisfied with them. Some of the repatriated Mexicans were called "gringos" in their native villages.[42]

The Second Wave of Immigrants

After World War II absorbed millions of Americans into the military services, labor shortages on the farm led to a federal program to bring in farm workers from Mexico. Contract laborers were brought in under the *bracero* program, initiated in 1942. The rationale for the program was that there were simply not "enough" Americans available during the wartime "emergency." The influx of Mexicans kept wages from rising sufficiently to attract "enough" Americans so that every year this "emergency" program was extended, until long after World

The Mexicans

War II. From about 50,000 in 1945, the number of Mexican contract laborers rose to a peak of over 400,000 a year in the late 1950s. The program was formally ended in 1964.

The wartime economy drew workers not only from Mexico. War industries also attracted Mexican Americans away from their traditional jobs and communities into the larger industrial economy and society. There were already more urban than rural Mexican Americans before the war, but jobs in war industries accelerated the urbanization of Mexican Americans. More than half the Mexican-American adult males in villages in New Mexico left their villages during World War II.[43] Employment barriers against Mexicans were relaxed during the labor shortages of World War II, as they were for other minorities.[44] Many Mexican Americans served in the military services, and seventeen earned the Congressional Medal of Honor. For many Mexican Americans, the military was their first experience in daily living in the mainstream American culture, and this accelerated their acculturation. The G.I. Bill later allowed Mexican-American veterans to attend colleges that might otherwise have been unattainable.

In Los Angeles, Mexican-American youth gang members often clashed with military service men, some of whom dated girls in their neighborhoods. The gang members wore zoot-suits—a highly exaggerated outfit of the times—and called themselves *pachucos*. Gang attacks on soldiers and sailors during wartime brought widespread condemnation on the young zoot-suiters, including condemnation from the older generation of Mexican Americans.[45] These gang attacks also brought retaliation by groups of soldiers and sailors in 1942, when they beat up any zoot-suiters they encountered on the streets. Decades later, the *pachucos* would be celebrated in retrospect as heroic militants.[46]

Mexican immigration to the United States was less than two thousand in 1940, but was more than six thousand by 1944, and was nearly ten thousand by 1952. From there on, the rise was even sharper. In 1956, more than 65,000 Mexican immigrants entered the United States—almost one-fourth of all immigrants from the rest of the world.[47] Not all of these were brought in by the *bracero* program. There were many forms of admission on a temporary or a permanent basis, as well as great amounts of illegal entry from Mexico. The second wave of immigration subsided, like the first, in mass deportations. The number expelled reached new heights in the postwar world. The expulsions in 1947 were about ten times the once record-breaking expulsions of 18,000 in 1930. And this was only the beginning of the great expulsions. In 1951, half a million Mexicans were expelled, and in 1954, more than 1 million were expelled.[48] Altogether, nearly 4 million people were sent back to Mexico in the postwar era. This time, citizenship was used instead of indigence as the basis for determining who would and would not be expelled.

The Third Wave of Immigration

Emigration from Mexico dropped in the wake of the great deportation drives of the 1950s, but it was not cut off as drastically as in the 1930s. A postwar peak of 65,000 Mexican immigrants in 1956 fell to about 23,000 in 1959, before slowly beginning to rise again.[49] By 1970, the old peak was surpassed. Altogether, about 440,000 people emigrated legally from Mexico during the 1960s.[50]

This third wave of immigration—which is still continuing—is based partly on explicit changes in immigration laws, partly on the growth of American legal and social agencies ready to protect and defend illegal aliens, and partly on political fears of offending the Mexican government or Mexican Americans by effective enforcement of existing restrictions on the border.

With the demise of the *bracero* program in 1964, the Mexican government ceased such efforts as it had made to control illegal border crossings into the United States. Before that, it had tried to protect the legally authorized Mexican contract laborers in the United States from the competition of the "wetbacks." There were now hundreds of thousands of former *braceros* in Mexico, as well as a rapidly growing Mexican population in general that had tripled in less than fifty years. Cities and towns near the border with the United States had grown especially rapidly.[51] There was a giant pool of potential illegal immigrants to the United States, where the pay remained several times as high as in Mexico.

American officials have devised various ways of attempting to relieve pressures on the border, without allowing unrestricted immigration. A joint project of the Mexican and American governments has attempted to economically develop the border zone on the Mexican side. This, however, has attracted a larger population influx, of whom about half a million are unemployed—and therefore potential border-crossers.[52] Commuters and shoppers from Mexico are allowed ready access to American border communities—from which many then move secretly into the interior to become illegal residents. Some pregnant Mexican women even come in on "shopping" trips and have their babies in American hospitals, often at public expense, and the children are then American citizens—able to facilitate the future legal emigration of family members from Mexico.

In addition to various evasions of immigration restrictions, there is massive outright illegal border crossing along the 2,000-mile boundary, only part of which is effectively covered by a small border patrol. More than 100,000 illegal immigrants are estimated to settle permanently in the United States from Mexico each year,[53] despite the fact that several hundred thousand a year are caught and turned back to Mexico.[54]

A number of factors prevent the United States from controlling emigration from Mexico as it does from the rest of the world. The long border and huge differences in income between the two countries are fundamental. Massive deportations have substituted for effective border control. The deportations have been made more difficult in recent years by the rise of American social agencies and civil rights organizations—often financed with government money—that challenge the investigations, raids, and arrests that lead to deportation proceedings.[55] Even when these organizations lose the cases, they raise the cost of deportation and therefore limit how many can be deported by the government with given resources. American employers of illegal Mexican aliens have both facilitated their evasions of the law and fought politically against effective border control or against any penalties against themselves for knowingly concealing illegal aliens. Illegal border-crossers from Mexico typically face nothing more serious than being sent back. The same person may try many times with little risk, and some have been caught by the border patrol more than once in the same night.

The policies of the Mexican government have also influenced immigration. Successive Mexican governments have put few, if any, restrictions on the movement of people from Mexico into the southwestern United States, which has sometimes been considered as "rightfully" part of their ancestral homeland. More practically, Mexican officials have seen the United States as a source of free training in job skills and more hygienic living patterns, which many of the immigrants have brought back as benefits to Mexico.[56] However, postrevolutionary governments in Mexico have also been committed to the principal of repatriating Mexicans from abroad and have even subsidized this repatriation in various ways—although aware that many seasonal Mexican workers in the United States used these subsidies to get a free trip home during the off season.[57] With the passing years, the repatriation program has become more selective. The Cardenas government of the

1930s was concerned not to bring back Mexicans who had become used to living on relief in the United States.[58] Since World War II, the program has encouraged the repatriation of people with industrial skills.[59] Generally, however, the Mexican government has treated the problem of enforcing immigration restrictions as an American problem. Its own concern has been largely limited to protecting Mexicans in the United States. It has joined with Mexican-American groups in the United States to oppose any vigorous ("repressive") activity by the border patrol—although Mexico itself is highly vigorous in its exclusion of illegal emigrants who attempt to cross its own southern border.[60]

SOCIAL AND ECONOMIC PROGRESS

The Mexican-American population is both diverse and fragmented. They are "concentrated" in the American Southwest, but this is an area larger than France, Germany, Italy, and Great Britain put together. The Los Angeles metropolitan area alone is larger than Belgium. Mexican-American communities are widely scattered in the region in which they are "concentrated." Moreover, substantial Mexican-American communities exist as far away as Chicago.

The widely separated waves of immigration mean that there are substantial differences among Mexican Americans in the length of time their families have been in the United States, in addition to all the other differences of class, education, and occupation that exist in any very large group. There have also been changes in Mexico itself, which affect the characteristics of the Mexican immigrants arriving in the United States at different times. Urbanization in Mexico has been reflected in the country's occupational structure. As of 1940, about two-thirds of all Mexican workers were in agriculture, livestock, or forestry, but by 1970, that proportion had fallen to less than half.[61]

Mexican Americans in the United States have likewise become urbanized. In 1950, 68 percent of Hispanics in the Southwest were urban. By 1960, that proportion had grown to 79 percent,[62] and by 1970 to 85 percent.[63] Mexican Americans are more urbanized than the American population as a whole. In another sense, however, they are less urbanized. Mexican Americans have become urban more recently, with all that that implies in terms of continuing adjustment. Moreover, Mexican Americans are not living in *metropolitan* areas quite so much as either blacks or whites.[64]

Both the economic and the social conditions of Mexican Americans reflect their great internal diversities. Nearly half the high-income Mexican-American family heads surveyed in Los Angeles in the mid-1960s had been born there, while most of the low-income Mexican-American family heads had been born outside of California, including 31 percent who had been born in Mexico. Less than 10 percent of the high-income Mexican-American family heads had been born in Mexico.[65] Another important difference is in location. In 1959, Mexican Americans in California earned more than twice as much as Mexican Americans in Texas.[66] Social class also makes a great difference in personal associations. Half the high-income Mexican Americans in Los Angeles live in areas that are predominantly white American,[67] and half the Mexican-American brides in high-status neighborhoods marry outside the Mexican-American group,[68] even though about three quarters of all marriages among Mexican Americans in general are with other Mexican Americans.[69]

Generations also differ greatly. The average age of first-generation Mexican Americans is forty-three; the second generation averages twenty-four years old; and the third generation is thirteen.[70] Internal divisions extend to the very name that Mexican Americans choose to call themselves—whether "Mexican," "Latin," "Spanish," "Chicano," or others. Names that are cherished by some segments are considered offensive by others. Genteel designations like "Spanish" or "Latin" that have long been used to disassociate higher classes from the masses of "Mexicans" are resented by many. Designations like "Chicano" are resented by others as exalting a boorish pattern of behavior. The degree of the sensitivities involved may be indicated by the fact that Mexican-American political groups have even refused to merge because they could not agree on what name would designate the group.[71]

Economic Conditions

The outdoor manual labor of early Mexican immigrants—as farm or railroad workers—has for most given way to urban occupations. By 1960, only 16 percent of Mexican-American males in the Southwest were farm laborers—the same as the proportion who were craftsmen and less than the 23 percent who were listed as "operatives." Only about 5 percent were clerical workers, and 4 percent were in the professions—less than among either blacks or whites. Unemployment among Mexican Americans was nearly twice the national average.[72] The average income of Mexican-American families was about 65 percent of that of white non-Hispanic families in the Southwest.[73]

These data conceal many important internal differences. Mexicans earned about 59 percent of the income of non-Hispanic whites in San Antonio and 84 percent in San Diego.[74] Mexicans in metropolitan Detroit earned more than double the income of Mexicans in the metropolitan area of Laredo or Brownsville.[75] Sometimes these differences reflect economic differences in the respective communities. The two largest Mexican-American urban populations—in Los Angeles and San Antonio—are in cities with very different economic histories and different occupational and income structures for its citizens in general.[76] Mexican Americans located in cities far from the Southwest tend to be people who left the migrant labor stream—and may therefore be a selective group of people—and may have higher earnings for this reason rather than because of location as such.

Over the years, Mexican-American incomes have risen, not only absolutely, but also relative to the rising incomes in American society in general. In 1949, the personal income of Mexican Americans was 57 percent of that of non-Hispanic whites in the Southwest. By 1959, this had risen to 62 percent.[77] In 1969, Mexican-American males between twenty-five and sixty-four years of age earned 66 percent of the incomes of non-Hispanic whites of the same age in the Southwest.[78] By 1971, they earned 73 percent of the U.S. average.[79]

Meaningful income comparisons are difficult because Mexican Americans are a decade younger than other Americans, and have lower levels of schooling, in both quantitative and qualitative terms, among other differences. In 1971, Mexican-American males, age twenty-five and up, had higher incomes than the U.S. average at all educational levels up to eight years, and 90 percent of the U.S. average for those who had attended high school and graduated from high school.[80] These precollege brackets include the great bulk (over 90 percent) of Mexican Americans.[81] Their incomes are very close to the incomes of other Americans of the same educational level, but the still large intergroup disparities reflect large disparities in years of schooling. In 1950, Mexican Americans in the Southwest completed only five years of school, compared to eleven for the non-Hispanic white population (and eight for blacks) in the same region. By 1960, this had risen to seven years for Mexican Americans compared to twelve for non-Hispanic whites and nine for blacks. Mexican-American education was growing faster than that of either blacks or whites but remained the lowest among the three groups.

Quality performances are also different—and to the disadvantage of Mexican Americans. Mexican-American youngsters scored lower on IQ and other standarized tests,[82] whether in separate schools or mixed schools, and whether their parents were laborers, white-collar workers, or skilled workers.[83] Double standards of grading Mexican children partly conceal these differences[84]—in part for the "emotional well-being" of the students and in part not to "rock the educational boat."[85] However, the accumulated educational deficiencies affect what kinds of colleges or courses of study in college can be pursued by those few Mexican-American young people who get there. Most Mexican Americans who have gone to college have attended the lower ranked colleges.[86] In Texas, for example, there were less than one-third as many Mexican Americans enrolled in the top state university at Austin than at lower ranked El Paso,[87] even though the number of students in general at Austin is much larger. Against this background, it is not surprising that Mexican-American men who have attended colleges earned only 77 percent of the U.S. average for all men who have attended college, whereas Mexican-American men hold their own very well against other men with similar educational backgrounds at the lower educational levels,[88] where the quality of the schooling itself often has little affect on job performance. The earnings of Hispanics in general show a higher rate of return to a given *quality* of schooling than among either blacks or whites.[89] That is, economically Hispanics make the most of what they have educationally, but they have less to begin with.

Other factors also complicate income comparisons. Labor force participation rates among Mexican-American females is much lower than among either black or white women,[90] which affects both personal and family income statistics. Unemployment among Mexican-American men is about double that among black men and three times that among white men.[91]

A family's economic standard of living depends not only on its income but also on how many people must be supported by it. Mexican Americans have far lower *per capita* income than would be indicated by their individual or family earnings. For example, Mexican-American per capita income was only 47 percent of that of non-Hispanic whites in the Southwest in 1959—and was lower than the per capita income of blacks.[92] This may partly explain why Mexican Americans, with higher incomes than blacks, nevertheless live in crowded housing more often and send their children to college less often.[93] The Mexicans simply have more mouths to feed. The large number of children per family among Mexican Americans may also help explain why the women are in the labor force less often than either black or white women. The proportion of people too old or too young to work is higher among Mexican Americans than among either blacks or whites.[94] This is due to larger numbers of children because there are smaller proportions of older Mexican Americans than among either blacks or whites.[95]

The economic progress of Mexican Americans affects different generations differently (see table below). First-generation Mexican-American men (born in Mexico) earn significantly less than either the second- or third-generation Mexican-American men. But the second generation earns about 14 percent higher average income than the third generation. This might seem to suggest that progress stops and retrogression sets in after the second generation. This is not true, however. The three generations differ substantially in age distribution—the first generation being the oldest, the second generation next, and the third generation the youngest. When age is taken into account, the first generation is at an even greater disadvantage than first appeared to be the case. For example, the third generation's mean income is about 11 percent higher than that of the first generation, but in all the prime earning years—from twenty-five to sixty-four—the third generation makes about 20 percent more than first-generation Mexican Americans of the same age. The paradox of apparently higher earnings in the second than in the third generation is due to age differences.

Mean Income of Mexican-American Males, 1969

AGE	First Generation		Second Generation		Third Generation	
	Income	% Population	Income	% Population	Income	% Population
16–19	$1,812	5	$1,372	12	$1,386	22
20–24	3,716	11	3,682	11	3,762	18
25–34	5,386	24	6,519	22	6,448	23
35–44	5,983	22	7,219	27	7,227	15
45–64	5,299	33	6,324	24	6,397	17
65+	2,502	5	2,693	4	2,693	5
ALL AGES	$4,668	100	$5,804	100	$5,103	100

Source: U.S. Bureau of the Census, 1970 Census of Population: Subject Reports, PC (2)-lb, pp. 42–43.

The Mexicans

More than half of the second generation is over thirty-five years of age, while most of the third generation is under thirty-five. Bracket for bracket, the second and third generations earn virtually the same incomes.

This does not mean that progress has halted. Both the second and the third generations share in the absolute rise of Mexican-American incomes and in its rise relative to that of other Americans. The first generation also progresses. Those who remain in the United States for fifteen years or more eventually overtake native-born Mexican Americans in income. After a decade, Mexican immigrants have incomes only 5 percent below those of native-born Mexican Americans, and after two decades, the immigrants surpass the native-born by 3 percent.[96] The long time required for emigrants from Mexico to equal native-born Mexican Americans in income suggests the importance of what economists call "human capital"—both specific skills and general experience in a given economy. It includes making contacts, learning to use existing institutions, knowing how to find better jobs, and how to get promoted. These internal patterns raise serious questions about common assertions that Mexican-Americans' income differences from general population are largely or solely caused by employer discrimination. As noted already, Mexican-American men have incomes about as high as, or higher than, other American men with similar educational qualifications, through the high school level.

A factor whose effect is difficult to gauge is that substantial numbers of Mexicans in the United States are illegal aliens. Many employers prefer them, for they are in no position to cause the employer trouble and may accept lower pay or poorer working conditions because they cannot usually invoke legal remedies without fear of exposing their illegal status—or having their employer do so in retaliation. During the *bracero* era, for example, legal migrants had numerous government protections as to their pay and treatment, but "wetbacks" did not. Many employers preferred "wetbacks" to *braceros*.[97] With the extension of the minimum wage law to agricultural workers in 1966, native Mexican Americans and Mexicans working in the United States with legal authorization had their costs to an employer raised further above those of illegal aliens.

Social Conditions

The family is central in Mexican-American culture. "Warmth inside the family and hostility to those outside the family"[98] has characterized the Mexican family, as it characterized the Italian immigrant family. Close friends complete a tight circle of social activity and relationships.[99] *Machismo* concepts give the family a male-dominated flavor, makes protection of the women's chastity a preoccupation, and inhibits their employment. About half of all Mexican-American married women were married in their teens.[100] This contributes to their even lower college attendance than Mexican men (although the sexes are evenly represented through high school) and to the very large families characteristic of Mexicans in either Mexico or the United States.

Family break-ups are much less common among Mexican Americans than among other low-income groups. The rate of divorce among Mexican-American women is lower than among whites and less than half the rate among blacks or Puerto Ricans.[101] Only 12 percent of Mexican-American families are female-headed, compared to 31 percent among blacks and 34 percent among Puerto Ricans. [102]

Mexican Americans average larger families than either black or white Americans, Puerto Ricans, or any other ethnic group.[103] In 1960, more than two-thirds of all Mexican-American children were born to mothers who had five or more children. The diversity of Mexican Americans, however, is indicated by the fact that while low-income women with less than a high school education averaged more than six children each, middle-class Mexican-American women who had completed high school averaged just two.[104] In short, family size reflects the degree of acculturation to American norms. This is also shown historically, for Mexican-American families in the past—while even larger than today—were no larger than the families of a number of other contemporary ethnic groups.[105] But after the severe immigration restrictions of 1924 led these other groups to become more Americanized, their fertility declined much faster than that of Mexican Americans, who continued to have their Mexican culture reinforced by continued massive inflows of people from Mexico.

Geographic differences drive home the same point. Heavy concentrations of Mexicans—enough to perpetuate a culture—have typically meant higher fertility rates than in places where the Mexican population is more scattered or is a smaller part of the general population. Metropolitan areas of Texas communities like Brownsville and Laredo—with heavy concentrations of Mexicans going back for many generations and with a strong separate subculture—average much higher fertility rates than newer and less concentrated Mexican populations in Los Angeles or Long Beach.[106] Although Los Angeles has the largest Mexican-American population of any American city, Mexican Americans are a smaller percentage of the total population than in Laredo or Brownsville or various other Texas cities.[107] Even within Los Angeles, Mexicans in the East Los Angeles *barrio* have a higher fertility rate than those in the city as a whole.[108] Mexican women in their mid-thirties to mid-forties in the Brownsville area have had more than five children, while Mexican women of the same age in Long Beach have had less than three.[109] About half the Mexican women in Long Beach have completed high school, compared to about one-sixth in Brownsville and less than 10 percent in Lubbock, Texas, where Mexican women in the same age bracket average 5.5 children.

Spanish is the language that is spoken in nearly half the Mexican-American homes. Nationally, about 47 percent of Mexican Americans grew up in homes where Spanish was the language spoken[110]—a high persistence of a foreign language compared to that of various European ethnic groups,[111] but not compared to the proportion among Puerto Ricans (72 percent) or Cubans (87 percent).[112] Language use, like other aspects of acculturation, varies greatly among Mexican Americans, from place to place and from class to class. Half of the higher income Mexican Americans living in predominantly non-Mexican neighborhoods in Los Angeles speak English mostly or solely to their children, and another 40 percent speak both Spanish and English to them. But among lower income Mexican Americans in the Los Angeles *barrios*, half of them speak Spanish solely or predominantly, and another 24 percent speak both. In San Antonio, almost three quarters of the low-income Mexican-American parents in the *barrios* there speak Spanish predominantly or exclusively to their children, and even higher income middle-income parents usually do not emphasize English.[113] About half the Mexican Americans in both cities consider themselves bilingual.[114]

The language spoken has both educational and economic impact. Hispanics whose mother tongue was English had completed high school about 50 percent more often than those whose mother tongue was Spanish, and had gone on to college about 70 percent more often.[115] Almost half of all low-income Mexican Americans in Los Angeles report difficulty in speaking English. The percentage is even higher in San Antonio.[116] The proportion of higher income Mexican Americans who had difficulty with English is much lower in both cities.[117]

Language choice and proficiency have in recent years become ideological issues, rather than simply pragmatic questions related to functioning in an English-speaking country. Attempts to teach English in school, and to get Hispanic youngsters to use English more, are seen by some—including non-Hispanic intellectuals—as an attempt to stigmatize Spanish as "inferior."[118] Even tragic situations growing out of an inability to communicate—with paramedics, firemen, or policemen, for example—have only led some to demand that all those in these occupations learn to speak Spanish.

At one time, public schools in the Southwest discouraged, forbade, and even punished the use of Spanish by Mexican-American students, in order to get them to learn English.[119] In more recent times, under political and federal court pressure, schools have instituted "bilingual" programs—often taught almost exclusively in Spanish. It remains to be seen what effect this will have on general acculturation or economic progress.

The Spanish spoken by Mexican Americans is not classic Castillian Spanish, but a folk dialect reflecting the language of the poorer people of Mexico, together with modifications of American words, in the manner of the early Italian immigrants. In order to get a "purer" Spanish, American television stations in the Spanish language usually import announcers from Latin America, although Mexican-American performers may be used for other purposes.[120] Spanish-language television and radio stations in the United States are preferred mainly by the poorer, less acculturated Mexican Americans,[121] but English-language newspapers are preferred to Spanish-language newspapers by Mexican Americans at various income levels and regardless of neighborhood.[122]

The goals and values of Mexican Americans have never centered on education. As of 1960, only 13 percent of Hispanics in the Southwest completed high school, compared to 17 percent for blacks in the same region, 28 percent among non-Hispanic whites, and 39 percent among Japanese Americans.[123] However, this too shows changes with time. As of 1950, only 8 percent of southwestern Hispanics had completed high school. In one decade, this rose to 13 percent and then to 29 percent in 1970.[124] Education has varied greatly among Mexicans with different exposures to American norms. Among third-generation Mexican Americans in these areas, 38 percent completed high school; but among those in the urban first generation (Mexican-born), only 13 percent had done so; and among the rural first generation, only 4 percent had completed high school.[125] Various attempts have been made to determine Mexican-American cultural values by questionnaires, rather than by actual behavior,[126] but answering a questionnaire costs nothing and therefore cannot test the depth of a commitment, particularly to a process like education that takes many years and that many find distasteful.

Among Mexican Americans, as among other ethnic groups, acculturation is not a simple one-way process. The larger society in the Southwest has adopted many Mexican features—not only such practical things as Mexican ranching equipment and practices, but such other cultural features as Mexican food and Spanish names. Many of the names of places in the Southwest have historically been preserved since Spanish times, but many other Spanish names of places and streets are quite recent, and were provided by non-Hispanics for other non-Hispanics. Marina del Rey, for example, is a relatively new community with very few Hispanic residents. There are also many new Spanish-named streets with few (if any) Hispanic residents (such as Avenida de Cortes in Pacific Palisades, as only one example).

The social pathology of Mexican Americans reflects their age composition. Mexican Americans have lower than average mortality from degenerative diseases that come with age—cancer, chronic heart disease, and vascular lesions—but high mortality rates from rheumatic heart disease, pneumonia, and automobile accidents. Fatal automobile accidents are a leading cause of death among Mexican-American young men—accounting for 43 percent of all deaths in the sixteen- to twenty-five-year-old bracket. Infant mortality is also very high.[127] Crime and violence take a heavy toll among Mexican Americans in general and urban youth gangs in particular. An estimated 13,000 Mexican-American youths belong to gangs in Los Angeles County alone, where there were 69 killings in 1977.[128]

Politics

For many years, Mexican Americans were both socially and politically "invisible." Working and living in isolated rural communities or in the separate world of urban *barrios*, Mexican Americans had little impact on the political system or on the life of the larger community. Because so few became naturalized citizens, and those who did seldom voted, political leaders paid little attention to them. In a pattern coming over from Mexico, many Mexican Americans tried to have as little as possible to do with the government. The fact that many were illegal aliens reinforced this tendency.

The post-World War II era saw this long-standing pattern begin to change. Mexican-American men serving in the armed forces saw a wider vision of the world and returned home after the war with broader aspirations and more assertiveness. The larger society's growing awareness of the problems and rights of minorities provided a setting in which political awareness could develop and express itself. By the 1960s, the civil rights movement and protest organizations of blacks and other ethnic groups provided a model and an impetus for similar developments among Mexican Americans.

Perhaps the best known of these political movements grew out of Cesar Chavez' labor union among agricultural workers, which emerged in the 1960s. Whatever the economic consequences of Chavez' union efforts—thousands of jobs have been eliminated by mechanization in the wake of union pay increases—he has become a nationally known figure whose political support therefore carries weight.

Mexican Americans achieved elective office late and in small numbers. But beginning in the 1950s, a number of Mexican Americans achieved high national office. Joseph Montoya became a congressman from New Mexico in 1957 and a U.S. senator in 1964, after a long career in state politics. Henry B. Gonzalez became a congressman from Texas in 1961, and then Edward R. Roybal was elected to Congress from California in 1962, Elio de la Garza from Texas in 1964, and Manuel Lujan from New Mexico in 1968. In 1974, Mexican Americans were elected governors in two states: Raul Hector Lopez becoming governor of Arizona and Jerry Apodaca governor of New Mexico.[129] At the state level, there were by 1967 just over 600 state legislators of Mexican ancestry in the Southwest.[130] In addition, many Mexican-American "spokesmen" emerged at the national or local level to lead organizations of various sizes and durability. Some of these were patterned after black protest movements—the Brown Berets after the Black Panthers, for example. However, most Mexican Americans have literally never heard of these various organizations,[131] however seriously the media treat their assertions in the name of "Chicanos."

Despite individual political achievements, Mexican Americans as a group are still not strong participants in politics. Rates of naturalization, registration, and voting are all low among Mexican Americans.[132] Moreover, political unity has been difficult to achieve among people from such a highly individualistic culture. One example of the difficulty of translating large numbers of Mexican Americans into voting strength is seen in Los Angeles, which has more Mexicans than most cities in Mexico but which has not had a Mexican elected to the City Council in nearly twenty years.[133] There are fewer Mexican-American members of the California Legislature than there are black members, although blacks are only half as large a portion of the population.[134]

The Mexicans

When Mexican Americans do vote, they vote overwhelmingly Demo-cratic. In 1960, for example, John F. Kennedy won 85 percent of the Mexican-American vote. Lyndon Johnson won 90 percent in 1964 and Hubert Humphrey 87 percent in 1968.[135] The lack of diversity in their voting makes it unnecessary for one party, and futile for the other, to exert itself to get the Mexican vote.

MEXICAN AMERICANS TODAY

The diverse elements of the Mexican-American population are at very different stages of acculturation and economic advancement. Never-theless, progress is apparent across broad economic, political, and so-cial areas. Compared to groups that have been here longer, or that arrived with more education and skills, Mexicans have not yet achieved the same economic levels. Compared to other groups emerg-ing from an agricultural past and with no tradition of education, Mexi-can Americans have more than held their own. As of 1979, Mexican-American family income was 18 percent higher than that of blacks and 54 percent higher than that of Puerto Ricans. It was 73 percent of the American national average.[136]

Numerous well-known Mexican Americans have emerged in sports and entertainment—the traditional areas of opportunity for emerging ethnic groups. Tennis champion Pancho Gonzales established an en-during reputation in the 1940s and 1950s. Joe Kapp and Jim Plunkett have become National Football League quarterbacks. Lee Trevino and Nancy Lopez are among the top golfers. Mexican-American singers have included Vikki Carr, Joan Baez, and Trini Lopez. Mexican-Ameri-can actors have a long line going back to Ramon Novarro and Gilbert Roland in the silent screen era and to Ricardo Montalban and Antho-ny Quinn in more recent times.

Similar achievements have not been made in scholarship, science, or the professions—all of which depend on higher education, which few Mexican Americans reach. As late as 1973, there were only three or four Mexican Americans with Ph.D.s in economics, eight with Ph.D.s in political science, and only two dozen with Ph.D.s in sociology.[137] Moreover, even among these very few, the tendency in recent years has been to devote themselves to social and political activism, rather

269

than to scholarship in their respective professions.[138] In broadly defined professions—ranging from physicians to schoolteachers—there were more than 90,000 persons of Spanish surname in the Southwest in 1970.[139] This was about the same as the total number of persons of Chinese and Japanese ancestry in the same professions,[140] but there were only about one-fourth as many persons of Chinese and Japanese ancestry in the United States as there were persons of Spanish surname in the Southwest.[141] The proportion of Mexican Americans in the professions is also lower than among blacks.

About half of all employed Mexican Americans today are native-born Americans whose parents were also born in the United States. The other half either came from Mexico themselves or their parents were Mexicans. This means that the people whose achievements are being repeatedly compared to the "national average" have been here about one-and-a-half generations. From the rural Mexican cultures of the 1920s to modern urban America today is a very long journey in human terms. Most Mexican Americans have come a long way on that journey.

VI

An Overview

Chapter 11

IMPLICATIONS

THE HISTORY of American ethnic groups has implications that reach beyond ethnicity. In an individualistic society, ethnic history reminds us of the enduring consequences of centuries-old cultural patterns into which each individual is born. As a noted historian once observed: "We do not live in the past, but the past in us."[1] Ethnic history, in addition, reflects how hard it is for differing human beings to get along with each other—not only when they carry such broad labels as Jews, Chinese, or Mexicans, but also in the many fragmented elements within these and other groups.

History is what happened, not what we wish had happened—nor what a theory or an ideology says should have happened. On the contrary, history can sometimes help to assess our beliefs about the past or about the present or future.

To seek for cause and effect in history is very different from seeking for justification and condemnation. Causal and moral analyses are each difficult enough without being confused with each other. For example, the extent to which one group's poverty is caused by another group's bigotry is a causal question, not a foregone conclusion because

273

of the moral repugnance of bigotry. It is not unknown for bigots to find themselves overtaken and left behind, economically and socially, by groups they have hated and stigmatized as inferior. Why this sometimes happens and sometimes does not is a causal question, but if bigotry alone was a sufficient causal explanation, Jews and Japanese would not be among the most prosperous American ethnic groups.

More generally, to seek the factors that advance and retard the progress of groups is in no way to morally or otherwise rank or grade these groups. Every human being is born into a world he never made, regardless of what ethnic label he carries. It is not personal merit but simply good fortune to be born into a group whose values and skills make life easier to cope with. But it is enormously important to get what insight we can into what those values and skills might be, and why.

Despite the obvious importance of money, some of the most economically successful ethnic groups—Jews being the classic example—began destitute when they first set foot on American soil. Despite the supposed prerequisite of political cohesion, some of the most remarkable advances in the face of adversity were made by groups that deliberately avoided politics—notably the Chinese and Japanese. Conversely, one of the slowest rises of any group with advantages of color and language was by the Irish—who were unexcelled in political success. Despite the supposedly crucial factor of the frontier in the history of opportunity in America, some of the most successful ethnic groups never came near the frontier or arrived after its closing had supposedly slammed the door on upward mobility. Among the most prominent people on the frontier were the Scotch-Irish, whose descendants now form one of the country's largest pockets of poverty, in the Appalachian region. The educational panacea is undermined by the history of groups like the Jews, the Chinese, and the Japanese, who first rose by their labor and their business sense and only later on could afford to send their children to college.

There are, however, some general patterns that do appear in history. Determining the reasons for those patterns and their implications may throw some light on ethnicity, on American society, and on human beings more generally.

Implications

PATTERNS

Perhaps the most striking pattern among American ethnic groups is their general rise in economic conditions with the passage of time. Progress is so generally taken for granted in the United States that it is necessary to realize that it is not automatic. In many parts of the world, people still live at an economic level not much above that of their ancestors. But in addition to absolute rises in living standards, political representation, and longevity, American ethnic groups have typically also risen in relative terms. Italian Americans who earned less than half the national income in the early twentieth century now receive more than the national average. The poverty-stricken Jews of the late nineteenth century now earn more than any other ethnic group, including Anglo-Saxons. There are wide variations in the rates of progress among American ethnic groups, but progress itself is pervasive.

Every ethnic group has encountered obstacles to its progress in the United States. But the obstacles and suffering they experienced before arriving here usually exceeded anything experienced on American soil. Anti-Semitism in the United States meant encountering snobbery and occupational restrictions, but not living under the threat of mass expulsions and massacres. Even the historic bitterness of slavery was worse for Africans enslaved to the Arabs or in the rest of the Western Hemisphere, where slaves died off faster then they could reproduce. In short, America has never been exempt from the ages-old sins that have plagued the human species. What has been distinctively American is the extent to which other factors have also been at work, usually for the better.

Comparison Problems

It has often been said that we are a nation of immigrants. In a sense, that is true; but the blanket term "immigrants" covers over many important distinctions among the various peoples who came to America. The famine Irish and the east European Jewish victims of pogroms were essentially refugees who fled in whole family units, burning their bridges behind them, and arrived in the United States committed to becoming Americans. Others have come as sojourners, mostly men, and with the intention of returning to their native lands, so that Americanization in language, culture, or citizenship had a low priority for them. The early emigrations from Italy, China, Japan, and Mexico

275

were largely of this character, as is much of today's migration back and forth between Puerto Rico and the mainland of the United States. There were also immigrants who were neither refugees nor sojourners, but simply people who chose to come to the United States to settle at a place and time of their choice. Such immigrants—the Germans or Scandinavians, for example—were far less likely to concentrate in the port cities where they landed and more likely to choose a long-run settlement site suited to their conditions. Finally, there were those who did not choose to come at all but who were brought as captives—African slaves—and whose geographic distribution and occupational roles were suited to the convenience of others.

Merely *comparing* the progress of these different kinds of groups is difficult—quite aside from the more complex task of assessing its meaning. Tracing the progress of a group that includes large proportions of sojourners is much more complex and uncertain than tracing the progress of groups that consist largely of the same people and their descendants over time. The Jews of 1970 were essentially the Jews of 1960, ten years later, but the Puerto Ricans in the continental United States in 1970 included substantial proportions who were living in Puerto Rico in 1960—and substantial proportions of the Puerto Ricans living on the mainland in 1960 were back on the island in 1970. Gross statistics collected in either location are misleading as to the progress of a given set of people.

The progress of Puerto Ricans who have remained permanently in the continental United States for more than a generation is very different from the progress of a changing mixture of people classified under the same label as "Puerto Ricans." There are substantial differences between them in incomes, occupations, and intermarriage rates. The same is true of Mexican Americans, who also move back and forth in substantial numbers. Comparing a sojourner group with a refugee group, or a conventional immigrant group, is difficult—whether the purpose is to measure group progress or discrimination by others. How can the living conditions of men who are seeking only a place to sleep, while they save money to take back home, be compared to the living conditions of a family of farmers in a home intended to last for generations? In short, how can progress be measured in the same units for people pursuing different goals? And how can others ("society") be held either causally or morally responsible for all these differences measured in the same units?

With the black population, it is not clear what is the appropriate time to even begin measuring their progress—whether at their initial

276

Implications

arrival in the seventeenth century, emancipation in the nineteenth century, or arrival in urban America in the twentieth century. Blacks are either some of the oldest Americans or some of the newest groups going through the adjustment process, according to which time is chosen—and their rate of progress has been substantial or slight, depending on the point from which it is measured.

Ethnic Succession

While each ethnic group is in some way unique, there has also been an historical pattern of one group replacing another in neighborhoods, jobs, leadership, schools, and other institutions.

Today's neighborhood changes have been dramatized by such expressions as "white flight," but these patterns existed long before black-white neighborhood changes were the issue. When the nineteenth-century Irish immigrants flooded into New York and Boston, the native Americans fled. With the first appearance of an Irish family in a neighborhood, "the exodus of non-Irish residents began."[2] According to a contemporary, property values "tremble" as "fear spreads," and panicky flight ensues.[3] As "the old occupants fled to the outskirts of town,"[4] in the mid-nineteenth century when immigration increased, New York City grew northward about one mile per decade. The built-up area extended only as far north as Fourteenth Street in 1840, but it grew to Thirty-fourth Street in a decade, and to Forty-second Street by 1860.[5]

"White flight" is a misleading term, not only because of its historical narrowness, but also because blacks too have fled when the circumstances were reversed. Blacks fled a whole series of neighborhoods in nineteenth-century New York, "pursued" by new Italian immigrants who moved in.[6] In nineteenth-century Detroit, blacks moved out of neighborhoods as Polish immigrants moved in.[7] The first blacks in Harlem were fleeing from the tough Irish neighborhoods in mid-Manhattan,[8] and avoided going north of 145th Street, for fear of encountering more Irish there.[9]

As the relative socioeconomic positions of ethnic groups changed with the passage of time, so did the neighborhood flight. In nineteenth-century nieghborhoods where Anglo-Saxons had once fled as the Irish moved in, the middle-class Irish later fled as the Jews and Italians moved in.[10]

When poor newcomers replaced older residents, the housing itself was drastically altered. The poor have seldom in history occupied brand-new housing, built specifically for them. They have inherited housing originally created for higher income people, who could afford more living space per person. Therefore, existing dwelling units have been broken up into smaller units for lower income tenants. Smaller apartments were created by partitions, and existing apartments were shared by more people, either cooperatively or through the device of renting rooms to help pay the rent. Virtually every ethnic group has passed through a stage where taking in roomers was a pervasive pattern. In 1880, there was an average of more than one roomer per family among Italian immigrants. By 1905, this had dropped to about one roomer for every two families—at the time about the same as among Jews.[11] This was still higher than among Harlem Negroes in the 1920s, when taking in roomers was considered a "notorious" widespread practice.[12] As in many other areas, the later practice was considered shocking and peculiar only because the history of the earlier pattern had been ignored or forgotten.

With the transfer of housing down the social scale came different maintenance policies. The pattern in the nineteenth century immigrant slums was to "allow old buildings to deteriorate" until they wore out and were torn down.[13] In other words, repairs were deliberately neglected on the theory that they would be wasted on the destructive tenants who now inhabited the building.[14] Nor were these beliefs about the immigrant tenants all hostile stereotypes. Even a sympathetic reformer said of them that "they carry their slums with them wherever they go. . . ."[15] Much the same would be said of various groups in the twentieth century. Often higher rents were charged for a given property as slum dwellings than in its previous, more "respectable" use.[16] Nevertheless, profit rates on slum properties were not particularly high,[17] despite much assertion to the contrary by social reformers.[18] The faster depreciation of slum housing was one factor. More fundamentally, however, profits are made on rents *paid*, not on rents *charged*. Evictions for nonpayment of rent were very widespread in nineteenth-century slums. Nonpayment of rent was also a pattern persisting among twentieth-century slum dwellers, although legal changes have made eviction more difficult in more recent times. "Exorbitant" rents for slum dwellings do not imply higher than average profit rates on slum property.

Ethnic succession did not end with neighborhoods. Early Irish immigrants were often used as strikebreakers and were hated and kept out of unions as a result. Later, the Irish were unionized and Italians, Negroes, and many others were used as strikebreakers, encountering in turn the same hostility and resistance to their admission to unions.

Implications

Still later, the Irish were union leaders, while Jews or Italians were rank-and-file union members. Today, there are unions where Jews are union leaders and blacks and Puerto Ricans are members. Similarly, in the schools, the Irish immigrant children in the mid-nineteenth century were taught by Protestant Anglo-Saxon teachers. Half a century later, Jewish immigrant children were far more likely to be taught by Irish Catholics than by Jewish teachers. A generation later, Negro children in Harlem were far more likely to be taught by Jewish teachers than by black teachers. Few children of rising ethnic groups have had "role models" of their own ethnicity. Some of the most successful—notably the Chinese and the Japanese—almost never did.

While various ethnic groups succeeded each other in neighborhoods, schools, jobs, etc., the country as a whole was also changing. The installation of underground sewage lines and indoor plumbing in the late nineteenth century meant that no other urban ethnic group had to endure as primitive and dangerous a set of living conditions as the Irish had in the mid-nineteenth century. Subways, trolleys, and eventually bus lines made it feasible for working people to spread out and still get to work in a reasonable time. The incredible overcrowding on New York's lower east side in the nineteenth century was never to be approached again in modern slums. Blacks, Puerto Ricans, and Mexican Americans today live in crowded housing conditions, compared to their contemporaries, but in no way so crowded as the conditions among Jews, Italians, or the Irish in the nineteenth century. "Overcrowded" schools today may have perhaps half as many students per class as in nineteenth century schools on New York's lower east side. The problems of today are very real, and sometimes severe, but they are by no means historically unprecedented.

Many of the problems of the poor and powerless remain the same, whatever group fills that role at a given time. *The Jewish Daily Forward* commented in 1907: "police in the Jewish quarter of New York are the most savage in America."[19] An Italian immigrant writer complained in the early twentieth century about his experiences with the "rudeness" and "inconsiderateness" of government officials, which he found "disgusting."[20] Many of the complaints against poor ethnic groups were also similar to those today—that "children are born with reckless regularity" among the Jews and Italians,[21] that murders are a result of "the wanton brutality of the moment,"[22] and that raising the immigrants to a decent level "implies a problem of such magnitude and such distant realization" that it can only be imagined.[23]

Despite many striking similarities over time, ethnic history is not a mere repetition of patterns, not even with an overlay of general progress. There are distinctive patterns—groups that behave very differently in very similar circumstances, as well as groups that the larger society has treated very differently.

Ethnic Differences

Perhaps the most striking difference among ethnic groups themselves is in their attitudes toward learning and self-improvement. Jews seized upon free schools, libraries, and settlement houses in America with a tenacity and determination unexcelled and seldom approached by others. They not only crowded into the public schools, but the adult night schools as well (after long days of work), paid to go to lectures out of their small wages, and kept the public libraries busy trying to keep them supplied with serious books. And still *The Jewish Daily Forward* castigated them for not doing enough![24] Living and working under very similar conditions to those of contemporary Jews, the Italian immigrants were among the most hostile of all Americans to the public schools, least interested in the public libraries, and most suspicious of the settlement houses. It would be difficult to explain this contrast on the basis of anything that had happened to these two groups in America. Yet the very different histories of the Jews and the Italians in Europe provide ample reason. Certainly, life in southern Italian villages produced little incentive for acquiring formal education, which would have been useless, if not counterproductive, for southern Italian peasants or laborers. Neither discrimination nor ability differences are necessarily implied by the very different academic performances of Italians and Jews in the same schools.

The family has also played very different roles in different groups. While poverty has been blamed for the large number of break-ups of Irish families in the nineteenth century, similar poverty among Italian immigrants at the turn of the century did not lead to any such result, nor did the Italians accept charity or resort to prostitution nearly as often as the Irish or other groups in such circumstances. Current circumstances are far from all-determining. It is not only the stability of the family—low rates of desertion or divorce—that is important, but also the values embodied in the family. Italians and Jews have both had highly stable families, but the values of the Jewish family drive the individual toward upward mobility, while Italian family values have—in the past, at least—often made the individual feel that he was somehow "betraying" the family by moving beyond its orbit into a wider world.

280

Implications

When the family is formed also has been an important factor in a group's history. Mexican-American families are highly stable but are formed very early in life. Half of all Mexican-American women have married in their teens, while only 10 percent of Japanese-American women have married that young.[25] This has obvious implications for the ability of the young women in these two groups to obtain education. Young men in these two groups likewise face very different prospects of getting higher education, when many more Mexican-American men are likely to have the responsibilities of fatherhood at a time when Japanese-American men are college students. The future careers of both men and women in these two groups are bound to differ.

Differences among ethnic groups themselves are seldom explicitly denied. They are, however, implicitly muted or ignored in political efforts centering on what the larger society can (or should) do for various ethnic groups. Why groups differ as much as they do, and in the particular ways that they do, is a complex question to which history gives some clues. Racial or genetic explanations of differences in group progress have also enjoyed varying amounts of popular and professional support over the years. Evidence has ranged from international comparisons of countries with racially different populations to differences in IQ levels and patterns among American ethnic groups.

International comparisons provide evidence both for and against genetic explanations of group differences. While European nations today are generally far in advance of most of the rest of the world in technology, income, and other widely used indices of progress, centuries ago the Chinese or Egyptians were in the forefront of civilization, with Europeans far behind. Substantial reshuffling of the rankings of nations and races at different stages of history undermine genetic explanations in general. A reshuffling of the IQ rankings of American ethnic groups within a period of half a century[26] undermines the theory of genetic determination of intelligence, even aside from questions about the tests themselves. The fact that black orphans raised by white families have IQs at or above the national average[27] is even stronger evidence against that theory.

Polish Americans had average IQs around 85 during the 1920s[28] (compared to a national norm of 100), but in the 1970s, their IQ level was 109.[29] This twenty-four-point rise in IQs was not only remarkable in itself but was also larger than the current black-white IQ difference (fifteen points). Italian Americans likewise rose over the years from

281

IQs averaging in the low to mid-eighties to IQs around the national average. Perhaps the most dramatic changes have been among Jewish Americans. Jewish soldiers in World War I averaged some of the lowest scores on mental tests of any of the numerous ethnic groups tested.[30] Yet within a decade, this economically rising and rapidly acculturating group had achieved an average IQ level above that of Americans in general.[31]

Controversy over the genetic component in intelligence has had a profound effect in history, whatever the intellectual merits or demerits of the theories themselves. Both proponents and opponents of theories of innate differences have often argued as if there was a direct correspondence between "ability" (however defined) and results—that is, as if the large intervening factor of cultural differences did not matter.

CULTURE

Whether in an ethnic context or among peoples and nations in general, much depends on the whole constellation of values, attitudes, skills, and contacts that many call a culture and that economists call "human capital." For more than a century, people have marveled at how quickly some nations recover economically from the utter devastation of war. The so-called German miracle after World War II was only the most recent example of something that has happened before in other places. What war destroys is the tangible physical capital of a nation—its cities, factories, farms, railroads, and highways. What it does not destroy is the human capital that built all these things in the first place—and can build them again. John Stuart Mill pointed out more than a century ago that the physical elements of an advanced economy wear out and are used up in a few years, and would have to be replaced anyway. What war does is speed up this process. But continued progress depends on what people know and will do.

The importance of human capital in an ethnic context is shown in many ways. Groups that arrived in America financially destitute have rapidly risen to affluence, when their cultures stressed the values and behavior required in an industrial and commercial economy. Even when color and racial prejudices confronted them—as in the case of the Chinese and Japanese—this proved to be an impediment but was ultimately unable to stop them. Nor was their human capital even a matter of bringing specific skills with them, such as those of the Jews in clothing production or of the Germans in beer production. The Chinese and Japanese came as unskilled young men working in the fields tending crops—but working harder and more relentlessly than anyone else. Later, the ubiquitous Chinese hand laundry did not require any technical skill not already possessed by the Irish or the black washerwoman of the same era. But the Irish and the blacks never set up laundries, or any other businesses, with the frequency of the Chinese or Japanese, although the two Asian groups were initially hampered by lack of money and lack of English, as well as by a lack of technical skills. Japanese gardeners did not have to master any equipment more technical than a lawnmower. What made these humble occupations avenues to affluence was the effort, thrift, dependability, and foresight that built businesses out of "menial" tasks and turned sweat into capital. In the same way, many Jewish pushcart peddlers eventually became storeowners, and sometimes owners of whole chains of stores.

International comparisons of ethnic group progress reinforce the importance of human capital. In the United States, Canada, Great Britain, and Israel, the same striking pattern emerges: immigrants begin economically below the level of existing members of their own ethnic group already in the country, but eventually rise to not only equal but surpass them.[32] In the United States, native-born Americans of Cuban, Japanese, Mexican, Negro, or Filipino ancestry are overtaken by immigrants of the *same* respective ancestry. Cuban immigrants reached the income level of native-born Cuban Americans after eighteen years and surpassed them thereafter. Mexican immigrants take fifteen years to overtake native-born Mexican Americans. Japanese immigrants take eighteen years to overtake native-born Japanese Americans. Immigrants from the Philippines overtake native-born Filipino Americans in thirteen years, and black West Indian immigrants overtake native black Americans in eleven years.[33]

The lengthy period required to equal the economic level of people of the same race or ethnicity born on American soil suggests something of the amount of human capital needed—not simply the technical skills (which could usually be acquired in much shorter time), but the whole spectrum of experience, contacts, personal and institutional savvy, confidence, and ease. However, the fact that immigrants not only equal but eventually surpass their native-born counterparts also suggests that they brought some advantage in terms of human capital, that migration is a *selective* process, bringing the more ambitious or venturesome or able elements of a population. Once they acquire all the other kinds of human capital they need, this advantage (or these advantages) begin to tell. This also implies a difference between selective immigration and unselective, wholesale refugee flight. The famine Irish of the 1840s were more like refugees, fleeing a national catastrophe in which people were literally dying in the streets. Their slow and difficult adjustment in the United States may in part reflect that. Immigrants from Meiji Japan may have had no more skills in the naïve sense, but were much more selectively chosen for personal qualities, as well as partially acculturated to American norms and goals in Japan itself.

Specific skills are a prerequisite in many kinds of work. But history shows new skills being rather readily acquired in a few years, as compared to the generations—or centuries—required for *attitude* changes. Groups today plagued by absenteeism, tardiness, and a need for constant supervision at work or in school are typically descendants of people with the same habits a century or more ago. The cultural inheritance can be more important than biological inheritance, although the latter stirs more controversy. In special isolated circumstances, where the necessary values and disciplines had developed, among small segments of blacks, for example, the skills and the economic results have followed. Among the more striking examples were the hundreds of small businesses established in the depths of the Great Depression by the very lowest income (and usually ill-educated) followers of Father Divine. The success of their businesses,[34] founded under such wholly unpromising circumstances, contrasts with the massive business failures under the government-sponsored "black capitalism" programs of the 1960s and 1970s.[35] Although the latter have had more financial support and/or "experts" available, the Father Divine cult developed more human capital in terms of both individual discipline and group cooperation. The Black Muslims have also achieved business success while drawing on the least educated and lowest income segments of the black population.[36] The importance of human capital is also shown in areas dealing with education. The most successful black high school, in terms of either student test scores or alumni career successes, was also a school with less absenteeism or tardiness than white schools in the same city.[37] It was not simply that either absenteeism or tardiness, as such, was so important, as that a set

Implications

of attitudes toward school caused students to be there consistently and on time.

It is sometimes believed that educational success requires that the children come from homes well stocked with books and magazines, and have the benefit of continual parent-child verbal interaction, after the model of Jewish immigrant homes. But Japanese-American homes did not meet any of these specifications,[38] and yet their children's achievements in school were outstanding. One of the great political and legal crusades of the twentieth century—school "integration"—has been based on the theory that the differences between being ethnically concentrated and being mixed with children from other ethnic backgrounds is so crucial as to make the whole educational experience itself inferior without them.[39] However, history shows that ethnic groups with different attitudes toward education perform as differently in the same school as in different schools. The differences between Japanese and Mexican-American children attending the same schools have been as great as differences between blacks and whites attending separate schools in the segregated South. Differences between Jewish and Puerto Rican children attending the same school for decades have been even greater.[40]

Diversities of culture have caused intergroup friction from both substantive differences in values and beliefs and from different forms of social coding to convey the same feelings or attitudes. A look, a gesture, a tone of voice, or a set of casual remarks may mean something very different in one culture than in another—causing continual misunderstandings and senses of uneasiness, affront, or hostility.[41] Moreover, personal clashes in an intergroup setting can readily spread from particular individuals to involve other members of each group in the vicinity. The educational and other social advantages of cultural diversity have varied with whether the association was voluntary or by force. For example, early studies of voluntarily integrated schools showed increased racial amity and educational benefits—providing a basis for *compulsory* integration under court orders, which produced opposite results.[42] Ethnically different families brought together in government housing projects—seeking low rents rather than diversity—have often socially segregated themselves, although statistically "integrated."[43]

Cultures are not "superior" or "inferior." They are better or worse adapted to a particular set of circumstances. The most successful of all American ethnic groups—the Jews—had a succession of utter failures in agriculture.[44] Their centuries of acculturation to urban society were as much a hindrance on the farm as they were an advantage in the city.

Personal blame seems especially out of place in dealing with historic forces beyond the control of any individual. It would be fatuous to blame emigrants from Mexico for not bringing with them the skills or other traits brought by emigrants from Germany. It seems equally fatuous to blame employers for not having Mexicans and Germans proportionally represented in jobs requiring such skills or traits.[45]

Acculturation has sometimes been depicted as a one-way process, in which racial and ethnic groups have been forced to surrender their respective cultures and conform to Anglo-Saxon practices. In reality, the American culture is built on the food, the language, the attitudes, and the skills from numerous groups. The old Anglo-Saxon Puritan resistance to social recreation was long ago overwhelmed by the German easygoing attitude of good clean fun, which is now considered the hallmark of Americans in general. American popular music has its roots in the black musical tradition that produced jazz and the blues. American political machines have been predominately Irish political machines. Nothing is more American than hamburgers or frankfurters, although both names derive from German cities. Pizza and tacos are not far behind. None of these features of American culture is descended from the British settlers. They are a common heritage, despite ethnic diversities that still exist. Budweiser is drunk in Harlem, Jews eat pizza, and Chinese restaurants are patronized by customers who are obviously not Chinese.

Groups that have the skills and entrepreneurship to be self-employed, or to employ one another, have not even had to learn English in order to prosper. The German farmers and Jewish garment industry workers of nineteenth-century America, or the Japanese-American farmers of the early twentieth century, were able to rise economically with little acculturation, and despite varying degrees of hostility. It is the groups that *lack* such skills and entrepreneurship that are dependant on others for employment and that have had to learn to speak their language and know enough of their culture to make working together reasonably comfortable.

The "melting pot" was once a popular image of American assimilation, but is now a disdained concept. Ironically, there was relatively little intermarriage during the era of "melting pot" theories, but such intermarriage is now much more widespread in the era when the concept is rejected by intellectuals. More than half of all marriages among

286

Implications

Americans of German, Irish, British, or Polish ancestry are with people of different ethnicity, and Italian and Japanese Americans are not far behind. Even groups with low rates of intermarriage—blacks, Jews, Hispanics—nevertheless have rising levels of intermarriage.

Internal Differences

While cultures are ways of accomplishing things,[46] they are also the focus of loyalties and emotions.[47] Attempts at acculturation for pragmatic reasons are often resented as denigrations of the group in question—sometimes as *nothing but* that[48]—so that it is seen as oppression when attempted by outsiders and as betrayal when attempted by members of the group. These attitudes have appeared to some extent among Jews, Mexicans, Negroes, Japanese, Italians,[49] and virtually every other ethnic group. Nevertheless, even the most resistant groups or segments of groups have acculturated—become "Americanized"—although at different rates.

Sometimes intragroup differences have been generational. After the struggles of the first and second generation have produced enough acculturation and affluence for the third generation to afford nostalgia for a vanishing ethnic culture, the younger members of the third generation especially may become fiercely concerned about a language they cannot speak, customs they have never followed, and an "identity" they have never had. This too has occurred in the most diverse groups—the Japanese,[50] Irish,[51] Mexicans,[52] Jews,[53] Negroes,[54] and others. Efforts may be made to deliberately or artificially acquire a "heritage" that they in fact never inherited.

Internal differences in acculturation have typically led to social and physical separation within the group—again, a pattern common to a variety of groups.[55] New or less acculturated members of the group continue to live at the initial settlement site, while more acculturated families distance themselves from them, and so on successively to the most acculturated and affluent families on the outer fringes of the ethnic neighborhood, leading its expansion into the surrounding larger community. This classic pattern of concentric rings of differently acculturated people of the same ethnic group has appeared in some cities, but various barriers (such as other groups that will not move) often mean that new ethnic communities of differently acculturated people are scattered at some distance from each other. Rising Jewish families who moved from the lower east side of Manhattan to newer middle-class communities in the Bronx were a typical example of a widespread pattern among many ethnic groups. Sometimes—especially in more recent years—more acculturated and affluent members of an ethnic group are individually scattered among the general population. Affluent Chinese no longer live in Chinatowns or in middle-class ethnic ghettos.

In the earlier immigrant period (or the earlier urban migration period, for blacks or Puerto Ricans), these residential separation patterns may reflect acculturation differences more so than simply economic differences as such. Some groups also had important Old World regional differences, such as among Italians from different provinces in Italy or Jews from different nations. These too were reflected in different residential concentrations in America.[56]

Various segments of the same group have not only separated but have engaged in mutual recriminations over their different degrees of acculturation. Some Jewish immigrant communities regarded other Jewish communities as too "Old World" or backward, or simply "too Jewish," while seeing others as too un-Jewish, half-Gentile, or outright turncoats.[57] Mexican Americans today likewise resent those among them who seem to be becoming "Anglo," while disdaining new arrivals from Mexico.[58] The painful readjustments of Mexican Americans who were deported to Mexico in the 1930s[59] further underscored the problems caused by different gradations of acculturation, as well as differences between a whole ethnic group and the larger society.

Sometimes the initial group differences have been recognized by employers—especially where work required extended periods of living together. Back at the turn of the century, employers of Italian work gangs learned that putting men together who came from different parts of Italy was an open invitation to violence.[60] The same was true to an even greater degree when Protestant and Catholic Irish work gangs dug canals in the nineteenth century.[61] In contemporary America, black migrant farm workers work and live in different camps when they are of West Indian rather than native origin.[62]

Whether at work places or in residential communities, the separation of people has a strong pragmatic basis that extends well beyond ethnicity. Older people generally do not want to live where there are many teenagers, and young adult apartment communities often have a "no children" policy. The point here is not to argue the advantages and disadvantages of diversity[63] but to show its pervasiveness in American history and the way people have coped with its frictions and problems by putting physical or social distance between themselves. In the old South, an elaborate racial ideology and tradition

Implications

made social distance to some extent a substitute for physical distance so that racial residential segregation was often less in southern cities than in northern cities. Physical proximity or contact with blacks in various settings was generally more acceptable to southern whites than to northern whites, for the same reason: the southern whites were more insistent on "white supremacy."

Against this background, the separation of groups at work or in neighborhood living patterns can be seen as a special case of a far more general phenomenon—and one not inherently dependent on an ideology of "superiority" or "inferiority," in either a cultural or biological sense. Such racist theories and ideologies have been intertwined with racial segregation and discrimination, especially in the South, but cannot be universally inferred whenever ethnic groups are not randomly distributed at work or at home. Even this late in history, half of all eastern and southern Europeans in American cities would have to be relocated to get a random distribution of them residentially.[64] Groups that have long enjoyed open access to housing are still not randomly distributed, in part because of their own preferences. Racially identifiable patterns in living, working, or attending schools are visible to the naked eye but are by no means unique otherwise. It is not even a question of whether one group is considered to behave or to perform "better" or to have innate "superiority." The two groups may *each* behave or perform *differently* when together than when separate—as among Italian railroad work groups or Irish canal-building crews, for example. This too has implications that reach beyond ethnicity. Men and women also behave differently when together than when separate[65]—and these differences may or may not facilitate the purposes of particular institutions. The issue is not inherently one of superiority, inferiority, or equality.

Ironically, intergroup hostility has usually been greatest among groups most alike in their social and economic conditions, and better relations have been more common among groups that are quite different. Prior to the Civil War, the most antislavery ethnic groups in the United States were the Germans and the Scotch-Irish, composed of skilled workers and independent farmers, and including some very wealthy elements as well, especially among the Germans. In the twentieth century, the black civil rights movement has been strongly supported by Jews, whose whole economic and cultural history is radically different from that of blacks. Conversely, the advancement of blacks has been bitterly fought at various stages of history by the Irish,[66] whose incomes and occupations were long similar to those of blacks and whose history and culture were parallel to those of blacks in many ways: the importance of expressive, pithy language,[67] the sports they dominated (boxing and baseball), the fields in which they advanced (sports, entertainment, religion, writing, politics), the fields they avoided (science and mathematics), the businesses in which they succeeded (life insurance, banking, publishing), the businesses in which they made little headway (manufacturing, merchandising), and their social pathologies (alcoholism, violence, broken homes). *A Raisin in the Sun* is a classic play about modern urban blacks but contains the classic elements of Irish plays—the strong woman, the immature man, religious faith, and conflicts between generations. One of the most popular movies about black militancy in the 1960s was a remake of a movie about Irish revolutionaries.[68] Yet despite these similarities—or perhaps because of them—blacks and the Irish have had the greatest hostility, violence, and bloodshed to exist between any two ethnic groups in American history. Such very dissimilar groups as the Chinese and the Italians have lived peacefully side by side for generations on New York's lower east side. It may also be indicative that the rise of more blacks to middle-class positions similar to those of Jews has been accompanied by reduced cooperation between these two groups and to more instances of intergroup conflict.

The importance of being with people from similar cultures is emphasized by the highly regionalized emigration patterns found among many groups. For example, in 1948, 70 percent of the emigrants from Hidaka District in Japan settled in Canada, and 90 percent of those from one village in Hidaka settled in one small part of Canada. Of the emigrants from Okinawa to the United States, more than 90 percent settled in Hawaii.[69] With Italian Americans, such regional patterns extended to the point of having people from particular Italian villages locate on the same streets in America.

Discrimination

Many discussions of group differences in income or occupation freely invoke such terms as "discrimination" or the even more emotionally charged (and empirically elusive) term "exploitation."[70] While clear instances of discrimination have been encountered by many ethnic groups at various periods in their history, determining how much of the group differences in income, occupations, or housing represent discrimination is a complex and uncertain process.[71] The very meaning of discrimination varies across a spectrum, from underpaying individuals for their current capabilities to the existence of historic barriers

290

that inhibited the development of capabilities. Employer discrimination as an explanation of current income differences usually means that a given group is underpaid relative to its current capabilities. Historical and current empirical evidence on this point is far from conclusive,[72] despite the axiomatic certainty of many assertions.

Employer discrimination cannot, for example, explain large income differences among various segments *within* a given ethnic group, if employers are generally unaware of these internal differences. The poverty that is as common among Hong Kong Chinese as affluence is among native-born Chinese Americans cannot be explained by the existence of racist employers, to whom Chinese "all look alike." The substantial differences in income between first- and third-generation Mexican Americans are likewise difficult to explain by employer attitudes, when generational information is unlikely to be sought from job applicants in the blue-collar occupations in which most Mexican Americans work. Employers are even less likely to seek genealogical information that would enable them to distinguish descendants of "free persons of color" from other blacks, and it is doubtful if most employers can tell a second-generation West Indian from other blacks, or would even be interested in trying.

The purely internal differences in income have implications for differences between the whole group and the larger society. In some cases, one social segment (the Hong Kong Chinese) earns lower incomes than the national average while another segment (native-born Chinese Americans) earns more than the national average. In the nineteenth century, eastern European Jews lived in poverty, while German Jews were affluent. Today, second-generation West Indians earn more than the national average, while native black Americans earn substantially less. When whole social segments of a group—not just some fortunate individuals—have above-average earnings, it is difficult to explain lower than average earning for the group as a whole by employer discrimination, if employers do not make such distinctions within the group.

The existence and effectiveness of economic discrimination depend on far more than the existence or degree of prejudice against a particular group.[73] The historic prejudice and legal discriminations encountered by the Japanese were at least as severe as those encountered by Puerto Ricans, and yet Japanese incomes are more than double the incomes of Puerto Ricans and are significantly above those of Anglo-Saxons. Not only history but also economics argues against the widespread assumption that group income differences are largely a function of discrimination, rather than human capital differences or differences in age, geographic distribution, and other factors. Translating subjective prejudice into overt economic discrimination is costly for profit-seeking competitive firms,[74] although less so for government, public utilities, regulated industries like banking, or nonprofit organizations such as universities or hospitals.[75] Just how costly was shown by the repeated failures of white employer cartels to control the wages of newly freed blacks after the Civil War—despite having almost every imaginable economic, legal, political, and social advantage.[76] Statistics that today compare the incomes of ethnic individuals with the "same" education, for example, as members of the general population usually ignore large *qualitative* differences in educational substance and performance.[77] Where these qualitative differences are even approximately taken into account, intergroup differences among comparable individuals shrink dramatically[78] or even disappear.[79]

Assertions of consumer discrimination—claims that "the poor pay more"[80]—likewise turn on group differences that are often ignored. Differences in crime rates, for example, affect the cost of running a store in many ways, leading to different prices for the same item in different ethnic neighborhoods. The honest consumer pays costs created by vandals, hoodlums, and criminals in his neighborhood, but that is different from saying that his neighborhood as a whole is being "exploited" by the store located there or by other ethnic groups. The steady exit of stores from high-crime neighborhoods suggests that there is no great profit being made there.

Ethnic groups also differ in credit repayment, and not always solely by income. Even low-income Italian Americans, for example, are considered good credit risks.[81] The revolving credit devices, used by the Chinese, Japanese, and West Indians to finance their businesses,[82] work only where prompt and full repayment can be relied on. Groups without the level of dependability that would enable them to use this device to raise capital among themselves are usually unable to raise capital from commercial sources for the same reason. Their failure to develop businesses cannot be arbitrarily attributed to lack of access to banks, for most small businesses (including those of Chinese, Japanese, and West Indians) are not launched with bank loans anyway.[83]

In housing markets as well, the high cost of slum dwellings has been denounced for years, going back to the nineteenth-century immigrant ghettos on the lower east side of New York. But despite bitter denunciations of slum landlords there,[84] the actual records show no particularly large profits being made on slums in general.[85] High rents were indeed *charged* for a given amount of space, but profits are made only on the rents actually *paid*—and thousands of evictions per year on the lower east side[86] indicate that the two are not only conceptually but also empirically very different. Again, the honest renter paid for the others, and the average profit rates indicate that the lower east side tenants *as a whole* were not "exploited."

Individuals may be devastated by discrimination, even if it does not explain the economic conditions of a group as a whole. W. E. B. Du Bois pointed out, at the turn of the century, that "the individual black workman is rated not by his own efficiency, but by the efficiency of a whole group of black fellow workmen which may often be low."[87] Race is one of many sorting devices used because of the costliness of individual knowledge.[88] The question of group discrimination is a question about whether the group as a whole is misjudged or under-paid—a question about average performance, not individual variation. The "representative Negroes"[89] were, according to Du Bois, "probably best fitted for the work they are doing,"[90] and if the racial prejudices of whites were to disappear overnight it "would not make very much difference in the positions occupied by Negroes" as a whole, although "some few would be promoted, some few would get new places" but "the mass would remain as they are...."[91] What Du Bois expected the lowering of racial barriers to accomplish was to provide incentives for successive generations of blacks to improve their skills and efforts.[92] Whatever the empirical validity of Du Bois' assessment, the important point here is that he distinguished discrimination against the individual from discrimination against the group.

Even where the current capability of the group is accurately assessed in the market, particular individuals in the group may still be grossly undervalued. Du Bois himself was perhaps the classic example. But no recitation of such examples provides evidence that discrimination against the group as a whole explains the group's poverty. The galling tragedy of a Du Bois or a Paul Robeson—men with superb educations and individual brilliance—was that they were held back solely by racial prejudice and eventually ended up embittered Communists.

In other groups as well, it has been precisely some of the most acculturated and talented members who have been the most bitter, militant, or extreme. The inference made by them and by others was that no amount of *group* acculturation, skills, or efforts would be any more successful than their individual development had been. Some of the Japanese interned during World War II reached the same despairing conclusion.[93] But however understandable their anger and despair, later events showed that the inference was neither logically conclusive nor historically correct. Within a generation after the internment, Japanese Americans were among the most affluent, socially accepted, and generally respected groups in the United States. This took about half a century from the beginning of Japanese immigration, and many of the virulent racists they encountered along the way could not have been changed by any conceivable thing the Japanese could have done. But the mortality of human beings, and therefore the turnover of individuals in the population, enabled the quiet persistence of the Japanese to ultimately win out on every economic, social, and political front.

Nevertheless, this approach, which proved successful with the Japanese (and Chinese and Jews), is often dismissed out of hand as naïve, while progress is thought to require more confrontationist methods— which failed repeatedly for Irish Americans in the nineteenth century, in areas ranging from public school controversies[94] to the military draft during the Civil War [95] to attempts to win economic advancement by terrorism[96] or to secure the independence of Ireland with a military expedition against Canada.[97] Among blacks in the twentieth century, the initial successes of the nonviolent civil rights movement slowed perceptibly as more militant, direct action tactics stiffened the resistance of the larger society and provoked backlashes extending from simple resentments to the resurgence of such organizations as the Ku Klux Klan (even in northern communities) and the Nazi fringe.

The point here is not to definitively solve the question as to how much of intergroup differences in income, social acceptance, etc., have been due to the behavior and attitudes of particular ethnic groups and how much to the behavior and attitudes of the larger society. The point is that this is a complex question, not a simple axiom.

Identity and Assimilation

The importance of ethnic identity has varied enormously within each ethnic group. For some individuals, it has been a badge to be worn proudly before the world. For others, it has been a way of life to be personally treasured, although not made a public issue. And for still others, ethnic identity has been incidental, or a curiosity—or a stigma to be forgotten, evaded, or escaped as much as possible. This whole spectrum of individual attitudes has existed historically in all ethnic groups. In short, ethnic identity has been a complex and elusive phenomenon. Its specific content has historically varied enormously, even within given groups. For example, the identity of nineteenth-

Implications

century Jewish immigrants centered on their religious observances and their ethnic and national cultural traditions, including Yiddish. From their perspective, it would seem incomprehensible how someone could be considered a Jew who—like many twentieth-century American Jews—pays little or no attention to religious observances and lives, dresses, and talks like Gentiles, among Gentiles. Yet no one would say that postholocaust, post-Israel Jews have lost their identity. Their voting records alone distinguish them sharply from other Americans of the same economic level. They do not live in the past, but the past in them.

Ethnic identity has sometimes been thought to be a potent—if not paramount—factor in group progress. But groups with much group identity—in such things as bloc voting or favoritism for political candidates or employees of one's own ethnicity—have not generally done better than groups with less concern over such things. No one exceeded the favoritism of the Irish for other Irishmen, whether in politics or in the church, but in general they advanced no faster than the Italians, who showed little of the same spirit in politics or elsewhere. Some groups (such as the Jews and the Japanese) have enjoyed and maintained their own special culture, but without making a public issue over it (as many blacks or Hispanics have). It is by no means clear that either cultural persistence or group advancement has been promoted by making cultural distinctiveness a controversial issue. The nineteenth-century Irish made more fuss about the Gaelic language than the nineteenth-century Jews did about Yiddish, but Yiddish was far more widely spoken among Jews than Gaelic among the Irish.

With many American ethnic groups, the accumulation of evolutionary changes has made the twentieth-century group very different from their nineteenth-century ancestors. Many of these profound changes are seldom discussed because of current ethnic etiquette and sensitivities. Both the testimony of contemporaries and the record of epidemics convey the historical fact that nineteenth-century Irish immigrants lived in filthy conditions, both in their homes and in their persons. But modern discussions of ethnicity usually omit any references to either cleanliness or its absence, except for using any mention or complaints along these lines as proof of the bias or hatred of the person quoted. Epidemics of filth-related diseases still move very selectively through ethnic neighborhoods, but ethnic differences in life expectancy are axiomatically attributed to the racism of the larger society.[98] Even extremely high automobile accident fatality rates among young men in a group that stresses machismo are automatically attributed to the group's poverty and to the older automobiles they drive as a result.[99]

Whatever justification these apologetics might have within a purely moralistic framework, within a cause-and-effect framework they simply blot out major factors at work. Historically, they prevent our knowing or understanding how progress was achieved—or is being achieved—in dealing with internal group problems whose very existence is ignored or denied. A group cannot be getting cleaner over time, if any suggestion that it was ever dirty was only a figment of bigots' imaginations. Their children could not have overcome their educational deficiencies in the schools, if their only problems were racist teachers and biased tests. No other internal problems—from alcoholism to violence—could be overcome by any group, if such things were only biased propaganda or the inevitable results of the failures of "society." As a corollary, some of the longest and hardest struggles for self-improvement must be denied—which is to say, history itself is denied.

Within the confines of the moralistic approach, progress (like poverty) can only be presented as a product of "society"—now grudgingly granting new "rights" or partial "acceptance." If the Irish were pariahs in the nineteenth century and fully accepted in the twentieth century, the moralistic approach sees only society's belated change to doing the right thing. It ignores the very possibility that the Irish who are accepted today may be very different from the nineteenth-century emigrants from Ireland whose personal behavior would still be wholly unacceptable to others today, including today's Irish Americans.

The history of American ethnic groups—which is to say, ultimately, the history of the American people—is the history of a complex aggregate of complex groups and individuals. It cannot be a simple morality play. It is a story of similar patterns and profound differences, of pain and pride and achievement. It is, in one sense, the story of many very different heritages. In another sense, it is the story of the human spirit in its many guises.

Notes

Chapter 1

1. U.S. Bureau of the Census, *Current Population Reports*, P-20, No. 249 (Washington, D.C.: U.S. Government Printing Office, 1973), p. 1.

2. The specific incomes are all listed in Thomas Sowell, ed., *Essays and Data on American Ethnic Groups* (Washington, D.C.: The Urban Institute, 1978), pp. 266, 284, 302, 320, 333, 337, 341, 350, 362, 374, 376, 386, 404. Income percentages for Japanese, Chinese, Filipino, West Indian, Puerto Rican, black, and American Indian families were based on 1969 incomes calculated from the 1970 Census Public Use Sample, using the U.S. national average as derived from the same source by the same definitions. Percentages for Jewish families were calculated from raw data supplied by the National Jewish Population Survey, tabulated using the same definitions as those of the groups listed above and of the U.S. national average. No 1969 income data were available for Polish, Italian, German, Irish, or Mexican families, but 1968 and 1970 income data were available from the Census Bureau's *Current Population Reports* (Series P-20, Nos. 213, 221, 224, and 249). Family income percentages for these five groups were calculated using the U.S. national average family income as reported in the same respective Census publications as the group incomes. An average of the 1968 and 1970 percentages was used as an estimate of the 1969 family income percentages for these five groups.

3. Thomas Sowell, "Ethnicity in a Changing America," *Daedalus*, Winter 1978, p. 221.

4. Ibid., pp. 226–227; Eric Hanushek, "Ethnic Income Variations: Magnitudes and Explanations," in *Essays and Data on American Ethnic Groups*, ed. Thomas Sowell, pp. 139–166.

5. Richard B. Freeman, *Black Elite* (New York: McGraw-Hill, 1977), Chapter 4.

6. Sowell, "Ethnicity in a Changing America," p. 232.

7. Ibid., pp. 217, 218; U.S. Bureau of the Census, *Current Population Reports*, P-20, No. 226 (Washington: U.S. Government Printing Office, 1971), p. 20.

8. Leo Grebler, et al., *The Mexican American People* (New York: The Free Press, 1970), pp. 181, 185.

9. Arthur R. Jensen, "How Much Can We Boost I.Q. and Scholastic Achievement?" *Harvard Educational Review*, Winter 1969, p. 95.

10. Sowell, "Ethnicity in a Changing America," p. 217.

11. Ernest van den Haag, *Punishing Criminals* (New York: Basic Books, Inc., 1975), p. 100.

12. Carl Brigham, *A Study of American Intelligence* (Princeton: Princeton University Press, 1923), p. 190.

13. Thomas Sowell, "Race and I.Q. Reconsidered," in *Essays and Data on American Ethnic Groups*, p. 207.

14. Ibid., p. 210.

15. Sowell, "Ethnicity in a Changing America," pp. 218–220.

16. J. C. Furnas, *The Americans* (New York: G. P. Putnam's Sons, 1969), pp. 522, 527, 700; Maldwyn Allen Jones, *American Immigration* (Chicago: University of Chicago Press, 1970), pp. 150, 151; Nathan Glazer and Daniel Patrick Moynihan, *Beyond the Melting Pot* (Cambridge: M.I.T. Press, 1963), p. 240; and Arthur Lewis, *Lament for the Molly Maguires* (New York: Pocket Books, 1964), p. 3.

17. Jones, *American Immigration*, pp. 157–163.

18. Diane Ravitch, *The Great School Wars* (New York: Basic Books, Inc. 1974), Chapters 4 and 5.

19. Glazer and Moynihan, *Beyond the Melting Pot*, p. 240.

20. Furnas, *The Americans*, pp. 65, 522; Daniel Boorstin, *The Americans* (New York: Random House, 1958), Vol. I, p. 37.

21. See Sowell, "Ethnicity in a Changing America," p. 226.

22. Jones, *American Immigration*, p. 179.

23. Sowell, ed., *Essays and Data on American Ethnic Groups*, pp. 210, 213, 214, 217, 257–258.

Chapter 2

1. Edward C. Banfield, *The Unheavenly City* (Boston: Little, Brown and Co., 1970), p. 58.

2. Thomas Sowell, *ed., Essays and Data on American Ethnic Groups* (Washington, D.C.: The Urban Institute, 1978), pp. 210, 257–258.

3. Quoted in Andrew M. Greeley, *That Distressful Nation* (New York: Quadrangle Books, 1972), pp. 34–35.

4. Oliver MacDonagh, "The Irish Famine Emigration to the United States," in *Perspectives in American History*, vol. X (1976), p. 366; Eugene D. Genovese, *Roll, Jordan, Roll* (New York: Pantheon Books, 1974), pp. 524–525.

5. Greeley, *That Most Distressful Nation*, p. 29.

6. Ibid.

7. Maire and Conor Cruise O'Brien, *A Concise History of Ireland* (Brooklyn, N.Y.: Beckman, 1972), p. 25.

8. Ibid., p. 47.

9. Ibid., p. 53.

10. Ibid., p. 56.

11. James G. Leyburn, *The Scotch-Irish* (Chapel Hill: University of North Carolina Press, 1962), p. 125.

12. Quoted in O'Brien, *A Concise History of Ireland*, p. 78.

13. George Potter, *To the Golden Door: The Story of the Irish in Ireland and America* (Westport, Conn.: Greenwood Press, 1960), pp. 106–109.

14. Oscar Handlin, *Boston's Immigrants* (New York: Atheneum, 1970), p. 41.

15. Greeley, *That Most Distressful Nation*, p. 129.

16. Ibid., p. 132.

17. Carl Wittke, *The Irish in America* (New York: Russell & Russell, 1970), p. 3.

18. MacDonagh, "The Irish Famine Emigration," p. 405.

19. Ibid., p. 365.

20. Ibid., pp. 405–406.

21. Simon Kuznets, "Immigration of Russian Jews to the United States: Background and Structure," in *Perspectives in American History*, vol. IX (1975), pp. 49–50.

22. MacDonagh, "The Irish Famine Emigration," pp. 402–403.

23. Ibid., p. 403.

24. Ibid., p. 410.

25. Philip D. Curtin, *The Atlantic Slave Trade* (Madison: University of Wisconsin Press, 1969), p. 280.

26. MacDonagh, "The Irish Famine Emigration," p. 402.

27. Ibid., p. 300.

28. Ibid., p. 369.

29. Ibid., p. 366.

30. Ibid., pp. 370–371.

31. Ibid., p. 425.

32. Ibid.

33. Ibid., pp. 394–395.

34. Ibid., p. 382.

35. Ibid., p. 380.

36. Leyburn, *The Scotch-Irish*, pp. 195, 202, 212.

37. Ibid., p. 200.

38. J. C. Furnas, *The Americans* (New York: G. P. Putnam's Sons, 1969), p. 703.

39. Ibid., p. 382.

40. Wittke, *The Irish in America*, pp. 23–24.

41. Ibid., p. 23.

42. Ibid., p. 147.

43. Ibid., p. 24.

44. Potter, *To the Golden Door*, pp. 173, 184, 185, 205.

Notes

45. Wittke, *The Irish in America*, p. 26.

46. Potter, *To the Golden Door*, p. 173.

47. Wittke, *The Irish in America*, Chapter VII.

48. Handlin, *Boston's Immigrants*, p. 114.

49. Potter, *To the Golden Door*, p. 181.

50. Wittke, *The Irish in America*, p. 44.

51. Handlin, *Boston's Immigrants*, p. 254.

52. Oscar Handlin, *The Newcomers* (New York: Anchor Books, 1962), p. 17.

53. Potter, *To the Golden Door*, p. 238.

54. Kathleen Neils Conzen, *Immigrant Milwaukee, 1836–1860* (Cambridge: Harvard University Press, 1976), p. 126.

55. Wittke, *The Irish in America*, p. 30.

56. Ibid., p. 39.

57. Furnas, *The Americans*, pp. 522, 527; M. A. Jones, *American Immigration* (Chicago: University of Chicago Press, 1960), pp. 150, 151; Wittke, *The Irish in America*, pp. 46, 120.

58. Wittke, *The Irish in America*, pp. 119–120; Maldwyn Allen Jones, *American Immigration*, (Chicago: University of Chicago Press, 1970), p. 56; Potter, *To the Golden Door*, pp. 285–286, 299, 311, 422, 426.

59. Potter, *To the Golden Door*, p. 520.

60. Jones, *American Immigration*, p. 130.

61. Ibid.

62. Conzen, *Immigration Milwaukee*, p. 73; Wittke, *The Irish in America*, p. 30.

63. Jones, *American Immigration*, p. 130; Conzen, *Immigrant Milwaukee*, pp. 66, 73.

64. Handlin, *Boston's Immigrants*, p. 253.

65. Ibid., pp. 60, 69–70, 84.

66. Wittke, *The Irish in America*, p. 37.

67. Frederick Law Olmsted, *The Cotton Kingdom* (New York: Modern Library, 1969), p. 215; Ulrich B. Phillips, *American Negro Slavery* (Baton Rouge: Louisiana State University Press, 1969), pp. 301–302; Ulrich B. Phillips, *Life and Labor in the Old South* (Boston: Little, Brown and Co., 1963), p. 186; Ulrich B. Phillips, *The Slave Economy of the Old South* (Baton Rouge: Louisiana State University, 1968), pp. 130n–131n; Lewis C. Gray, *History of Agriculture in the Southern United States* (Washington, D.C.: Carnegie Institution of Washington, 1933), vol. II, p. 520; Furnas, *The Americans*, p. 394; Daniel Boorstin, *The Americans* (New York: Random House, 1965), vol. II, p. 101; Potter, *To the Golden Door*, p. 203.

68. Handlin, *Boston's Immigrants*, p. 42.

69. Ibid., p. 240.

70. Ibid., p. 45.

71. Ibid.

72. Oscar Handlin, *The Newcomers* (New York: Anchor Books, 1962). p. 17.

73. Banfield, *The Unheavenly City*, p. 72.

74. MacDonagh, "The Irish Famine Emigration," p. 394; Wittke, *The Irish in America*, p. 51.

75. Alice Kessler-Harris and Virginia Yans–McLaughlin, "European Immigrant Groups," in *Essays and Data on American Ethnic Groups*, ed. Thomas Sowell, p. 120.

76. Handlin, *Boston's Immigrants*, p. 111.

77. Ibid., p. 113.

78. Ibid., p. 109.

79. Wittke, *The Irish in America*, p. 27.

80. Handlin, *Boston's Immigrants*, p. 113.

81. Diane Ravitch, *The Great School Wars* (New York: Basic Books, 1974), p. 28.

82. Handlin, *Boston's Immigrants*, pp. 115–116.

83. Ibid., p. 114.

84. Ibid.

85. Furnas, *The Americans*, pp. 698–699.

86. Nathan Glazer and Daniel Patrick Moynihan, *Beyond the Melting Pot* (Cambridge: M.I.T. Press, 1963), p. 222.

87. Stephan Thernstrom, *The Other Bostonians* (Cambridge: Harvard University Press, 1973), p. 132.

88. Glazer and Moynihan, *Beyond the Melting Pot*, pp. 222–223.

89. Wittke, *The Irish in America*, p. 107.

90. Ibid., p. 108.

91. Ibid., p. 112.

92. Ibid.

93. Glazer and Moynihan, *Beyond the Melting Pot*, p. 224.

94. Boorstin, *The Americans*, vol. III, p. 260.

95. Jones, *American Immigration*, p. 234.

96. Glazer and Moynihan, *Beyond the Melting Pot*, p. 226.

97. Humbert S. Nelli, *Italians in Chicago, 1880–1930* (New York: Oxford University Press, 1970), Chapter 4.

98. Ibid., pp. 89, 91–112; Wittke, *The Irish in America*, p. 189; Herbert J. Gans, *The Urban Villagers* (New York: The Free Press, 1962), p. 174.

99. Irving Howe, *World of Our Fathers* (New York: Harcourt, Brace, Jovanovich, 1976), pp. 367–368.

100. Nelli, *Italians in Chicago*, pp. 91–112.

101. Howe, *World of Our Fathers*, p. 368.

102. Ibid., p. 370.

103. Nelli, *Italians in Chicago*, p. 87.

104. William Foote Whyte, *Street Corner Society* (Chicago: University of Chicago Press, 1955), p. 211; Gerald D. Suttles, *The Social Order of the Slum* (Chicago: University of Chicago Press, 1968), p. 100.

105. Nelli, *Italians in Chicago*, Chapter 4; Suttles, *The Social Order of the Slum*, p. 120; Rudolf Glanz, *Jew and Irish* (New York: Ktav, 1966), p. 91.

106. Wittke, *The Irish in America*, pp. 193–194.

107. Ibid., pp. 202–227, 233, 236, 241–252.

108. Jones, *American Immigration*, p. 143.

109. U.S. Bureau of the Census, *Historical Statistics of the United States, From Colonial Times to 1970* (Washington, D.C.: U.S. Government Printing Office, 1975), p. 106.

110. Jones, *American Immigration*, p. 155; Wittke, *The Irish in America*, p. 154.

111. Wittke, *The Irish in America*, p. 114; Jones, *American Immigration*, p. 154; Glanz, *Irish and Jew*, p. 51.

112. Handlin, *Boston's Immigrants*, p. 177.

113. Jones, *American Immigration*, p. 157.

114. Wittke, *The Irish in America*, p. 116; Jones, *American Immigration*, p. 159; Handlin, *Boston's Immigrants*, p. 200.

115. Wittke, *The Irish in America*, p. 23.

116. Thernstrom, *The Other Bostonians*, p. 131.

117. Ibid., p. 133.

118. Ibid., p. 186.

119. Ibid., pp. 187, 188.

120. Ibid., pp. 132–133.

121. Ibid., p. 135.

122. Jacob Riis, *How the Other Half Lives* (Cambridge: Harvard University Press, 1970), p. 19.

123. Francesco Cordasco, ed., *Jacob Riis Revisited* (New York: Anchor Books, 1968), p. 336; Ravitch, *The Great School Wars*, p. 108; Joseph Lopreato, *Italian Americans* (New York: Random House, 1970), pp. 110–111; Charles H. Trout, *Boston, the Great Depression, and the New Deal* (New York: Oxford University Press, 1977), p. 10.

124. Howe, *World of Our Fathers*, pp. 271–272, 274.

125. Wittke, *The Irish in America*, pp. 126, 225; Jones, *American Immigration*, p. 222; Lorenzo J. Greene and Carter G. Woodson, *The Negro Wage Earner* (New York: AMS Press, 1970), p. 140.

126. Kessler-Harris and Yans-McLaughlin, "European Ethnic Groups," p. 116.

127. Ibid., pp. 113–114; Thernstrom, *The Other Bostonians*, Chapter 7.

128. Thernstrom, *The Other Bostonians*, p. 137.

129. Trout, *Boston, the Great Depression, and the New Deal*, p. 16.

130. Wittke, *The Irish in America*, p. 230.

131. Glazer and Moynihan, *Beyond the Melting Pot*, p. 225. See also Wittke, *The Irish in America*, p. 230; Potter, *To the Golden Door*, p. 548.

Notes

132. Wittke, *The Irish in America*, p. 233.

133. O'Brien, *A Concise History of Ireland*, p. 25. See also Gerhand Herm, *The Celts* (New York: St. Martin's Press, 1976), pp. 239–240.

134. Glazer and Moynihan, *Beyond the Melting Pot*, p. 232.

135. Greeley, *That Most Distressful Nation*, p. 250. See also Potter, *To the Golden Door*, p. 606.

136. Ravitch, *The Great School Wars*, p. 179.

137. Robert M. Yerkes, *Psychological Examining in the United States Army* (Washington, D.C.: U.S. Government Printing Office, 1921), p. 697.

138. Thernstrom, *The Other Bostonians*, p. 137.

139. Ibid., p. 166.

140. Ibid., p. 167.

141. Ibid., pp. 172–173.

142. Wittke, *The Irish in America*, pp. 125–132, 168–169; Williston H. Lofton, "Northern Labor and the Negro during the Civil War," *Journal of Negro History* (July 1949), pp. 256–261, 262, 268–270, David Katzman, *Before the Ghetto: Black Detroit in the Nineteenth Century* (Urbana: University of Illinois Press, 1973), pp. 44–45, 101; Gilbert Osofsky, *Harlem: The Making of a Ghetto* (New York: Harper & Row, 1968), pp. 45–46; Constance M. Green, *The Secret City* (Princeton: Princeton University Press, 1970), pp. 49, 93, 128, 134; Greene and Woodson, *The Negro Wage Earner*, p. 23; St. Clair and Horace B. Clayton, *Black Metropolis* (New York: Harcourt, Brace and World, Inc., 1970), vol. I, pp. 44, 62, 66, 110n; Stephen Birmingham, *Certain People* (Boston: Little, Brown and Co., 1977), pp. 185–186; Leon Litwack, *North of Slavery* (Chicago: University of Chicago Press, 1962), pp. 162, 166.

143. Glazer and Moynihan, *Beyond the Melting Pot*, p. 233; James McCague, *The Second Rebellion* (New York: The Dial Press, 1968), p. 74.

144. Wittke, *The Irish in America*, pp. 183, 184.

145. Luciano J. Iorizzo and Salvatore Mondello, *The Italian Americans* (Boston: Twayne Publishers, Inc., 1971), p. 35; Wittke, *The Irish in America*, p. 189; Whyte, *Street Corner Society*, p. 195; Stanley Feldstein and Lawrence Costello, ed., *The Ordeal of Assimilation* (New York: Anchor Books, 1974), pp. 127–131.

146. Wittke, *The Irish in America*, p. 190.

147. Ibid., pp. 191–192.

148. Ronald H. Bayor, "Italians, Jews and Ethnic Conflict," *International Migration Review* (Winter 1972), pp. 377–391.

149. Wittke, *The Irish in America*, pp. 183, 184.

150. Ibid., pp. 119–120; Jones, *American Immigration*, p. 150.

151. Gans, *The Urban Villagers*, p. 167; Glanz, *Jew and Irish*, p. 89.

152. Feldstein and Costello, *The Ordeal of Assimilation*, p. 373.

153. Greeley, *That Most Distressful Nation*, p. 93.

154. Wittke, *The Irish in America*, p. 91.

155. Ibid. p. 187.

156. Ibid., p. 95; Carter G. Woodson, *The Education of the Negro Prior to 1961* (Washington, D.C.: The Associated Publishers, Inc., 1919), pp. 11, 108, 138, 183; Joseph Butsch, "Catholics and the Negro," *Journal of Negro History* (October 1917), p. 404.

157. Thomas Sowell, "Patterns of Black Excellence," *The Public Interest* (Spring 1976), pp. 41–47.

158. U.S. Bureau of the Census, *Current Population Reports*, Series P-20, No. 221 (Washington: U.S. Government Printing Office, 1971), p. 7.

159. Ibid., p. 22; ibid., No. 249, pp. 33, 34. A very different picture of Irish income—and progress in general—is presented in the writings of Andrew Greeley—different not only from the census data but also from other studies of the Irish in America.

160. Sowell, "Race and I.Q. Reconsidered," in *Essays and Data on American Ethnic Groups*, p. 210.

161. Greeley, *That Most Distressful Nation*, pp. 132, 134.

162. U.S. Bureau of the Census, *Current Population Reports*, Series P-20, No. 249 (Washington, D.C.: U.S. Government Printing Office, 1973), p. 22.

163. Ibid., p. 19.

164. Mark R. Kramer and Michael S. Kramer, *The Ethnic Factor* (New York: Simon and Schuster, 1972), p. 124.

165. Greeley, *That Most Distressful Nation,* Chapter 7.

166. Ben J. Wattenberg, *The Real America* (New York: Doubleday, 1974), p. 194.

Chapter 3

1. Virginia Brainard Kunz, *The Germans in America* (Minneapolis: Lerner Publications Co., 1966), pp. 63–72.

2. Ibid., pp. 48–55, 60–62.

3. U.S. Bureau of the Census, *Historical Statistics of the United States, Colonial Times to 1976* (Washington, D.C.: U.S. Government Printing Office, 1975), pp. 105–106.

4. William H. Harris and Judith S. Leven, *The New Columbia Encyclopedia* (New York: Columbia University Press, 1975), p. 1071.

5. Michael Grant, *The Fall of the Roman Empire* (University Park, Pa.: The Annenberg School Press, 1976), p. 33.

6. Ibid., pp. 31–39.

7. Ibid., pp. 56, 68, 75–76, 81–87, 203–204.

8. Glanville Downey, *The Late Roman Empire* (Huntington, N.Y.: Robert E. Krieger Publishing Co., 1976).

9. Grant, *The Fall of the Roman Empire,* p. 225.

10. Ibid., p. 216.

11. Ibid., p. 219.

12. Ibid., p. 220.

13. Wolfgang Köllmann and Peter Marschalck, "German Emigration to the United States," in *Perspectives in American History,* vol. VII (1975) pp. 509–511.

14. Ibid., p. 514.

15. Ibid., pp. 509, 511.

16. Ibid., p. 519.

17. Ibid., p. 518.

18. Ibid.; U.S. Bureau of the Census, *Historical Statistics of the United States, Colonial Times to 1970,* p. 106.

19. Köllmann and Marschalck, "German Emigration," p. 519.

20. U.S. Bureau of the Census, *Historical Statistics of the United States, Colonial Times to 1970,* p. 106.

21. Köllmann and Marschalck, "German Emigration," pp. 543, 548.

22. Kunz, *The Germans in America,* pp. 56–59.

23. Köllmann and Marschalck, "German Emigration," p. 511. See also Oscar Handlin, *The Newcomers* (New York: Anchor Books, 1962), p. 5.

24. Köllmann and Marschalck, "German Emigration," p. 511.

25. Ibid., p. 512. See also Carl Wittke, *The Germans in America* (New York: Teachers College, Columbia University Press, 1967), p. 2.

26. Wittke, *The Germans in America,* p. 1.

27. Ibid., p. 2.

28. Kunz, *The Germans in America,* p. 14.

29. Theodore Heubner, *The Germans in America* (Radnor, PA.: Chilton Co., 1962), pp. 45–47.

30. Kunz, *The Germans in America,* p. 9.

31. Daniel Boorstin, *The Americans* (New York: Random House, 1958), vol. I, pp. 55–56; J. C. Furnas, *The Americans* (New York: G. P. Putnam's Sons, 1969), pp. 90–91.

32. Kunz, *The Germans in America,* pp. 21–22.

33. Abbot Emerson Smith, *Colonists in Bondage* (Magnolia, Maine: Peter Smith, 1965), pp. 3–4.

34. Ibid., p. 51.

35. Köllmann and Marschalck, "German Emigration," p. 513.

36. Abbot Emerson Smith, *Colonists in Bondage,* p. 23.

37. Warren B. Smith, *White Servitude in Colonial South Carolina* (Chapel Hill: University of South Carolina Press, 1961), pp. 52–53, 58–59.

38. Abbot Emerson Smith, *Colonists in Bondage,* p. 215.

39. Ibid., p. 214.

40. Ibid., p. 216.

Notes

41. Ibid., pp. 221–222
42. Maldwyn Allen Jones, *American Immigration* (Chicago: University of Chicago Press, 1960), p. 67.
43. Kunz, *The Germans in America*, p. 22.
44. Abbot Emerson Smith, *Colonists in Bondage*, p. 223.
45. Furnas, *The Americans*, pp. 84–85.
46. Warren B. Smith, *White Servitude in Colonial South Carolina*, p. 52.
47. Abbot Emerson Smith, *Colonists in Bondage*, pp. 21–22.
48. Kunz, *The Germans in America*, pp. 11–12.
49. Ibid., p. 10.
50. Boorstin, *The Americans*, vol. I, p. 225.
51. Furnas, *The Americans*, p. 86.
52. Kunz, *The Germans in America*, p. 24.
53. Heubner, *The Germans in America*, p. 21.
54. Furnas, *The Americans*, p. 86. See also Kunz, *The Germans in America*, p. 14.
55. Furnas, *The Americans*, pp. 87–88.
56. Ibid., p. 88.
57. Wittke, *The Germans in America*, p. 3; Huebner, *The Germans in America*, pp. 21–41, passim; James G. Leyburn, *The Scotch-Irish* (Chapel Hill: University of North Carolina Press, 1962), pp. 201–204, 211, 216; Kunz, *The Germans in America*, p. 9.
58. Furnas, *The Americans*, p. 84.
59. Heubner, *The Germans in America*, p. 28.
60. Leyburn, *The Scotch-Irish*, pp. 191, 228, 230.
61. Charles H. Anderson, *White Protestant Americans*, (Englewood Cliffs, N.J.: Prentice-Hall, Inc., 1970), p. 80.
62. Leyburn, *The Scotch-Irish*, pp. 190–191, 216.
63. Ibid., pp. 190–191, 221, 222–223, 228, 229, 230, 231.
64. Ibid., p. 191.
65. Anderson, *White Protestant Americans*, p. 81.
66. Kunz, *The Germans in America*, pp. 17–19.
67. Jacob M. Price, "Economic Function and the Growth of American Port Towns in the Eighteenth Century," in *Perspectives in American History*, vol. VIII (1974), p. 155.
68. Kunz, *The Germans in America*, p. 19.
69. Ibid., pp. 19–20; Boorstin, *The Americans*, vol. I, pp. 350–351.
70. Huebner, *The Germans in America*, p. 42.
71. Ibid., pp. 42–43.
72. Kunz, *The Germans in America*, p. 25.
73. Huebner, *The Germans in America*, pp. 45–46.
74. Ibid., p. 52.
75. Kunz, *The Germans in America*, pp. 30–31.
76. Huebner, *The Germans in America*, p. 54.
77. Ibid., p. 57.
78. Ibid., p. 58.
79. Ibid., p. 60.
80. Wittke, *The Germans in America*, p. 5.
81. Kunz, *The Germans in America*, p. 34.
82. Ibid., pp. 35–37.
83. Huebner, *The Germans in America*, p. 46.
84. Kunz, *The Germans in America*, pp. 38–39.
85. Furnas, *The Americans*, p. 362.
86. Kunz, *The Germans in America*, p. 38.
87. Ibid., p. 39; Wittke, *The Germans in America*, p. 6.
88. U.S. Bureau of the Census, *Historical Statistics of the United States, Colonial Times to 1970*, p. 106.
89. Köllmann and Marschalck, "German Emigration," p. 520.
90. Ibid., p. 518.
91. Ibid., pp. 516–517.
92. Ibid., pp. 524–526.
93. Ibid., p. 527.

94. Ibid., pp. 527–528; Huebner, *The Germans in America,* p. 61.

95. Furnas, *The Americans,* p. 387.

96. Huebner, *The Germans in America,* pp. 62–67.

97. Ibid., p. 134. See also U.S. Bureau of the Census, *Historical Statistics of the United States, Colonial Times to 1970,* p. 106.

98. Köllmann and Marschalck, "German Emigration," p. 529.

99. Ibid., p. 530.

100. Ibid., pp. 530–531.

101. Ibid., pp. 537, 539.

102. Hildegard Binder Johnson, "The Location of German Immigrants in the Middle West," *Annals of the Association of American Geographers,* vol. XLI, No. 1 (March 1951), pp. 3, 4, 11, 18, 34–35.

103. Huebner, *The Germans in America,* p. 87.

104. Ibid., p. 84.

105. Johnson, "The Location of German Immigrants," p. 25.

106. Jones, *American Immigration,* p. 119.

107. Wittke, *The Germans in America,* pp. 8–9; Kunz, *The Germans in America,* pp. 42–43.

108. Jones, *American Immigration,* p. 118.

109. Johnson, "The Location of German Immigrants," p. 4.

110. Anderson, *White Protestant Americans,* p. 80.

111. Huebner, *The Germans in America,* p. 124.

112. Kathleen Neils Conzen, *Immigrant Milwaukee, 1836–1860* (Cambridge: Harvard University Press, 1976), p. 152.

113. Ibid., p. 132.

114. Anderson, *White Protestant Americans,* p. 82.

115. Wittke, *The Germans in America,* p. 11.

116. Ibid., p. 9.

117. Anderson, *White Protestant Americans,* p. 83.

118. "German Immigration," in *The Ordeal of Assimilation,* ed. Stanley Feldstein and Lawrence Costello (New York: Anchor Books, 1974), p. 13.

119. Furnas, *The Americans,* p. 390.

120. Wittke, *The Germans in America,* p. 11.

121. Anderson, *White Protestant Americans,* p. 83.

122. Furnas, *The Americans,* p. 391.

123. Huebner, *The Germans in America,* pp. 125–126.

124. Conzen, *Immigrant Milwaukee,* p. 73.

125. Alice Kessler-Harris and Virginia Yans McLaughlin, "European Immigrant Groups," in *Essays and Data on American Ethnic Groups,* ed. Thomas Sowell (Washington, D.C.: The Urban Institute, 1978), p. 111.

126. Conzen, *Immigrant Milwaukee,* p. 14.

127. Ibid., pp. 104–105.

128. Ibid., p. 109.

129. Kunz, *The Germans in America,* pp. 63–64.

130. Ibid., pp. 64–65.

131. Huebner, *The Germans in America,* p. 128.

132. Kunz, *The Germans in America,* pp. 66–69, 71.

133. Wittke, *The Germans in America,* p. 10; Furnas, *The Americans,* pp. 390–391.

134. Carl Wittke, *The Irish in America,* (New York: Russell & Russell, 1970), p. 182.

135. E. V. Smalley, "The German Element in the United States," in *The Ordeal of Assimilation,* ed. Stanley Feldstein and Lawrence Costello., p. 105.

136. Ibid.

137. Kunz, *The Germans in America,* p. 84.

138. Huebner, *The Germans in America,* p. 106; Kunz, *The Germans in America,* p. 72.

139. Kunz, *The Germans in America,* p. 72.

140. Huebner, *The Germans in America,* p. 137.

141. Ibid., p. 138.

142. Wittke, *The Germans in America,* pp. 10–12.

143. Anderson, *White Protestant Americans,* p. 84.

144. Huebner, *The Germans in America,* p. 23.

Notes

145. Jones, *American Immigration*, p. 139.

146. Wittke, *The Germans in America*, p. 13.

147. Jones, *American Immigration*, p. 138.

148. Wittke, *The Irish in America*, p. 186.

149. Ibid., p. 187.

150. See, for example, Conzen, *Immigrant Milwaukee*, p. 167; Louis Wirth, *The Ghetto* (Chicago: University of Chicago Press, 1956), p. 246; Moses Rischin, *The Promised City* (Cambridge: Harvard University Press, 1967), pp. 96–97.

151. Frances Butwin, *The Jews in America* (Minneapolis: Lerner Publications Company, 1969), p. 45.

152. Clement Eaton, *The Freedom-of-Thought Struggle in the Old South* (New York: Harper & Row, 1964), pp. 33, 166, 178, 180, 182–183, 190, 238–240, 242, 253–260, 267–299.

153. Kunz, *The Germans in America*, p. 50.

154. Ibid., pp. 49–50.

155. Ibid., pp. 47–48.

156. Ibid., pp. 77–78.

157. Carrol C. Calkins, ed., *The Story of America*, (Pleasantville, N.Y.: The Reader's Digest Association, 1975), p. 361.

158. Kunz, *The Germans in America*, p. 75.

159. Ibid., p. 54.

160. Ibid.

161. Anderson, *White Protestant Americans*, p. 85.

162. Ibid.

163. U.S. Bureau of the Census, *Current Population Reports*, Series P-20, No. 221 (Washington, D.C.: U.S. Government Printing Office, 1971), p. 7.

164. David S. Neft, et al., *The Sports Encyclopedia: Baseball* (New York: Grosset & Dunlap, 1974), p. 476.

165. Ibid., p. 482.

166. Kunz, *The Germans in America*, p. 82.

167. U.S. Bureau of the Census, *Current Population Reports*, Series P-20, No. 249 (Washington, D.C.: U.S. Government Printing Office, 1973), p. 25.

168. Ibid., p. 24.

Chapter 4

1. Thomas Sowell, *Knowledge and Decisions* (New York: Basic Books, 1980), pp. 67–69.

2. Louis Wirth, *The Ghetto* (Chicago: University of Chicago Press, 1956), p. 30.

3. Ibid., p. 32.

4. Ibid., p. 34.

5. Ibid., pp. 68–69.

6. Ibid., p. 89.

7. Ibid., pp. 112, 116.

8. Ibid., p. 114.

9. Ibid., pp. 114, 115.

10. Ibid., p. 107.

11. Stephen H. Haliczer, "The Castilian Urban Patriciate and the Jewish Expulsions of 1480–92," *American Historical Review*, February 1973, pp. 38n, 39.

12. Bernard S. Bachrach, "A Reassessment of Visigothic Jewish Policy, 589–711," *American History Review*, February 1973, pp. 11–34.

13. Haliczer, "The Castilian Urban Patriciate," pp. 35–58.

14. Solomon Grayzel, *A History of the Jews* (New York: Mentor Books, 1968), p. 365.

15. Wirth, *The Ghetto*, p. 132.

16. Ibid., p. 134.

17. Ibid., p. 136.

18. Ibid., p. 135.

19. Nathan Glazer, *American Judaism* (Chicago: University of Chicago Press, 1957), p. 15.

20. Ernest van den Haag, *The Jewish Mystique* (New York: Stein & Day, 1969), pp. 21–22.

Notes

21. Wirth, *The Ghetto*, p. 141.

22. Frances Butwin, *The Jews in America* (Minneapolis: Lerner Publications Co., 1969), p. 38.

23. Maldwyn Allen Jones, *American Immigration* (Chicago: University of Chicago, 1970), p. 120.

24. Butwin, *The Jews in America*, p. 40; J. C. Furnas, *The Americans* (New York: G. P. Putnam's Sons, 1969), p. 393.

25. Butwin, *The Jews in America*, p. 40.

26. Furnas, *The Americans*, p. 393.

27. Butwin, *The Jews in America*, pp. 42–43.

28. Ibid., p. 45.

29. Moses Rischin, *The Promised City* (Cambridge: Harvard University Press, 1962), p. 52.

30. Alice Kessler-Harris and Virginia Yans-McLaughlin, "European Immigrant Groups," in *Essays and Data on American Ethnic Groups,* ed. Thomas Sowell (Washington, D.C.: The Urban Institute, 1978), pp. 111–112.

31. Grayzel, *A History of the Jews,* pp. 389–392; Butwin, *The Jews in America,* pp. 32–33.

32. Butwin, *The Jews in America*, pp. 50–51.

33. Simon Kuznets, "Immigration of Russian Jews to the United States: Background and Structure," in *Perspectives in American History,* vol. IX (1975), p. 39; Rischin, *The Promised City*, p. 20.

34. Kuznets, "Immigration of Russian Jews," p. 44.

35. Ibid., p. 80.

36. Ibid., p. 73.

37. Ibid., p. 76.

38. Rischin, *The Promised City*, p. 20.

39. Kessler-Harris and Yans-McLaughlin, "European Immigrant Groups," p. 116.

40. Rischin, *The Promised City*, Chapter 6; Wirth, *The Ghetto*, p. 181.

41. Wirth, *The Ghetto*, p. 183.

42. Rischin, *The Promised City*, p. 97.

43. Irving Howe, *World of Our Fathers* (New York: Harcourt, Brace, Jovanovich, 1976), p. 230.

44. Ibid., p. 231.

45. Rischin, *The Promised City*, p. 97.

46. Ibid., p. 98.

47. Ibid., p. 100.

48. Ibid., p. 106.

49. Ibid., p. 102.

50. Ibid., p. 104.

51. Ibid., p. 105.

52. Wirth, *The Ghetto*, p. 160.

53. Ibid., pp. 172–173.

54. Ibid., p. 173.

55. Ibid., p. 184.

56. Ibid., p. 181.

57. Ibid., p. 180.

58. Rischin, *The Promised City*, p. 100.

59. E. Digby Batlzell, "The Development of a Jewish Upper Class in Philadelphia, 1782–1940," in *The Jews: Social Patterns of an American Group,* ed. Marshall Sklare (New York: The Free Press, 1958), p. 274.

60. Rischin, *The Promised City*, p. 111.

61. Wirth, *The Ghetto*, p. 184.

62. Ibid., p. 224.

63. Howe, *World of Our Fathers*, p. 177.

64. Butwin, *The Jews in America*, p. 54.

65. Rischin, *The Promised City*, pp. 261–263.

66. Ibid., p. 265.

67. Ibid., p. 79.

Notes

68. Ibid., p. 80.

69. Howe, *World of Our Fathers*, p. 69.

70. Thomas Kessner, *The Golden Door* (New York: Oxford University Press, 1977), p. 61.

71. Howe, *World of Our Fathers*, pp. 177–179.

72. Rischin, *The Promised City*, p. 84.

73. Howe, *World of Our Fathers*, pp. 55–56.

74. Kessler-Harris and Yans-McLaughlin, "European Immigrant Groups," p. 116.

75. Howe, *World of Our Fathers*, p. 69.

76. Rischin, *The Promised City*, Chapter 5.

77. Jacob Riis, *How the Other Half Lives* (Cambridge: Harvard University Press, 1970), p. 82.

78. Daniel Boorstin, *The Americans* (New York: Random House, 1958), vol. III, p. 99.

79. Ibid., pp. 95–100.

80. Howe, *World of Our Fathers*, p. 82.

81. Ibid., p. 80.

82. Riis, *How the Other Half Lives*, pp. 80–81.

83. Ibid., p. 84.

84. Kessner, *The Golden Door*, p. 60.

85. Howe, *World of Our Fathers*, p. 80.

86. Kessner, *The Golden Door*, p. 61.

87. Ibid., p. 33.

88. Rischin, *The Promised City*, p. 86.

89. Ibid., p. 87.

90. Lawrence Friedman, *Government and Slum Housing* (Skokie, Ill.: Rand McNally, 1968), p. 30.

91. Rischin, *The Promised City*, pp. 56–57.

92. Ibid., p. 57.

93. Howe, *World of Our Fathers*, p. 229.

94. Rischin, *The Promised City*, pp. 80, 84.

95. Ibid., p. 82.

96. Howe, *World of Our Fathers*, p. 148.

97. Wirth, *The Ghetto*, Chapter VI: van den Haag, *The Jewish Mystique*, Chapter 1.

98. Stanley Feldstein and Lawrence Costello, *The Ordeal of Assimilation* (New York: Anchor Books, 1974), pp. 122–123. See also Irving Howe and Kenneth Libo, *How We Lived* (New York: Richard Marek Publishers, 1979), p. 204.

99. Howe, *World of Our Fathers*, p. 248. See also Howe and Libo, *How We Lived*, pp. 279–316.

100. Howe, *World of Our Fathers*, p. 260.

101. Ibid., p. 271.

102. Diane Ravitch, *The Great School Wars* (New York: Basic Books, 1974), p. 115; Selma C. Berrol, "Education and Economic Mobility: The Jewish Experience in New York City, 1880–1920," *American Jewish Historical Quarterly*, March 1976, p. 260.

103. Berrol, "Education and Economic Mobility," p. 259.

104. Ravitch, *The Great School Wars*, p. 89.

105. Ibid., p. 176.

106. Ibid.; Howe, *World of Our Fathers*, p. 278.

107. Ravitch, *The Great School Wars*, p. 177.

108. Ibid.; See also Berrol, "Education and Economic Mobility," p. 270.

109. Howe, *World of Our Fathers*, p. 271.

110. Clifford Kirkpatrick, *Intelligence and Immigration* (Baltimore: The Williams and Wilkins Co., 1926), p. 40.

111. Report of the Immigration Committee, 61st Congress, 3rd Session, *The Children of Immigrants in Schools* (Washington, D.C.: U.S. Government Printing Office, 1911), vol. I, p. 64.

112. L.P. Ayres, *Laggards in Our Schools* (Charities Publishing Co., 1912), p. 107.

113. Robert M. Yerkes, *Psychological Examining in the United States Army*, Memoirs of the National Academy of *Sciences*, vol. 15 (Washington, D.C.: U.S. Government Printing Office, 1921), p. 697.

114. Carl Brigham, *A Study of American Intelligence* (Princeton, N.J.: Princeton University Press, 1923), p. 190.

115. Rischin, *The Promised City*, p. 73.

116. Kessner, *The Golden Door*, p. 60.

117. Ibid., p. 64.

118. Stephan Thernstrom, *The Other Bostonians* (Cambridge: Harvard University Press, 1973), p. 152.

119. Sidney Goldstein, "American Jewry, 1970: A Demographic Profile," in *American Jewish Yearbook, 1971*, ed. Morris Fine and Milton Himmelfarb (New York: American Jewish Committee and the Jewish Publication Society of America, 1971), p. 74.

120. Rischin, *The Promised City*, p. 93.

121. Goldstein, "American Jewry, 1970: A Demographic Profile," p. 40.

122. Wirth, *The Ghetto*, pp. 198-199.

123. Ibid., p. 199.

124. Goldstein, "American Jewry, 1970: A Demographic Profile," p. 41.

125. Ibid., p. 9.

126. Ibid., p. 35.

127. Ibid., p. 82.

128. Ibid., p. 63.

129. Ibid., p. 81.

130. Van den Haag, *The Jewish Mystique*, p. 19; Loehlin et al., *Race Differences in Intelligence*, pp. 179-184; Nathan Glazer, "The American Jew and the Attainment of Middle-Class Rank: Some Trends and Explanations," in *The Jews*, ed. Marshall Sklare, p. 145.

131. Van den Haag, *The Jewish Mystique*, pp. 22-23.

132. Butwin, *The Jews in America*, pp. 91-95; Howe, *World of Our Fathers*, pp. 164-165.

133. Howe, *World of Our Fathers*, p. 539.

134. Ibid., p. 543.

135. Butwin, *The Jews in America*, p. 91.

136. Jerold S. Auerbach, "From Rags to Robes: The Legal Profession, Social Mobility and the American Jewish Experience," *American Jewish Historical Quarterly*, December 1976, pp. 249-284.

137. Kessner, *The Golden Door*, pp. 59-70.

138. Berrol, "Education and Economic Mobility," p. 261.

139. Ravitch, *The Great School Wars*, p. 178.

140. Howe, *World of Our Fathers*, p. 165.

141. Berrol, "Education and Economic Mobility," p. 262.

142. Howe, *World of Our Fathers*, p. 270.

143. Berrol, "Education and Economic Mobility," pp. 262-263.

144. Jones, *American Immigration*, pp. 212-213.

145. Howe, *World of Our Fathers*, pp. 374-377.

146. Ibid., p. 378.

147. Ibid., Chapter 9; Arthur Liebman, "The Ties that Bind: The Jewish Support for the Left in the United States," *American Jewish Historical Quarterly*, December 1976, pp. 285-321.

148. Butwin, *The Jews in America*, p. 95.

149. Glazer, "The American Jew and the Attainment of Middle-Class Rank," p. 144

150. Ibid., p. 145.

151. Goldstein, "American Jewry, 1970: A Demographic Profile," p. 21.

152. Ibid., p. 27.

153. Ibid., p. 28.

154. Thomas Sowell, "Ethnicity in a Changing America," *Daedalus*, Winter 1978, p. 217. See also Thernstrom, *The Other Bostonians*, p. 166; Kessner, *The Golden Door*, pp. 93n, 132, 170. A contrary view is expressed by the distinguished demographer, Goldstein ("American Jewry, 1970: A Demographic Profile," pp. 15-16), but his data for the turn of the century is limited to Rhode Island.

155. Sowell, "Ethnicity in a Changing America," p. 217.

156. Ibid., p. 221.

157. Rudolf Glanz, *Jew and Irish* (New York: Ktav, 1966), p. 41.

Notes

158. See, for example, Wirth, *The Ghetto*, p. 230; Jeffrey S. Gurock, *When Harlem Was Jewish, 1870-1930* (New York: Columbia University Press, 1979), pp. 147-148.

159. Glanz, *Jew and Irish*, p. 75.

160. Mark R. Levy and Michael S. Kramer, *The Ethnic Factor* (New York: Simon and Schuster, 1972), p. 102.

161. Ibid., p. 103.

162. Ibid., pp. 118-119.

163. Ibid., p. 119.

164. Ibid., pp. 120-121. This was by no means unprecedented. In 1932, liberal Robert Wagner, Sr., not only won the Jewish vote against a Jewish opponent for the Senate; he carried a higher percentage of the Jewish vote than did Jewish liberal Herbert Lehman. Nathan Glazer and Daniel Patrick Moynihan, *Beyond the Melting Pot* (Cambridge: M.I.T. Press, 1963), p. 167.

165. Glanz, *Jew and Irish*, p. 99.

166. Rischin, *The Promised City*, p. 89.

167. Ibid.

168. Ibid., p. 90.

169. Ibid., p. 91.

170. Howe, *World of Our Fathers*, p. 337.

171. See Chapter 1 of this book.

172. Sowell, ed., *Essays and Data on American Ethnic Groups*, pp. 364-365. The comparison was with tabulations from the 1970 Public Use Sample, using the same definitions.

173. Everett Ladd and Seymour Martin Lipset, *The Divided Academy* (New York: McGraw-Hill, 1975), pp. 88, 150.

174. Sowell, ed., *Essays and Data on American Ethnic Groups*, p. 363. Compare ibid., pp. 267, 285, 303, 321, 351, 387, 405.

175. Ibid., p. 362. Compare pp. 266, 284, 302, 320, 350, 386, 404.

176. Van den Haag, *The Jewish Mystique*, p. 118.

177. Alan Fisher, "Continuity and Erosion of Jewish Liberalism," *American Jewish Historical Quarterly*, December 1976, p. 326.

178. Paula Goldman Leventman and Seymour Leventman, "Congressman Drinan S.J., and His Jewish Constituents," *American Jewish Historical Quarterly*, December 1976, p. 218.

179. Alan Fisher, "Continuity and Erosion of Jewish Liberalism," p. 218.

180. Goldstein, "American Jewry, 1970: A Demographic Profile," p. 80.

Chapter 5

1. U.S. Bureau of the Census, *Historical Statistics of the United States, Colonial Times to 1970* (Washington, D.C.: U.S. Government Printing Office, 1975), p. 105.

2. Robert F. Foerster, *The Italian Emigration of Our Times* (New York: Arno Press, 1969), p. 7.

3. Ibid., p. 3; Nathan Glazer and Daniel Patrick Moynihan, *Beyond the Melting Pot* (Cambridge: M.I.T. Press, 1963), p. 182.

4. Richard Gambino, *Blood of My Blood* (New York: Anchor Books, 1974), pp. 70-71.

5. Ibid., p. 71.

6. Joseph Lopreato, *Italian Americans* (New York: Random House, 1970), p. 102.

7. Edward C. Banfield, *The Moral Basis of a Backward Society* (New York: The Free Press, 1958), pp. 35, 47.

8. Lopreato, *Italian Americans*, p. 26. See also Foerster, *The Italian Emigration of Our Times*, p. 51.

9. Lopreato, *Italian Americans*, p. 26.

10. Foerster, *The Italian Emigration of Our Times*, p. 51.

11. Ibid., p. 53-59.

12. Ibid., p. 60.

13. Ibid., p. 61.

14. Shepard B. Clough, *The Economic History of Modern Italy* (New York: Columbia University Press, 1964), p. 4.

15. Lopreato, *Italian Americans*, p. 26.

16. Clough, *The Economic History of Modern Italy*, p. 4.

17. Ibid.

18. Edward Gibbon, *The Decline and Fall of the Roman Empire* (New York: Modern Library, no date), vol. III, p. 344.

19. Ibid., pp. 344–390.

20. Ibid., pp. 344, 347, 349. See also Gambino, *Blood of My Blood*, p. 4.

21. Gibbon, *The Decline and Fall of the Roman Empire*, vol. III, pp. 347, 348, 354, 358, 359, 387, 389.

22. Ibid., p. 817.

23. Ibid., vol. II, p. 747.

24. Lopreato, *Italian Americans*, p. 102.

25. Clough, *The Economic History of Modern Italy*, pp. 6–7. See also Foerster, *The Italian Emigration of Our Times*, p. 107.

26. Foerster, *The Italian Emigration of Our Times*, p. 108.

27. Ibid.

28. Clough, *The Economic History of Modern Italy*, pp. 8–9, 371.

29. Ibid., p. 371.

30. Ibid., p. 9.

31. Ibid., pp. 3–4; Banfield, *The Moral Basis of a Backward Society*, pp. 35, 45, 56.

32. Banfield, *The Moral Basis of a Backward Society*, pp. 75–76.

33. Quoted in Lopreato, *Italian Americans*, p. 28.

34. Banfield, *The Moral Basis of a Backward Society*, p. 61.

35. Ibid., pp. 19, 86.

36. Foerster, *The Italian Emigration of Our Times*, pp. 347, 361–362.

37. Lopreato, *Italian Americans*, p. 31.

38. Ibid., p. 33.

39. Banfield, *The Moral Basis of a Backward Society*, p. 83; Glazer and Moynihan, *Beyond the Melting Pot*, p. 194.

40. Gambino, *Blood of My Blood*, p. 247.

41. Ibid., p. 252.

42. Ibid., p. 188.

43. Banfield, *The Moral Basis of a Backward Society*, p. 109.

44. Lopreato, *Italian Americans*, p. 57.

45. Gambino, *Blood of My Blood*, pp. 214, 218.

46. Ibid., p. 228.

47. Ibid., p. 130.

48. Ibid., pp. 10, 105–106.

49. Luciano J. Iorizzo and Salvatore Mondello, *The Italian-Americans* (Boston: Twayne Publishers, Inc., 1971), p. 4.

50. Foerster, *The Italian Emigration of Our Times*, Chapters XIII–XVI.

51. Ibid., p. 320.

52. Ibid., p. 323.

53. W.P.A. Writers' Project, *The Italians of New York* (New York: Random House, 1938), pp. 2, 3. See also Foerster, *The Italian Emigration of Our Times*, pp. 40, 325, 340; Humbert S. Nelli, *The Italians in Chicago* (New York: Oxford University Press, 1970), p. 22.

54. Foerster, *The Italian Emigration of Our Times*, p. 325; Nelli, *The Italians in Chicago*, p. 22.

55. W.P.A. Writers' Project, *The Italians of New York*, p. 3; Lopreato, *Italian Americans*, p. 33; Foerster, *The Italian Emigration of Our Times*, p. 369.

56. Iorizzo and Mondello, *The Italian-Americans*, p. 30.

57. Foerster, *The Italian Emigration of Our Times*, p. 325; Lopreato, *Italian Americans*, p. 102.

58. Gambino, *Blood of My Blood*, p. 85.

59. Lopreato, *Italian Americans*, p. 103.

60. Samuel L. Baily, "Italians and Organized Labor in the United States and Argentina: 1880–1910," in *The Italian Experience in the United States*, ed. Silvano M. Tomasi and Madeline H. Engel (Englewood, N. J.: Center for Migration Studies, Inc., 1970), p. 112.

61. Gambino, *Blood of My Blood*, p. 85.

62. Glazer and Moynihan, *Beyond the Melting Pot*, p. 206.

Notes

63. *Journal of Economic History,* June 1971, p. 424.

64. Foerster, *The Italian Emigration of Our Times,* p. 23.

65. Ibid., p. 28.

66. Ibid., p. 32.

67. Ibid., p. 35.

68. Ibid., p. 39.

69. Nelli, *The Italians in Chicago,* p. 72; Iorizzo and Mondello, *The Italian-Americans,* p. 95.

70. Foerster, *The Italian Emigration of Our Times,* pp. 399–400. See also Lopreato, *Italian Americans,* p. 158.

71. Lopreato, *Italian Americans,* pp. 56, 66.

72. Ibid., p. 57. See also Iorizzo and Mondello, *The Italian-Americans,* p. 89; Foerster, *The Italian Emigration of Our Times,* p. 409; Gambino, *Blood of My Blood,* p. 318; Nelli, *The Italians in Chicago,* p. 161.

73. Foerster, *The Italian Emigration of Our Times,* p. 393; Lopreato, *Italian Americans,* pp. 41–42; Humbert S. Nelli, "Italians in Urban America," in *The Italian Experience in the United States,* pp. 79, 91; William H. Whyte, *Street Corner Society* (Chicago: University of Chicago Press, 1955), pp. xvii, 201; Glazer and Moynihan, *Beyond the Melting Pot,* p. 186; Iorizzo and Mondello, *The Italian-Americans,* pp. 88–89; Foerster, *The Italian Emigration of Our Times,* p. 393.

74. Foerster, *The Italian Emigration of Our Times,* p. 272.

75. Ibid., p. 393.

76. Ibid.

77. Lopreato, *Italian Americans,* p. 42.

78. Stephan Thernstrom, *The Other Bostonians* (Cambridge: Harvard University Press, 1973), p. 209.

79. Ronald H. Bayor, "Italians, Jews and Ethnic Conflict," *International Migration Review,* Winter 1972, pp. 377–391.

80. Rudolf Ganz, *Jew and Italian* (Shulsinger Bros., Inc., 1970), p. 60.

81. George E. Cunningham, "The Italian, A Hindrance to White Solidarity in Louisiana, 1890–1898," *Journal of Negro History,* January 1965, pp. 22–36; Iorizzo and Mondello, *The Italian-Americans,* p. 68.

82. Herbert J. Gans, *The Urban Villagers* (New York: The Free Press, 1962), p. 35; Nelli, *The Italians in Chicago,* pp. 195–196.

83. Nelli, *The Italians in Chicago,* pp. 195–196; Thomas Kessner, *The Golden Door* (New York: Oxford University Press, 1977), p. 16.

84. Nelli, *The Italians in Chicago,* p. 198. See also Lopreato, *Italian Americans,* p. 85.

85. Foerster, *The Italian Emigration of Our Times,* pp. 343, 359; Iorizzo and Mondello, *The Italian-Americans,* p. 61.

86. Lopreato, *Italian Americans,* p. 147; Foerster, *The Italian Emigration of Our Times,* pp. 350, 354, 358.

87. Kessner, *The Golden Door,* p. 58.

88. Alice Kessler-Harris and Virginia Yans-McLaughlin, "European Ethnic Groups," in *Essays and Data on American Ethnic Groups,* ed. Thomas Sowell (Washington, D.C.: The Urban Institute, 1978), p. 112.

89. Foerster, *The Italian Emigration of Our Times,* pp. 333, 360.

90. Ibid., p. 333.

91. Gambino, *Blood of My Blood,* p. 86.

92. George Potter, *To the Golden Door* (Boston: Little, Brown and Co., 1960), pp. 513–517.

93. Francesco Cordasco, ed., *Jacob Riis Revisited* (New York: Anchor Books, 1968), pp. 142, 180.

94. See, for example, Nelli, *The Italians in Chicago,* pp. 66–67.

95. Foerster, *The Italian Emigration of Our Times,* pp. 36, 362; Luciano J. Iorizzo, "The Padrone and Immigrant Distribution," in *The Italian Experience in the United States,* p. 70.

96. Foerster, *The Italian Emigration of Our Times,* pp. 361, 362; Kessner, *The Golden Door,* p. 57n; Gambino, *Blood of My Blood,* p. 87.

97. Foerster, *The Italian Emigration of Our Times,* p. 267.

98. Gambino, *Blood of My Blood,* p. 339.

Notes

99. Foerster, *The Italian Emigration of Our Times*, pp. 356–357, 362, 402; Iorizzo and Mondello, *The Italian-Americans*, p. 169; Kessner, *The Golden Door*, p. 57n.

100. Nelli, *The Italians in Chicago*, pp. 195–196.

101. Iorizzo, "The Padrone and Immigrant Distribution," p. 54.

102. Ibid., p. 53.

103. Ibid., p. 55. See also Stanley Feldstein and Lawrence Costello, eds., *The Ordeal of Assimilation* (New York: Anchor Books, 1974), pp. 255–261.

104. Iorizzo, "The Padrone and Immigrant Distribution," p. 56.

105. Nelli, *The Italians in Chicago*, p. 66.

106. Iorizzo, "The Padrone and Immigrant Distribution," p. 61.

107. Ibid., pp. 56–57.

108. Ibid., pp. 73–74.

109. Ibid., p. 27; J. C. Furnas, *The Americans* (New York: G. P. Putnam's Sons, 1969), p. 843.

110. See Jacob Riis, *How the Other Half Lives* (Cambridge: Harvard University Press, 1970), pp. 36–37, 38; Feldstein and Costello, eds., *The Ordeal of Assimilation*, pp. 230–236, 285–290.

111. Foerster, *The Italian Emigration of Our Times*, p. 391.

112. Nelli, *The Italians in Chicago*, p. 66.

113. Lopreato, *Italian Americans*, p. 87.

114. Rudolph J. Vecoli, "Prelates and Peasants: Italian Immigrants and the Catholic Churches," *Journal of Social History*, Spring 1969, p. 238.

115. Lopreato, *Italian Americans*, pp. 89–90; Iorizzo and Mondello, *The Italian-Americans*, pp. 179–192; Nelli, *The Italians in Chicago*, p. 181.

116. Glazer and Moynihan, *Beyond the Melting Pot*, p. 204.

117. Iorizzo and Mondello, *The Italian-Americans*, p. 182.

118. Nelli, *The Italians in Chicago*, p. 67.

119. Diane Ravitch, *The Great School Wars* (New York: Basic Books, 1974), p. 179.

120. Ibid., p. 192.

121. Silvano M. Tomasi, C.S., "The Ethnic Church and the Integration of Italian Immigrants in the United States," in *The Italian Experience in the United States*, p. 167.

122. Vecoli, "Prelates and Peasants," p. 235.

123. Foerster, *The Italian Emigration of Our Times*, p. 406.

124. Gans, *The Urban Villagers*, p. 171; Whyte, *Street Corner Society*, p. 196.

125. Martin Arnold, "The City's Italian-American Needy: Too Proud to Take Aid They 'Earned,' " *New York Times*, September 29, 1972, pp. 39ff.

126. Whyte, *Street Corner Society*, p. xviii; Nelli, "Italians in Urban America," p. 91.

127. Baily, "Italians and Organized Labor," p. 119.

128. Foerster, *The Italian Emigration of Our Times*, p. 393. See also Baily, "Italians and Organized Labor," pp. 115–116, 119.

129. Glazer and Moynihan, *Beyond the Melting Pot*, p. 194.

130. Nelli, "Italians in Urban America," p. 89.

131. Kessner, *The Golden Door*, p. 94.

132. Iorizzo and Mondello, *The Italian-Americans*, pp. 79–80.

133. Lopreato, *Italian Americans*, pp. 106–107. See also Gans, *The Urban Villagers*, pp. 81, 89–110.

134. W.P.A. Writers' Project, *Italians of New York*, pp. 50–51; Oscar Handlin, *Race and Nationality in American Life* (New York: Anchor Books, 1957), p. 102.

135. Riis, *How the Other Half Lives*, p. 39.

136. Ibid., p. 36.

137. Lopreato, *Italian Americans*, p. 111.

138. See, for example, James McCague, *The Second Rebellion* (New York: Dial Press, 1968), pp. 37–38.

139. Lopreato, *Italian Americans*, p. 130; Foerster, *The Italian Emigration of Our Times*, pp. 404–405.

140. Glazer and Moynihan, *Beyond the Melting Pot*, p. 210.

141. Ibid.; Lopreato, *Italian Americans*, p. 134; Francis A. J. Lanni, "Mafia and the Web of Kinship," in *An Inquiry into Organized Crime*, ed. Luciano J. Iorizzo, The American

Notes

Italian Historical Association, Proceedings of the Third Annual Conference, October 24, 1970, p. 17.

142. Lopreato, "Italian Americans," p. 126.

143. Rudolf Glanz, *Jew and Italian*, (New York: Ktav, 1970), p. 61.

144. Glazer and Moynihan, *Beyond the Melting Pot*, p. 197; Gans, *The Urban Villagers*, p. 52.

145. Glazer and Moynihan, *Beyond the Melting Pot*, p. 188; Gambino, *Blood of My Blood*, p. 14.

146. Gambino, *Blood of My Blood*, pp. 129–182. See also Lopreato, *Italian Americans*, p. 58.

147. Lopreato, *Italian Americans*, p. 120.

148. Gambino, *Blood of My Blood*, p. 247.

149. Quoted in Kessner, *The Golden Door*, p. 40.

150. Ibid., p. 84; Nelli, *The Italians in Chicago*, p. 67.

151. Nelli, *The Italians in Chicago*, p. 68; Lopreato, *Italian Americans*, p. 64.

152. Cordasco, ed., *Jacob Riis Revisited*, p. 139.

153. Nelli, *The Italians in Chicago*, p. 69.

154. Glazer and Moynihan, *Beyond the Melting Pot*, p. 199.

155. Reports of the Immigration Commission, *The Children of Immigrants in School* (Washington, D.C.: U.S. Government Printing Office, 1911), vol. I, p. 64.

156. Sr. Mary Fabian Matthews, "The Role of the Public School in the Assimilation of the Italian Immigrant Child in New York City, 1900–1914," in *The Italian Experience in the United States*, p. 131.

157. Ibid., p. 136.

158. Ravitch, *The Great School Wars*, p. 178.

159. Gambino, *Blood of My Blood*, p. 256.

160. Sowell, "Race and I.Q. Reconsidered," in *Essays and Data on American Ethnic Groups*, p. 207.

161. Ibid., pp. 210, 211.

162. Ibid., p. 208.

163. Gans, *The Urban Villagers*, pp. 132–133.

164. U.S. Bureau of the Census, *Current Population Reports*, Series P-20, No. 221 (Washington, D.C.: U.S. Government Printing Office, 1971), p. 19.

165. Gambino, *Blood of My Blood*, p. 227.

166. Ibid., pp. 257, 264–265.

167. Ibid., p. 264; Glazer and Moynihan, *Beyond the Melting Pot*, p. 202.

168. Kessner, *The Golden Door*, p. 107.

169. Thernstrom, *The Other Bostonians*, p. 136.

170. Lopreato, *Italian Americans*, p. 148.

171. W.P.A. Writers' Project, *The Italians in New York*, p. 64.

172. Nelli, *The Italians in Chicago*, p. 75.

173. Ibid., p. 76.

174. Ibid., p. 77.

175. Foerster, *The Italian Emigration of Our Times*, p. 354.

176. Ibid., p. 353.

177. Ibid., pp. 354–355.

178. Iorizzo and Mondello, *The Italian-Americans*, p. 112.

179. Ibid., p. 121.

180. Iorizzo, "The Padrone and Immigrant Distribution," pp. 63–68.

181. Ibid., pp. 67, 70.

182. Iorizzo and Mondello, *The Italian-Americans*, pp. 117, 118, 127.

183. Ibid., pp. 126–127.

184. Thernstrom, *The Other Bostonians*, p. 131.

185. Ibid., pp. 139–141.

186. Sowell, ed., *Essays and Data on American Ethnic Groups*, pp. 336–337, 340–341.

187. This is attested to not only by observers (Gans, *The Urban Villagers*, p. 123; Gambino, *Blood of My Blood*, pp. 84, 273, 319), but also by such objective indices as a high proportion of males with jobs (Foerster, *The Italian Emigration of Our Times*, p. 342; Gam-

bino, *Blood of My Blood*, p. 337) and a high proportion of families with multiple jobholders (Gambino, *Blood of My Blood*, p. 339).

188. Gambino, *Blood of My Blood*, p. 37.

189. Ibid., p. 89.

190. Ibid., p. 88.

191. Lopreato, *Italian Americans*, p. 51.

192. Gambino, *Blood of My Blood*, p. 238.

193. Thomas Sowell, "Ethnicity in a Changing America," *Daedalus*, Winter 1978, p. 217.

194. Daniel Bell, *The End of Ideology* (New York: The Free Press, 1962), p. 141–148.

195. Glazer and Moynihan, *Beyond the Melting Pot*, p. 210.

196. Ibid., p. 213.

197. U.S. Bureau of the Census, *Current Population Reports*, P-20, No. 249 (Washington, D.C.: U.S. Government Printing Office, 1973), pp. 26, 34.

198. Gambino, *Blood of My Blood*, p. 87.

199. U.S. Bureau of the Census, *Current Population Reports*, P-20, No. 221 (Washington, D.C.: U.S. Government Printing Office, 1971), p. 19.

200. Ibid., pp. 23–24.

201. Gambino, *Blood of My Blood*, pp. 269–270.

202. Ibid., pp. 266–267.

203. U.S. Bureau of the Census, *Current Population Reports*, P-20, No. 249 (Washington, D.C.: U.S. Government Printing Office, 1973), p. 23.

204. U.S. Bureau of the Census, *Current Population Reports*, P-20, No. 221, p. 22.

205. Iorizzo, "The Padrone and Immigrant Distribution," p. 57.

206. Gambino, *Blood of My Blood*, pp. 15, 16.

207. Martin Arnold, "The City's Italian American Needy: Too Proud to Take Aid They 'Earned,' " *New York Times*, September 29, 1972, pp. 39ff.

208. Gambino, *Blood of My Blood*, p. 33.

209. Mark R. Kramer and Michael S. Levy, *The Ethnic Factor* (New York: Simon and Schuster, 1972), pp. 173–174.

210. Gambino, *Blood of My Blood*, pp. 33, 336.

211. Ibid., pp. 345–346; Gerald D. Suttles, *The Social Order of the Slum* (Chicago: University of Chicago Press, 1973), pp. 66, 128.

212. Gambino, *Blood of My Blood*, p. 342.

213. Ibid., p. 11.

214. Ibid., p. 319.

215. Kramer and Levy, *The Ethnic Factor*, p. 180.

216. Ibid., pp. 180–181.

217. Ibid., p. 179.

218. Ibid., p. 178.

219. Ibid., pp. 182–183.

220. Ibid., p. 173.

221. Ibid., p. 177.

222. Ibid.

223. Gambino, *Blood of My Blood*, p. 255.

224. Glazer and Moynihan, *Beyond the Melting Pot*, pp. 214–216; Gambino, *Blood of My Blood*, pp. 315–316.

225. Nelli, *The Italians in Chicago*, p. 202.

226. Gambino, *Blood of My Blood*, p. 84.

Chapter 6

1. Stanford M. Lyman, *Chinese Americans* (New York: Random House, 1974).

2. Barry Newman, "Discreet Elite," *Wall Street Journal*, April 26, 1980, pp. 1 ff.

3. Lyman, *Chinese Americans*, p. 7.

4. Ibid., pp. 4, 7.

5. Yuan-li Wu and Chun-hsi Wu, *Economic Development in Southeast Asia: The Chinese Dimension* (Hoover Institution Press, 1980), pp. 58–59.

Notes

6. Charles O. Hucker, *China's Imperial Past* (Stanford, Calif.: Stanford University Press, 1975), pp. 434–435.

7. Ibid., p. 342.

8. Ibid., p. 336.

9. Ibid., p. 65.

10. Ibid., p. 352.

11. Ibid., p. 333.

12. Ibid., p. 356.

13. Ibid.

14. Ibid., p. 296.

15. Ivan H. Light, *Ethnic Enterprise in America* (Berkeley: University of California Press, 1972), p. 81.

16. Betty Lee Sung, *The Story of the Chinese in America* (New York: Collier Books, 1967), p. 8.

17. Hucker, *China's Imperial Past*, p. 9.

18. Ibid., p. 6.

19. Ibid., pp. 2–3

20. Lyman, *Chinese Americans*, p. 10.

21. Hucker, *China's Imperial Past*, pp. 296, 337–338.

22. Ibid., p. 338.

23. Lyman, *Chinese Americans*, pp. 37–42.

24. Sung, *The Story of the Chinese in America*, pp. 124–125.

25. Ibid., p. 14.

26. Ibid., pp. 15–16.

27. Lyman, *Chinese Americans*, pp. 35–36.

28. Sung, *The Story of the Chinese in America*, p. 22.

29. Ibid., p. 52.

30. Lyman, *Chinese Americans*, p. 5; Monica Boyd, "Oriental Immigration: The Experience of the Chinese, Japanese, and Filipino Populations in the United States," *International Migration Review*, Spring 1971, p. 48.

31. Sung, *The Story of the Chinese in America*, p. 33.

32. Roger Daniels, *Concentration Camps, U.S.A., Japanese Americans and World War II* (New York: Holt, Rinehart and Winston, 1972), p. 4.

33. J. C. Furnas, *The Americans* (New York: G. P. Putnam's Sons, 1969), p. 699.

34. Light, *Ethnic Enterprise in America*, p. 1; Lyman, *Chinese Americans*, p. 60.

35. Lyman, *Chinese Americans*, pp. 60, 61.

36. Ibid., pp. 61–62.

37. Daniels, *Concentration Camps, U.S.A.*, p. 4.

38. Lyman, *Chinese Americans*, p. 81.

39. Light, *Ethnic Enterprise in America*, p. 6.

40. Daniels, *Concentration Camps, U.S.A.*, p. 4.

41. Lyman, *Chinese Americans*, p. 71.

42. Sung, *The Story of the Chinese in America*, p. 56.

43. Boyd, "Oriental Immigration," p. 49; *American Sociological Review*, December 1969, pp. 865–867.

44. William Petersen, "Chinese American and Japanese Americans," in *Essays and Data on American Ethnic Groups*, ed. Thomas Sowell (Washington, D.C.: The Urban Institute, 1978), p. 73.

45. Sung, *The Story of the Chinese in America*, p. 68.

46. Ibid., p. 31.

47. Ibid., p. 75.

48. Light, *Ethnic Enterprise in America*, p. 7.

49. Sung, *The Story of the Chinese in America*, pp. 203, 209.

50. Ibid., p. 237.

51. Ibid., p. 240.

52. Ibid., p. 139.

53. Light, *Ethnic Enterprise in America*, p. 97.

54. Lyman, *Chinese Americans*, p. 98; Sung, *The Story of the Chinese in America*, p. 137.

55. Sung, *The Story of the Chinese in America*, p. 320.
56. Ibid., p. 269.
57. Lyman, *Chinese Americans*, p. 30.
58. Ibid., p. 31.
59. Ibid., p. 33.
60. Ibid., p. 94.
61. Ibid., p. 106.
62. Ibid., p. 89.
63. Ibid., p. 91.
64. Sung, *The Story of the Chinese in America*, p. 259.
65. Lyman, *Chinese Americans*, p. 90.
66. Sung, *The Story of the Chinese in America*, p. 16.
67. Ibid., pp. 16–17.
68. Ibid., p. 18.
69. Ibid., p. 282.
70. Lyman, *Chinese Americans*, p. 102.
71. Ibid., p. 104.
72. Ibid., p. 152.
73. Sung, *The Story of the Chinese in America*, p. 87.
74. Lyman, *Chinese Americans*, p. 88.
75. Sung, *The Story of the Chinese in America*, p. 156.
76. Ibid., p. 159.
77. Ibid., pp. 156–157.
78. Ibid., p. 157.
79. Light, *Ethnic Enterprise in America*, p. 87.
80. Ibid., pp. 88, 191–192.
81. Ibid., p. 88.
82. Ibid., p. 174.
83. Lyman, *Chinese Americans*, p. 119.
84. Thomas Sowell, "Ethnicity in a Changing America," *Daedalus*, Winter 1978, pp. 213, 218–220.
85. Lyman, *Chinese Americans*, p. 130.
86. Boyd, "Oriental Immigration," p. 59.
87. Light, *Ethnic Enterprise in America*, p. 8.
88. Lyman, *Chinese Americans*, p. 133.
89. Ibid., p. 137.
90. Light, *Ethnic Enterprise in America*, p. 120.
91. Lyman, *Chinese Americans*, p. 120.
92. Light, *Ethnic Enterprise in America*, p. 8.
93. Sung, *The Story of the Chinese in America*, p. 128.
94. Ibid., p. 322.
95. Ibid., p. 150.
96. Lyman, *Chinese Americans*, p. 5.
97. Sung, *The Story of the Chinese in America*, p. 111.
98. Ibid., p. 171.
99. Thomas Sowell, "Assumptions versus History in Ethnic Education," *Teachers College Record* (forthcoming).
100. Thomas Sowell, "Race and I.Q. Reconsidered," in *Essays and Data on American Ethnic Groups*, p. 213.
101. Betty Lee Sung, *The Story of the Chinese in America*, p. 171.
102. William Petersen, "Chinese Americans and Japanese Americans," in *Essays and Data on American Ethnic Groups*, p. 93.
103. Sung, *The Story of the Chinese in America*, p. 167.
104. Ibid., p. 169.
105. Ibid., p. 177.
106. Lyman, *Chinese Americans*, p. 114. Just as some writers have tended to project back into history the peacefulness of mid-twentieth-century Chinatowns, Lyman has tried to project forward the criminality of Chinese youths in the earlier era.
107. Hucker, *China's Imperial Past*, p. 11.
108. Sung, *The Story of the Chinese in America*, pp. 163–165.

Notes

109. Sowell, ed., *Essays and Data on American Ethnic Groups*, p. 309.

110. Ibid., p. 310.

111. Ivan Light and Charles Choy Wong, "Protest or Work: Dilemmas of the Tourist Industry in American Chinatowns," *American Journal of Sociology*, May 1975, p. 1350.

112. Ibid.

113. Ibid., p. 1351.

114. Ron Chernow, "Chinatown, Their Chinatown: The Truth Behind the Facade," *New York*, June 11, 1973, p. 39.

115. Ibid.; Sung, *The Story of the Chinese in America*, p. 184.

116. Ibid., p. 179.

117. Ibid., p. 184.

118. Chernow, "Chinatown, Their Chinatown," p. 44.

119. Ibid.

120. Nathaniel Shepard, Jr., "Youth Gangs Involving 200 Members Become Growing Menace in Chinatown," *New York Times*, August 18, 1973, p. 25.

121. Light and Wong, "Protest or Work," p. 1353.

122. Ibid.

123. Chernow, "Chinatown, Their Chinatown," p. 42.

124. Ibid.

125. Ibid.

126. Ibid.

127. Ibid., p. 43.

128. Light and Wong, "Protest or Work," p. 1352.

129. Chernow, "Chinatown, Their Chinatown," p. 44; Shephard, "Youth Gangs," p. 25.

130. Shephard, "Youth Gangs."

131. Light and Wong, "Protest or Work," p. 1359.

132. Ibid.

133. Ibid., p. 1361.

134. Sowell, ed., *Essays and Data on American Ethnic Groups*, p. 299.

135. Ibid., pp. 266, 284, 302, 386.

136. Thomas Sowell, ed., *Affirmative Action Reconsidered* (Washington, D.C.: American Enterprise Institute, 1975), pp. 16, 17, 21, 22.

137. Ibid., pp. 16, 17.

138. Claire Jones, *Chinese Americans* (Minneapolis: Lerner Publications, 1972), pp. 91–93.

139. Ibid., p. 86.

140. Ibid., p. 87.

141. Ibid., pp. 85–86.

142. Ibid., p. 85.

143. Barry Chiswick, "The Economic Progress of Immigrants: Some Apparently Universal Patterns," in *Contemporary Economic Problems*, ed. William Fellner (Washington, D.C.: American Enterprise Institute, 1979), p. 374.

144. William Petersen, "Chinese Americans and Japanese Americans," in *Essays and Data on American Economic Groups*, p. 86.

145. Sung, *The Story of the Chinese in America*, p. 120.

146. U.S. Bureau of the Census, *1970 Census of Population: Subject Reports PC(2)-1G*, p. 68.

147. Ibid., p. 76.

148. Ibid.

Chapter 7

1. William Petersen, "Chinese Americans and Japanese Americans," in *Essays and Data on American Ethnic Groups*, ed. Thomas Sowell (Washington, D.C.: The Urban Institute, 1978), p. 66.

2. Yasuo Wakatsuki, "Japanese Emigration to the United States, 1866–1924," in *Perspectives in American History*, vol. XII (1979), p. 465.

3. Ibid., p. 438.

4. Ibid., p. 418.
5. Ibid., p. 431.
6. Ibid., p. 432.
7. Ibid., pp. 434, 435.
8. Ibid., p. 440.
9. Ibid., p. 443.
10. Ibid., p. 441.
11. Ibid., p. 442.
12. Ibid., p. 443.
13. Ibid.
14. Ibid., p. 397.
15. Ibid., p. 399.
16. Ibid., p. 396.
17. Ibid., p. 397.
18. Ibid., pp. 398, 395.
19. Ibid., p. 400.
20. Ibid.
21. Ibid., pp. 401–402.
22. Ibid., p. 410.
23. Ibid., p. 444–447.
24. Ibid., p. 428.
25. Ibid.
26. Ibid., p. 429.
27. Ibid., p. 446.
28. Ibid., p. 429.
29. Ibid., p. 416.
30. William Petersen, *Japanese Americans* (New York: Random House, 1971), p. 11.
31. Ibid.
32. Ibid., p. 15.
33. Ibid., p. 196.
34. Wakatsuki, "Japanese Emigration to the United States," p. 495.
35. Petersen, *Japanese Americans*, p. 196.
36. Wakatsuki, "Japanese Emigration to the United States," pp. 463–464.
37. Ibid., p. 449.
38. Ibid., p. 450.
39. Ibid., pp. 450–451.
40. Ibid., p. 451.
41. Ibid., p. 454.
42. Ibid., p. 452.
43. Petersen, *Japanese Americans*, p. 28.
44. Ibid.; Harry H. L. Kitano, *Japanese Americans* (Englewood Cliffs, N.J.: Prentice-Hall, 1969), p. 15.
45. Petersen, *Japanese Americans*, p. 28; Robert Higgs, "Landless by Law: Japanese Immigrants in California Agriculture to 1941," *Journal of Economic History*, March 1978, p. 208.
46. Petersen, *Japanese Americans*, p. 23.
47. Ibid., p. 28.
48. Ibid., pp. 24–25.
49. Higgs, "Landless by Law," p. 208.
50. Ibid.
51. Petersen, *Japanese Americans*, p. 33.
52. Higgs, "Landless by Law," p. 207.
53. Petersen, *Japanese Americans*, p. 196.
54. Kitano, *Japanese Americans*, p. 62; Roger Daniels, *Concentration Camps, U.S.A.* (New York: Holt, Rinehart and Winston, 1972), p. 17.
55. Petersen, *Japanese Americans*, p. 16.
56. Ibid., p. 14.
57. Kitano, *Japanese Americans*, p. 13.
58. Petersen, *Japanese Americans*, p. 143.

Notes

59. Robert Higgs, "Race, Skills and Earnings: American Immigrants in 1909," *Journal of Economic History*, June 1971, pp. 420–428.

60. Gene N. Levine and Darrel M. Montero "Socioeconomic Mobility among Three Generations of Japanese Americans," *Journal of Social Issues*, vol., 29, no. 2 (1973), p. 40.

61. Petersen, *Japanese Americans*, pp. 32–33, 34.

62. U.S. Bureau of the Census, *Historical Statistics of the United States* (Washington, D.C.: U.S. Government Printing Office, 1976), pp. 107, 108.

63. Ibid., pp. 105, 197.

64. Petersen, *Japanese Americans*, p. 16.

65. Ibid., p. 30.

66. Higgs, "Landless by Law," p. 215.

67. Petersen, *Japanese Americans*, p. 46.

68. Ibid., pp. 23, 24.

69. Ibid., p. 27.

70. Higgs, "Landless by Law," pp. 208–209.

71. Ibid., p. 209.

72. Petersen, *Japanese Americans*, p. 52.

73. Ibid.

74. Higgs, "Landless by Law," pp. 216, 217.

75. Ibid., p. 218.

76. Ibid., p. 219.

77. Ibid., p. 221.

78. Ibid., p. 222.

79. Daniels, *Concentration Camps, U.S.A.*, p. 21.

80. Higgs, "Landless by Law," p. 207.

81. Kitano, *Japanese Americans*, p. 22.

82. Ivan H. Light, *Ethnic Enterprise in America* (Berkeley: University of California Press, 1972), p. 17.

83. Ibid., p. 10.

84. Ibid.; Kitano, *Japanese Americans*, p. 19.

85. Levine and Montero, "Socioeconomic Mobility among Three Generations of Japanese Americans," p. 39.

86. Petersen, *Japanese Americans*, p. 199.

87. Ibid., p. 201.

88. Daniels, *Concentration Camps, U.S.A.*, pp. 22–23.

89. Kitano, *Japanese Americans*, pp. 23–24.

90. Petersen, *Japanese Americans*, pp. 134–135.

91. Ibid., p. 165.

92. Kitano, *Japanese Americans*, pp. 81–82.

93. Light, *Ethnic Enterprise in America*, p. 63.

94. Ibid., p. 88.

95. Petersen, *Japanese Americans*, p. 202.

96. Ibid., p. 183.

97. Ibid., p. 204.

98. Ibid., p. 60.

99. Ibid., p. 58.

100. Ibid., p. 207.

101. Daniels, *Concentration Camps, U.S.A.*, pp. 23–24.

102. Ibid., pp. 24–25.

103. Ibid., pp. 34–35.

104. Ibid., pp. 70–71.

105. Ibid., p. 96.

106. Ibid.

107. Ibid., pp. 36–37.

108. Ibid., p. 46n.

109. Petersen, *Japanese Americans*, pp. 79–81.

110. Daniels, *Concentration Camps, U.S.A.*, pp. 68–70.

111. Petersen, *Japanese Americans*, pp. 75–76.

112. Daniels, *Concentration Camps, U.S.A.*, p. 79.

113. Ibid.

114. Petersen, *Japanese Americans,* p. 79.

115. Petersen, "Chinese Americans and Japanese Americans," p. 84.

116. Daniels, *Concentration Camps, U.S.A.,* Chapter 6.

117. S. I. Hayakawa, *Through the Communication Barrier* (New York: Harper & Row, 1979), p. 132.

118. Petersen, *Japanese Americans,* p. 71.

119. Hayakawa, *Through the Communication Barrier,* p. 132.

120. Petersen, *Japanese Americans,* p. 84.

121. Hayakawa, *Through the Communication Barrier,* p. 132.

122. Petersen, *Japanese Americans,* p. 83.

123. Daniels, *Concentration Camps, U.S.A.,* pp. 149, 151, 159, 160.

124. Petersen, *Japanese Americans,* p. 84.

125. Ibid., p. 87; Kitano, *Japanese Americans,* p. 42.

126. Petersen, *Japanese Americans,* p. 87.

127. Ibid.

128. Hayakawa, *Through the Communication Barrier,* p. 133.

129. Daniels, *Concentration Camps, U.S.A.,* p. 155.

130. Ibid., pp. 158–165; Petersen, *Japanese Americans,* pp. 101–104.

131. Kitano, *Japanese Americans,* p. 42.

132. Levine and Montero, "Socioeconomic Mobility among Three Generations of Japanese Americans," p. 42.

133. Petersen, *Japanese Americans,* p. 114.

134. Ibid., p. 120.

135. Levine and Montero, "Socioeconomic Mobility among Three Generations of Japanese Americans," p. 35.

136. Petersen, "Chinese Americans and Japanese Americans," p. 258.

137. Petersen, *Japanese Americans,* p. 126; Hayakawa, *Through the Communication Barrier,* pp. 131–132.

138. Monica Boyd, "Oriental Immigration: The Experience of the Chinese, Japanese, and Filipino Populations in the United States," *International Migration Review,* Spring 1971, p. 59.

139. Thomas Sowell, "Ethnicity in a Changing America," *Daedalus,* Winter 1978, p. 213.

140. Levine and Montero, "Socioeconomic Mobility among Three Generations of Japanese Americans," pp. 44–45.

141. Ibid., p. 69.

142. Ibid., p. 73.

143. Ibid., p. 45.

144. Ibid.

145. Ibid., p. 34.

146. Hayakawa, *Through the Communication Barrier,* p. 140.

147. Petersen, "Chinese Americans and Japanese Americans," p. 94.

148. U.S. Bureau of the Census, *1970 Census of Population, Subject Reports PC (2)-IG* (Washington, D.C.: U.S. Government Printing Office, 1973), p. x.

149. Ibid., p. 1.

150. Barry R. Chiswick, "The Economic Progress of Immigration: Some Apparently Universal Patterns," in *Contemporary Economic Problems, 1979,* ed. William Fellner (Washington, D.C.: American Enterprise Institute, 1979), p. 384.

151. U.S. Bureau of the Census, *1970 Census of Population, Subject Reports PC (2)-IG,* p. 44; U.S. Bureau of the Census, *1970 Census of Population, General Social and Economic Characteristics, California PC (1)-C6* (Washington, D.C.: U.S. Government Printing Office, 1972), p. 384.

152. U.S. Bureau of the Census, *1970 Census of Population, Subject Reports PC (2)-IG,* p. 44; U.S. Bureau of the Census, *1970 Census of Population, General Social and Economic Characteristics, California, PC (1)-C6,* p. 403.

153. The male labor force participation rate of Japanese Americans is virtually the same as the national average, while the rate for Japanese-American females is substantially above the national average for females.

Notes

U.S. Bureau of the Census, *1970 Census of Population, Subject Reports PC(2)-IG*, p. 13; U.S. Bureau of the Census, *Pocket Data Book* (Washington, D.C.: U.S. Government Printing Office, 1976), p. 157.

154. Sowell, ed., *Essays and Data on American Ethnic Groups.*, p. 347.

155. More than 60 percent of Japanese-American families, compared to half of all U.S. families. Source, 1970 Census, Public Use Sample.

156. Thomas Sowell, *Affirmative Action Reconsidered* (Washington, D.C.: American Enterprise Institute, 1975), p. 17.

157. Sowell, *"Ethnicity in a Changing America,"* p. 217.

158. Sowell, ed., *Essays and Data on American Ethnic Groups.*, p. 359.

159. U.S. Bureau of the Census, *1970 Census of Population, Subject Report PC(2)-IG*, p. 17.

160. Akemi Kihumura and Harry H. L. Kitano, "Interracial Marriage: A Picture of the Japanese Americans," *Journal of Social Issues*, vol. 29, no. 2 (1973), p. 69.

161. Ibid., p. 73.

162. Kitano *Japanese Americans*, p. 24.

163. Noel L. Leathers, *The Japanese in America* (Minneapolis: Lerner Publications, 1974), p. 23.

164. Ibid., pp. 62–63.

Chapter 8

1. Ulrich B. Phillips, *Life and Labor in the Old South* (Boston: Little, Brown and Co., 1963), p. 6.

2. William L. Westermann, *The Slave Systems of Greek and Roman Antiquity* (Philadelphia: The American Philosophical Society, 1955).

3. Phillips, *Life and Labor in the Old South*, p. 9.

4. Eric Hoffer, *In Our Time.* (New York: William Morrow, 1977), p. 75.

5. Robert W. Fogel and Stanley L. Engerman. *Time on the Cross* (Boston: Little, Brown and Co., 1974), p. 13.

6. Phillips, *Life and Labor in the Old South*, pp. 11–13.

7. Philip D. Curtin, *The Atlantic Slave Trade* (Madison: University of Wisconsin Press, 1969), p. 266.

8. Ibid., p. 265.

9. Ibid., p. 268.

10. Ibid.

11. Benjamin Brawley, *A Social History of the American Negro* (New York: Collier Books, 1970), p. 17.

12. Frank Wesley Pitman, "Slavery on British West India Plantations in the Eighteenth Century," *Journal of Negro History*, October 1926, pp. 589–590.

13. Curtin, *The Atlantic Slave Trade*, pp. 277, 279, 280, 281.

14. Ibid., p. 276.

15. Philip D. Curtin, "Epidemiology and the Slave Trade," *Political Science Quarterly*, vol. 83 (1968), pp. 190–216.

16. J. C. Furnas, *The Americans* (New York: G. P. Putnam's Sons, 1969), pp. 122–123.

17. Stanley M. Elkins, *Slavery* (Chicago: University of Chicago Press, 1969), pp. 51n, 78; Ulrich B. Phillips, *American Negro Slavery*, (Baton Rouge: Louisiana State University, 1969), p. 52; Lewis C. Gray, *History of Agriculture in the Southern United States* (Washington, D.C.: Carnegie Institution of Washington, 1933), vol. 2, p. 519; David Lowenthal, "Race and Color in the West Indies," *Daedalus*, Spring 1967, pp. 610–611. See also David Brion Davis, *The Problem of Slavery in Western Culture* (Ithaca, N.Y.: Cornell University Press, 1966), Chapter 8. Let me also take this opportunity to explicitly repudiate my own conclusions to the contrary in Thomas Sowell, *Race and Economics* (New York: David McKay Co., 1975), pp. 24–28, 31, passim.

18. Herbert G. Gutman, "The World Two Cliometricians Made," *Journal of Negro Education*, January 1975, pp. 67– 85; Phillips, *American Negro Slavery*, p. 328.

19. Herbert G. Gutman, *The Black Family in Slavery and Freedom, 1750–1925* (New York: Vintage Books, 1977), pp. 146, 148–149, 318–319, 570.

20. Ibid., p. 147.

21. Ibid., p. 83; Eugene D. Genovese, *Roll, Jordan, Roll* (New York: Pantheon, 1974), p.

72; John Hope Franklin, *From Slavery to Freedom* (New York: Vintage Books, 1969), p. 207.

22. Fogel and Engerman, *Time on the Cross,* pp. 109–115.

23. Genovese, *Roll, Jordan, Roll,* pp. 524–526; Oliver MacDonagh, "The Irish Famine Emigration to the United States," *Perspectives in American History,* vol. X (1976), p. 366.

24. Fogel and Engerman, *Time on the Cross,* p. 125.

25. Frederick Law Olmsted, *The Cotton Kingdom* (New York: Modern Library, 1969), p. 215; Phillips, *American Negro Slavery,* pp. 301–302; Phillips, *Life and Labor in the Old South,* p. 186; Gray, *History of Agriculture in the Southern United States,* vol. 2, p. 520; Furnas, *The Americans,* p. 394.

26. Phillips, *American Negro Slavery,* p. 305.

27. Gutman, *The Black Family in Slavery and Freedom,* p. 263.

28. Ibid., p. 264.

29. Olmsted, *The Cotton Kingdom,* pp. 28, 32, 42, 78, 100, 101, 140, 219, 254, 303, 306, 367; Phillips, *American Negro Slavery,* p. 287; Genovese, *Roll, Jordan, Roll,* pp. 285–324; Franklin, *From Slavery to Freedom,* p. 208.

30. Genovese, *Roll, Jordan, Roll,* pp. 609–612.

31. Ibid., pp. 599–609.

32. Ibid., pp. 622–624.

33. Ibid., pp. 365–388.

34. Gutman, *The Black Family in Slavery and Freedom,* pp. 88–91.

35. Genovese, *Roll, Jordan, Roll,* p. 761, note 34.

36. Gutman, *The Black Family in Slavery and Freedom,* p. 217; Genovese, *Roll, Jordan, Roll,* p. 360.

37. Gutman, *The Black Family in Slavery and Freedom,* p. 218.

38. Genovese, *Roll, Jordan, Roll,* p. 471.

39. Zelma George, "Negro Music in American Life," in *The American Negro Reference Book,* ed. John P. Davis (Englewood Cliffs, N.J.: Prentice-Hall, 1970), pp. 731–765.

40. Ibid., p. 755.

41. Gutman, *The Black Family in Slavery and Freedom,* pp. 12–15, 51, 151, 273.

42. Ibid., p. 271.

43. Ibid., p. 12.

44. Leon F. Litwack, *Been in the Storm So Long* (New York: Alfred A. Knopf, 1979), p. 243.

45. Gutman, *The Black Family in Slavery and Freedom,* p. 150.

46. Ibid., p. 146.

47. Many discovered their spouse remarried. Gutman, Ibid., pp. 418–425.

48. Ibid., p. 349.

49. Litwack, *Been in the Storm So Long,* p. 139.

50. Gutman, *The Black Family in Slavery and Freedom,* pp. 32, 45.

51. Ibid., p. 59.

52. Ibid., p. 149.

53. Ibid., pp. 231, 236, 238; Litwack, *Been in the Storm So Long,* p. 248.

54. Gutman, *The Black Family in Slavery and Freedom,* pp. 217–218; Litwack, *Been in the Storm So Long,* p. 238.

55. Gutman, *The Black Family in Slavery and Freedom,* pp. 230, 236–237.

56. Ibid., pp. 230, 231–232, 241, 245.

57. Ibid., pp. 157, 190.

58. Ibid., p. 200.

59. Ibid., p. 192.

60. Ibid., p. 128.

61. Ibid., p. 190.

62. Clement Eaton, *The Freedom-of-Thought Struggle in the Old South* (New York: Harper and Row, 1964), pp. 39–40.

63. Genovese, *Roll, Jordan, Roll,* p. 7.

64. Fogel and Engerman, *Time on the Cross,* pp. 38, 95.

65. Bureau of the Census, *Negro Population: 1790–1915* (Washington, D.C.: U.S. Government Printing Office, 1918), p. 41.

66. *Journal of Negro History,* January 1975, p. 154.

Notes

67. Ibid.

68. Fogel and Engerman, *Time on the Cross*, p. 48.

69. Herbert G. Gutman, "The World Two Cliometricians Made," *Journal of Negro History*, January 1975, p. 156.

70. Ulrich B. Phillips, *The Slave Economy of the Old South* (Baton Rouge: Louisiana State University Press, 1968), pp. 4–5.

71. See Thomas Sowell, *Markets and Minorities* (forthcoming), Chapter 5.

72. Phillips, *Life and Labor in the Old South*, pp. 125–127.

73. Ibid., pp. 10, 11.

74. Ibid., p. 12.

75. Eaton, *The Freedom-of-Thought Struggle in the Old South*, pp. 178, 180, 182.

76. Ibid., p. 166.

77. John Hope Franklin, *The Free Negro in North Carolina* (New York: W. W. Norton and Co., 1971), p. 26.

78. Ibid., pp. 113–114.

79. Eaton, *The Freedom-of-Thought Struggle in the Old South*, pp. 86–87.

80. Carter G. Woodson, *A Century of Negro Migration* (New York: A.M.S. Press, 1970), p. 31.

81. Maldwyn Allen Jones, *American Immigration* (Chicago: University of Chicago Press, 1970), pp. 13, 32; Franklin, *From Slavery to Freedom*, p. 71.

82. Franklin, *From Slavery to Freedom*, pp. 71–72.

83. Ibid., p. 72.

84. Fogel and Engerman, *Time on the Cross*, pp. 29–30; Westermann, *The Slave Systems of Greek and Roman Antiquity*, pp. 1, 74, 149–159.

85. Brawley, *A Social History of the American Negro*, p. 15.

86. Franklin, *From Slavery to Freedom*, pp. 237–241.

87. Karl E. Taeuber and Alma F. Taeuber, "The Negro Population in the United States," in *The American Negro Reference Book*, p. 103.

88. Alexis de Tocqueville, *Democracy in America* (New York: Alfred A. Knopf, 1966), vol. I, pp. 357–360; Franklin, *From Slavery to Freedom*, pp. 279–280.

89. Edward Gibbon, *The Decline and Fall of the Roman Empire* (New York: Modern Library, no date), vol. I., p. 303.

90. Phillips, *American Negro Slavery*, pp. 122–124; Eaton, *The Freedom-of-Thought Struggle in the Old South*, p. 19.

91. Eaton, *The Freedom-of-Thought Struggle in the Old South*, Chapter 1.

92. Ibid., Chapter 8.

93. Bureau of the Census, *Negro Population: 1790–1915*, p. 53.

94. E. Franklin Frazier, *Black Bourgeoisie* (New York: The Free Press, 1962), pp. 18–19.

95. David W. Cohen and Jack P. Greene, eds., *Neither Slave Nor Free* (Baltimore: Johns Hopkins University Press, 1972), pp. 7, 31, 62, 221, 229, 286, 317–318.

96. Ibid., pp. 29, 40, 41, 209; Ira Berlin, *Slaves Without Masters* (New York: Pantheon, 1974), pp. 109–110.

97. Carter G. Woodson, *The Education of the Negro Prior to 1861* (New York: Arno Press, 1968), pp. 227–228.

98. U. S. Bureau of the Census, *Historical Statistics of the United States, Colonial Times to 1970* (Washington, D.C.: U.S. Government Printing Office, 1975), Part 1, p. 382; *The Seventh Census of the United States: 1850*, pp. xliii, lxi.

99. Wilbur Zelinsky, "The Population Geography of the Free Negro in Ante-Bellum America," *Population Studies*, March 1950, p. 387; Reynolds Farley, "The Urbanization of Negroes in the United States," *Journal of Social History*, Spring 1968, p. 255.

100. Thomas Sowell, "Three Black Histories," in *Essays and Data on American Ethnic Groups*, ed. Thomas Sowell (Washington, D.C.: The Urban Institute, 1978), pp. 12–13.

101. Thomas Sowell, "Black Excellence: The Case of Dunbar High School," *The Public Interest*, Spring 1974, pp. 1–21.

102. Stephen Birmingham, *Certain People* (Boston: Little, Brown and Co., 1977), pp. 70, 71, 130–131, 160; Edward Vyron Reuter, *The Mulatto in the United States* (Richard G. Badger, 1918).

103. See Birmingham, *Certain People*, passim.

104. Litwack, *Been in the Storm So Long*, p. 97.

105. Ibid., p. 100.

106. Ibid., p. 99.

107. Ibid., pp. 162–163.

108. Ibid., pp. 89, 119.

109. Ibid., p. 239.

110. Robert Higgs, *Competition and Coercion* (Cambridge: Cambridge University Press, 1977), p. 9.

111. *Dred Scott v. Sanford, 60 U.S. 393* (1857).

112. Litwack, *Been in the Storm So Long*, Chapter 2.

113. Ibid., p. 305.

114. Ibid., p. 230.

115. Ibid., p. 305.

116. Ibid., p. 235.

117. Ibid., p. 232.

118. Ibid., Chapter 7.

119. Lorenzo J. Greene and Carter G. Woodson, *The Negro Wage Earner* (New York: A.M.S. Press, 1970), p. 37.

120. Ibid., p. 38.

121. Ibid., p. 39.

122. Ibid., p. 45.

123. Litwack, *Been in the Storm So Long*, pp. 244–245; Higgs, *Competition and Coercion*, p. 40.

124. Litwack, *Been in the Storm So Long*, p. 244.

125. See, for example, Olmsted, *Cotton Kingdom*, pp. 218–219.

126. W. E. B. Du Bois, *The Philadelphia Negro* (New York: Schocken Books, 1967), p. 178; Nathan Glazer and Daniel Patrick Moynihan, *Beyond the Melting Pot* (Cambridge: M.I.T. Press, 1963), p. 34; E. Franklin Frazier, *The Negro in the United States* (New York: The Macmillan Co., 1971), p. 303.

127. Higgs, *Competition and Coercion*, p. 53.

128. Ibid., p. 41.

129. Litwack, *Been in the Storm So Long*, p. 421.

130. Higgs, *Competition and Coercion*, p. 54.

131. Ibid., p. 74; Litwack, *Been in the Storm So Long*, p. 421.

132. Higgs, *Competition and Coercion*, p. 57.

133. Ibid., pp. 48–49.

134. Olmsted, *Cotton Kingdom*, pp. 28, 32, 42, 100, 101, 102–103, 104–105, 143–146, 254, 402–403, 564–565; Genovese, *Roll, Jordan, Roll*, pp. 295–309.

135. Higgs, *Competition and Coercion*, p. 42; Litwack, *Been in the Storm So Long*, pp. 372–373.

136. Higgs, *Competition and Coercion*, p. 53.

137. Ibid., p. 48.

138. Ibid., p. 56.

139. Ibid., p. 49.

140. Ibid., p. 51.

141. Frazier, *The Negro in the United States*, p. 166.

142. Higgs, *Competition and Coercion*, p. 109.

143. Ibid., p. 110.

144. Ibid., p. 111.

145. Ibid., pp. 47–48.

146. Ibid., pp. 48–49.

147. Ibid., p. 117.

148. Ibid., pp. 64–65.

149. Ibid., pp. 65, 71.

150. Ibid., pp. 65–66.

151. Constance Baker Motley, "The Legal Status of the Negro in the United States," in *American Negro Reference Book*, p. 516.

152. Bureau of the Census, *Historical Statistics of the United States, Colonial Times to 1970*, p. 422.

153. Berlin, *Slaves Without Masters*, pp. 305–306.

Notes

154. Woodson, *The Education of the Negro Prior to 1861*, Chapter 4.

155. Constance M. Green, *The Secret City* (Princeton, N.J.: Princeton University Press, 1970), p. 17.

156. Woodson, *The Education of the Negro Prior to 1861*, pp. 128–129.

157. Ibid., p. 141.

158. Ibid., p. 11.

159. Ibid.

160. *The Seventh Census of the United States: 1850*, pp. xliii, lxi.

161. Frazier, *The Negro in the United States*, p. 74.

162. Litwack, *Been in the Storm So Long*, pp. 68, 472–476; Booker T. Washington, W. E. B. Du Bois, and James Weldon Johnson, *Three Negro Classics* (New York: Avon Books, 1965), pp. 44–45.

163. James M. McPherson, *The Abolitionist Legacy* (Princeton, N.J.: Princeton University Press, 1975), pp. 168, 184–185; Frazier, *Black Bourgeoisie*, pp. 73–74; Thomas Sowell, *Black Education: Myths and Tragedies* (New York: David McKay Co., 1972), pp. 40–41, 65–69, 222.

164. McPherson, *The Abolitionist Legacy*, p. 143.

165. Ibid., p. 159.

166. W. E. B. Du Bois, *Black Reconstruction* (West Orange, N.J.: Albert Saifer, 1935), p. 648.

167. Thomas Sowell, "Patterns of Black Excellence," *The Public Interest*, Spring 1976, pp. 29, 35, 38.

168. Gunnar Myrdal, *An American Dilemma* (New York: McGraw-Hill, 1964), vol. 2, p. 1266.

169. Frazier, *The Negro in the United States*, p. 429.

170. McPherson, *The Abolitionist Legacy*, p. 206.

171. Gunnar Myrdal, *An American Dilemma*, p. 1266.

172. McPherson, *The Abolitionist Legacy*, p. 367.

173. Ibid.

174. Ibid., p. 165.

175. Ibid., p. 174.

176. Ibid., p. 168.

177. Ibid., p. 166.

178. Ibid., p. 198.

179. Ibid., p. 199.

180. Woodson, *The Education of the Negro Prior to 1861*, p. 265.

181. Charles S. Johnson, *The Negro College Graduate* (Chapel Hill: University of North Carolina Press, 1938), p. 8.

182. David C. Rankin. "The Impact of the Civil War on the Free Colored Community of New Orleans," in *Perspectives in American History*, vol. XI (1977–78), p. 382.

183. Ibid., p. 385.

184. Ibid., p. 387.

185. Ibid., p. 391.

186. Ibid., p. 410.

187. Ibid., p. 414.

188. Thomas Sowell, "Three Black Histories," pp. 14–15.

189. Birmingham, *Certain People*, Chapters 1, 8; G. Franklin Edwards, ed., *E. Franklin Frazier on Race Relations* (Chicago: University of Chicago Press, 1968), pp. 267–279; Sowell, *Black Education: Myths and Tragedies*, p. 121.

190. Myrdal, *An American Dilemma*, pp. 695–700; Birmingham, *Certain People*, Chapters 1, 8, 11; Frazier, *Black Bourgeoisie*, p. 99; E. Franklin Frazier, *The Negro Family in the United States* (Chicago: University of Chicago Press, 1969), Chapter XII.

191. Birmingham, *Certain People*, pp. 14–15. See also Elliott M. Rudwick, *W. E. B. Du Bois* (New York: Atheneum, 1969), pp. 118, 132.

192. See Thomas Sowell, *Knowledge and Decisions* (New York: Basic Books, 1980), pp. 87–89; Reuter, *The Mulatto in the United States*, pp. 368–369.

193. Louis R. Harlan, *Booker T. Washington* (New York: Oxford University Press, 1972), p. 212.

194. Ibid., p. 225.

195. Washington, et al., *Three Negro Classics*, p. 79.
196. Ibid., p. 86.
197. Harlan, *Booker T. Washington*, p. 280.
198. Washington, et al., *Three Negro Classics*, p. 141.
199. Ibid., p. 149.
200. Ibid., p. 157.
201. Ibid., p. 75.
202. Sowell, "Three Black Histories," pp. 32–33; Elliott M. Rudwick, *W. E. B. Du Bois*, p. 82.
203. Washington, et al., *Three Negro Classics*, p. 78.
204. Frazier, *The Negro in the United States*, p. 459; Myrdal, *An American Dilemma*, p. 889n; Thomas Sowell, "The Plight of Black Students in the United States," *Daedalus*, Spring 1974, p. 189.
205. W. E. B. Du Bois, *The Education of Black People*, ed. Herbert Aptheker (Amherst: University of Massachusetts Press, 1973), pp. 68–69. Booker T. Washington, *The Future of the American Negro* (New York: The New American Library, 1969), Chapters IV, V.
206. Washington, *The Future of the American Negro*, pp. 79–80; Du Bois, *The Education of Black People*, pp. 17–30.
207. Birmingham, *Certain People*, p. 144.
208. Ibid., p. 15.
209. Zelinsky, "The Population Geography of the Free Negro in Ante-Bellum America," p. 287.
210. Farley, "The Urbanization of Negroes in the United States," p. 245.
211. Sowell, "Three Black Histories," pp. 10–11.
212. Farley, "The Urbanization of Negroes in the United States," p. 247.
213. Ibid., p. 251.
214. Ibid.
215. Taeuber and Taeuber, "The Negro Population in the United States," p. 110.
216. U.S. Burean of the Census, *Historical Statistics of the United States, Colonial Times to 1970*, p. 106.
217. Farley, "The Urbanization of Negroes in the United States," pp. 252–253.
218. Sowell, "Three Black Histories," p. 35.
219. Taeuber and Taeuber, "The Negro Population in the United States," p. 111.
220. Ibid.; Farley, "The Urbanization of Negroes in the United States," pp. 253–254.
221. Taeuber and Taeuber, "The Negro Population in the United States," p. 113.
222. Daniel O. Price, "Urbanization of the Blacks," *The Milbank Memorial Fund Quarterly*, April 1970, p. 49.
223. Birmingham, *Certain People*, p. 186.
224. Sowell, *Race and Economics*, p. 38.
225. Sowell, "Three Black Histories," p. 17.
226. Ibid., p. 35.
227. Oscar Handlin, *Boston's Immigrants*, (New York: Atheneum, 1970), pp. 69–70, 133.
228. Robert Ernst, "The Economic Status of New York City Negroes, 1850–1863," in *The Making of Black America*, eds. August Meier and Elliott Rudwick (New York: Atheneum, 1969), vol. I, pp. 257–258.
229. Richard Gambino, *Blood of My Blood* (New York: Anchor Books, 1974), p. 77.
230. Oscar Handlin, *The Newcomers* (New York: Anchor Books, 1962), p. 47.
231. Jacob Riis, *How the Other Half Lives* (Cambridge: Harvard University Press, 1970), p. 99; Du Bois, *The Philadelphia Negro*, pp. 33–36, 119–121.
232. Gilbert Osofsky, *Harlem: The Making of a Ghetto* (New York: Harper and Row, 1966), p. 12.
233. David M. Katzman, *Before the Ghetto* (Urbana: University of Illinois Press, 1975), p. 26. See also pp. 55, 69, 73.
234. St. Clair Drake and Horace R. Cayton, *Black Metropolis* (New York: Harcourt, Brace & World, 1970), vol. I, p. 176n. See also Allan H. Spear, *Black Chicago* (Chicago: University of Chicago Press, 1970), Chapter 1.
235. Du Bois, *The Philadelphia Negro*, p. 7; Green, *The Secret City*, p. 127.
236. Du Bois, *The Philadelphia Negro*, pp. 33–35.
237. Katzman, *Before the Ghetto*, p. 128.

Notes

238. Ibid., pp. 160–161.

239. Drake and Cayton, *Black Metropolis*, vol. 1, pp. 44–45.

240. William Julius Wilson, *The Declining Significance of Race* (Chicago: University of Chicago Press, 1978), p. 62.

241. Spear, *Black Chicago*, p. 168; Frazier, *The Negro in the United States*, pp. 284–285; Florette Henri, *Black Migration: Movement North, 1900–1920* (New York: Anchor Books, 1976), pp. 96–97; Osofsky, *Harlem: The Making of a Ghetto*, p. 44; Ivan H. Light, *Ethnic Enterprise in America* (Berkeley: University of California Press, 1972), Figure 1 (after p. 100).

242. Drake and Cayton, *Black Metropolis*, vol. I, pp. 66–67, 73–76.

243. Henri, *Black Migration*, pp. 17, 86.

244. Taeuber and Taeuber, "The Negro Population in the United States," p. 110.

245. Frazier, *The Negro in the United States*, pp. 281–285; Green, *The Secret City*, p. 207.

246. Greene and Woodson, *The Negro Wage Earner*, p. 47.

247. Du Bois, *The Philadelphia Negro*, p. 161.

248. Ibid., pp. 161–162.

249. Frazier, *The Negro in the United States*, pp. 568, 592. See also Myrdal, *An American Dilemma*, p. 142.

250. Myrdal, *An American Dilemma*, p. 142. See also Taeuber and F. Taeuber, "The Negro Population in the United States," p. 154.

251. Mydral, *An American Dilemma*, pp. 142, 173.

252. Taeuber and Taeuber, "The Negro Population in the United States," p. 157.

253. Sowell, *Black Education: Myths and Tragedies*, p. 4. See also Frazier, *The Negro in the United States*, pp. 440–441.

254. Osofsky, *Harlem: The Making of a Ghetto*, p. 20. See also Gutman, *The Black Family in Slavery and Freedom*, pp. 450, 451, 453.

255. Gutman, *The Black Family in Slavery and Freedom*, p. 453.

256. Henri, *Black Migration*, p. 142.

257. Ibid., p. 149.

258. Ibid., p. 164.

259. Gutman, *The Black Family in Slavery and Freedom*, p. 452.

260. Ibid., p. 455.

261. Taeuber and Taeuber, "The Negro Population in the United States," p. 122.

262. James P. Smith and Finis Welch, *Race Differences in Earnings: A Survey and New Evidence* (Santa Monica, Calif.: The Rand Corporation, 1978), p. 19.

263. U.S. Bureau of the Census, *Historical Statistics of the United States, Colonial Times to 1970*, p. 49.

264. Thomas Sowell, "Ethnicity in a Changing America," *Daedalus*, Winter 1978, p. 217.

265. U.S. Bureau of the Census, *Historical Statistics of the United States, Colonial Times to 1970*, p. 49.

266. Sowell, *Race and Economics*, pp. 135–136.

267. Ibid.; see also Frazier, *The Negro in the United States*, pp. 330–331.

268. U.S. Bureau of the Census, *Historical Statistics of the United States, Colonial Times to 1970*, p. 382.

269. Smith and Welch, *Race Differences in Earnings*, p. 1.

270. Finis Welch, "Black-White Differences in Returns to Schooling," *American Economic Review*, December 1973.

271. Frazier, *The Negro in the United States*, p. 427.

272. Ibid., p. 434.

273. Henri, *Black Migration*, p. 178.

274. Sowell, "Patterns of Black Excellence," p. 29.

275. Virgil A. Clift, "Educating the American Negro," in *The American Negro Reference Book*, p. 369.

276. Edwards, *E. Franklin Frazier on Race Relations*, p. 54.

277. Frazier, *The Negro in the United States*, pp. 465–466.

278. Sowell, *Black Education: Myths and Tragedies*, pp. 256–257. See also Christopher Jencks and David Riesman, "The American Negro College," *Harvard Educational Review*, Winter 1967, pp. 3–60.

279. Frazier, *The Negro in the United States*, pp. 480, 483.

280. Allen B. Ballard, *The Education of Black Folk* (New York: Harper and Row, 1973), p. 65.

281. Birmingham, *Certain People*, p. 8.

282. Ibid., Chapter 4.

283. The term "West Indian" is used in many different senses. Here it will mean persons of Negro ancestry from the islands of Jamaica, Barbados, Trinidad, and other parts of the British West Indies. It will not include Puerto Ricans, Cubans, Haitians, or others sometimes encompassed within that term.

284. Osofsky, *Harlem: The Making of a Ghetto*, p. 131.

285. Thomas Sowell, "Three Black Histories," p. 42.

286. Johnson, *The Negro College Graduate*, pp. 71, 73.

287. Light, *Ethnic Enterprise in America*, p. 37.

288. Philip D. Curtin, *The Atlantic Slave Trade* (Madison: University of Wisconsin Press, 1969), p. 26; Franklin, *From Slavery to Freedom*, p. 69.

289. Franklin, *From Slavery to Freedom*, p. 63.

290. Claude Levy, "Slavery and the Emancipation Movement in Barbados, 1650–1833," *Journal of Negro History*, January 1970, p. 5.

291. Genovese, *Roll, Jordan, Roll*, p. 7; Philip D. Curtin, *Two Jamaicas* (New York: Atheneum, 1970), p. 11.

292. Curtin, *Two Jamaicas*, pp. 14, 15.

293. Charles H. Wesley, "The Negro in the West Indies, Slavery and Freedom," *Journal of Negro History*, January 1932, p. 58.

294. Curtin, *Two Jamaicas*, p. 16.

295. Compare Phillips, *American Negro Slavery*, p. 62, with Fogel and Engerman, *Time on the Cross*, p. 123.

296. Pitman, "Slavery on British West India Plantations in the Eighteenth Century," pp. 634–635; Eric Williams, *The Negro in the Caribbean* (Westport, Conn.: Negro Universities Press, 1971), p. 57; Curtin, *Two Jamaicas*, p. 18; Douglas Hall, "Jamaica," in *Neither Slave Nor Free*, eds. David W. Cohen and Jack T. Greene (Baltimore: Johns Hopkins University Press, 1972), pp. 208–209.

297. Wesley, "The Negro in the West Indies, Slavery and Freedom," pp. 56–57; Curtin, *Two Jamaicas*, p. 18; Hall, "Jamaica," pp. 208–209.

298. Genovese, *Roll, Jordan, Roll*, p. 421.

299. Pitman, "Slavery on British West India Plantations," p. 610. ⌐

300. Ibid., p. 611.

301. Charles H. Wesley, "The Emancipation of the Free Colored Population in the British Empire," *Journal of Negro History*, April 1934, pp. 137, 140–141, 144.

302. Wesley, "The Negro in the West Indies, Slavery and Freedom," pp. 51–52, 55, 66.

303. Genovese, *Roll, Jordan, Roll*, pp. 536–537; Levy, "Slavery and the Emancipation Movement in Barbados, 1650–1833," p. 6; Wesley, "The Negro in the West Indies, Slavery and Freedom," p. 54; Pitman, "Slavery on British West India Plantations," p. 608; Curtin, *Two Jamaicas*, p. 19.

304. Pitman, "Slavery on British West India Plantations," p. 608; Genovese, *Roll, Jordan, Roll*, p. 536.

305. Ira De A. Reid, *The Negro Immigrant* (New York: A.M.S. Press, 1970), p. 244.

306. Ibid., pp. 44–237.

307. Ibid., p. 233.

308. Ibid., p. 236.

309. Ibid., p. 241.

310. Ibid., p. 244.

311. Ibid., p. 89.

312. Glazer and Moynihan, *Beyond the Melting Pot*, p. 35; Light, *Ethnic Enterprise in America*, p. 33.

313. Reid, *The Negro Immigrant*, pp. 226–227.

314. Ibid., pp. 138–140, 141–142.

315. Nancy Foner, "West Indians in New York City and London: A Comparative Analysis," *International Migration Review*, Summer 1979, p. 287.

Notes

316. Reid, *The Negro Immigrant*, pp. 25, 167–169; Osofsky, *Harlem: The Making of a Ghetto*, pp. 134–135.

317. Ibid.; Reid, *The Negro Immigrant*, pp. 25–26, 109, 114–115, 150–151, 152, 159, 168–169, 198, 223; Lennon Raphael, "West Indians and Afro-Americans," *Freedomways*, Summer 1946, pp. 438–444.

318. Osofsky, *Harlem: The Making of a Ghetto*, pp. 134–135; Harold Cruse, *The Crisis of the Negro Intellectual* (New York: William Morrow, 1967), pp. 44–47.

319. Foner, "West Indians in New York and London," p. 290.

320. Sowell, "Three Black Histories," p. 43.

321. Ibid., p. 42.

322. Ibid., p. 44.

323. Ibid., p. 42.

324. Sowell, ed., *Essays and Data on American Ethnic Groups*, pp. 257, 258.

325. Foner, "West Indians in New York City and London," p. 285.

326. Ibid., pp. 293–294.

327. Sowell, "Ethnicity in a Changing America," pp. 213, 218–220.

328. Franklin, *From Slavery to Freedom*, p. 584.

329. Ibid., p. 587.

330. U.S. Bureau of the Census, *Historical Statistics of the United States, Colonial Times to 1970*, p. 297.

331. Ibid., p. 57.

332. U.S. Bureau of the Census, *Current Population Reports*, Series P-23, No. 46. (Washington, D.C.: U.S. Government Printing Office, 1973), p. 19.

333. Ben J. Wattenberg, *The Real America* (New York: Capricorn Books, 1976), p. 134.

334. U.S. Bureau of the Census, *Current Population Reports*, Series P-23, No. 46, p. 49.

335. Wattenberg, *The Real America*, p. 132.

336. U.S. Bureau of the Census, *Current Population Reports*, Series P-23, No. 42, p. 118.

337. U.S. Bureau of the Census, *Current Population Reports*, Series P-23, No. 46, p. 10.

338. Ibid., p. 18.

339. U.S. Bureau of the Census, *U.S. Census of Population, 1970*, Subject Reports PC(2)-1b (Washington, D.C.: U.S. Government Printing Office, 1971), pp. 149–150.

340. U.S. Bureau of the Census, *Current Population Reports*, P-23 No. 46, p. 24.

341. Sowell, ed., *Essays and Data on American Ethnic Groups*, pp. 257–258.

342. By 1967, black family income outside the South already exceeded the level reached by Puerto Rican income in 1968. U.S. Bureau of the Census, *Current Population Reports*, Series P-23, No. 46, p. 18; U.S. Bureau of the Census, *Current Population Reports*, Series P-20, No. 213, p. 34.

343. U.S. Bureau of the Census, *Current Population Reports*, P-20, No. 224, p. 5.

344. Compare ibid. and U.S. Bureau of the Census, *Current Population Reports*, P-23, No. 38, p. 27.

345. Wattenberg, *The Real America*, p. 137.

346. Perhaps the most famous discussion of this popular thesis was the so-called Moynihan Report. See U.S. Department of Labor, *The Negro Family: The Case for National Action*, March 1965.

347. Gutman, *The Black Family in Slavery and Freedom*, passim.

348. Wattenberg, *The Real America*, pp. 129, 138.

349. Walter E. Williams, *Youth and Minority Unemployment* (Stanford, Calif.: Hoover Institution Press, 1977), p. 14.

350. Ibid.

351. Smith and Welch, *Race Differences in Earnings*, pp. ix, 20–21, 24, 49; Orley Ashenfelter, "Comments," in *Frontiers of Quantitative Economics*, ed., M. D. Intriligator and D. A. Kendrick (New York: North-Holland Publishing Co., 1974), vol. 2, p. 558; Sowell, *Affirmative Action Reconsidered*, p. 23.

352. Birmingham, *Certain People*, p. 69.

Chapter 9

1. U.S. Bureau of the Census, *Current Population Reports*, Series P-20, No. 224 (Washington, D.C.: U.S. Government Printing Office, 1971), p. 4n.

2. Nathan Glazer, *Affirmative Discrimination* (New York: Basic Books, 1975), p. 155.

3. Thomas Sowell, ed., *Essays and Data on American Ethnic Groups* (Washington, D.C.: The Urban Institute, 1978), pp. 257, 258.

4. Ronald J. Larsen, *The Puerto Ricans in America* (Minneapolis: Lerner Publications, 1973), p. 9.

5. Ibid., pp. 9, 14.

6. Ibid., pp. 12–14.

7. Ibid., p. 18.

8. Joseph P. Fitzpatrick, *Puerto Rican Americans* (Englewood Cliffs, N.J.: Prentice-Hall, 1971), p. 103.

9. Larsen, *The Puerto Ricans in America*, p. 20.

10. Ibid., p. 24.

11. Ibid., pp. 26–27.

12. Fitzpatrick, *Puerto Rican Americans*, p. 47.

13. Larsen, *The Puerto Ricans in America*, p. 27.

14. Ibid., p. 34.

15. Ibid., p. 36.

16. Ibid., p. 35.

17. Lloyd G. Reynolds and Peter O. Gregory, *Wages, Productivity and Industrialization in Puerto Rico* (Homewood, Ill.: Richard D. Irwin, Inc., 1965), pp. 52–53. See also Carlos J. Lastra, *The Impact of Minimum Wages on a Labor-Oriented Industry* (Government Development Bank for Puerto Rico, 1969), p. 3; Jaime Santiago, "One Step Forward," *The Wilson Quarterly*, Spring 1980, pp. 132, 136.

18. Larsen, *The Puerto Ricans in America*, p. 38.

19. Ibid., pp. 36–37.

20. Virginia R. Dominguez, *From Neighbor to Stranger: The Dilemma of Caribbean Peoples in the United States* (New Haven, Conn.: Antilles Research Program, Yale University, 1975), p. 99.

21. Larsen, *The Puerto Ricans in America*, p. 44.

22. Ibid.

23. Dominguez, *From Neighbor to Stranger*, p. 101.

24. Ibid., p. 102.

25. Oscar Handlin, *The Newcomers* (New York: Anchor Books, 1962), pp. 56–57; Nathan Glazer and Daniel Patrick Moynihan, *Beyond the Melting Pot* (Cambridge: MIT Press, 1963), pp. 93–94.

26. Fitzpatrick, *Puerto Rican Americans*, pp. 12, 13; Dominguez, *From Neighbor to Stranger*, p. 99. It should be noted that migration data vary considerably when reported by calendar year or by fiscal year. See Fitzpatrick, *Puerto Rican Americans*, p. 12n.

27. Dominguez, *From Neighbor to Stranger*, p. 26.

28. U.S. Bureau of the Census, *Current Population Reports*, Series P-20, No. 213, p. 5.

29. Fitzpatrick, *Puerto Rican Americans*, p. 61.

30. Glazer and Moynihan, *Beyond the Melting Pot*, p. 89.

31. Ibid., pp. 87–88.

32. Fitzpatrick, *Puerto Rican Americans*, p. 51.

33. Glazer and Moynihan, *Beyond the Melting Pot*, p. 88.

34. Ibid., p. 89.

35. Ibid., pp. 88–90; Fitzpatrick, *Puerto Rican Americans*, pp. 82–83.

36. Glazer and Moynihan, *Beyond the Melting Pot*, p. 89.

37. Dominguez, *From Neighbor to Stranger*, p. 98.

38. Glazer and Moynihan, *Beyond the Melting Pot*, p. 94.

39. Ibid., p. 90.

40. Fitzpatrick, *Puerto Rican Americans*, p. 164n.

41. Dominguez, *From Neighbor to Stranger*, p. 119.

42. Fitzpatrick, *Puerto Rican Americans*, p. 133.

43. Dominguez, *From Neighbor to Stranger*, p. 119.

44. U.S. Bureau of the Census, *Current Population Reports*, Series P-20, No. 213, p. 14.

45. *Harper's Magazine*, February 1979, pp. 29, 32.

46. Fitzpatrick, *Puerto Rican Americans*, p. 132.

47. Diane Ravitch, *The Great School Wars* (New York: Basic Books, 1974), p. 403.

Notes

48. Thomas Sowell, "Race and IQ Reconsidered," in *Essays and Data on American Ethnic Groups*, pp. 215, 217.

49. Dominguez, *From Neighbor to Stranger*, pp. 117–118.

50. Fitzpatrick, *Puerto Rican Americans*, Chapter 7.

51. Ibid., pp. 102–103.

52. Ibid., p. 103; Glazer and Moynihan, *Beyond the Melting Pot*, p. 132.

53. Geoffrey Godsell, "The Puerto Ricans," *The Christian Science Monitor*, May 1, 1980, pp. 12–13.

54. Handlin, *The Newcomers*, pp. 60, 96.

55. Ibid., p. 60.

56. Fitzpatrick, *Puerto Rican Americans*, p. 107.

57. Glazer and Moynihan, *Beyond the Melting Pot*, p. 133.

58. Handlin, *The Newcomers*, p. 60.

59. Fitzpatrick, *Puerto Rican Americans*, p. 111.

60. Ibid., p. 112.

61. U.S. Bureau of the Census, *Current Population Reports*, Series P-20, No. 213, p. 7.

62. Fitzpatrick, *Puerto Rican Americans*, p. 95.

63. Dominguez, *From Neighbor to Stranger*, pp. 115–116.

64. Fitzpatrick, *Puerto Rican Americans*, p. 155.

65. Ibid., p. 158.

66. U.S. Bureau of the Census, *Current Population Reports*, Series P-20, M. 224, p. 14.

67. Larsen, *The Puerto Ricans in America*, p. 45.

68. Elena Padilla, "Concepts of Work and Situational Demands on New York City Puerto Ricans," in *American Minorities and Economic Opportunity*, ed. H. Roy Kaplan (Itasca, Ill.: F. E. Peacock Publishers, 1977), p. 157.

69. Ibid., p. 158.

70. Ibid.

71. Fitzpatrick, *Puerto Rican Americans*, p. 61.

72. Larsen, *The Puerto Ricans in America*, p. 41.

73. U.S. Bureau of the Census, *Current Population Reports*, Series P-20, No. 213, p. 29.

74. Some studies show Puerto Ricans with slightly higher income than blacks and others, and vice versa, but the differences are small either way. Sowell, *Essays and Data on American Ethnic Groups*, pp. 284, 386; Dominguez, *From Neighbor to Stranger*, p. 112.

75. Glazer and Moynihan, *Beyond the Melting Pot*, p. 116.

76. Compare Thomas Sowell, "Three Black Histories," in *Essays and Data in American Ethnic Groups*, p. 43; Padilla, "Concepts of Work," p. 159.

77. Ibid., p. 158; Glazer and Moynihan, *Beyond the Melting Pot*, p. 11.

78. Thomas Sowell, "Ethnicity in a Changing America," *Daedalus*, Winter 1978, pp. 220–225.

79. 1970 Census, Public Use Sample.

80. U.S. Bureau of the Census, *Current Population Reports*, Series P-20, No. 224, p. 6.

81. Ibid., p. 5.

82. Sowell, ed., *Essays and Data on American Ethnic Groups*, p. 386.

83. Ibid., pp. 284, 350, 386.

84. U.S. Bureau of the Census, *Current Population Reports*, Series P-20, No. 224, p. 9.

85. Sowell, ed., *Essays and Data on American Ethnic Groups*, pp. 292, 396–397.

86. U.S. Bureau of the Census, *Current Population Reports*, Series P-20, No. 224, p. 13.

87. Ibid., p. 5; U.S. Bureau of the Census, *Current Population Reports*, Series P-20, No. 213, p. 34.

88. Sowell, ed., *Essays and Data on American Ethnic Groups*, pp. 386, 404.

89. U.S. Bureau of the Census, *Current Population Reports*, Series P-20, No. 224, p. 5.

90. Fitzpatrick, *Puerto Rican Americans*, p. 58; Glazer and Moynihan, *Beyond the Melting Pot*, pp. 100–101.

91. Mark R. Levy and Michael S. Kramer, *The Ethnic Factor* (New York: Simon and Schuster, 1972), p. 89.

92. Ibid., p. 91.

93. Ibid., p. 77.

94. Ibid., p. 79.

95. Ibid., p. 88.

96. Ibid.

97. Glazer and Moynihan, *Beyond the Melting Pot*, pp. 102–103.

98. See, for example, Thomas Sowell, *Knowledge and Decisions* (New York: Basic Books, 1980), pp. 126–129.

99. Martin Anderson, *The Federal Bulldozer* (Cambridge: MIT Press, 1965), pp. 64–65.

100. Williams, *Youth and Minority Unemployment* (Stanford, Calif.: Hoover Institution, 1977)

101. Walter E. Williams, "Government-Sanctioned Restraints that Reduce Economic Opportunities for Minorities," *Policy Review*, Fall 1977, pp. 7–30.

102. Fitzpatrick, *Puerto Rican Americans*, p. 61.

103. Board of Education, City of New York, *The Puerto Rican Study, 1953–1957* (Board of Education, 1958), pp. 74–75.

104. Fitzpatrick, *Puerto Rican Americans*, p. 95.

105. Godsell, "The Puerto Ricans," p. 12.

106. Larsen, *The Puerto Ricans in America*, pp. 71–84, passim.

107. Godsell, "The Puerto Ricans," p. 12.

108. Sowell, ed., *Essays and Data on American Ethnic Groups*, p. 394.

109. Ibid., p. 397.

110. Glazer and Moynihan, *Beyond the Melting Pot*, pp. 98–99.

111. Sowell, ed., *Essays and Data on American Ethnic Groups*, pp. 280, 382.

112. U.S. Bureau of the Census, *Current Population Reports*, Series P-20, No. 224, p. 12.

113. Ibid.

114. Fitzpatrick, *Puerto Rican Americans*, p. 133.

115. Godsell, "The Puerto Ricans," p. 12.

116. U.S. Bureau of the Census, *Current Population Reports*, Series P-20, No. 224, p. 5.

117. Godsell, "The Puerto Ricans," p. 12.

118. Ibid.

119. Ibid., p. 13.

Chapter 10

1. Arthur F. Corwin, "Causes of Mexican Emigration to the United States: A Summary View," in *Perspectives in American History*, vol. VII (1973), p. 571.

2. U.S. Bureau of the Census, *Current Population Reports*, Series P-20, no. 224 (Washington, D.C.: U.S. Government Printing Office), p. 3.

3. Corwin, "Causes of Mexican Emigration," p. 596.

4. U.S. Bureau of the Census, 1970 Census of Population, General Social and Economic Characteristics, PC(1)-C6 (Washington, D.C.: U.S. Government Printing Office, 1972), p. 385. Cf. Corwin, "Causes of Mexican Emigration," p. 598.

5. Jane Pinchot, *The Mexicans in America* (Minneapolis: Lerner Publications, 1973), p. 12.

6. Ellywyn R. Stoddard, *Mexican Americans* (New York: Random House, 1973), p. 12.

7. Pinchot, *The Mexicans in America*, p. 12.

8. Leo Grebler, Joan W. Moore, Ralph C. Guzman, *The Mexican-American People* (New York: The Free Press, 1970), p. 321.

9. Stoddard, *Mexican Americans*, p. 75; Grebler, et al., *The Mexican-American People*, pp. 320–321.

10. Grebler, et al., *The Mexican-American People*, p. 334.

11. Pinchot, *The Mexicans in America*, p. 16.

12. Ibid.

13. U.S. Commission on Civil Rights, *The Excluded Student: Educational Practices Affecting Mexican Americans in the Southwest* (Washington, D.C.: U.S. Government Printing Office, 1972), pp. 76–82.

14. Stoddard, *Mexican Americans*, pp. 165–166. See also Grebler, et al., *The Mexican-American People*, p. 321.

15. Corwin, "Causes of Mexican Emigration," pp. 558–559.

16. Ibid., p. 559.

17. Ibid., pp. 558–559.

18. Ibid., p. 560.

Notes

19. Ibid., pp. 561–562.
20. Pinchot, *The Mexican in America*, p. 29.
21. Carey McWilliams, "The Borderlands Are Invaded," in *The Mexican Americans: An Awakening Minority*, ed. Manuel P. Servin (Encino, Calif.: Glencoe Press, 1970), p. 32.
22. Pinchot, *The Mexican in America*, p. 29.
23. Stoddard, *Mexican Americans*, p. 28.
24. Ibid., p. 22.
25. Corwin, "Causes of Mexican Emigration," p. 566.
26. Ibid., p. 565.
27. Maldwyn Allen Jones, *American Immigration* (Chicago: University of Chicago Press, 1960), p. 291.
28. Corwin, "Causes of Mexican Emigration," p. 590.
29. Ibid., p. 566.
30. McWilliams, "The Borderlands Are Invaded," p. 48.
31. Ibid., p. 47.
32. Pinchot, *The Mexicans in America*, pp. 31–32.
33. Ibid., p. 45.
34. Grebler, et al., *The Mexican-American People*, p. 323.
35. Joan Moore, *Mexican Americans* (Englewood Cliffs, N.J.: Prentice-Hall, 1971), p. 115.
36. Thomas Sowell, "Ethnicity in a Changing America," *Daedalus*, Winter 1978, p. 217.
37. Moore, *Mexican Americans*, p. 25.
38. Ibid., p. 42; Pinchot, *The Mexicans in America*, p. 43.
39. Corwin, "Causes of Mexican Emigration," p. 570.
40. Ibid.
41. Moore, *Mexican Americans*, p. 42.
42. Pinchot, *The Mexicans in America*, p. 44.
43. Ibid.
44. Stoddard, *Mexican Americans*, p. 186.
45. Manuel P. Servin, "The Post-World War II Mexican American, 1925–1965: A Non-Achieving Minority," in *The Mexican-American: An Awakening Minority*, p. 155.
46. Perhaps the most striking example of this was a play entitled *Zoot Suit*, which ran in the late 1970s. Among the writers who made themselves partisans of the *pachuchos* are Pinchot, *The Mexicans in America*, pp. 48–49, and Robin F. Scott, "The Zoot-Suit Riots," in *The Mexican-American: An Awakening Minority*, pp. 116–124.
47. Moore, *Mexican Americans*, p. 41.
48. Corwin, "Causes of Mexican Emigration," p. 570.
49. Moore, *Mexican Americans*, p. 41.
50. Corwin, "Causes of Mexican Emigration," p. 632.
51. Ibid., pp. 578–579.
52. Ibid., p. 580.
53. Ibid., p. 631.
54. Ibid., p. 570.
55. Ibid., p. 587.
56. Ibid., p. 612.
57. Ibid.
58. Ibid., p. 613.
59. Ibid., p. 614.
60. Georgie Anne Gayer, "Are Mexico and Chicanos Trying to Use Each Other?" *Los Angeles Times*, March 6, 1978, Part II, p. 7.
61. Corwin, "Causes of Mexican Emigration," p. 575.
62. Grebler, et al., *The Mexican-American People*, p. 113.
63. U.S. Bureau of the Census, *1970 Census of Population, Subject Reports PC(2)-1D*, p. 1.
64. Grebler, et al., *The Mexican-American People*, pp. 113–114.
65. Ibid., p. 340.
66. Moore, *Mexican Americans*, p. 60.
67. Grebler, et al., *The Mexican-American People*, p. 327.
68. Moore, *Mexican Americans*, p. 115.
69. Grebler, et al., *The Mexican-American People*, p. 411.

70. Ibid., pp. 137–138.

71. Ibid., pp. 385–387.

72. Ibid., pp. 208, 209.

73. Ibid., p. 181.

74. Ibid., p. 182.

75. U.S. Bureau of the Census, *1970 Census of Population, Subject Reports, PC(2)-1C*, pp. 170, 171.

76. Grebler, et al., *The Mexican-American People*, pp. 297–307.

77. Ibid., p. 190.

78. Vernon Briggs, Jr., Walter Fogel, and Fred H. Schmidt, *The Chicano Worker* (Austin, University of Texas Press, 1977), p. 50.

79. U.S. Bureau of the Census, *Current Population Reports*, Series P-20, No. 224, p. 6.

80. Briggs, Jr., et al., *The Chicano Worker*, p. 54.

81. Thomas Sowell, ed., *Essays and Data on American Ethnic Groups*, p. 375.

82. Grebler, et al., *The Mexican-American People*, p. 161. Thomas Sowell, "Race and IQ Reconsidered," in *Essays and Data on American Ethnic Groups*, p. 214.

83. Thomas Sowell, "Assumptions versus History in Ethnic Education," *Teachers College Record* (forthcoming).

84. Grebler, et al., *The Mexican-American People*, pp. 166, 167, 169.

85. Ibid., p. 167.

86. Moore, *Mexican Americans*, p. 69.

87. Stoddard, *Mexican Americans*, p. 133.

88. Briggs, Jr., et al., *The Chicano Worker*, p. 54.

89. Eric Hanushek, "Ethnic Income Variations: Magnitudes and Explanations," in *Essays and Data on American Ethnic Groups*, p. 157.

90. U.S. Bureau of the Census, *Current Population Reports*, Series P-20, No. 224, p. 10.

91. Ibid.

92. Grebler, et al., *The Mexican-American People*, p. 185.

93. Ibid., p. 144.

94. Ibid., pp. 123–125.

95. U.S. Bureau of the Census, *Current Population Reports*, Series P-20, No. 224, p. 4.

96. Barry R. Chiswick, "The Economic Progress of Immigrants: Some Apparently Universal Patterns," in *Contemporary Economic Problems*, ed. William Fellner (Washington, D.C.: American Enterprise Institute, 1979), p. 379.

97. Arthur F. Corwin, "Causes of Mexican Emigration," p. 582.

98. Morre, *Mexican Americans*, p. 105.

99. Ibid., p. 104.

100. Grebler, et al., *The Mexican-American People*, p. 414; Peter Uhlenberg, "Demographic Correlates of Group Achievement: Contrasting Patterns of Mexican-Americans and Japanese-Americans," in *Race, Creed, Color, or National Origin*, ed. Robert K. Yin (Itasca, Ill.: F. E. Peacok Publishers, 1973), p. 91.

101. U.S. Bureau of the Census, *Current Population Reports*, Series P-20, No. 224, p. 15.

102. Ibid., p. 14.

103. Ibid.; Sowell, "Ethnicity in a Changing America," p. 217.

104. Uhlenberg, "Demographic Correlates," p. 88.

105. Sowell, "Ethnicity in a Changing America," p. 217.

106. U.S. Bureau of the Census, *1970 Census of Population, Subject Reports, PC(2)-1D*, pp. 87–88.

107. Grebler, et al., *The Mexican-American People*, pp. 115–116.

108. U.S. Bureau of the Census, *1970 Census of Population, Subject Reports, PC(2)-1D*, pp. 90, 91.

109. Ibid., pp. 87, 91.

110. U.S. Bureau of the Census, *Current Population Reports*, Series P-20, No. 213, p. 14.

111. Ibid., Series P-20, No. 221, p. 10.

112. Ibid., Series P-20, No. 213, p. 14.

113. Grebler, et al., *The Mexican-American People*, p. 426.

114. Ibid., p. 424.

115. U.S. Bureau of the Census, *Current Population Reports*, Series P-20, No. 213, p. 21.

116. Grebler, et al., *The Mexican-American People*, p. 424.

Notes

117. Ibid., p. 425.

118. See, for example, Stoddard, *Mexican Americans*, pp. 108, 117, 119, 122.

119. Moore, *Mexican Americans*, pp. 121–124.

120. Grebler, et al., *The Mexican American People*, p. 432.

121. Ibid., p. 429.

122. Ibid., p. 431.

123. Ibid., p. 143.

124. U.S. Bureau of the Census, *1970 Census of Population, Subject Reports, PC(2)-1D*, p. 21.

125. Ibid., pp. 26, 27, 31.

126. See, for example, Stoddard, *Mexican Americans*, p. 43; Moore, *Mexican Americans*, p. 131; Grebler, et al., *The Mexican-American People*, pp. 372n, 433–437.

127. Moore, *Mexican Americans*, p. 73.

128. "It's Your Turn in the Sun," *Time*, October 16, 1978, p. 53.

129. Pinchot, *The Mexicans in America*, p. 84–87.

130. Grebler, et al., *The Mexican American People*, p. 561.

131. Ibid., p. 547.

132. Ibid., pp. 558, 563–568; "It's Your Turn in the Sun," p. 51.

133. Grebler, et al., *The Mexican-American People*, p. 562.

134. "It's Your Turn in the Sun," p. 55.

135. Mark R. Levy and Michael S. Kramer, *The Ethnic Factor* (New York: Simon and Schuster, 1972), p. 77.

136. Geoffrey Godsell, "The Puerto Ricans," *Christian Science Monitor*, May 1, 1980, p. 12.

137. Stoddard, *Mexican Americans*, p. 212.

138. Ibid., pp. 212–213; Servin, "The Post-World War II Mexican American," p. 157.

139. U.S. Bureau of the Census, *1970 Census of Population, Subject Reports, PC(2)-1D*, p. 60.

140. U.S. Bureau of the Census, *1970 Census of Population, General Social and Economic Characteristics, PC(1)-C6*, pp. 31, 90.

141. Ibid., pp. 1, 60; *1970 Census of Population, Subject Reports, PC(2)-1D*, p. 1.

Chapter 11

1. Ulrich B. Phillips, *The Slave Economy of the Old South* (Baton Rouge: Louisiana State University Press, 1968), p. 269.

2. George Potter, *To the Golden Door* (Westport, Conn.: Greenwood Press, 1960), p. 169.

3. J. C. Furnas, *The Americans* (New York: G. P. Putnam's Sons, 1969), pp. 698–699.

4. Oscar Handlin, *The Newcomers* (New York: Anchor Books, 1962), p. 14.

5. Ibid., p. 13.

6. Jacob Riis, *How the Other Half Lives* (Cambridge: Harvard University Press, 1970), p. 21.

7. David M. Katzman, *Before the Ghetto* (Urbana: University of Illinois, 1975), p. 73.

8. Gilbert Osofsky, *Harlem: The Making of a Ghetto* (New York: Harper Torchbooks, 1968).

9. Ibid., p. 45; Jeffrey S. Gurock, *When Harlem Was Jewish, 1870–1930* (New York: Columbia University Press, 1970), p. 146.

10. Francesco Cordasco, ed., *Jacob Riis Revisited* (New York: Anchor Books, 1968), p. 336; Diane Ravitch, *The Great School Wars* (New York: Basic Books, 1974), p. 108; Joseph Lopreato, *Italian Americans* (New York: Random House, 1970), pp. 110–111; Charles H. Trout, *Boston, the Great Depression and the New Deal* (New York: Oxford University Press, 1977), p. 10.

11. Thomas Kessner, *The Golden Door* (New York: Oxford University Press, 1977), p. 101.

12. Ibid., p. 102. See also Osofsky, *Harlem: The Making of a Ghetto*, p. 138.

13. Handlin, *The Newcomers*, p. 14.

14. Riis, *How the Other Half Lives*, p. 8.

15. Ibid., p. 21.

16. Handlin, *The Newcomers*, p. 14.

17. Riis, *How the Other Half Lives,* p. 6n.

18. Ibid., p. 6; Cordasco, ed., *Jacob Riis Revisited,* p. 321.

19. Irving Howe and Kenneth Libo, *How We Lived, 1880–1930* (New York: Richard Marek, 1979), p. 226.

20. Stanley Feldstein and Lawrence Costello, ed., *The Ordeal of Assimilation* (New York: Anchor Books, 1974), p. 76.

21. Ibid., p. 179.

22. Ibid., p. 208.

23. Ibid., p. 215.

24. Howe and Libo, *How We Lived, 1880–1930,* p. 193.

25. Peter Uhlenberg, "Demographic Correlates of Group Achievement: Contrasting Patterns of Mexican-Americans and Japanese-Americans," in *Race, Creed, Color, or National Origin,* ed., Robert K. Yin (Itasca, Ill.: F. E. Peacock, 1973), p. 91.

26. Thomas Sowell, "Race and I.Q. Reconsidered," in *Essays and Data on American Ethnic Groups* (The Urban Institute, 1978), pp. 207–214.

27. Sandra Scarr and Richard Weinberg, "I.Q. Test Performance of Black Children Adopted by White Families," *American Psychologist,* October 1976, pp. 726–739.

28. Sowell, "Race and I.Q. Reconsidered," p. 209.

29. Ibid., p. 210.

30. Ibid., p. 208.

31. Ibid., pp. 210, 211–212.

32. See the path-breaking research of Barry Chiswick, "The Economic Progress of Immigrants: Some Apparently Universal Patterns," in *Contemporary Economic Problems, 1979,* ed. William Fellner (Washington, D.C.: American Enterprise Institute, 1979), pp. 357–399.

33. Ibid., pp. 333–334.

34. Ivan H. Light, *Ethnic Enterprise in America* (Berkeley: University of California Press, 1972), pp. 141–151.

35. Some of the misconceptions behind this concept are explored in Walter E. Williams, "Some Hard Questions on Minority Business," *Negro Educational Review,* April–July 1974, pp. 123–142.

36. Theodore Draper, *The Rediscovery of Black Nationalism* (New York: The Viking Press, 1970), p. 84.

37. Thomas Sowell, "Patterns of Black Excellence," *The Public Interest,* Spring 1976, p. 51.

38. Harry H. L. Kitano, *Japanese Americans* (Englewood Cliffs, N.J.: Prentice-Hall, 1969), p. 72.

39. *Brown v. Board of Education of Topeka,* 347 VS 483 (1954).

40. Thomas Sowell, "Assumptions Versus History in Ethnic Education," in *The State of American Education,* ed. Diane Ravitch (forthcoming).

41. Gerald D. Suttles, *The Social Order of the Slum* (Chicago: University of Chicago Press, 1973), pp. 62, 63, 66, 103, 128; Stephen Birmingham, *Certain People* (Boston: Little, Brown and Co., 1977), p. 67; Richard Gambino, *Blood of My Blood* (New York: Anchor Books, 1974), pp. 235–236.

42. Norman Miller and H. B. Gerard, "How Busing Failed at Riverside," *Psychology Today,* June 1976, pp. 66–67ff.

43. Suttles, *The Social Order of the Slum,* pp. 28, 56.

44. Maldwyn Allen Jones, *American Immigration* (Chicago: University of Chicago Press, 1960), pp. 212–213.

45. See Thomas Sowell, *"Weber* and *Bakke* and the Presuppositions of 'Affirmative Action,'" *Wayne Law Review,* July 1980, pp. 1309–1336.

46. Thomas Sowell, *Knowledge and Decisions* (New York: Basic Books, 1980), pp. 100–110.

47. Many writers have regarded the politicization of these emotions as the *sine qua non* for group advancement. For a different view see Thomas Sowell, *Race and Economics,* pp. 116–127.

48. For examples of this attitude, see Stephen S. Baratz and Joan C. Baratz, "Early Childhood Intervention: The Social Science Basis of Institutional Racism," *Harvard Educational Review,* February 1970, pp. 29–50; Jane Pinchot, *The Mexicans in America* (Minne-

Notes

apolis: Lerner Publishing Co., 1973), p. 60; Joan Moore, *Mexican Americans* (Englewood Cliffs, N.J.: Prentice-Hall, 1970), pp. 81, 121.

49. Louis Wirth, *The Ghetto* (Chicago: University of Chicago Press, 1956), pp. 205, 207, 214, 215; Marshall Sklare, "Aspects of Religious Worship in the Contemporary Conservative Synagogue," in *The Jews*, (New York: The Free Press, 1958), pp. 374–375; Moses Rischin, *The Promised City* (Cambridge: Harvard University Press, 1962), pp. 97–98; Leo Grebler et al., *The Mexican-American People* (New York: The Free Press, 1970), pp. 317–318, 375; Moore, *Mexican Americans*, p. 123; Ellwyn R. Stoddard, *Mexican Americans* (New York: Random House, 1973), pp. 65, 241; Thomas Sowell, "The Plight of Black Students in the United States," *Daedalus*, Spring 1974, p. 192; Birmingham, *Certain People*, p. 99; William Petersen, *Japanese Americans* (New York: Random House, 1971), pp. 60, 86; S. I. Hayakawa, *Through the Communication Barrier* (New York: Harper & Row, 1979), pp. 140, 141; Herbert J. Gans, *The Urban Villagers* (New York: The Free Press, 1962), p. 153; Gambino, *Blood of My Blood*, pp. 257–260.

50. Hayakawa, *Through the Communication Barrier*, pp. 140–141.

51. Nathan Glazer and Daniel Patrick Moynihan, *Beyond the Melting Pot* (Cambridge: MIT Press, 1963), pp. 241, 252–254.

52. Stoddard, *Mexican Americans*, p. 67; Moore, *Mexican Americans*, p. 127.

53. Irving Howe, *World of Our Fathers* (New York: Harcourt, Brace, Jovanovich, 1976), pp. 614, 616.

54. Charles E. Silberman, *Crisis in Black and White* (New York: Random House, 1964), pp. 71, 169–170; Thomas Sowell, *Black Education: Myths and Tragedies* (New York: David McKay, 1972), pp. 121–122.

55. E. Franklin Frazier, *The Negro in the United States* (Chicago: University of Chicago Press, 1969), pp. 258–266; Wirth, *The Ghetto*, Chapter XII; Leo A. Grebler, et al., *The Mexican-American People*, pp. 327–335; Humbert Nelli, *The Italians in Chicago* (New York: Oxford University Press, 1970), pp. 24, 28, 36.

56. Robert F. Foerster, *The Italian Emigration of Our Times*, (New York: Arno Press, 1969), p. 393; Rischin, *The Promised City*, p. 76.

57. Wirth, *The Ghetto*, pp. 205, 207, 214, 215.

58. Stoddard, *Mexican Americans*, pp. 67, 228.

59. Pinchot, *The Mexicans in America*, pp. 43–44.

60. Foerster, *The Italian Emigration of Our Times*, pp. 393–394.

61. Furnas, *The Americans*, p. 382.

62. N. Foner and R. Napoli, "Jamaican and Black-American Migrant Farm Workers: A Comparative Analysis," *Social Problems*, 1978.

63. See Sowell, *Knowledge and Decisions*, p. 83.

64. Nathan Glazer, *Affirmative Discrimination* (New York: Basic Books, 1975), p. 154.

65. Thomas Sowell, "Status versus Behavior," *Washington University Law Quarterly*, Winter 1979, p. 186.

66. Carl Wittke, *The Irish in America* (Baton Rouge: Louisiana State University Press, 1956), Chapter XII; Williston H. Lofton, "Northern Labor and the Negro During the Civil War," *Journal of Negro History*, July 1949, pp. 256–261, 262, 268–270; David M. Katzman, *Before the Ghetto* (Urbana: University of Illinois Press, 1973), p. 44–45; Birmingham, *Certain People*, pp. 185–186.

67. Potter, *To the Golden Door*, p. 101; Wittke, *The Irish in America*, p. 194; Gunnar Myrdal, *An American Dilemma* (New York: McGraw-Hill, 1964), vol. 2, pp. 960–961.

68. "Uptight," *Ebony*, November 1968, pp. 46–54.

69. Yasuo Wakatsuki, "Japanese Emigration to the United States, 1866–1924," in *Perspectives in American History*, vol. XII (1979), p. 428.

70. Gordon F. Bloom, "A Reconsideration of the Theory of Exploitation," *Readings in the Theory of Income Distribution*, ed. William Fellner and Bernard F. Haley (The Blakiston Co., 1951), pp. 245–277.

71. See Thomas Sowell, *Markets and Minorities* (forthcoming).

72. See, for example, Robert Higgs, "Race, Skills and Earnings: American Immigrants in 1909," *Journal of Economic History*, June 1971, pp. 420–428. Thomas Sowell, *Affirmative Action Reconsidered* (Washington, D.C.: American Enterprise Institute, 1975), pp. 15–20; Robert Higgs, "Firm-Specific Evidence on Racial Wage Differentials and Work Force Segregation," *American Economic Review*, vol. 67, no. 2, pp. 236–245.

73. See Gary S. Becker, *The Economics of Discrimination* (Chicago: University of Chicago Press, 1971); Sowell, *Race and Economics,* Chapters 6, 7.

74. Sowell, *Race and Economics,* Chapter 6.

75. Ibid., Chapter 7.

76. Robert Higgs, *Competition and Coercion* (Cambridge: Cambridge University Press, 1977), pp. 47–54.

77. Thomas Sowell, "Ethnicity in a Changing America," *Daedalus,* Winter 1978, pp. 231–232.

78. Eric Hanushek, "Ethnic Income Variations: Magnitudes and Explanations," in *Essays and Data on American Ethnic Groups,* p. 157.

79. Sowell, *Affirmative Action Reconsidered,* pp. 15–20.

80. David Caplovitz, *The Poor Pay More* (New York: The Free Press, 1967). But see Sowell, *Race and Economics,* pp. 173–178; Walter Williams, "Why the Poor Pay More: An Alternative Explanation," *Social Science Quarterly,* September 1973, pp. 375–379; Walter E. Williams, "Racial Price Discrimination: A Note," *Economic Inquiry,* June 1977, pp. 147–150.

81. Gambino, *Blood of My Blood,* p. 33.

82. Light, *Ethnic Enterprise in America,* Chapter 2.

83. Ibid., pp. 19–20.

84. Cordasco, ed., *Jacob Riis Revisited,* pp. 321, 324, 333, 334, 344, 355; Riis, *How the Other Half Lives,* p. 6.

85. Riis, *How the Other Half Lives,* p. 6n.

86. Rischin, *The Promised City,* p. 84.

87. W. E. B. Du Bois, *The Philadelphia Negro* (New York: Schocken Books, 1970), p. 323.

88. Sowell, *Knowledge and Decisions,* pp. 87–88; Walter E. Williams, "Racial Price Discrimination," *Economic Inquiry,* June 1977, pp. 147–150.

89. Du Bois, *The Philadelphia Negro,* p. 315.

90. Ibid., p. 316.

91. Ibid., p. 395.

92. Ibid., p. 355.

93. Roger Daniels, *Concentration Camps, U.S.A.* (New York: Holt, Rinehart and Winston, 1972), pp. 79–80, 107.

94. Ravitch, *The Great School Wars,* Chapters 4–7.

95. Wittke, *The Irish in America,* pp. 143–146.

96. Ibid., pp. 220–222.

97. Ibid., p. 150–160.

98. Alphonso Pinkney, *Black Americans* (Englewood Cliffs, N.J.: Prentice-Hall, 1969), p. 44. See also Pinchot, *The Mexicans in America,* p. 77.

99. Moore, *Mexican Americans,* p. 73.

Index

Index

Index

Index

Index

Index

Index

Index

Index

Index

353